JEROME, *EPISTLE* 106
(*ON THE PSALMS*)

WRITINGS FROM THE GRECO-ROMAN WORLD

JEROME, *EPISTLE* 106 (*ON THE PSALMS*)

Introduction, translation, and commentary by

Michael Graves

Library of Congress Control Number: 2022936956

Dedicated to
The Pines School of Graduate Studies,
Hebrew Union College–Jewish Institute of Religion

Contents

Abbreviations

Primary Sources

2 Amm.	Dionysius of Halicarnassus, *Epistula ad Ammaeum ii* (*Letters to Ammaeus*)
2 Regn.	Dio Chrysostom, *De regno ii* (*Kingship 2*)
A.J.	Josephus, *Antiquitates judaicae* (*Antiquities of the Jews*)
Ad.	Terence, *Adelphi* (*Brothers*)
Ann.	Tacitus, *Annales* (*Annals*)
Ars	Horace, *Ars poetica* (*Art of Poetry*)
Att.	Cicero, *Epistulae ad Atticum* (*Letters to Atticus*)
Civ.	Augustine, *De civitate Dei* (*City of God*)
Comm. Agg.	Jerome, *Commentariorum in Aggaeum liber* (*Commentary on Haggai*)
Comm. Am.	Jerome, *Commentariorum in Amos libri III* (*Commentary on Amos*)
Comm. Dan.	Jerome, *Commentariorum in Danielem libri III* (*Commentary on Daniel*)
Comm. Eccl.	Jerome, *Commentarii in Ecclesiasten* (*Commentary on Ecclesiastes*)
Comm. Eph.	Jerome, *Commentariorum in Epistulam ad Ephesios libri III* (*Commentary on Ephesians*)
Comm. Ezech.	Jerome, *Commentariorum in Ezechielem libri XVI* (*Commentary on Ezekiel*)
Comm. Gal.	Jerome, *Commentariorum in Epistulam ad Galatas libri III* (*Commentary on Galatians*)
Comm. Hab.	Jerome, *Commentariorum in Habacuc libri II* (*Commentary on Habakkuk*)
Comm. Jer.	Jerome, *Commentariorum in Jeremiam libri VI* (*Commentary on Jeremiah*)

Comm. Mal.	Jerome, *Commentariorum in Malachiam liber* (*Commentary on Malachi*)
Comm. Matt.	Jerome, *Commentariorum in Matthaeum libri IV* (*Commentary on Matthew*)
Comm. Mich.	Jerome, *Commentariorum in Michaeum libri II* (*Commentary on Micah*)
Comm. not.	Plutarch, *De communibus notitiis contra stoicos* (*On Common Notions against the Stoics*)
Comm. Os.	Jerome, *Commentariorum in Osee libri III* (*Commentary on Hosea*)
Comm. Phlm.	Jerome, *Commentariorum in Epistolam ad Philemonem liber* (*Commentary on Philemon*)
Comm. Ps.	Jerome, *Commentarioli in Psalmos* (*Commentaries on the Psalms*)
Comm. Soph.	Jerome, *Commentariorum in Sophoniam libri III* (*Commentary on Zephaniah*)
Comm. Tit.	Jerome, *Commentariorum in Epistulam ad Titum liber* (*Commentary on Titus*)
Comp.	Dionysius of Halicarnassus, *De compositione verborum* (*On Literary Composition*)
De or.	Cicero, *De oratore* (*On Oratory*)
Diatr.	Epictetus, *Diatribai* (*Discourses*)
Doctr. chr.	Augustine, *De doctrina christiana* (*Christian Instruction*)
Enarrat. Ps.	Augustine, *Enarrationes in Psalmos* (*Enarrations on the Psalms*)
Ep.	*Epistulae* (*Epistles*)
Exod. Rab.	Exodus Rabbah
Exp.	Cassiodorus, *Expositio Psalmorum* (*Explanation of the Psalms*)
Exp. Luc.	Ambrose, *Expositio Evangelii secundum Lucam* (*Commentary on Luke*)
Fab.	Babrius, *Fabulae* (*Fables*)
Fin.	Cicero, *De finibus* (*On Ends*)
Frat. amor.	Plutarch, *De fraterno amore* (*On Brotherly Love*)
Fug.	Ambrose, *De fuga saeculi* (*Flight from the World*)
GPsal	Jerome, Gallican Psalter
Haer.	Irenaeus, *Adversus haereses* (*Against Heresies*)
Hist. eccl.	Eusebius, *Historia ecclesiastica* (*Ecclesiastical History*)
Hom. Num.	Origen, *Homiliae in Numeros* (*Homilies on Numbers*)

Inst.	Quintilian, *Institutio oratoria* (*Institutes of Oratory*)
Instr.	Commodian, *Instructiones* (*Instructions*)
Jov.	Jerome, *Adversus Jovinianum libri II* (*Against Jovinianus*)
Let. Aris.	Letter of Aristeas
Laps. virg.	Pseudo-Ambrose, *De lapsu virginis consecratae* (*On Lapsed Virgins*)
Ling.	Varro, *De lingua latina* (*On the Latin Language*)
Locut. Hept.	Augustine, *Locutionum in Heptateuchum libri septem* (*Expressions in the Heptateuch*)
Marc.	Tertullian, *Adversus Marcionem* (*Against Marcion*)
Mos.	Philo, *De vita Mosis* (*On the Life of Moses*)
Myst.	Iamblichus, *De mysteriis* (*On the Mysteries*)
Nat. d.	Cicero, *De natura deorum* (*On the Nature of the Gods*)
Nom. hebr.	Jerome, *De nominibus hebraicis* (*On Hebrew Names*)
Non parc.	Lucifer of Cagliari, *De non parcendo in Deum delinquentibus* (*On Not Sparing Those Who Commit Offenses against God*)
Off.	Cicero, *De officiis* (*On Duties*)
Opt. gen.	Cicero, *De optimo genere oratorum* (*On the Best Kind of Orator*)
P.Bod.	Papyrus Bodmer
P.Oxy.	Oxyrynchus Papyrus
P.Ryl.	Rylands Papyrus
Pon.	Ovid, *Epistulae ex Ponto* (*Letters from the Black Sea*)
Praep. ev.	Eusebius, *Praeparatio evangelica* (*Preparation for the Gospel*)
Pref. Chron.	Preface to Jerome's translation of Eusebius's *Chronicon*
Pref. Ezra	Jerome, *Preface to Ezra*
Pref. Gos.	Jerome, *Preface to the Gospels*
Pref. GPsal.	Jerome, *Preface to the Gallican Psalter*
Pref. IH Chron.	Jerome, *Preface to Chronicles iuxta Hebraicum*
Pref. IH Job	Jerome, *Preface to Job iuxta Hebraicum*
Pref. IH Ps.	Jerome, *Preface to Psalms iuxta Hebraicum*
Pref. Isa.	Jerome, *Preface to Isaiah*
Pref. Josh.	Jerome, *Preface to Joshua*
Pref. Kings	Jerome, *Preface to Kings*
Pref. Pent.	Jerome, *Preface to the Pentateuch*
Pun.	Appian, *Punica* (*Punic Wars*)
Pyrrh.	Plutarch, *Pyrrhus*

Qu. hebr. Gen. Jerome, *Quaestionum hebraicarum liber in Genesim* (*Hebrew Questions on Genesis*)
Quaes. Ambrosiaster, *Quaestiones Veteris et Novi Testamenti* (*Questions on the Old Testament and New Testament*)
Ruf. Jerome, *Adversus Rufinum libri III* (*Against Rufinus*)
Somn. Philo, *De somniis* (*On Dreams*)
Test. Cyprian, *Ad Quirinum testimonia adversus Judaeos* (*To Quirinus: Testimonies against the Jews*)
Tg. Ps.-J. Targum Pseudo-Jonathan
Tract. Marc. Jerome, *Tractatus in Evangelium Marci* (*Treatise on the Gospel of Mark/Homilies on Mark*)
Vir. ill. Jerome (with additions by Gennadius), *De viris illustribus* (*Concerning Illustrious Men*)
Vit. Diogenes Laertius, *Vitae philosophorum* (*Lives of Eminent Philosophers*)
Vit. Hil. Jerome, *Vita S. Hilarionis eremitae* (*Life of Hilarion*)
Vit. poes. Hom. Pseudo-Plutarch, *De vita et poesi Homeri* (*The Life and Poetry of Homer*)

Secondary Sources

Amelli Amelli, Ambrogio M., ed. *Liber Psalmorum iuxta antiquissimam latinam versionem nunc primum ex Casinensi Cod. 557.* Collectanea Biblica Latina 1. Rome: Pustet, 1912.
Aug *Augustinianum*
BASP *Bulletin of the American Society of Papyrologists*
BDAG Danker, Frederick W., Walter Bauer, William F. Arndt, and F. Wilbur Gingrich. Greek-English Lexicon of the New Testament and Other Early Christian Literature. 3rd ed. Chicago: University of Chicago Press, 2000.
BHS *Biblia Hebraica Stuttgartensia*
Bib *Biblica*
BWANT Beiträge zur Wissenschaft vom Alten und Neuen Testament
Caloz Caloz, Masséo. *Étude sur la LXX origénienne du Psautier.* OBO 19. Fribourg: Éditions universitaires; Göttingen: Vandenhoeck & Ruprecht, 1978.
CC Corpus Christianorum

CC 2	Reifferscheid, August, and Georg Wissowa, eds. *Quinti Septimi Florentis Tertuliani Opera, Pars II: Opera Montanistica. De Ieiunio Adversus Psychicos.* Turnhout: Brepols, 1954.
CC 3	Weber, Robert, ed. *Sancti Cypriani Episcopi Opera: Ad Quirinum.* Turnhout: Brepols, 1972.
CC 8	Diercks, G. F., ed. *De non parcendo in deum delinquentibus.* Turnhout: Brepols, 1978.
CC 9A	Étaix, Raymond, and Joseph Lemarié, eds. *Chromatii Aquileiensis Opera.* Turnhout: Brepols, 1974.
CC 14	Adriaen, Marcus, ed. *Sancti Ambrosii Mediolanensis Opera, Pars IV. Expositio Evangelii Secundum Lucam. Fragmenta in Esaiam.* Turnhout: Brepols, 1957.
CC 33	Fraipont, Jean, ed. *Sancti Aurelii Augustini. Locutiones in Heptateuchum Libri VII.* Turnhout: Brepols, 1958 .
CC 38	Dekkers, Eligius, and Jean Fraipont, eds. *Sancti Aurelii Augustini Opera, Pars 10, 1. Enarrationes in Psalmos I–L.* Turnhout: Brepols, 1956.
CC 39	Dekkers, Eligius, and Jean Fraipont, eds. *Sancti Aurelii Augustini Opera, Pars 10, 2. Enarrationes in Psalmos LI–C.* Turnhout: Brepols, 1956.
CC 48	Dombart, Bernhard, and Alphonse Kalb, eds. *Aurelii Augustini Opera, Pars 14, 2: De Civitate Dei Libri XI–XXII.* Turnhout: Brepols, 1955.
CC 61	Doignon, Jean, ed. *Sancti Hilarii Pictaviensis Episcopi Opera, Pars 1, 1. Tractatus Super Psalmos, Instructio Psalmorum in Psalmos I–XCI.* Turnhout: Brepols, 1997.
CC 61A	Doignon, Jean, ed. *Sancti Hilarii Pictaviensis Episcopi Opera, Pars 1, 2. Tractatus Super Psalmos, In Psalmum CXVIII.* Turnhout: Brepols, 2002.
CC 61B	Doignon, Jean, ed. *Sancti Hilarii Pictaviensis Episcopi Opera, Pars 1, 3. Tractatus Super Psalmos, In Psalmos CXIX–CL.* Turnhout: Brepols, 2009.
CC 68A	Callens, P. ed. *Prosperi Aquitani Opera, Pars 2. Expositio Psalmorum. Liber Sententiarum.* Turnhout: Brepols, 1972.
CC 69	Günther, Otto, ed. *Gregorius. Iliberritanus. Faustinus Luciferianus: Marcellinus et Faustinus Presbyteri, De Confessione Verae Fidei.* Turnhout: Brepols, 1967.

CC 72	Lagarde, Paul de, and Germain morin, eds. *S. Hieronymi Presbyteri Opera, Pars I: Opera Exegetica I. Liber Interpretationis Hebraicorum Nominum.* Turnhout: Brepols, 1959.
CC 73	Adriaen, Marcus, ed. *Commentariorum in Esaiam libri I–XI.* Turnhout: Brepols, 1963.
CC 75	Glorie, Franciscus., ed. *S. Hieronymi Presbyteri Opera, Pars I: Opera Exegetica IV. Commentariorum in Hiezechielem Libri XIV.* Turnhout: Brepols, 1964.
CC 76	Adriaen, Marcus, ed. *S. Hieronymi Presbyteri Opera, Pars I: Opera Exegetica VI. Commentarii in Prophetas Minores.* Turnhout: Brepols, 1969.
CC 77	Hurst, David, and Marcus Adriaen, eds. *S. Hieronymi Presbyteri Opera, Pars I: Opera Exegetica VII. Commentariorum in Matheum Libri IV.* Turnhout: Brepols, 1969.
CC 77A	Raspanti, Giacomo, ed. *S. Hieronymi Presbyteri Opera, Pars 1. Opera Exegetica 6. Commentarii in Epistulam Pauli Apostoli ad Galatas.* Turnhout: Brepols, 2006.
CC 78	Morin, Germain, ed. *S. Hieronymi Presbyteri Opera, Pars 2. Opera Homiletica.* Turnhout: Brepols, 1958.
CC 79	Lardet, Pierre, ed. *S. Hieronymi Presbyteri Opera, Pars III: Opera Polemica I. Contra Rufinum.* Turnhout: Brepols, 1982.
CC 97	Adriaen, Marcus, ed. *Magni Aurelii Cassiodori Senatoris Opera, Pars 2, 1. Expositio Psalmorum I–XX.* Turhout: Brepols, 1958.
CC 98	Adriaen, Marcus, ed. *Magni Aurelii Cassiodori Senatoris Opera, Pars 2, 2. Expositio Psalmorum LXXI–CL.* Turhout: Brepols, 1958.
CC 128	Martin, Joseph, ed. *Commodianus. Claudius Marius Victorius. Commodiani Instructionum.* Turnhout: Brepols, 1960.
CH	Colomo, Daniela, and W. B. Henry. "Septuagint (5101)." Pages 1-11 in vol. 77 of *The Oxyrhynchus Papyri.* Edited with Translation and Notes by Amin Benaissa. Graeco-Roman Memoirs 98. London: Egypt Exploration Society, 2011.
CRAI	*Comptes rendus de l'Académie des inscriptions et belles-lettres*
CSEL	Corpus Scriptorum Ecclesiasticorum Latinorum

CSEL 32	Schenkl, Karl, ed. *Sancti Ambrosii Opera, Pars Altera.* Vienna: Tempsky, 1897.
CSEL 50	Souter, Alexander, ed. *Pseudo-Augustini: Quaestiones Veteris et Novi Testamenti CXXVII.* Vienna: Tempsky, 1908.
CSEL 54	Hilberg, Isidorus, ed. *Epistulae I–LXX.* Vol. 1 of *Sancti Eusebii Hieronymi Epistulae.* Vienna: Österreichischen Akademie der Wissenschaften, 1996.
CSEL 55	Hilberg, Isidorus. *Epistulae LXXI–CXX.* Vol. 2 of *Sancti Eusebii Hieronymi Epistulae.* Vienna: Verlag der Österreichischen Akademie der Wissenschaften, 1996.
CSEL 56.1	Hilberg, Isidorus. *Epistulae CXXI–CLIV.* Vol. 3 of *Sancti Eusebii Hieronymi Epistulae.* CSEL 56.1. Vienna: Österreichischen Akademie der Wissenschaften, 1996.
CSEL 78	Faller, Otto, ed. *Sancti Ambrosii Opera, Pars Octava. De Fide [Ad Gratianum Augustum].* Vienna: Hölder-Pichler-Tempsky, 1962.
CSEL 94.1	Müller, Hildegund, ed. *Sancti Augustini Opera. Enarrationes in Psalmos 51–100, Pars 1: Enarrationes in Psalmos.* Vienna: Österreichischen Akademie der Wissenschaften, 2004.
CSEL 95.1	Gori, Franco, and Claudio Pierantoni, eds. *Sancti Augustini Opera. Enarrationes in Psalmos 101–150, Pars 1: Enarrationes in Psalmos 101–109.* Vienna: Österreichischen Akademie der Wissenschaften, 2011.
CSEL 95.2	Gori, Franco, ed. *Augustinus. Enarrationes in Psalmos 101–150, Pars 2: Enarrationes in Psalmos 110–118.* Berlin: de Gruyter, 2015.
CSEL 95.4	Gori, Franco, and Francisca Recanatini, eds. *Sancti Augustini Opera. Enarrationes in Psalmos 101–150, Pars 4: Enarrationes in Psalmos 134–140.* CSEL 95.4. Vienna: Österreichischen Akademie der Wissenschaften, 2002.
DCH	Clines, David J. A., ed. *Dictionary of Classical Hebrew.* 9 vols. Sheffield: Sheffield Phoenix, 1993–2014.
De-Rossi	Vol. 4 of Giovanni Bernardo De-Rossi, *Variae Lectiones Veteris Testamenti.* 5 vols. Parma: Ex Regio Typographeo, 1784–1798.
ECF	Eary Church Fathers

Field	Field, Frederick. *Origenis Hexaplorum Quae Supersunt: Sive Veterum Interpretum Graecorum in Totum Vetus Testamentum Fragmenta*. 2 vols. Oxford: Clarendon, 1875.
Gasquet	Gasquet, Francis A., et al. *Liber Psalmorum ex recensione sancti Hieronymi cum praefationibus et Epistula ad Sunniam et Fretelam*. Vol. 10 of *Biblia Sacra iuxta latinam vulgatam versionem ad codicum fidem*. Rome: Libreria Editrice Vaticana, 1953.
GCS	Griechischen Christlichen Schriftsteller
GELS	Muraoka, Takamitsu. *A Greek-English Lexicon of the Septuagint*. Leuven: Peeters, 2009.
GKC	Kautzsch, Emil, ed. *Gesenius' Hebrew Grammar*. Translated by Arther E. Cowley. 2nd ed. Oxford: Clarendon, 1910.
GL	Gildersleeve, Basil L., and Gonzalez Lodge. *Gildersleeve's Latin Grammar*. 3rd ed. New York: University Publishing, 1900.
GPsal	Gallican Psalter
HALOT	Koehler, Ludwig, Walter Baumgartner, and Johann J. Stamm. *The Hebrew and Aramaic Lexicon of the Old Testament*. Translated and edited under the supervision of Mervyn E. J. Richardson. 4 vols. Leiden: Brill, 1994–1999.
Heb	Hebrew
Hilberg	Hilberg, Isidorus, ed. *Epistulae LXXI–CXX*. Vol. 2 of *Sancti Eusebii Hieronymi Epistulae*: CSEL 55. Vienna: Österreichischen Akademie der Wissenschaften, 1996.
Hill	Hill, Robert C., trans. *Theodore of Mopsuestia: Commentary on Psalms 1-81*. WGRW 5. Atlanta: Society of Biblical Literature, 2006.
HRCS	Hatch, Edwin, and Henry A. Redpath. *Concordance to the Septuagint and Other Greek Versions of the Old Testament*. 2 vols. Oxford: Clarendon, 1897.
HSCP	*Harvard Studies in Classical Philology*
IH	Jerome's *iuxta Hebraicum* translation
Jastrow	Jastrow, Marcus. *A Dictionary of the Targumim, the Talmud Babli and Yerushlami, and the Midrashic Literature*. 2 vols. London: Luzac, 1903.
JSCS	*Journal of Septuagint and Cognate Studies*

JSOTSup	Journal for the Study of the Old Testament Supplement Series
Kennicott	Kennicott, Benjamin. *Vetus Testamentum Hebraicum, cum Variis Lectionibus.* 2 vols. Oxford: Clarendon, 1776–1780.
KT	Kasser, Rodolphe, and Michel Testuz, eds. *Papyrus Bodmer XXIV: Psaumes XVII–CXVIII.* Cologny-Geneva: Bodmer Library, 1967.
LCL	Loeb Classical Library
LD	Lewis, Charles T., and Charles Short. *A Latin Dictionary.* Oxford: Clarendon, 1879.
LSJ	Liddell, Henry George, Robert Scott, and Henry Stuart Jones. *A Greek-English Lexicon.* 9th ed. with revised supplement. Oxford: Clarendon, 1996.
LXX	Septuagint
MS(S)	manuscript(s)
MT	Masoretic Text
NA^{28}	*Novum Testamentum Graece*, Nestle-Aland, 28th ed.
OBO	Orbis Biblicus et Orientalis
OCM	Oxford Classical Monographs
OECS	Oxford Early Christian Studies
OL	Old Latin
OrChrAn	Orientalia Christiana Analecta
P.BYU	The Brigham Young University Papyri
Pesh	Peshiṭta Institute, Leiden. *The Book of Psalms.* Part 2, fascicle 3 of *The Old Testament in Syriac according to the Peshiṭta Version.* Leiden: Brill, 1980.
PG	Migne, Jacques-Paul, ed. Patrologia Graeca [= *Patrologiae Cursus Completus*: Series Graeca]. 162 vols. Paris: Migne, 1857–1886.
PL	Migne, Jacques-Paul, ed. Patrologia Latina [= *Patrologiae Cursus Completus*: Series Latina]. 217 vols. Paris: Migne, 1844–1864.
PTS	Patristische Texte und Studien
Rahlfs	Rahlfs, Alfred. *Psalmi cum Odis.* SVTG 10. Göttingen: Vandenhoeck & Ruprecht, 1979.
RBén	*Revue Bénédictine*
REAug	*Revue des études augustiniennes*
RH	Vol. 2 of Alfred Rahlfs and Robert Hanhart. *Septuaginta, Id est Vetus Testamentum graece iuxta LXX interpretes.*

	Editio altera. 2 vols. in 1. Stuttgart: Deutsche Bibelgesellschaft, 2006.
RTL	*Revue théologique de Louvain*
Sabatier	Vol. 2. of Pierre Sabatier, *Bibliorum Sacrorum Latinae Versiones Antiquae, seu Vetus Italica*. Paris: Apud Franciscum Didot, 1751.
SC	Sources chrétiennes
SC 100	Rousseau, A., B. Hemmerdinger, C. Mercier, and L. Doutre-leau, eds. *Irénée de Lyon: Contre les hérésies, Livre IV*. 2 vols. Lyon: Vitte; Paris: Cerf, 1965.
SC 412	Labrousse, Mireille, ed. *Traité contre les Donatistes, Livres I et II*. Paris: Cerf, 1995.
SC 592	Canellis, Aline, ed. *Jérôme: Préfaces aux livres de la Bible*. Paris: Cerf, 2017.
SCS	Septuagint and Cognate Studies
StPatr	Studia Patristica
StT	Studi e Testi, Biblioteca apostolica vaticana
SVTG	Septuaginta: Vetus Testamentum Graecum Auctoritate Academiae Scientiarum Gottingensis editum
Thibaut	Thibaut, André, ed. *Le Psautier latin du Sinaï*. Vetus Latina: Die Reste der Altlateinischen Bibel 39. Freiburg: Herder, 2010.
TZ	*Theologische Zeitschrift*
Ulrich	Vol. 3 of Eugene Ulrich, *The Biblical Qumran Scrolls: Transcriptions and Textual Variants*. 3 vols. Leiden: Brill, 2013
Van Ess	Part 2 of Leander van Ess, *Biblia Sacra Vulgatae Editionis iuxta Exemplar ex Typographia Apostolica Vaticana, Romae 1592*. 3 parts in 1 vol. Tübingen: Fues, 1824.
VC	*Vigiliae Christianae*
VCSup	Supplements to Vigiliae Christianae
VLR	*Vetus Latina, die Reste der Altlateinischen Bibel*
Weber	Weber, Robert. *Le Psautier Romain et les autres anciens psautiers latins*. Collectanea Biblica Latina 10. Rome: Abbaye Saint-Jérôme, 1953.
WG	Weber, Robert, and Roger Gryson, eds. *Biblia Sacra iuxta vulgatam versionem*. 5th ed. Stuttgart: Deutsche Bibelgesellschaft, 2007.
WGRW	Writings from the Greco-Roman World

White   White, Emanuel. "A Critical Edition of the Targum of
               Psalms: A Computer Generated Text of Books I and II."
               PhD diss., McGill University, 1988. https://tinyurl.com/
               SBLPress1656a1.

YCS   Yale Classical Studies

ZNW   *Zeitschrift für die Neutestamentliche Wissenschaft und die
               Kunde der Älteren Kirche*

INTRODUCTION

Jerome of Stridon (ca. 347–ca. 419 CE), author of many commentaries on Scripture, student of Latin, Greek, and Hebrew, and translator of the Latin Vulgate, was the most learned biblical scholar of the early church. Through his exegetical works, translations, and reference books (such as his *Book of Hebrew Names*), Jerome established a paradigm for biblical scholarship that inspired imitators throughout the Middle Ages and into the Renaissance.[1] In the Roman Catholic Church, Jerome is honored on his feast day (June 30) as *Doctor in exponendis sacris scripturis maximus*, "the greatest teacher of the church in expounding the Sacred Scriptures."[2] Jerome's work is of interest not only to students of Christianity and culture in late antiquity but also to those engaged in biblical criticism, translation, and exegesis.

The book of Psalms played a central role in early Christian worship.[3] The Greek and Latin texts of the Psalter were regularly recited, widely copied, and in the early centuries often revised by Christians in different regions. Jerome's work on the Psalter includes a short treatise on linguistic

---

1. See Eugene F. Rice Jr., *Saint Jerome in the Renaissance* (Baltimore: Johns Hopkins University Press, 1985), 31–35, 84–136.

2. For example, the encyclical *Divino Afflante Spiritu,* given by Pope Pius XII in order to promote biblical studies, was delivered on June 30, 1943, in recognition of Jerome's contribution to Christian biblical scholarship.

3. Communal recitation of Psalms was probably adopted by early Christians from Jewish practice. By the fourth century, the role of Psalms in Christian worship expanded and became more fixed as a result of the extensive use of the Psalter in Christian monastic communities; see Andrew B. McGowan, *Ancient Christian Worship* (Grand Rapids: Baker Academic, 2014), 204–10; and Robert F. Taft, *The Liturgy of the Hours in East and West* (Collegeville, MN: Liturgical Press, 1986), 33–56, 141–63. The Psalms are the most frequently cited Old Testament book among the *Sayings of the Desert Fathers*; see Douglas Burton-Christie, *The Word in the Desert: Scripture and the Quest for Holiness in Early Christian Monasticism* (New York: Oxford University Press, 1993), 97, 111–13, 117–18, 126–27.

difficulties in the Psalms (the *Commentarioli in Psalmos*), numerous homilies on the Psalms (*Tractatus sive Homiliae in Psalmos*), three translations
of the Psalter into Latin, and many discussions of specific passages from the
Psalms in exegetical letters. One special "letter" that deals with the Psalms
is Jerome's *Ep.* 106, which is not a letter in the conventional sense but a long
treatise on the text and interpretation of the Psalms. *Epistle* 106 was written
as a defense of Jerome's Gallican Psalter, a Latin version of Origen's Greek
text based on the Hexapla. It is this Gallican Psalter that later became the
official Psalter of the Latin Vulgate. In *Ep.* 106, Jerome discusses different
textual and exegetical options according to various Greek and Latin copies
of the Psalms with input from the Hebrew. *Epistle* 106 provides insightful
commentary on the Gallican Psalter, offers a unique window into the complex textual state of the Psalter in the late fourth century, and serves as an
outstanding example of ancient philological scholarship on the Bible. The
present volume offers the first accessible English translation and the first
commentary on this important work of biblical interpretation.

1. Jerome's Life and Writings

1.1. Early Life

Jerome was born around 347 CE and spent his early life in Stridon, a small
town in the Roman province of Dalmatia.[4] He received his primary education in his hometown under the supervision of his Christian parents,
who were wealthy enough to employ teachers for Jerome and his brother.
His parents sent Jerome to Rome at the age of eleven or twelve in order
to study literature and rhetoric. Among Jerome's teachers was the prominent scholar Aelius Donatus, who composed widely read commentaries on
classical authors and a popular Latin grammatical textbook.[5] Later, Jerome
also studied rhetoric and had some exposure to philosophical writers as
part of his formal education. Jerome's parents were obviously intent on
preparing their son for life in the church and in Roman public service. As
he later recollected, "From my cradle, I have been nourished on Catholic
milk" (*Ep.* 82.2.2), and also, "Almost from the cradle, my life has been spent

---

4. On the date of Jerome's birth, see Michael Graves, *Jerome's Hebrew Philology*,
VCSup 90 (Leiden: Brill, 2007), 13 n. 3.

5. On Jerome, Donatus, and the study of γραμματική in antiquity, see Graves,
Jerome's Hebrew Philology, 13–75.

in the company of grammarians, rhetoricians, and philosophers" (*Pref. IH Job* 4).[6]

1.2. Travels in the East

In the late 360s, Jerome traveled to the city of Trier in Gaul, the residence of the emperor Valentinian. But instead of pursuing his career in civil service, Jerome decided to give up his plans for secular advancement and devote his life to Christian ideals. In around 372, Jerome went east to Antioch, and from there in 375 he ventured into the desert of Chalcis in Syria in order to try out the monastic life of withdrawal from society; but Jerome never took to this lifestyle, and within a year or two he returned to Antioch. While in Antioch, Jerome heard lectures by Apollinaris of Laodicea, whom he later claimed proudly as a teacher in scriptural interpretation even though he rejected Apollinaris's teaching on the person of Christ (*Ep.* 84.3.1). To this period belong Jerome's earliest literary productions, including many letters, a lost allegorical commentary on Obadiah, and his *Life of Paul the First Hermit*, an inventive narrative about the supposed monastic predecessor of St. Anthony (ca. 251–356 CE).

Jerome eventually journeyed to Constantinople in order to attend the church council of 381. In Constantinople, Jerome deepened his understanding of Greek theology and cultivated his early admiration for Origen through interactions with Gregory of Nazianzus. While in the East, Jerome significantly improved his command of Greek, picked up some Syriac, and began his study of Hebrew under the tutelage of a Jewish convert to Christianity. During this period, Jerome composed an exegetical letter on Isa 6, a Latin translation and update of Eusebius of Caesarea's *Chronicon*, and translations into Latin of Origen's homilies on Isaiah, Jeremiah, and Ezekiel.

---

6. For a more detailed treatment of Jerome's life and works along the lines given here, see Michael Graves, trans., *Jerome: Commentary on Jeremiah*, Ancient Christian Texts (Downers Grove, IL: IVP Academic, 2011), xxiv–xlvi. An excellent introduction to Jerome's life can be found in Stefan Rebenich, *Jerome*, ECF (New York: Routledge, 2002), 3–59. The most thorough study of Jerome's life is still Ferdinand Cavallera, *Saint Jérôme: Sa vie et son œuvre*, 2 vols. (Paris: Champion, 1922). For an extremely useful catalog of Jerome's works with bibliography, see Alfons Fürst, *Hieronymus: Askese und Wissenschaft in der Spätantike* (Freiberg: Herder, 2003), 283–304. The best biography of Jerome in English remains J. N. D. Kelly, *Jerome: His Life, Writings, and Controversies* (London: Duckworth, 1975).

1.3. Career in Rome

In 382, Jerome returned to Rome. With his knowledge of Greek language
and theology, Eastern monastic experience, and basic Hebrew competence
he quickly found favor with Pope Damasus, whom he served as a secre-
tary. While in Rome, Jerome continued his Hebrew studies by reading with
Jews and by studying the Hebrew text of the Bible alongside the Greek
hexaplaric versions. With encouragement from the Roman bishop, Jerome
translated Origen's homilies on the Song of Songs, and he also produced
lightly revised versions of the Latin Psalms and Gospels based on the best
Greek texts he could obtain in Rome. This first Latin Psalter (ca. 384) is
not extant, but it probably bears some close relationship to the Roman
Psalter (see introduction, §2.1). Jerome also showed enthusiasm for rigorous ascetic ideals, promoting poverty, fasting, self-denial, and virginity.
Unfortunately for Jerome, some important members of the Christian com-
munity in Rome rejected his rigorous ascetic teaching and even criticized
his biblical scholarship, complaining, for example, that his revision of the
Latin Gospels changed too much of the traditional Latin wording. After
Damasus' death, Jerome was forced to leave Rome in 385.[7]

1.4. Residence in Bethlehem

Following his stay in Rome, Jerome decided to return to the East. For a
time, he resided in Egypt, where he listened to the teaching of Didymus
of Alexandria and visited monks in the Egyptian desert. Finally, in 386
Jerome returned to Bethlehem together with his wealthy friend Paula, who

---

7. Jerome's extreme views on Christian self-denial came under sharp scrutiny
after a young woman died in 384 as a result of the harsh regimen of fasting that she
practiced at Jerome's direction. Jerome not only promoted severe forms of piety but
also wrote sarcastically about the majority of Christians in Rome, who failed to live up
to the standards he prescribed. Moreover, Jerome cultivated friendships with several
wealthy widows in Rome who were instrumental in financing his scholarly projects.
This led to suspicions of legacy hunting, or perhaps even relational misconduct with
a wealthy widow, Paula, who eventually traveled with him to the East. After Damasus
died, formal ecclesiastical charges were brought against Jerome. The details of these
proceedings are not fully clear, but it appears that Jerome was given no choice but to
leave Rome. See Andrew Cain, *The Letters of Jerome: Asceticism, Biblical Exegesis, and
the Construction of Christian Authority in Late Antiquity*, OECS (Oxford: Oxford University Press, 2009), 99–128; and Kelly, *Jerome*, 104–15.

had accompanied him from Rome on his eastern trek. Through Paula's resources they established a pair of monasteries, one for men supervised by Jerome and the other for women overseen by Paula. These monasteries served as centers of refuge for the poor and for pilgrims from the West, where aid was given to those in need and Jerome was afforded the time he needed to write.

Jerome lived in Bethlehem for the rest of his life, and his arrival in 386 marked the beginning of a productive time for him as an author. Early in his residence in Bethlehem, Jerome produced commentaries on Galatians, Ephesians, Titus, and Philemon, and also rendered into Latin Didymus' treatise *On the Holy Spirit*. In the late 380s, Jerome translated several biblical books into Latin based on Origen's hexaplaric Septuagint text, including Psalms, Job, Song of Songs, Proverbs, Ecclesiastes, and 1–2 Chronicles. Because Origen's text was a version of the LXX that included adaptations to the Hebrew, it represented a middle path between popular LXX texts on the one hand and a fresh translation from the Hebrew on the other. This second translation of the Psalms is known today as the Gallican Psalter because of its reception in Gaul, and it became the official Psalter of the Latin Vulgate (see introduction, §2.2). The late 380s and early 390s also saw Jerome write several works intended to promote the value of Hebrew scholarship, such as his *Book of Hebrew Names, Book of Hebrew Place Names,* and *Hebrew Questions on Genesis.* Jerome also wrote exegetical works on Ecclesiastes (late 380s) and the Psalms (*Commentarioli,* early 390s), which reflected his ever-increasing interest in Hebrew and Jewish traditions. The monastic life continued to hold Jerome's attention, as he wrote two more lives of idealized ascetic characters, *The Life of Hilarion,* and *The Life of Malchus the Captive Monk.* Jerome likewise continued his work as a translator, rendering into Latin Origen's homilies on Luke. Throughout all his years in Bethlehem, Jerome stayed in constant contact with friends in Rome through letters. Most of his works were written with this audience in mind.

1.5. IH Edition, Hebrew Scholarship, and Controversies

A new phase of Jerome's scholarship began in 391 with the start of his translation of the Old Testament from Hebrew into Latin.[8] Partly because

---

8. In the early years of his translation project based on the original Hebrew, Jerome

of the newness of translating directly from the Hebrew, and partly because
of his reliance on Jewish sources, Jerome was sharply criticized for making
this translation. One of his prominent critics was Augustine, who only later
in life came to recognize the value of Jerome's version.[9] Jerome completed
his translation *iuxta Hebraicum* (IH) in 405, and for each biblical book
he included a preface where he explained his work and defended himself
against detractors. The book of Psalms was one of the first books Jerome
translated from the Hebrew. This third of Jerome's Latin Psalters was completed by 393. Although it did not ultimately win a place in the medieval
Vulgate Bible, the IH Psalter continued to be copied and studied as a scholarly resource (see introduction, §2.3).

Jerome engaged in many theological controversies in his career. His
harshest and most personal controversy erupted in 393, when Bishop
Epiphanius of Salamis came to Palestine in order to secure signatures on a
document condemning Origen for some of his speculative theological ideas.
In spite of Jerome's former praise of Origen and his earlier enthusiasm for
translating Origen's exegetical writings, Jerome agreed to sign the condem-
nation.[10] But Rufinus, Jerome's former friend who also translated Origen's
works and who now lived in Jerusalem, refused to condemn Origen. This

---

stated, "Therefore, with full knowledge and recognition (of the difficulties and potential criticisms), I send forth my hand into the flame" (*Pref. Isa.* 3).

9. Augustine first criticized Jerome for his Hebrew translation project in *Ep.* 28
(written in 394 or 395), in which he wonders how Jerome could possibly improve on
the Septuagint. Augustine spelled out his belief in the authority of the Septuagint in
Doctr. chr. 2.15 (written in 396). Later, in *Ep.* 71 (written in 403), Augustine expressed
concern that Jerome's Hebrew-based translation could cause a rift between East and
West, and he also raised the problem of how Jerome's work could be checked for accuracy, since no other Christian knew Hebrew. Augustine also recounted the story of
a bishop in the town of Oea who introduced Jerome's translation of Jonah into his
congregation and almost lost control of his church because of the strife that resulted.
Jerome answered Augustine point by point in his *Ep.* 112 in 404, defending his translation of the plant in Jonah 4:6 as "ivy" rather than the traditional Septuagint (and Old
Latin) translation, "gourd." Augustine showed only slight concessions to Jerome's position in his *Ep.* 82 (written in 405), yet in *Civ.* 18.42–44 (written sometime after 420),
Augustine allows for both the Septuagint and the Hebrew text to be inspired, and he
refers to Jerome as "a most learned man, skilled in all three languages" (i.e., Hebrew,
Greek and Latin). Moreover, in *Doctr. chr.* 4.7.15 (composed in the late 420s), Augustine quotes Amos in Jerome's IH version rather than the Septuagint.

10. E.g., Jerome's earlier comment that Origen was "the greatest teacher of the
churches after the apostles" (*Nom. hebr.*, Pref.).

caused a public feud between Jerome and Rufinus, which involved not only the Eastern bishops Epiphanius (against Origen) and John of Jerusalem (in favor of Origen) but also significant members of the church in Rome and their networks in the Latin-speaking world.[11] After a brief reconciliation in 397, arguments and allegations erupted again in 398, culminating in 401 with Rufinus's *Apology against Jerome* and Jerome's *Apology against Rufinus* (401–402), in which both men attacked each other, Jerome being particularly virulent in assailing his opponent's integrity and orthodoxy. Jerome became more and more outspoken against Origen's doctrinal errors from this time forward, even though he continued to consult Origen's exegetical works and profit from them. Furthermore, Jerome continued to attack Rufinus for following the heresies of Origen, even after Rufinus's death. Despite such turmoil, however, this period was not lacking in biblical scholarship. In addition to the IH translations he was producing, Jerome also completed a commentary on Matthew in 397–398, and sometime in the mid-390s he began his series of commentaries on the Minor Prophets.

Jerome's last years kept him busy with controversy and scholarship. Examples of Jerome's engagement in theological controversy include his *Against Vigilantius* (406) and *Dialogue against the Pelagians* (415). Remarkably, such conflicts did not prevent Jerome from continuing to write biblical commentaries, although these later commentaries show clear indications of the Pelagian debate while still keeping the errors of Origen in view. The final fifteen years of Jerome's life saw him reach his full measure of competence as a Hebraist and interpreter of the Old Testament. Jerome completed his commentary on the Minor Prophets in 401, wrote an abbreviated commentary on Daniel in 407, and then followed up with commentaries on Isaiah (408–410), Ezekiel (410–414), and Jeremiah. Jerome began his commentary on Jeremiah in 414, and reached the end of chapter thirty-two by the time of his death in 419 (or 420).

2. Jerome's Three Translations of the Psalms

As noted in the previous section, Jerome produced three different Latin translations of the Psalter. It will be useful here to list these three Latin Psalters together and highlight their differences.

---

11. E.g., in his *Ep.* 73.6 Augustine reports that the conflict between Jerome and Rufinus was widely known, even in North Africa.

2.1. The Roman Psalter

In the preface to his Gallican Psalter, Jerome states: "A short time ago when I was at Rome, I emended the Psalter; I corrected it, although hastily, for the most part based on the Seventy translators."[12] Jerome proceeds to justify the need for his Gallican Psalter by explaining that this first revision had already suffered corruption at the hands of copyists. This first Psalter was thus produced in Rome around 384, and Jerome seems to have completely ignored it once he composed the Gallican Psalter. In fact, it is unclear whether any trace of this first Latin Psalter survives. There is a tradition going back centuries that identifies Jerome's Roman Psalter with the traditional Roman Psalter still used liturgically in St. Peter's Basilica in Rome. Although some still defend this identification, the most common view is that the preserved Roman Psalter is not the same as Jerome's Roman Psalter, which is essentially lost.[13] J. N. D. Kelly suggested that the preserved Roman Psalter might represent the text that Jerome revised in producing his own (now lost) Roman Psalter.[14]

2.2. The Gallican Psalter

Between around 386 and around 392, Jerome translated several books into Latin based on Origen's hexaplaric recension of the Septuagint. The books for which we have evidence are Psalms, Job, and the Song of Songs (all extant), and also Proverbs, Ecclesiastes, and 1–2 Chronicles (known from the surviving prefaces). It is unclear whether Jerome completed the rest of the Old Testament from the Hexapla or whether he abandoned this project when he started his IH edition.[15] The hexaplaric LXX Psalter came to

---

12. *Psalterium Romae dudum positus emendaram et iuxta Septuaginta interpretes, licet cursim, magna illud ex parte correxeram* (*Pref. GPsal* 1). See also **12.2.10**.

13. See Aline Canellis, ed., *Jérôme: Préfaces aux livres de la Bible*, SC 592 (Paris: Cerf, 2017), 406–7; and Colette Estin, *Les Psautiers de Jérôme à la lumière des traductions juives antérieures*, Collectanea Biblica Latina 15 (Rome: San Girolamo, 1984), 25–28.

14. Kelly, *Jerome*, 89.

15. On the one hand, Jerome sometimes wrote as if he had revised the entire Old Testament according to the hexaplaric text (e.g., *Ruf.* 2.24, 3.25; *Ep.* 71.5; *Ep.* 106.2.2; *Ep.* 134.2), and Cassiodorus (d. 583) claimed to have used Jerome's hexaplaric translation in the production of a large one-volume Bible. Furthermore, Jerome's LXX translation in his *Commentary on Isaiah* looks like a Latin version of the hexaplaric

be known as the Gallican Psalter due to its popular reception in Gaul. In his own original edition of the Gallican Psalter, Jerome employed asterisks to mark additions from the hexaplaric versions (typically Theodotion) to match the Hebrew, and obeli to mark passages that were absent from the Hebrew (see introduction, §8.2; and **7.2.5–12**). Jerome essentially copied these signs from the hexaplaric LXX, although it is possible that he occasionally used these critical signs creatively to mark his own observations based on the Hebrew, without direct warrant in the hexaplaric edition (see **55.2.21–22**). Unfortunately, soon after its initial publication, the Gallican Psalter came to be copied without the critical signs; as a result, most preserved copies of the Gallican Psalter lack these signs altogether.[16]

Although the famous Codex Amiatinus produced in Northumbria around 700 used Jerome's IH Psalter, the Bible published by Alcuin in the early ninth century combined Jerome's IH translation for most books (except for the Psalms) with the Gallican Psalter. It was Alcuin's configuration with the Gallican Psalter that became the standard Latin Bible of the Middle Ages. Given the familiarity most Christians had with the wording of the Psalms according to some version of the Vetus Latina, it was natural that the Gallican Psalter would gain general acceptance rather than the IH Psalter, even as Jerome's IH translations became standard for other books. By the early Renaissance period, the standard medieval Bible (including the Gallican Psalter) was known as the *editio vulgata*, the "common edi-

---

Isaiah text. This could be taken as evidence that Jerome finished the hexaplaric translation project. See Gryson, VLR 12, 18–19; and Gryson., ed., *Commentaire de Jérôme sur le Prophète Isaïe, Livres I–IV* (Freiburg: Herder, 1993), 52. On the other hand, Jerome never mentions any other hexaplaric revisions beyond Psalms, Job, Song of Songs, Proverbs, Ecclesiastes, and 1–2 Chronicles, not even in the prefaces to IH books; and Jerome makes no mention of the hexaplaric revision in *On Illustrious Men* (see Kelly, *Jerome*, 159). The apparently "hexaplaric" translation in a work such as the *Commentary on Isaiah* might simply show that Jerome was translating directly from the hexaplaric LXX when he wrote the commentary; see Pierre Jay, *L'exégèse de saint Jérôme d'après son "Commentaire sur Isaïe"* (Paris: Études Augustiniennes, 1985), 118, 125. Jerome's statements that suggest he revised the entire Old Testament according to the LXX might be nothing more than exaggeration. These statements might have misled Cassiodorus into thinking that texts he had at hand were Jerome's complete hexaplaric edition.

16. Two copies of the Gallican Psalter that preserve critical signs are the Cathach Psalter of St. Columba (seventh century) and Vatican, Reg. lat. 11 (eighth century). See introduction, §4.3.

tion" or "Vulgate."[17] The following fact should be noted, however: when Jerome uses the term *editio vulgata*, he is referring to the popular edition of his day, either the common Septuagint text or the common Vetus Latina version.

2.3. The IH Psalter

Jerome referred to this translation as his version *iuxta Hebraicum* ("according to the Hebrew"), or as the rendering *apud Hebraeos* ("among the Hebrews"), or else as *mea interpretatio* ("my translation") or *editio nostra* ("our edition").[18] Jerome probably began translating the IH edition in 391. As *Ep.* 48.4 (394) indicates, the sixteen prophetic books (including Daniel) were already circulating at Rome in 394, Samuel–Kings had been available for some time, and Job had recently been completed. Although *Ep.* 48.4 does not mention the Psalms, Jerome's *On Illustrious Men* 134 (393) shows that the Prophets and the IH Psalter were already complete. Thus, we know that IH Psalms, the Prophets, and Samuel–Kings were finished by at least 393, and Job was just completed in 394. Some consider Samuel–Kings to be the first translation because the extended preface to these books, the *Prologus Galeatus* or "Helmeted Preface," could have served as an introduction to the whole project.[19] Others argue that the Prophets preceded Samuel–Kings, since the preface to IH Isaiah introduces the presentation of the text *per cola et commata*, "by clauses and phrases," as if perhaps introducing it for the whole series of translations. If the Prophets indeed came before Samuel–Kings, the discussion of canon in the preface to Daniel may have inspired Jerome to begin his next translation (i.e., Samuel–Kings) with a preface dealing with the canon, namely, the *Prologus Galeatus*.[20] It is unclear how IH Psalms fits in chronologically with these other early translations. On the basis of *On Illustrious Men*, one might conclude that IH Psalms along with IH Prophets were the first IH translations. The lack of reference to IH Psalms in *Ep.* 48.4 could be explained by supposing that Jerome had

---

17. See Edmund F. Sutcliffe, "The Name 'Vulgate,'" *Bib* 29 (1948): 345–52.

18. E.g., see *Comm. Jer.* Pref.; 31:21–22; 31:37; *Pref. IH Job*; *Pref. Ezra*; *Pref. IH Ps.*; *Ep.* 78:20.

19. See Kelly, *Jerome*, 161; and H. F. D. Sparks, "The Latin Bible," in *The Bible in its Ancient and English Versions*, ed. Henry W. Robinson (Oxford: Clarendon, 1940), 112.

20. See Pierre Jay, "La datation des premières traductions de l'Ancien Testament sur l'hébreu par saint Jérôme," *REAug* 28 (1982): 208–12.

published this edition early (391 or 392) and that his substantial changes to the traditional wording received an unfavorable reception.[21] The fact that the prologue to IH Psalms does not appear to have been written to serve as an introduction to the IH edition as a whole could be taken to mean that it was translated second after the Prophets, but it could also be explained by supposing that Jerome translated IH Psalms first and published it before he was ready to announce his intentions for the project as a whole. I will return to the question of the date and context of Jerome's translation of IH Psalms in the introduction, §6.2.

In the preface to his IH Psalter, Jerome defends his decision to translate from the Hebrew by claiming that the work's primary purpose is to assist Christians in debating with Jews and that he does not necessarily expect the work to be read in churches. Whether or not this argument represents Jerome's genuine sentiment in light of his commitment to the Hebrew text as the standard of truth (the *hebraica veritas*), it certainly accords with his customary respect for the traditional wording of the Latin Bible (see introduction, §7.2.2), especially where singing the Psalms is concerned (see **46.5.1–4**). Jerome also announces in the preface to IH Psalms that, following in the wake of Aquila, Symmachus, and Theodotion, he will render the Hebrew Psalter into Latin as a *novam editionem* ("new edition"). In reality, Jerome relies heavily on the hexaplaric versions in translating the IH Psalter, although he does not follow the interpretation of any one consistently, and sometimes he is independent of all three, thus showing that the Hebrew as he understands it is the final authority. Still, at this early stage of his production of the IH edition, Jerome is more dependent on the hexaplaric versions for his understanding of the Hebrew than he will be in later years.[22] Obviously, Jerome's competence in Hebrew in the early 390s at the start of his IH project was not as strong as it became by the end of this project in 405.

---

21. In his preface to IH Psalms, Jerome devotes considerable space (even for him) to denouncing those who criticize his learned work, probably because he received negative feedback from those who had heard about his IH Psalter and perhaps had even seen early excerpts.

22. Justin Rogers summarizes: "Although in translating PsH, Jerome did not have the benefit of the Hebraic learning he would acquire over the next several decades, the translation is generally faithful to the Hebrew"; see "Psalms: 10.3.7 Vulgate," in *Writings*, vol. 1C of *Textual History of the Bible: The Hebrew Bible*, ed. Armin Lange (Leiden: Brill, 2017), 106.

As noted in the previous section on the Gallican Psalter, the IH Psalter did not become the standard version of the Psalms for the medieval Latin Bible. Over time, it was the Gallican Psalter, not the IH Psalter, that displaced the Vetus Latina version. Still, Jerome's IH Psalter was copied throughout the Middle Ages, often being employed as a scholarly tool.[23] In the early ninth century, for example, Theodulf of Orlean supervised the production of scholarly Latin Bibles that employed Jerome's IH Psalter. Later, Remigius of Auxerre (d. 908) in his commentary on the Gallican Psalter used the IH Psalter as a source of information about the Hebrew text. In the twelfth century, Herbert of Bosham (ca. 1120–ca. 1195) composed a commentary on IH Psalms in which he demonstrated his own functional knowledge of Hebrew. The IH Psalter never fell out of usage, even if it did not typically serve as the primary Psalter for liturgical purposes. The relationship between the IH Psalter and *Ep.* 106 is addressed below (introduction, §§5.3 and 6.2).

3. Jerome's *Epistle* 106

3.1. Content and Type of Letter

Jerome's letters have long been noted for the extensive amount of biblical exegesis and criticism they contain. In 1904, when Eugène Tisserant (later Cardinal Tisserant) arrived at the Biblical School of the Dominican Fathers in Jerusalem, he asked archaeologist Fr. Louis-Hughes Vincent what he should read in order to prepare for serious study of the Old Testament. The corpus of Jerome's letters was one of the three works recommended to him.[24] As it turns out, the substantial biblical content of Jerome's letters, along with their frequent emphasis on ascetic themes, makes perfect sense once it is realized that most of these letters are not simply personal com-

---

23. See Michael Graves, "Glimpses into the History of the Hebrew Bible through the Vulgate Tradition, with Special Reference to Vulgate MS θ^G," in *The Text of the Hebrew Bible and Its Editions*, ed. Andrés P. Otero and Pablo T. Morales (Leiden: Brill, 2017), 217–54.

24. Eugène Cardinal Tisserant, foreword to *A Monument to St. Jerome*, ed. Francis X. Murphy (New York: Sheed & Ward, 1952), ix. The three works recommended were Jerome's letters, Emil Schürer's *History of the Jewish People in the Age of Jesus Christ*, and a French translation of the *Zend-Avesta*. According to Tisserant, he read the first two of these works.

munications between friends but stylized compositions intended to promote Jerome's status as an expert in biblical scholarship and ascetic practice.[25] When we read Jerome's letters, on the whole, we are not peering into the inner workings of his relationships; instead, we are reading carefully crafted short notes and treatises that champion Jerome's viewpoints on select topics and Jerome himself as the expert on these topics. In this light, *Ep.* 106 is best understood as a scholarly treatise on the Gallican Psalter.

In terms of epistolary type, Andrew Cain rightly classifies *Ep.* 106 as "Apologetic" (ἀπολογητικός).[26] This treatise offers a sustained response to criticisms leveled against Jerome's Gallican Psalter. Jerome's treatment of every biblical passage, whether it deals with the form of the text or its meaning, is intended to show that the rendering Jerome gave in the Gallican Psalter is correct or at least defensible as an informed option.

3.2. Structure and Rhetoric of *Epistle* 106

The structure of *Ep.* 106 is simple and its style highly formulaic. The treatise begins with a paragraph in which Jerome praises Sunnia and Fretela, using scriptural imagery for their interest in the "Hebrew truth" (*hebraica veritas*). Next, Jerome explains his preference for the hexaplaric Septuagint over the popular or Lucianic Septuagint on the grounds that the hexaplaric text agrees more with the Hebrew. It was this hexaplaric edition of the Septuagint that served as the basis for Jerome's Gallican Psalter. After this follows the body of *Ep.* 106, which consists of textual examinations of 177 select passages from the Psalms. In each case, the discourse unit begins with a quotation from the Gallican Psalter about which Sunnia and Fretela had asked a question (*Prima ... quaestio*; **3.1**). Jerome then reports the content of the challenge that the two Gothic clergymen raised, typically using language such as "in place of this, in Greek it has" (*pro quo habetur in Graeco*), "you say that you have found" (*invenisse vos dicitis*), or "you say that you have read" (*legisse vos dicitis*). In other words, as the letter presents itself, Sunnia and Fretela wrote to Jerome and asked him to explain for each of these 177 passages why he translated as he did in the Gallican Psalter given that the Greek text has a different reading or requires a different translation. Jerome's explanations for some passages are more than a page

---

25. See Cain, *The Letters of Jerome*.
26. Cain, *The Letters of Jerome*, 209–10.

in length, and in other cases Jerome dismisses the objection in a sentence. This central section, with 177 sections comprising (1) a quotation from Jerome's version, (2) the proposed alternative based on the Greek, and (3) Jerome's justification for his translation choice, takes up roughly forty out of forty-three total pages in the CSEL edition. *Epistle* 106 concludes with Jerome's explanations of six Greek words: νεομηνία, ἔρημος, θρόνος, νυκτικόραξ, κυνόμυια, and λαξευτήριον, the meanings of which Jerome says were requested by Sunnia and Fretela and also by a certain Avitus, who is similarly mentioned at the start of *Ep.* 106 (see **2.2.25**). The authenticity of *Ep.* 106 as a letter is addressed below (introduction, §6.1).

The first passage discussed is from Ps 5:6 (Heb 5:5b), and the final passage is from Ps 146:10 (Heb 147:10). Generally, Jerome works through the Psalter in order, from earlier chapters and verses to later ones, the only exceptions occurring at **63.1** (Ps 101:8) and **63.2** (Ps 101:7), and **65.3** (Ps 103:25) and **65.4** (Ps 103:14), where in each case Jerome takes a verse out of order. See table 1 below for a list of passages discussed; the references given are according to the Gallican Psalter, followed by Hebrew versification in parentheses.

In the vast majority of cases the text that begins the discussion, which presumably was cited back to Jerome together with an objection, is Jerome's Gallican Psalter translation. A select number of passages present complications or exceptions. In several instances, the text quoted back to Jerome as his own reflects a miscopying of the Gallican Psalter, and Jerome points out that the supposed objection is actually based on his interlocutors' faulty text (see **12.1**; **29.3**; **30.3**; **33.4**; **41.1**; **41.2**; **46.3**; **52.1**; **57.3**; **69.1**). In other instances, the text quoted as Jerome's translation differs from the Gallican Psalter in some small way that is not relevant to the question, and it is unclear whether the difference represents a transmission error in *Ep.* 106 or the Gallican Psalter (manuscript evidence is often conflicted), or whether Sunnia and Fretela misquoted the text and Jerome failed to notice (see **14.1**; **23.2**; **33.3**; **35.2**; **36.1**; **64.1**; **67.4**).[27] Otherwise, in one passage Jerome begins not with his own rendering but with the text suggested by Sunnia and Fretela (**15.1**); in one passage Jerome intentionally gives the Greek form of a loanword (**63.2**); and in another passage the difference is simply one of spelling: *herodii* versus *erodii* (**65.5**). An

---

27. In three cases where manuscript evidence for *Ep.* 106 and the Gallican Psalter is complex (**37.1**; **75.2**; **75.4**), I argue in the commentary that in their original forms they matched.

intriguing complication occurs at **71.1**, which involves not only a miscopying of the Gallican Psalter text by Sunnia and Fretela but also a quiet correction of the Gallican Psalter by Jerome. Apart from these complications and exceptions, the standard pattern of *Ep.* 106 is that Jerome's Gallican Psalter is quoted back to him, an objection is stated, and then he answers the objection. The consistent rhetorical thrust of *Ep.* 106 is the justification of the Gallican Psalter.

Table 1: Psalms Passages Discussed in *Epistle* 106 (177 total)

5:6 (5:5b)	30:23 (31:23)	55:3–4 (56:3–4)
5:9 (5:9)	31:2 (32:2)	55:8 (56:8)
6:11 (6:11)	31:4 (32:4)	58:10 (59:10)
7:9 (7:9)	34:10 (35:10)	58:11 (59:11)
8:4 (8:4)	36:23 (37:23)	58:12a (59:11b)
16:2 (17:2)	38:12 (39:11)	58:12 (59:12)
16:8 (17:8)	39:9 (40:9)	58:14 (59:14)
16:13 (17:13)	39:14 (40:14)	59:11 (60:11)
17:14 (18:14)	40:7 (41:7)	60:6 (61:6)
17:34 (18:34)	41:6–7 (42:6–7)	60:9 (61:9)
17:36 (18:36)	41:11 (42:11)	61:9 (62:9)
17:40 (18:40)	41:12 (42:12)	62:2 (63:2)
17:47 (18:47)	43:10 (44:10)	63:8 (64:8)
17:48 (18:49)	43:15 (44:15)	64:8 (65:8)
18:6 (19:6)	43:26 (44:27)	64:10 (65:10)
19:5 (20:5)	44:6 (45:6)	65:15 (66:15)
19:10 (20:10)	47:5 (48:5)	65:19 (66:19)
21:20 (22:20)	47:9 (48:9)	67:5 (68:5)
21:24 (22:24)	47:10 (48:10)	67:19 (68:19)
22:5 (23:5)	48:15 (49:15)	67:19–20 (68:19–20)
24:4a (25:3b)	48:16 (49:16)	67:25a (68:25a)
24:21 (25:21)	48:21 (49:21)	67:25b (68:25b)
26:6 (27:6)	49:20 (50:20)	67:33 (68:33)
26:8 (27:8)	49:22 (50:22)	68:31 (69:31)
27:2 (28:2)	49:23 (50:23)	70:12 (71:12)
28:9 (29:9)	54:9a (55:9a)	70:17 (71:17)
28:10 (29:10)	54:9b (55:9b)	70:18 (71:18)
30:5 (31:5)	54:13 (55:13)	71:11 (72:11)

71:18 (72:18)

71:19 (72:19)

72:7 (73:7)

72:11 (73:11)

72:17 (73:17)

72:26 (73:26)

72:28 (73:28)

73:1 (74:1)

73:3 (74:3)

73:8 (74:8)

73:13–14 (74:13–14)

73:23 (74:23)

74:2 (75:2)

75:6 (76:6)

75:12–13 (76:12–13)

76:7 (77:7)

76:9 (77:9)

77:6 (78:6)

77:31 (78:31)

77:36 (78:36)

77:38 (78:38)

77:54 (78:54)

77:57 (78:57)

77:69b (78:69b)

77:72 (78:72)

78:1 (79:1)

79:10 (80:10)

82:13 (83:13)

83:3 (84:3)

83:6 (84:6)

83:7 (84:9)

84:2 (85:2)

84:11a (85:11a)

85:14 (86:14)

85:15 (86:15)

88:8 (89:8)

88:20 (89:20)

88:39 (89:39)

89:2 (90:2)

89:10 (90:10)

90:2 (91:2)

93:12 (94:12)

93:23 (94:23)

97:3 (98:3)

100:6 (101:6)

101:7 (102:7)

101:8 (102:8)

101:11 (102:11)

101:15 (102:15)

102:9 (103:9)

103:4 (104:4)

103:7 (104:7)

103:25 (104:25)

103:14 (104:14)

103:17 (104:17)

103:18 (104:18)

104:30 (105:30)

104:33 (105:33)

104:42 (105:42)

105:1 (106:1)

105:7a (106:7a)

105:7b (106:7b)

105:44 (106:44)

106:29 (107:29)

106:30 (107:30)

107:3 (108:3)

107:10 (108:10)

109:2a (110:2a)

109:2b (110:2b)

110:1 (111:1)

113:11 (115:3)

114:2 (116:2)

114:9 (116:9)

117:10 (118:10)

118:47 (119:47)

118:48 (119:48)

118:59a (119:59a)

118:59b (119:59b)

118:69 (119:69)

118:109 (119:109)

118:136 (119:136)

118:172 (119:172)

119:2 (120:2)

126:5 (127:5)

129:4 (130:4–5)

131:2 (132:2)

135:7 (136:7)

137:2 (138:2)

138:4 (139:4)

139:6 (140:6)

139:14 (140:14)

140:7 (141:7)

146:10 (147:10)

4. The Text of the Psalms in Jerome's Time

Because the primary topic of *Ep.* 106 is the text of the Psalter, it will be useful to set forth some basic information about the textual evidence for the book of Psalms in order to comprehend Jerome's arguments and fit them into their broader framework. Throughout *Ep.* 106, Jerome discusses possible Latin translations of the Greek Psalter, with constant reference to different Greek readings and regular appeals to the Hebrew. Below are brief summaries of the current state of research on the Hebrew, Greek, and Latin texts of the Psalms along with explanations of the manuscript witnesses for these texts that are cited in my commentary to illuminate Jerome's discussions.

4.1. The Hebrew Text of the Psalms

The base text for research on the Hebrew Bible, including the Hebrew Psalter, is the medieval Masoretic Text (MT). This is typically represented by the Leningrad Codex (1009 CE) as given in *Biblia Hebraica Stuttgartensia* (eds. Elliger and Rudolph, 1977). In a few difficult passages, the text was confirmed in *The Leningrad Codex: A Facsimile Edition* (eds. Freedman, Beck, and Sanders, 1998). Another important witness to the MT is the Aleppo Codex (ca. 925 CE), which I checked for each contested Hebrew passage in *Jerusalem Crown*.[28] In addition, I occasionally report readings from the apparatus of Benjamin Kennicott's *Vetus Testamentum cum Variis Lectionibus* (1780) and from Giovanni de-Rossi's *Variae Lectiones Veteris Testamenti* (1788), both of which list variants taken from mostly late masoretic manuscripts. These two substantial eighteenth-century collections of Hebrew readings were assembled in the hope that different recensions of biblical books might be discovered through the collation of all preserved Hebrew manuscripts. This hope did not materialize, since all the manuscripts discovered represent the MT type, and the vast majority of variant readings are secondary vis-à-vis earlier MT witnesses such as the Leningrad and Aleppo codices.[29] Overall, the text-critical value of these late manuscripts is

---

28. See Yosef Ofer and Mordechai Glatzer, eds, *Jerusalem Crown: The Bible of the Hebrew University of Jerusalem*, 2nd ed. (Jerusalem: N. Ben-Zvi, 2004).

29. See Moshe H. Goshen-Gottstein, "Hebrew Biblical Manuscripts: Their History and Their Place in the HUBP Edition," *Bib* 48 (1967): 243–90. Goshen-Gottstein

not great.[30] Nevertheless, this does not mean that early readings are totally
lacking in these texts. For example, Jerome sometimes presupposes or even
spells out a Hebrew word that matches a reading from Kennicott rather
than the Leningrad Codex.[31] Such agreements are also found in Hebrew-
based glosses registered in the margins of ninth-century Theodulfian Latin
Bibles.[32] Therefore, I cite medieval Hebrew variants from Kennicott and
De-Rossi wherever they lend meaningful support to earlier readings or else
illuminate the text's history in relation to notable errors or corrections.

The discovery of the Qumran scrolls has provided fresh insight into
the early text of the Hebrew Psalter, yet the Qumran evidence has generated different interpretations. On the one hand, deviations from the
MT in Qumran fragments, especially when interpreted next to specific
textual variants in the Septuagint, suggest that the proto-MT was not the
only textual tradition for the Psalms in the first century BCE.[33] On the
other hand, the proto-MT is clearly represented at Qumran, and overall
the Hebrew consonantal text presumed by the Septuagint is close to the
proto-MT. Scholars debate how diverse the text of the book of Psalms was
in the first century BCE.[34] By the second century CE, however, the proto-
MT was established, and the consonantal Hebrew text of Jerome's time was
definitely of the proto-MT type. Major deviations from MT do not factor
into our analysis of the Hebrew text underlying Jerome's Latin translation. Still, in numerous passages the evidence for the Greek Psalter raises

----

correctly recognized the limited value of these late masoretic manuscripts, but his *tout
court* dismissal of this body of readings is probably too extreme.

30. For a cautious assessment of the value of the readings listed in Kennicott and
De-Rossi, see Emanuel Tov, *Textual Criticism of the Hebrew Bible*, 3rd ed. (Minneapolis: Fortress, 2011), 36–39.

31. E.g., see מחסיה at *Comm. Jer.* 32:12 (Jerome and Kennicott: מעשיה), and אנש
at *Comm. Jer.* 17:9 (Jerome and Kennicott: אנוש); see Graves, *Jerome: Commentary on
Jeremiah*, 208, 107; and Kennicott 2:137, 115.

32. E.g., see לביתו at 1 Sam 23:18 (θ[G] gloss and Kennicott: לדרכו), and at 1 Sam
25:17 the omission of כל in θ[G] (gloss) and Kennicott; see Graves, "Glimpses into the
History," 238–41; and Kennicott 1:550, 553.

33. In particular, the Qumran scrolls offer some variations in the order of Psalms
within collections and the inclusion or exclusion of certain Psalms. It is not clear, however, that all of these texts are meant to be copies of the book of Psalms, rather than
liturgical texts.

34. See Brent A. Strawn, "10.1 Textual History of the Psalms," in Lange, *Writings*, 5–23; Armin Lange and Brent A. Strawn, "Psalms 10.2 Ancient Hebrew Texts," in
Lange, *Writings*, 24–81.

questions about the Hebrew text, and even some Latin texts presuppose a vocalization that differs from MT. Where Hebrew evidence from Qumran is relevant, the scrolls are cited according to *The Biblical Qumran Scrolls: Transcriptions and Textual Variants* (ed. Ulrich, 2013).

In addition to MT and Qumran Hebrew readings, other witnesses to the Hebrew include Cairo Genizah manuscripts (cited from BHS), the Arabic version (cited from BHS), the Syriac Peshitta (cited from the Leiden Peshiṭta Institute edition, 1980), and the Aramaic Targums (cited from the edition of White, 1988).

4.2. The Greek Text of the Psalms

Various Greek readings are discussed in *Ep.* 106. Typically, Jerome reports the Greek text as quoted by Sunnia and Fretela, who appealed to the Greek as the basis for their criticism of the Gallican Psalter. Jerome either accepts the Greek as given and defends his version based on translation principles, or else he rejects their "popular" Greek text in favor of the "hexaplaric" Greek text that underlies the Gallican Psalter. In order to set Jerome's comments in their context and clarify the logic of his arguments, I identify (as much as possible) the Greek readings cited in *Ep.* 106 with reference to major witnesses to the Septuagint. Generally speaking, I do not attempt to reconstruct the Old Greek reading, although I sometimes need to distinguish between the prerevised Greek text and the corrected form. Moreover, my analysis of Greek witnesses is not systematic enough to allow for any conclusions about the affiliations between witnesses, although I hope that my analysis will make it easier for Septuagint scholars to integrate *Ep.* 106 into the history of the Greek Psalter. Below (introduction, §5.1) I present what conclusions I can based on my comparison of *Ep.* 106 with the Greek evidence. It should be clear from the commentary that the readings presented by Jerome in this treatise map directly to the actual state of the Greek text of the book of Psalms in Jerome's time.

The Greek Psalter is attested by more manuscripts than any other book of the Greek Bible.[35] Most scholars place the translation of the Greek Psalter in the second century BCE, although some favor the first century BCE.

---

35. On the current state of scholarship on the Greek Psalter, see James K. Aitkin, "Psalms," in *The T&T Clark Companion to the Septuagint*, ed. James K. Aitkin (London: Bloomsbury T&T Clark, 2015), 320–34; Jannes Smith, "Psalms: 10.3.1 Septuagint," in Lange, *Writings*, 82–88; and Eberhard Bons and Ralph Brucker, "*Psalmoi*/The Book

The translator of Greek Psalms apparently made use of the Greek Pentateuch and therefore came later than the Greek Pentateuch. Translation
technique studies support the conclusion that one translator is respon-
sible for the entire Greek Psalter. Most scholars view Egypt as the likely
place of origin, but others have suggested that the translation was made in
Palestine.[36] Overall, the Greek book of Psalms is a relatively literal representation of its Hebrew *Vorlage* (e.g., word order, lexical correspondence),
which is close to the MT. Certain Hebraizing features of the Greek Psalms
resemble translation techniques associated with the so-called kaige movement, although the Greek Psalter appears to be an independent work that
predates the activity of kaige revision.[37] The general closeness of the Greek

---

of Psalms," in *Introduction to the Septuagint*, ed. Siegfried Kreuzer, trans. David A.
Brenner and Peter Altmann (Waco, TX: Baylor University Press, 2019), 297–316.

36. One piece of evidence cited in favor of Palestine as the place where the Greek
Psalter was produced is Jerome's comment in *Ep.* 65.14.7 that there is a word βᾶρις
(often "boat") used "up to today" in Palestine for buildings that are enclosed all around
and fortified with walls and towers. Jerome does not say anything about how the word
is used elsewhere, but if one takes the meaning "boat" to reflect Egyptian usage (see
LSJ, s.v. "βᾶρις": "*flat-bottomed boat*, used in Egypt") and Jerome's "fortified building" to reflect Palestinian usage, then, because this word appears in the Greek Psalter
with the meaning "palace, fortress" (LXX Ps 44:9; 47:4, 14), one might conclude that
the Greek Psalter was translated in Palestine. Jerome's comment, however, should not
be pressed too far. It would hardly be surprising if a "Palestinian" word usage was
employed by Jewish biblical translators in Egypt (or elsewhere). Furthermore, even if
Jerome's knowledge of linguistic usage is relatively accurate (Jerome lived for a brief
time in Egypt and was fluent in Greek), one can hardly expect him to possess exhaustive information about how a given word was used in all other regions and in previous
centuries. In reality, Jerome's comment in *Ep.* 65.14.7 suggests nothing more than that
there was a word βᾶρις used in Palestine with the meaning "fortified building." One
cannot conclude from this that βᾶρις was not used in this sense elsewhere.

37. See Peter J. Gentry, "The Greek Psalter and the καίγε Tradition: Methodological
Questions," in *The Old Greek Psalter: Studies in Honor of Albert Pietersma*, ed. Robert
J. V. Hiebert, Claude E. Cox, and Peter J. Gentry (Sheffield: Sheffield Academic, 2001),
74–97. It should be noted that Eugene Ulrich explains the overall closeness of Greek
Psalms witnesses to the proto-MT by positing that the Old Greek (now mostly lost)
has secondarily been brought into conformity with the Hebrew; see Eugene Ulrich,
"The Dead Sea Scrolls and Their Implications for an Edition of the Septuagint Psalter,"
in *Der Septuaginta-Psalter und seine Tochterübersetzungen*, ed. Anneli Aejmelaeus and
Udo Quast (Göttingen: Vandenhoeck & Ruprecht, 2000), 323–36. Of course, adjustments of the Old Greek toward the Hebrew are at least part of the broader transmission
picture for the Greek Psalter.

Psalter to the MT does not preclude the existence of numerous differences in individual passages between the Greek and Hebrew witnesses due to factors such as translation mistakes, interpretive renderings, scribal errors in transmission, editorial activity (e.g., hexaplaric insertions), and differences in the underlying Hebrew. Most Septuagint scholars operate as if the Old Greek translation can be reconstructed from the surviving evidence. On the positive side, there are a great many witnesses. On the negative side, the manuscripts offer a plethora of different readings.

The primary resource for information about the text of the Greek Psalter is Rahlfs's Göttingen edition, *Psalmi cum Odis* (1931, 3rd ed. 1979). I supplemented Rahlfs's apparatus with the following resources: (1) P.Bod 24 (third century CE), edited by Kasser and Testuz; (2) P.Oxy. 5101 (first–second century CE), edited by Colomo and Henry; (3) Origen's new homilies on the Psalms, edited by Perrone; (4) new fragments preserved for Didymus of Alexandria's commentary on the Psalms; (5) more extensive interaction with sources representing the Vetus Latina (see introduction, §4.3); and (6) wider engagement with Greek exegetical sources, especially through modern editions of Catenae.[38]

The theoretical framework that Rahlfs employed to organize his textual witnesses has received considerable attention. Many of his basic insights remain starting points for discussion. Rahlfs grouped his witnesses into six categories. On one side are three groups of early witnesses, and on the other side are two groups of later witnesses. Outside of this continuum is a group of purportedly mixed texts.[39]

---

38. The most important catena source for the Psalms is the Palestinian Catena (sixth century), which preserves exegetical extracts for Eusebius of Caesarea, Didymus of Alexandria, Theodoret, Origen, John Chrysostom, Apollinaris of Laodicea, and some others. Difficulties in relying on this material include the ancient compiler's practice of abridging sources and mistakes in the manuscripts regarding attributions. Attributions confirmed in modern editions (e.g., Curti, Mühlenberg) are more reliable than attributions based on older collections (e.g., Eusebius in PG 23). On the sources consulted for this commentary, see the bibliography. On the Psalms Catenae, see Carmelo Curti and Maria A. Barbàra, "Greek Exegetical Catenae," in *Patrology: The Eastern Fathers from the Council of Chalcedon (451) to John of Damascus (†750)*, ed. Angelo Di Berardino, trans. Adrian Walford. (Cambridge: James Clarke, 2006), 605–26; and Natalio F. Marcos, *The Septuagint in Context: Introduction to the Greek Versions of the Bible*, trans. Wilfred G. E. Watson (Leiden: Brill, 2001), 287–301.

39. See Alfred Rahlfs, ed., *Psalmi cum Odis*, 3rd ed., SVTG 10 (Göttingen: Vandenhoeck & Ruprecht, 1979), 21–71.

1. The mixed texts include Codex Alexandrinus (fifth century), MS 1219 Washington (fifth century), MS 55 Rome (tenth century), MS 2011 Cambridge (eighth century), Papyrus 2025 (P.Oxy. 1226; third–fourth century), and MS 2029 Sinai (fourth century).

2. The two later groups are as follows: (1) The recension of Origen, including MS 1098 (tenth century) and the Gallican Psalter (along with Jerome's text in *Ep.* 106); and (2) the Lucianic recension, including over one hundred manuscripts cited from the Holmes-Parsons edition of the Septuagint (1823).[40] This group also includes Theodoret's *Commentary*, the Syro-Hexapla, the Zürich Greek Psalter (seventh century), quotations from the commentaries of Hesychius of Jerusalem, Theodore of Mopsuestia, John Chrysostom, and the text proposed by Sunnia and Fretela in Jerome's *Ep.* 106.

3. The three early groups include the following: (1) the Lower Egyptian group, including Codex Vaticanus, Codex Sinaiticus, the Bohairic Coptic version, Papyrus 2008 (fifth/sixth century), and Papyrus 2014 (third century); (2) the Upper Egyptian group, including London Brit. Mus. Papyrus 37 (seventh century), the Sahidic Coptic version, the Leipzig Papyrus 2013 (fourth century), and MS 1220 (fourth century); and (3) the Western group, including the Greek text of the Verona Psalter (sixth century), and the Vetus Latina tradition as represented by the Latin text of the Verona Psalter, Codex Sangermanensis, and North African authors such as Tertullian, Cyprian, and Augustine.

I cite these witnesses in the commentary where they illuminate Jerome's discussion of the Greek texts known to him. Rahlfs's comprehensive system of classification, although valuable because of its author's deep familiarity with the sources, does not necessarily represent the current thinking among Septuagint specialists. Of the many criticisms and qualifications that have been offered to Rahlfs's system, the following are especially pertinent:

1. Albert Pietersma expressed appreciation for Rahlfs's great contribution to our understanding of the text of the Greek Psalter, but he also raised several points of concern.[41] These concerns include the following. (1) Rahlfs's bipolar model, with Vaticanus on one side and the popular text on

---

40. Robert Holmes and James Parsons, eds., *Vetus Testamentum Graecum cum Variis Lectionibus*, vol. 3 (Oxford: Clarendon, 1823).

41. Albert Pietersma, "The Present State of the Critical Text of the Greek Psalter," in Aejmelaeus and Quast, *Der Septuaginta-Psalter*, 12–32.

the other, along with the entire organizational scheme that flows from this, is not sufficiently established and should be entirely rethought. Pietersma is doubtful whether enough evidence exists to group any early (fourth–fifth century or older) witnesses. Also, the connection of many fragmentary texts with a specific textual group (especially Upper and Lower Egyptian) seems too uncertain. (2) The bipolar model fails to capture the idea that the original Old Greek Psalter underlies all surviving witnesses. Pietersma prefers the metaphor of a tree with a single stump at the base (i.e., the Old Greek) and various branches growing out (i.e., the families of witnesses). (3) Any determination of manuscript affiliation needs to be based on indicative secondary readings, which requires that one already knows the original reading.[42] (4) The regular treatment of manuscripts representing the popular text (Lucianic manuscripts) as an undifferentiated mass is problematic. Ideally, we would want to create subgroups and report the readings of these subgroups more accurately and systematically. It would also be ideal to review the manuscript evidence fresh and not simply rely on Holmes-Parsons. (5) Rahlfs's organizational scheme and criteria for evaluating readings undervalue the Antiochene (popular, Lucianic) group as a potential witness to the Old Greek. (6) Decisions about which reading represents the Old Greek should be grounded in stronger analysis of the translation technique of the various witnesses.

2. Boyd-Taylor, Austin, and Feuerverger reiterated and expanded on many points raised by Pietersma, and they also conducted a pilot study on manuscript affiliations in the Greek Psalter aimed at establishing guidelines for revising Rahlfs's critical apparatus.[43] In this study, they found evidence in favor of the affiliation between Codex Vaticanus and the Bohairic Coptic version as well as between Codex Vaticanus and Codex Sinaiticus (i.e., Rahlfs's Lower Egyptian group). Furthermore, they did not find evidence for close affiliation between Codex Vaticanus, on the one hand, and Codex Alexandrinus, the Sahidic Coptic version, and the Greek text of the

---

42. The circularity of this argument (i.e., that we must first know the original text before we can identify manuscript affiliations, which we use to identify the original) is acknowledged and addressed by Cameron Boyd-Taylor, Peter C. Austin, and Andrey Feuerverger, "The Assessment of Manuscript Affiliation within a Probabilistic Framework: A Study of Alfred Rahlfs's Core Manuscript Groupings for the Greek Psalter," in *The Old Greek Psalter*, 104.

43. Boyd-Taylor, Austin, and Feuerverger, "Assessment of Manuscript Affiliation," 98–124.

Verona Psalter, on the other. These results are what one would expect based on Rahlfs's organizational scheme.

3. As Reinhart Ceulemans has explained, the edition of Theodoret's *Commentary on the Psalms* that Rahlfs consulted was based on poor manuscripts that sometimes give inaccurate readings for the biblical lemmata in the commentary.[44] It appears that the original biblical lemmata in the commentary were of the Antiochene type, that is, the Greek text current in the region of Antioch in the fourth–fifth centuries. (Whether or not this text is connected to Lucian of Antioch is another matter.) This Antiochene text served as the basis for the popular Byzantine text (which is identified in Rahlfs as Lucianic), but the Antiochene text of the fourth–fifth centuries is not precisely the same as the later popular text. Unfortunately, in the edition of Theodoret's commentary used by Rahlfs, the popular Byzantine text was sometimes substituted for Theodoret's original lemma. As a result, Theodoret's commentary as cited by Rahlfs sometimes reflects not Theodoret's original text but the later popular version of this textual family. In other words, Theodoret's commentary as cited in Rahlfs (and in the only edition presently available) may represent either his original text (i.e., the Antiochene text) or else the later, popular text known from the bulk of Byzantine manuscripts (the Lucianic manuscripts in Rahlfs). A new critical edition of Theodoret's *Commentary on the Psalms* would be a great help to scholarship on the Greek Psalter.

4. Regarding the Syro-Hexapla, Robert Hiebert has clarified its relationship to Greek manuscripts.[45] In the specific case of the book of Psalms, there are no manuscripts of the Syro-Hexapla that offer a fundamentally hexaplaric text. Instead, the Syro-Hexapla Psalter appears to be a revision of the Philoxenian Syriac version. Hiebert was able to identify some variations among Syro-Hexapla Psalter witnesses, but none of these variations indicate different underlying Greek texts. Based on a comparison involving the main body of Lucianic (i.e., popular Byzantine) manuscripts and the Syro-Hexapla majority text (including the Ambrosian Codex, eighth–ninth century), the Syro-Hexapla was found to agree with the Lucianic text

---

44. Reinhart Ceulemans, "Theodoret and the Antiochene Text of the Psalms," in *XV Congress of the International Organization for Septuagint and Cognate Studies*, ed. Wolfgang Kraus, Michaël N. van der Meer, and Martin Meiser, SCS 64 (Atlanta: SBL Press, 2016), 149–64.

45. Robert J. V. Hiebert, "The 'Syrohexaplric' Psalter: Its Text and Textual History," in Aejmelaeus and Quast, *Der Septuaginta-Psalter*, 123–46.

in 85.2 percent of the cases. This accords with Rahlfs's placement of the Syro-Hexapla in his Lucianic recension group.

5. Jonathan Hong in a recent book on the Greek text of select Psalms offers a perspective on reconstructing the Old Greek Psalter that differs from that presented in Rahlfs.[46] Whereas Rahlfs saw Vaticanus and Sinaiticus as strong witnesses to the Old Greek, Hong thinks that the Antiochene (Lucianic) witnesses are closer to the Old Greek. According to Hong, the Antiochene text, as represented not only by witnesses in Rahlfs's Lucianic group but also in some cases by Codex Alexandrinus, is a freer translation aimed at producing an understandable text. This text-type often gives the Old Greek reading, although it was subject to some quantitative adjustments toward the Hebrew through hexaplaric influence. According to Hong, the fact that this Antiochene text was already widespread in the fourth century is confirmed by Jerome's comments at the beginning of *Ep.* 106. As for Vaticanus and Sinaiticus, they exhibit extensive Hebraizing corrections in line with P.Oxy. 5101 and P.Bod. 24, which show corrections to the Hebrew that resemble the kaige revision movement but lack the distinctive features of kaige. The texts in Rahlfs's Upper and Lower Egyptian groups reflect this Hebraizing tendency and therefore stand further from the Old Greek than does the Antiochene group.

In light of the above discussion, I cite manuscript evidence with sensitivity to the groupings assigned by Rahlfs, but not strictly according to those groupings. I do not presuppose that witnesses belong together merely because Rahlfs connected them, although textual agreements in the passages addressed in *Ep.* 106 often reflect the categorization scheme suggested by Rahlfs. In the commentary, when I refer to the Lucianic text, I mean by this the popular Byzantine text as reflected in manuscripts cited as Lucianic in Holmes-Parsons, without necessarily assuming a historical connection to Lucian of Antioch. When I reference Theodoret's commentary on the Psalms, I mark the word "Commentary" with an asterisk (i.e., Theodoret, *Commentary**) in order to indicate that the reading in question represents Theodoret's text as given in the flawed edition currently available and may not always represent Theodoret's original text.

---

46. Jonathan Hong, *Der ursprüngliche Septuaginta-Psalter und seine Rezensionen: Eine Untersuchung anhand der Septuaginta-Psalmen 2; 8; 33; 49 und 103*, BWANT 224 (Stuttgart: Kohlhammer, 2019), 333–40.

4.3. The Latin Text of the Psalms

Most scholars trace the origins of the Old Latin Bible (Vetus Latina) to
North Africa in the second century CE. By the third century, evidence
exists for both an African family (e.g., Tertullian and Cyprian) and a Euro-
pean family (e.g., Novatian) of the Vetus Latina. Translations were not
made all at once, but specific texts were apparently translated as needed
and then expanded into complete books until the whole Bible was available
in Latin. The translations were produced anonymously and were routinely
revised according to the Greek. As Greek texts evolved, this resulted in
adjustments to the Old Latin tradition. Latin Christian writers refer to the
Old Latin translation with terms such as *vetus editio* ("old edition") and
antiqua interpretatio ("ancient translation") as if it were a unified version.
Many scholars argue that a single translation stands behind all Vetus Latina
readings, but some doubt that there was only one original Latin translation
for every book. By the late fourth century, the situation of textual diversity
was magnified by the fact that many Latin writers who knew Greek felt free
to make their own translations.[47] Because witnesses to the Vetus Latina
Psalter often give widely divergent readings, I generally refer to the "tradition" of the Vetus Latina in the commentary without assuming one original
Latin version.[48]

Textual evidence for the Vetus Latina comes from manuscripts and
quotations in patristic authors. The fundamental text for the Vetus Latina
Psalter is still that of Pierre Sabatier, *Bibliorum Sacrorum Latinae Versiones Antiquae, seu Vetus Italica* (1751), which uses Codex Sangermanensis
(sixth century; VL[303]) as its base. A useful sample of Vetus Latina readings
can be found in the critical apparatus of Robert Weber, *Le Psautier Romain*

---

47. See Augustine's comments in *Doctr. chr.* 2.11.16 and *Ep.* 71.6.

48. On the history of the Vetus Latina, see Pierre-Maurice Bogaert, "The Latin
Bible," in *From the Beginnings to 600*, vol. 1 of *The New Cambridge History of the Bible*,
ed. James C. Paget and Joachim Schaper (Cambridge: Cambridge University Press,
2013), 505–26; Eva Schulz-Flügel, "The Latin Old Testament Tradition," in *Antiquity*,
part 1 of *From the Beginnings to the Middle Ages (until 1300)*, vol. 1 of *Hebrew Bible/
Old Testament: The History of Its Interpretation*, ed. Magne. Sæbø (Göttingen: Vandenhoeck & Ruprecht, 1996), 642–62; Michael Graves, "21.8 Latin Church Fathers,"
in Lange, *Writings*, 759–63; Jean Gribomont, "Les plus anciennes traductions latines,"
in *Le monde latin antique et la Bible*, ed. Jacques Fontaine and Charles Pietri (Paris:
Beauchesne, 1985), 43–65; and Victor Saxer, "La Bible chez les Péres latin du IIIe
siècle," in Fontaine and Pietri, *Le monde latin antique*, 339–64.

et les autres anciens psautiers latins (1953). Where Old Latin passages from outside the Psalter are quoted, I have consulted where available the editions published in the series Vetus Latina: Die Reste Der Altlateinischen Bibel. For two important Latin Psalters, Codex Casinensis 557 (twelfth century; VL[136]) edited by Amelli, and the Sinai Psalter (twelfth century; VL[460]) edited by Thibaut, I checked each passage discussed in *Ep.* 106 and included significant readings in the commentary. Codex Casinensis 557 is distinctive as being a Vetus Latina Psalter that appears to reflect hexaplaric (Hebraizing) influence. The Sinai Psalter warrants special attention because of its recent publication date (2010).

The following constitute the main manuscripts for the Vetus Latina that are cited in the commentary, organized generally by region as described by Pierre-Maurice Bogaert:[49]

1. *The Regional Psalters*: Related but different textual traditions for the Psalms are preserved in numerous manuscripts from three key regions: the Roman Psalter (England and Italy, with manuscripts as early as the eighth century); the Ambrosian Psalter (Milan, close to the quotations of Ambrose); and the Mozarabic Psalter (Iberia). The Roman Psalter appears alongside the Gallican Psalter and the IH Psalter in the *Psalterium Augiense triplex* (ninth century; VL[316]).

2. *A witness from Italy*. An important Psalter from Italy with a distinct text is Saint Zenon of Verona's Psalter (seventh–eighth century; VL[306]).

3. *The Italian Psalter in Africa*. Important witnesses for this tradition include the Latin text of the Verona Psalter (sixth century; VL[300]), the Saint-Gall Psalter (eighth century; VL[304]), and the Sinai Psalter (twelfth century; VL[460]).

4. *Psalters connected to Gaul of Lyon*. These are Codex Sangermanensis (sixth century; VL[303], related to the text of Hilary of Poitiers) and the Corbie Psalter (eighth century; VL[325]).

---

49. See Pierre-Maurice Bogaert, "Le psautier latin des origines au XIIe siècle. Essai d'histoire," in Aejmelaeus and Quast, *Der Septuaginta-Psalter*, 51–81, esp. 69–70. See also José M. Cañas Reíllo, "Psalms 10.4.1 Vetus Latina," in Lange, *Writings*, 115–19. Manuscripts are identified according to the number assigned in Roger Gryson, *Altlateinische Handschriften/Manuscrits vieux latins, Première partie: Mss 1–275*, VLR 1/2A (Freiburg: Herder, 1999); Gryson, *Altlateinische Handschriften/Manuscrits vieux latins, Deuxième partie: Mss 300–485*, VLR 1/2B (Freiburg: Herder, 2004).

5. *A mixed Psalter text.* The Lyon Psalter (fifth–sixth century; VL[421]) offers a text that appears to be mixed, giving readings both from the Vetus Latina and the Gallican Psalter.

6. *Psalters connected to Gaul of Narbonne.* The Coislin Psalter (seventh century; VL[333]) and the *Psalterium Augiense* 2 (seventh century; VL[302]).

7. *An Old Latin tradition with hexaplaric influence.* Codex Casinensis 557 (twelfth century; VL[136]).

The following are important patristic sources for the Vetus Latina: Tertullian and Cyprian (North African), Ambrose (close to the text of Milan), Hilary of Poitiers, Ambrosiaster, Rufinus (close to the Roman Psalter, but with hexaplaric influence), Augustine (close to the Verona Psalter), Cassiodorus (reflects the Roman Psalter with influence from Augustine and the Gallican Psalter), and Prosper of Aquitaine.[50]

The Old Latin text as presented in Augustine's *Enarrations on the Psalms* requires special attention. Augustine's text was essentially an Italian text that he brought back with him to North Africa (see *Doctr. chr.* 2.15.22). If one compares Augustine's citations with previous African Latin readings, it is possible to think that Augustine revised the text himself. But this is unlikely for several reasons. First, Augustine's knowledge of Greek was not strong enough to permit him to produce his own complete translation of the Psalms, although he was certainly able to check the Greek and make his own translation decisions when different options were available. Second, Augustine depicted himself not as a translator but as an interpreter of the Latin text who occasionally appealed to the Greek. Third, the similarity between Augustine's quotations and the Verona Psalter shows that in the Verona Psalter we have testimony to the kind of Italian text that Augustine appropriated for use in his *Enarrations on the Psalms.*[51] In other words, Augustine's text in the *Enarrations* should be seen as a version of the Vetus Latina that originated in Italy and that sometimes exhibits distinctive readings because Augustine intervened in the text based on his consultation of the Greek and other Latin sources. One of Augustine's Latin sources

---

50. For a recent discussion of patristic witnesses for the Latin Bible in relation to the New Testament, see H. A. G. Houghton, *The Latin New Testament: A Guide to Its Early History, Texts, and Manuscripts* (Oxford: Oxford University Press, 2016), 3–68.

51. See Bogaert, "Le psautier latin des origines au XIIe siècle. Essai d'histoire," 69–70; "Les bibles d'Augustin," *RTL* 37 (2006): 513–31, esp. 522–23. For the view that Augustine revised the Psalter himself, see Donatien De Bruyne, *Saint Augustin: Reviseur de la Bible* (Rome: Tipografia Poliglotta Vaticana, 1931).

was Jerome, whose Gallican Psalter Augustine employed in composing the *Enarrations on the Psalms*.[52]

As for Jerome's Latin Psalter, we must account for his two preserved Latin translations and two exegetical works on the Psalms.

Critical editions of the Gallican Psalter and IH Psalter are presented in Weber-Gryson (5th ed., 2007). The Benedictine edition (*Biblia Sacra iuxta latinam vulgatam versionem*, 1953) offers a slightly different reconstructed text for the Gallican Psalter with a larger number of variants. Both editions of the Gallican Psalter are referenced in the commentary. The IH Psalter was edited with a substantial apparatus by Sainte-Marie (1954). I consulted this edition alongside Weber-Gryson for the IH translation. On occasion, I trace out the trajectory of a reading by stating how the passage was later handled in the Sixto-Clementine Vulgate, for which I use the critical edition by Van Ess (1824).

For the manuscript evidence related to Jerome's Psalters, the editions noted were consulted. For the Gallican Psalter, I mention the following manuscripts in the commentary: the Lyon Psalter (fifth–sixth century; mixed OL and GPsal text); the Cathach Psalter of St. Columba (seventh century; contains some asterisk and obelus signs); Vatican, Reg. lat. 11 (eighth century; IH and GPsal; the GPsal contains some asterisk and obelus signs); the Dagulf Psalter, Vienna Lat. 1861 (eighth century); the *Psalterium Augiense triplex* (ninth century); the Psalter of St. Gallen, Stiftsbibl. 20 (ninth century); and the Double Psalter of Rouen (tenth century; IH and GPsal). As for the IH Psalter, in addition to the manuscripts already listed that contain the IH edition (i.e., Vatican, Reg. lat. 11; the *Psalterium Augiense triplex*; Double Psalter of Rouen), important texts include Codex Amiatinus (ca. 700), manuscripts produced under the supervision of Theodulf (eighth–ninth century), and Codex Toletanus (tenth century).

Jerome produced two exegetical works dealing with the Psalms. (1) Sometime prior to 393 Jerome published a collection of short notes on select passages in the Psalms. Jerome based this *Commentarioli on the*

52. Colette Estin, "Les traductions du Psautier," in Fontaine and Pietri, *Le monde latin antique*, 67–88, esp. 70. On Augustine's use of Jerome's IH translation as early as 395 or 397, see Simone Deléani, "Un emprunt d'Augustin à l'Écriture: 'Redite, praevaricatores, ad cor' (Isaïe 46, 8b)," *REAug* 38 (1992): 29–49, esp. 33; and Anne-Marie La Bonnardière, "Did Augustine Use Jerome's Vulgate?" in *Augustine and the Bible*, ed. Paula Bright (Notre Dame, IN: University of Notre Dame Press, 1986), 42–51.

Psalms on exegetical notes written by Origen.[53] The *Commentarioli* comments on a Latin text that represents Jerome's rendering (in keeping with the Vetus Latina tradition) of the Greek text Origen used in his treatise. In the *Commentarioli* we can see information about the Greek text that Jerome learned in the process of adapting his Origenian model. On the *Commentarioli on the Psalms*, see especially **11.2.18–19; 7.1.1**; see also **4.1.13–14; 5.1.6; 8.2.3–4; 10.1.9–10; 17.2.11–12; 26.1.16–17; 37.1.21; 41.2.2–3; 54.1.17–18; 54.3.5; 57.2.20; 57.3.26; 65.3.25–26; 73.2.3–4; 77.1.25; 84.1.21–22**.

(2) Jerome produced two series of homilies on the Psalms. These were published by Germain Morin originally in 1897–1903 and appear in the Corpus Christianorum series as *S. Hieronymi Presbyteri Opera, Pars 2. Opera Homiletica* (CC 78:195). Because these homilies represent Jerome's preaching in Bethlehem, refer to the Origenist controversy, and yet do not address Pelagianism, Morin dated them to the early 400s. According to Vittorio Peri, Jerome is not the author of these homilies but merely their translator, the true author being Origen.[54] Given their style and perspective throughout, they certainly appear to be based on expositions composed by Origen.[55] At the same time, Pierre Jay has shown substantial traces of Jerome's own hand in these homilies.[56] Perhaps it is best to say that Jerome's *Homilies on the Psalms* transmit Origen's ideas as adapted and often supplemented by Jerome as translator/author. I refer to these homilies in the commentary to illustrate Jerome's later exegesis, with the understanding that the monk of Bethlehem borrowed heavily from his Greek model (see **41.2.2–3; 53.1.12–13; 57.1.8; 57.2.20; 59.1.16–17; 73.1.1–2; 76.1.21–22**).

In the majority of biblical citations shared between *Ep.* 106 and the *Homilies on the Psalms*, the lemma of the homilies matches the Gallican Psalter. This is true for Ps 5:6; 5:9; 7:9; 67:19; 67:20; 67:25; 67:33–34; 82:13; 83:3; 83:6 (first and second series); 83:7 (first and second series); 84:2

---

53. Siegfried Risse, trans. and intro., *Hieronymus. Commentarioli in Psalmos: Anmerkungen zum Psalter*, Fontes Christiani 79 (Turnhout: Brepols, 2005), 29–30.

54. Vittorio Peri, *Omelie origeniane sui Salmi: Contributo all'identificazione del testo latino*, StT 289 (Vatican City: Biblioteca Apostolica Vaticana, 1980).

55. See Marie-Josèphe Rondeau, *Les travaux des Pères grecs et latins sur le Psautier. Recherches et bilan*, vol. 1 of *Les Commentaires patristiques de Psautier (IIIe–Ve siècles)*, OrChrAn 219 (Rome: Pontificium Institutum Studiorum Orientalium, 1982), 158–61.

56. Pierre Jay, "Jérôme à Bethléem: Les *Tractatus in psalmos*," in *Jérôme entre l'Occident et l'Orient*, ed. Yves-Marie Duval (Paris: Études Augustiniennes, 1988), 367–80.

(first and second series); 84:11; 89:10; 93:12 (first and second series); 97:3; 101:7; 101:11; 101:15; 103:1; 103:4; 103:5; 103:7; 103:17; 103:18; 103:25; 105:1; 109:2; 110:1; 131:2;[57] 135:7; 139:14; and 140:7. In other cases, the biblical lemma in the homilies deviates from the Gallican Psalter. Some of these deviations are probably nothing more than slips due to the oral context: 76:7 (*exercitabar* missing); 77:6 (*ea* added); 83:3 (*exultaverunt* for *exultavit*); 88:8 (*metuendus* for *horrendus*); 88:20 (*filiis* for *sanctis*);[58] 100:6 (*super* for *ad*); 103:3 (*pennas* for *pinnas*); 103:10 (*emittit* for *emittis*); 119:2 (*et* added); 146:10 (*est* for *erit*). Nevertheless, some deviations constitute adjustments toward the IH edition: 75:12–13 (*spiritum* for *spiritus*); 76:9 (*et generatione* for *in generationem*); 82:13 (*nobis* added); 89:2 (*et usque* for *usque*); 90:2 (*tu* omitted); 103:14 (*educat* for *educas*); 114:2 (*te* omitted); 114:9 (*coram* added).

5. Textual Agreement Trends in *Epistle* 106

Jerome believed that distinct families of texts existed for the Greek Old Testament in his day. An important passage on this topic is Jerome's account of the "threefold diversity" (*trifaria varietas*) that existed among copies of the Septuagint: "Alexandria and Egypt extol [the copies of] Hesychius as their authority in the LXX; Constantinople to Antioch approves the copies of Lucian the martyr; between these, the provinces of Palestine read the codices prepared by Origen that Eusebius and Pamphilius published. And all the world contends among these in this threefold diversity" (*Pref. IH Chron.* 2). Jerome's perception that different text-types prevailed in the regions of (1) Egypt, (2) Constantinople-to-Antioch, and (3) Palestine has been used as a benchmark for identifying and organizing LXX witnesses into families, although Jerome's failure to elaborate on the recension of

---

57. Jerome makes an interesting comment on the Hebrew text of this verse in his homily on Ps 131. As Jerome explains, where the LXX has ὡς ὤμοσεν, "as he swore" (GPsal: *sicut iuravit*), the Hebrew has the relative pronoun: *In hebraico non habet ὡς, hoc est "sicut," nec est sensus; sed habet ὅς, hoc est "qui."* ("In Hebrew, it does not have ὡς, that is 'just as,' nor is this the meaning; but it has ὅς, that is, 'who' "; see CC 78:274). This accurately reflects the preserved Hebrew text (אשר), and Jerome made this clear in his IH translation *qui iuravit*.

58. In his second homily series, Jerome quotes Ps 88:20 as *in aspectu filiis tuis*; see **57.2.20**.

Hesychius in particular leaves us uncertain as to the identity of this textual tradition or even what Jerome believed about it.[59]

In *Ep.* 106, Jerome identifies only two text-types for the Psalms: a "Lucianic" (Λουκιάνειος) edition, and another edition found in the "hexaplaric" (ἑξαπλοῖς) codices (**2.2**). It is interesting that Jerome refers to the first of these as the "common" (κοινή or *communis*) and "popular" (*vulgata*) edition, which "nowadays is referred to by most as Lucianic" (*a plerisque nunc Λουκιάνειος dicitur*). In other words, Jerome claims that this edition is the most widely available, and he implies that calling this text-type "Lucianic" is a recent phenomenon (see **2.2.22**). As for the hexaplaric edition, Jerome says that this is the version of the Psalter that is recited "both in Jerusalem and in the churches of the East." This hexaplaric Psalter was a translation of Origen's edition based on the fifth column of the Hexapla. In his edition, Origen presented the LXX text marked with critical signs to indicate where the Greek contained material that was lacking in the Hebrew and where additions from Theodotion were made in order to supply material that was present in the Hebrew but lacking in the Greek (see **7.2.5–12**; **7.2.12–13**; and introduction, §8.2).[60]

According to Jerome, the Greek text upon which Sunnia and Fretela base many of their questions is the popular or Lucianic text, whereas the Gallican Psalter was translated from the hexaplaric Greek text. The difference between the popular Greek text of Sunnia and Fretela and Jerome's hexaplaric Greek is one of the primary topics addressed by *Ep.* 106. Another

---

59. Jerome also speaks disparagingly of the codices of Lucian and Hesychius in the preface to his translation of the Four Gospels, perhaps in this case only addressing the New Testament (*Pref. Gos.* 1). Cf. **2.2.24–25**. On the role that Jerome's comments have played in the history of scholarship on the Septuagint, see Sidney Jellicoe, *The Septuagint and Modern Study* (Oxford: Oxford University Press, 1968), 134–71; and Siegfried Kreuzer, "The Origins and Transmission of the Septuagint," in Kreuzer, *Introduction to the Septuagint*, 3–56, esp. 41–43. On a possible Hesychian recension, see Marcos, *Septuagint in Context*, 239–46.

60. On the fifth column (i.e., the LXX column) of Origen's Hexapla, see Peter J. Gentry, "Did Origen Use the Aristarchian Signs in the Hexapla?," in *XV Congress of the International Organization for Septuagint and Cognate Studies*, 133–47; Adrian Schenker, "L'apport durable des Hexaples d'Origène. Bilan de la Lettre à Africanus, bilan aujourd'hui," in *Eukarpa: Études sur la Bible et ses exégètes en hommage à Gilles Dorival*, ed. Mireille Loubet and Didier Pralon (Paris: Cerf, 2011), 385–94; and Joachim Schaper, "The Origin and Purpose of the Fifth Column of the Hexapla," in *Origen's Hexapla and Fragments*, ed. Alison Salvesen (Tübingen: Mohr Siebeck, 1998), 3–15.

topic of recurring interest for Jerome is the Hebrew text, either as an ally of the hexaplaric Septuagint or sometimes (especially later in *Ep.* 106) as a witness that is independent of the Septuagint.

In this section, I present brief summaries and highlights from the commentary that describe trends of agreement between sources on three different fronts: (1) the Greek text of Jerome and the Greek text of Sunnia and Fretela; (2) the Vetus Latina, Jerome, and Sunnia-Fretela; (3) the Hebrew in *Ep.* 106 and the Hebrew in the IH edition.

5.1. The Greek Text of Jerome and the Greek Text of Sunnia and Fretela

In my commentary on *Ep.* 106, I report as much evidence on the Greek as I could obtain from published sources that might help in contextualizing and assessing Jerome's claims about the Greek text of Sunnia and Fretela and his own Greek text. The central object of comparison is always the Greek as reported in *Ep.* 106. Obviously, the information provided in my commentary on *Ep.* 106 cannot establish affiliations among Septuagint witnesses. Furthermore, because in many passages the Septuagint is said to agree uniformly (or almost uniformly) with a certain reading, and thus even major witnesses are not listed by name at every relevant passage, one cannot simply count up the number of mentions for a given witness to find its comprehensive agreement statistics. It is hoped, however, that the present brief overview and the discussion of agreements throughout the commentary will facilitate the use of *Ep.* 106 in the study of the Septuagint.

Epistle 106 discusses 177 passages on which Sunnia and Fretela challenged the Gallican Psalter. Not every contested passage can be traced back to a difference in the underlying Greek. In some cases, the text that Sunnia and Fretela reject is not really Jerome's Gallican Psalter but a miscopying of it, and Jerome simply corrects the mistake. In other cases, both sides agree on the Greek and simply disagree on how to translate it. According to my count, roughly one third of the disagreements are resolved without reference to different Greek texts. Among the passages where the difference goes back to the underlying Greek, the various sources often intersect in multiple ways that elude easy summary. Sometimes important Greek witnesses do not match any text reported in *Ep.* 106. Many early Greek sources for the Psalms are so fragmentary that they are referenced only a handful of times. Nevertheless, a few general trends of agreement emerge from the commentary that are worth mentioning.

Among passages where the Greek text is in dispute, in approximately thirty-five cases I indicate that the Septuagint uniformly (or almost uniformly) agrees with either Jerome or Sunnia and Fretela. The general trend is that these majority-LXX readings agree more often with Sunnia and Fretela, although there are a few that match Jerome.[61]

Certain key witnesses frequently favor the Greek text of Sunnia and Fretela against Jerome in passages where the Greek evidence is divided. These witnesses are Codex Alexandrinus, MS 1219 Washington, MS 55 Rome, the Greek text of the Verona Psalter, the Lucianic manuscripts, Theodoret's *Commentary**, and the Syro-Hexapla.[62] For several other key

---

61. The majority reading of the LXX agrees with Sunnia and Fretela at, e.g., **7.1**; **8.1**; **8.2**; **9.1**; **9.2**; **9.4**; **13.1**; **14.2**; **15.1**; **19.1**; **25.3**; **26.3**; **27.1**; **28.3**; **31.2**; **33.1**; **40.1**; **44.2**; **46.2**; **46.7**; **57.2**; **58.2**; **61.1** (but not Sinaiticus); **66.2** (but not Sinaiticus or P.Bod. 24); **71.1**; **75.1**; **75.3**; **75.5**; **76.1**; **80.1** (but not MS 1219, Sahidic Coptic, or Syro-Hexapla); **83.2**. The majority-reading of the LXX agrees with Jerome at, e.g., **6.1** (a few exceptions noted); **9.5**; **24.1** (but not Alexandrinus); **43.3**; **45.1**; **50.3** (a few exceptions noted); **65.2**.

62. Codex Alexandrinus agrees with Sunna and Fretela against Jerome at, e.g., **4.1**; **18.1**; **20.1**; **21.1**; **22.1**; **23.2**; **24.1**; **25.1**; **25.2**; **26.1**; **29.1**; **60.1**; **61.1**; **65.6**; **68.2**; **72.1**; **75.2**; **75.7**; **78.1**; **81.1**; **84.1** (a correction). Agreements between Codex Alexandrinus and Jerome include **5.1**; **14.1** (but text under obelus); **33.4**; **83.2**. MS 1219 Washington agrees with Sunna and Fretela against Jerome at, e.g., **25.2**; **26.1**; **29.1**; **31.1**; **34.1**; **39.1**; **43.1**; **44.1**; **49.3**; **50.7**; **56.2**; **60.1**; **68.2**; **75.6**; **75.7**; **77.1**; **82.1**; **84.1**. Agreements between MS 1219 Washington and Jerome include **46.1**; **80.1**. MS 55 Rome agrees with Sunna and Fretela against Jerome at, e.g., **4.1**; **5.1**; **6.1**; **16.1**; **18.1**; **28.2**; **29.1**; **32.1**; **33.3**; **33.4**; **42.1**; **65.6**; **67.2**; **68.2**; **75.7**; **84.1**. Agreements between MS 55 Rome and Jerome include **41.6**. The Greek Text of the Verona Psalter agrees with Sunna and Fretela against Jerome at, e.g., **4.1**; **5.1**; **25.1**; **26.1**; **28.2**; **29.1**; **33.3**; **33.4**; **33.5**; **34.1**; **41.2**; **43.1**; **44.1**; **46.2**; **48.1**; **50.7**; **67.2**; **68.1**; **75.6**; **81.1**; **82.1**. Agreements between the Greek of the Verona Psalter and Jerome include **14.1** (but text under obelus); **68.2**; **78.1** (matches GPsal, but not Jerome's Hebrew meaning). The Lucianic manuscripts agree with Sunna and Fretela against Jerome at, e.g., **4.1**; **5.1**; **6.1** (a few manuscripts); **8.1b**; **16.1**; **18.1**; **20.1**; **21.1**; **23.2** (many manuscripts); **25.1**; **25.2**; **26.1**; **28.2**; **29.1**; **31.1**; **32.1**; **33.4**; **33.5**; **34.1**; **35.2**; **39.1**; **39.2**; **41.2**; **42.1**; **43.1**; **43.2**; **44.1**; **49.3**; **50.3** (many manuscripts); **56.2**; **60.1**; **65.6**; **68.1** (a few manuscripts); **68.2**; **75.6**; **75.7** (most manuscripts); **77.1**; **78.1**; **82.1**; **84.1**. Agreements between the Lucianic manuscripts and Jerome include: **13.1** (a few manuscripts); **41.6**; **46.1**; **50.7**; **57.2** (a few manuscripts). Theodoret's *Commentary** agrees with Sunna and Fretela against Jerome at, e.g., **4.1**; **5.1**; **8.1b**; **16.1**; **18.1**; **20.1**; **21.1**; **25.1**; **25.2**; **26.1** (some manuscripts); **28.2**; **29.1**; **31.1**; **32.1**; **33.4**; **33.5**; **34.1**; **35.2**; **39.1**; **39.2**; **41.2**; **42.1**; **43.1**; **43.2**; **44.1**; **49.3**; **56.2**; **60.1**; **65.6**; **67.2**; **68.2**; **75.6**; **77.1**; **78.1**; **82.1**; **84.1**. Agreements between Theodoret's *Commentary** and Jerome include **41.6**; **46.1**; **50.7**. The Syro-Hexapla agrees with Sunna and Fretela against Jerome at, e.g., **4.1**; **5.1**; **8.1b**; **16.1**; **17.2**; **18.1**; **21.1**; **25.1**; **25.2**; **28.2**;

witnesses, such as Codex Vaticanus and Codex Sinaiticus, the number of agreements with Sunnia and Fretela on the one hand and Jerome on the other are more balanced, although a slight trend in favor of Sunnia and Fretela seems evident.

Two recently discovered papyri deserve specific mention, especially because they exhibit a closer relationship to Jerome's Gallican Psalter. First, P.Oxy. 5101, a fragmentary text that preserves only a few passages, contains two passages discussed in *Ep.* 106. In both cases, P.Oxy. 5101 agrees with Jerome's Greek text against Sunnia and Fretela (**27.1** and **29.1**). Second, P.Bod. 24 agrees with Sunnia and Fretela on eight occasions, and it agrees with Jerome's Gallican Psalter on ten occasions, with four independent renderings.[63]

The fact that the uniform (or almost uniform) Septuagint readings tend to agree with Sunnia and Fretela more often than with Jerome lends support to Jerome's claim that the text employed by Sunnia and Fretela was "popular." This conclusion is reinforced by the strong tendency for the Lucianic manuscripts, Theodoret's *Commentary**, and the Syro-Hexapla to agree with Sunnia and Fretela. In fact, a wide variety of witnesses discussed in the commentary regularly match the Greek text proposed by Sunnia and Fretela. Especially important as sources that converge often with Sunnia and Fretela are Codex Alexandrinus, MS 1219 Washington, and MS 55. Interestingly, whereas Rahlfs classified all three of these witnesses as mixed texts, Jonathan Hong grouped Alexandrinus together with the Lucianic manuscripts as belonging to the Antiochene text (see introduction, §4.2). Of course, there are also many instances of agreement with Jerome's Gallican Psalter. Some of these agreements may reflect the widespread influence of hexaplaric readings.[64]

29.1; 31.1; 32.1; 33.5; 39.1; 41.2; 43.1; 43.2; 48.1; 49.3; 56.2; 60.1; 65.6 (mixed text); 67.2; 68.2; 75.6; 75.7; 77.1; 78.1; 82.1; 84.1. Agreements between the Syro-Hexapla and Jerome include: 25.3; 41.6; 46.1; 50.7; 80.1.

63. Sunnia and Fretela: 25.3; 33.4; 34.1; 39.2; 43.1; 44.1; 56.1; 65.6. Jerome: 14.2; 23.2; 41.6; 50.5; 50.6 (matches Jerome's Greek text; the issue is translation); 50.7; 54.1; 60.2 (uniquely close to Jerome); 66.2; 68.2. Independent: 28.1 (this reading is mentioned by Jerome); 33.5 (fits with Jerome's paraphrase in *Ep.* 106); 47.1 (omits "all" like Jerome, but gives verb like Sunnia and Fretela) 50.1 (uses a word closely related to both Sunnia-Fretela and Jerome).

64. On several occasions, Jerome speaks of the widespread attestation of hexaplaric readings; for example, in *Ep.* 112.19.2, Jerome says that if Augustine wanted to reject the passages added under asterisk, he would need to condemn all the libraries of

To sum up, it seems reasonable to conclude that the Greek text consulted by Sunnia and Fretela belonged to a widely available text-type. At the same time, the Greek evidence is diverse enough to suggest considerable textual plurality for the Greek Psalter in the late fourth century.

5.2. The Vetus Latina, Jerome, and Sunnia-Fretela

The evidence for the Vetus Latina Psalter is even more diverse than for the Septuagint. For textual witnesses that show distinctive agreements with either Sunnia and Fretela or the Gallican Psalter, trends of agreement are less pronounced than for the Greek. The number of passages for which there is a consensus Vetus Latina reading are fewer, and the number of Vetus Latina readings that are independent of both Jerome and Sunnia and Fretela are greater.

Based on how Jerome reports their objections, it seems that Sunnia and Fretela primarily based their criticisms of the Gallican Psalter on the Greek text. Consequently, there are instances when Jerome preserves a common Vetus Latina reading in the Gallican Psalter, whereas Sunnia and Fretela suggest correcting this toward the Greek. In other instances, Sunnia and Fretela propose a reading that matches the standard Vetus Latina, and Jerome deviates from this in the Gallican Psalter due to hexaplaric influence. Nevertheless, even in the midst of this variation, there seems to be a modest trend for Vetus Latina witnesses to agree with Sunnia and Fretela more often than with Jerome. Among passages in *Ep.* 106 where a majority Vetus Latina rendering exists and offers support one way or the other, there is a slight preference for Sunnia and Fretela.[65]

In addition, several other important Vetus Latina witnesses tend to agree more often with Sunnia and Fretela than with Jerome, as seen in passages discussed in the commentary where the evidence for the Old Latin is significantly divided. These witnesses include Codex Sangermanensis, the Verona Psalter, the Roman Psalter, and Augustine's *Enarrations*.[66] I have

---

the churches, because "scarcely will you find even one book that does not have these." See also *Pref. IH Job* 4; *Pref. Ezra* 3.

65. As the commentary shows, the evidence is relatively balanced but slightly favors Sunnia and Fretela. Agreements with Sunnia and Fretela include **9.2; 14.1; 17.2; 25.1; 26.3; 31.2; 33.5; 44.2; 46.1; 46.2; 50.2; 53.1; 57.2; 58.2; 76.1; 83.2**. Agreements with Jerome include **9.5; 23.1; 23.2; 32.2; 43.3; 46.3; 50.1; 50.5; 55.1; 65.2; 67.3; 84.1**.

66. Agreements between Codex Sangermanensis and Sunnia and Fretela include

not provided exhaustive comparisons on these sources in the commentary, but the passages discussed provide representative samples. Especially noteworthy in its agreements with Sunnia and Fretela is the Sinai Psalter.[67] Several witnesses to the Vetus Latina are cited in the commentary on a more limited basis, generally because they offer few readings that add to the testimony of the primary witnesses. Among these, some tend to favor Sunnia and Fretela (e.g., Hilary's *Tractatus* and the Ambrosian Psalter), while others are more balanced in their agreements (e.g., Cassiodorus's *Explanation* and the Corbie Psalter).

The Vetus Latina manuscript that shows the highest level of agreement with Jerome's Gallican Psalter is Codex Casinensis 557.[68] What makes this manuscript unique, however, are its seven readings that appear to be Hebraizing revisions of the Vetus Latina tradition and are independent of the Gallican Psalter.[69] Codex Casinensis 557 illustrates the fact that people other than Jerome were correcting Vetus Latina texts by means of the hexaplaric versions.

The general tendency of Vetus Latina witnesses to agree more often with Sunnia and Fretela than with Jerome is not surprising. Jerome's object

---

4.1; 8.1b; 11.1; 24.1; 27.1; 28.3; 30.1; 33.4; 44.1; 44.3; 48.1; 50.6; 50.7; 54.3; 60.1; 63.4; 67.2; 72.1 (close); 75.1; 75.2; 75.6; 82.1. Agreements between Codex Sangermanensis and Jerome include 9.4; 9.6; 14.2; 46.6; 59.1; 67.1; 68.2. Agreements between the Verona Psalter and Sunnia and Fretela include 4.1; 5.1; 11.1; 15.1; 24.1; 26.1; 27.1 (close); 28.3; 33.3; 33.4; 43.1; 44.1; 48.1; 50.7; 75.1; 75.6. Agreements between the Verona Psalter and Jerome include 67.1; 68.2. Agreements between the Roman Psalter and Sunnia and Fretela include 8.1b; 18.1; 21.1; 22.1; 26.1; 27.1; 28.2; 33.1; 33.3; 33.4; 34.1; 42.1; 44.1; 44.3; 48.1; 50.6; 50.7; 56.2; 59.1; 67.2; 75.1; 75.6; 82.1. Agreements between the Roman Psalter and Jerome include 28.3; 54.2; 54.3; 60.2; 63.4; 67.1; 68.2; 73.2. Agreements between Augustine's *Enarrations* and Sunnia and Fretela include 5.1; 8.1b; 11.1; 15.1; 16.1 (some manuscripts); 17.1; 24.1; 26.1; 27.1 (close); 28.2; 28.3; 31.3; 32.2; 33.3; 33.4; 43.1; 44.1; 50.7; 54.3; 72.1 (close); 75.1; 75.6; 82.1. Agreements between Augustine's *Enarrations* and Jerome include 9.4; 46.6; 50.6; 53.1; 66.3; 68.2; 81.1; 83.2.

67. Agreements with Sunnia and Fretela are 11.1; 15.1; 17.1; 21.1; 22.1; 23.2; 24.1; 26.1; 26.3; 28.2; 30.1; 33.1; 32.2; 33.3; 33.4; 34.1; 44.1; 44.3; 48.1; 50.1; 50.6; 50.7; 53.1; 54.3; 63.4; 67.2. Agreements with Jerome are 9.6; 28.3; 67.1. Not aligned: 12.1; 15.1b; 41.1; 65.6.

68. Agreements with Sunnia and Fretela: 4.1; 9.5; 22.1; 23.2; 25.2; 44.1; 50.7; 55.1; 67.2. Agreements with Jerome: 9.2; 9.4; 14.2; 17.2; 24.1; 26.3; 28.3; 33.1; 39.2; 41.1; 46.6; 50.2; 54.3; 57.2; 63.4; 67.1.

69. Independent, Hebraizing: 9.6; 31.2; 32.2; 33.2; 47.1; 66.3; 74.1. Independent, not Hebraizing: 15.1.

in the Gallican Psalter was to revise the received Latin text in the direction of the hexaplaric Septuagint. Consequently, we should expect that his version will deviate from the Vetus Latina in many places where the Latin translation suggested by Sunnia and Fretela does not. On the other hand, Jerome's Gallican Psalter was not a new translation but a revision of the Old Latin with an avowed conservative bent (see **12.2**; **30.4**; **66.1**), and the Latin renderings suggested by Sunnia and Fretela are occasionally idiosyncratic. As a result, Jerome's translation can sometimes be more traditional. Given the diverse nature of the Vetus Latina tradition, there are many Latin readings referenced in the commentary that agree neither with Jerome nor with Sunnia and Fretela.

5.3. The Hebrew in *Epistle* 106 and the Hebrew in the IH Edition

Jerome refers to the Hebrew throughout *Ep.* 106 and transcribes numerous Hebrew words (see introduction, §6.2). He frequently indicates the meaning of a single Hebrew word or phrase, usually by reporting Greek hexaplaric evidence. I have identified fourteen places where Jerome offers a full Latin translation from the Hebrew that is not simply a rendering of his Greek sources. In nine of these cases, Jerome's translation of the Hebrew in *Ep.* 106 conflicts with his translation in the IH edition, whereas in five cases the Hebrew-based translation in *Ep.* 106 matches the IH edition. In addition, there are many passages in *Ep.* 106 where Jerome's argument in favor of a particular translation runs counter to what he gives in the IH Psalter. Below I list (1) points of explicit disagreement over the Hebrew between *Ep.* 106 and the IH Psalter, (2) passages that illustrate the tension that frequently exists between *Ep.* 106 and the IH edition, and (3) points of agreement between *Ep.* 106 and the IH Psalter on how to translate the Hebrew.

    1. *Disagreements with IH.* The nine places where Jerome gives a translation of the Hebrew that conflicts with the IH edition are: Ps 17:48 (**9.6.24**); Ps 43:15 (**26.2.18–19**); Ps 58:11 (**33.2.19–20**); Ps 60:9 (**35.2.15**); Ps 63:8 (**38.1.56**); Ps 67:33 (**41.6.7–8**); Ps 101:7 (**63.2.8–9**); Ps 103:17 (**65.5.13**); Ps 137:2 (**81.1.4–6**). For example, at Ps 17:48 (**9.6.24**), Jerome says, "In the Hebrew it has nothing except 'my deliverer from my enemies'" (*liberator meus ab inimicis meis*), whereas in the IH edition he translates this phrase as "you who rescues me from my enemies" (*qui servas me ab inimicis meis*). Again, at Ps 43:15 (**26.2.18–19**), after justifying his Gallican Psalter translation, Jerome comments, "Alternately, it is found written thus in

the Hebrew: 'You have made us a proverb among the nations'" (*posuisti nos proverbium in gentibus*). But in the IH edition, Jerome translates, "You have made us an illustration among the nations" (*posuisti nos similitudinem in gentibus*), which is close to the translation suggested by Sunnia and Fretela in *Ep.* 106 that Jerome calls κακόφωνον. As a third example, at Ps 101:7 (**63.2.8–9**), Jerome explains what he put in the Gallican Psalter based on the Greek and then adds, "Among the Hebrews it says, 'I became like a night-owl (*noctua*) among ruins.' Most who interpret this stringently think the 'horned-owl' (*bubo*) is meant." In other words, Jerome says that the Hebrew says "night-owl" (*noctua*), although stringent translators use the word "horned-owl" (*bubo*). Typically when Jerome speaks of translating "stringently" (*contentiose*), he means this in a negative sense (see **55.1**; cf. *Ep.* 57.11.2–4). But in his IH edition, Jerome decides to translate this word as "horned-owl" (*bubo*).

2. *Tensions with IH.* In many passages in *Ep.* 106, Jerome makes an argument in favor of a particular way of translating the biblical text that stands in tension with what we find in the IH edition. These are treated in detail in the commentary, but some clear examples include Ps 39:14 (**23.2.15**), Ps 48:15 (**29.2.3**), Ps 58:10 (**33.1.13–14**), Ps 62:2 (**37.1.21**), Ps 72:7 (**45.1.11**), Ps 74:2 (**47.1.25–26**), Ps 75:12–13 (**48.2.3–4**), Ps 76:9 (**49.3.2**), Ps 77:54 (**50.5.2–3**), Ps 77:69b (**50.6b.14–15**), Ps 77:72 (**50.7.23–24**), Ps 82:13 (**53.1.12–13**), Ps 83:3 (**54.1.17–18**), Ps 104:30 (**66.1.6**), and Ps 114:9 (**73.2.3–4**). Thus, at Ps 48:15 (**29.2.3**), Jerome in the Gallican Psalter translated οἱ εὐθεῖς as *iusti*, "just," whereas Sunnia and Fretela proposed *recti*, "upright." In *Ep.* 106, Jerome defends *iusti* as in the Gallican Psalter, but in the IH edition he gives *recti*, as Sunnia and Fretela suggested. At Ps 58:10 (**33.1.13–14**), where Jerome in the Gallican Psalter translated "because God is my protector" (third person), Sunnia and Fretela said the text should be second person: "You are my protector." In *Ep.* 106, Jerome defends the Gallican Psalter by saying that neither "God" nor "you" is written in the Hebrew, but in the IH edition Jerome translates this sentence as second person. At Ps 72:7 (**45.1.11**), Sunnia and Fretela question Jerome's singular verb, claiming that the verb should be plural. In *Ep.* 106 Jerome says that the plural verb is incorrect (*quod falsum est*), but in the IH edition Jerome uses the plural. Again, at Ps 82:13 (**53.1.12–13**), Sunnia and Fretela stated that the Greek κληρονομήσωμεν ἑαυτοῖς should be translated, "let us inherit for ourselves (*nobis*)," whereas Jerome did not include the word "for ourselves" (*nobis*) in the Gallican Psalter. In *Ep.* 106, Jerome justifies his decision to omit "for ourselves" thus: "This is a superfluous point of discus-

sion, because when someone says, 'let us inherit,' 'for ourselves' is implied."
In the IH edition, however, Jerome includes the word *nobis*, "for ourselves,"
which agrees not only with the Greek but also with the Hebrew. *Epistle* 106
contains many discussions of this kind, in which Jerome's argument for a
certain translation contradicts what he does in the IH Psalter.

3. *Agreements with IH.* There are five passages in *Ep.* 106 where
Jerome translates the Hebrew and this translation agrees with the IH edition. These are: Ps 54:9b (**31.2.13–14**), Ps 76:7 (**49.1.9–10**), Ps 118:136
(**75.7.10–11**), Ps 118:172 (**75.8.15–16**), and the explanation of λαξευτήριον
(**86.3.18**). In the first two cases, Jerome's way of introducing the Hebrew
translation does not suggest that he has already translated the passage
previously: Ps 54:9b (**31.2.13–14**): "in Hebrew it is written *merucha*, and
the sense of the whole passage according to them reads like this"; and
Ps 76:7 (**49.1.9–10**): "In place of this in Hebrew we read, 'I remembered
my songs in the night, with my heart I spoke, and I searched my spirit.'"
The next two instances of agreement occur back to back near the end of
Ep. 106: Ps 118:136 (**75.7.10–11**): "In the Hebrew it reads, 'Streams of
water flowed from my eyes, because they did not keep your law'"; and Ps
118:172 (**75.8.15–16**): "In fact, we translate thus from the Hebrew: 'My
tongue will speak your word.'" In the latter case, Jerome actually states
"we translate" (*vertimus*). The final instance of agreement is found in
the very last discussion at the end of the treatise in his explanation of
λαξευτήριον (**86.3.18**): "So, translating from the Hebrew we said thus." In
this concluding example, we might easily take Jerome to be referring to a
translation he made in the past.

The patterns of agreement and disagreement between the Hebrew-
based translations in *Ep.* 106 and the IH Psalter raise the question of the
relative chronology of the two works. For much of *Ep.* 106, Jerome makes
no reference to a previous translation according to the Hebrew, he offers
renderings of the Hebrew that differ from the IH edition, and he regularly takes up positions that contradict how he translates in the IH edition. Based on most of *Ep.* 106, one would assume that Jerome had not yet
produced the IH Psalter and that the changes we find in the IH Psalter vis-
à-vis *Ep.* 106 reflect Jerome's more mature viewpoints. Nevertheless, the
body of *Ep.* 106 contains some agreements with the IH edition (on Ps 54:9b
and Ps 76:7), although these renderings are not introduced as an "edition,"
and the very end of the letter seems to allude in the past tense to a translation matching the IH edition. The date of *Ep.* 106 and its relationship to the
IH Psalter will be taken up below (§6.2).

6. The Authenticity and Date of *Epistle* 106

The content of *Ep.* 106 is technical. It contains no references to recognizable historical events, and the two individuals mentioned incidentally in the letter (Avitus and Firmus) add little to our understanding of the context. Moreover, Sunnia and Fretela are known today only from this work. Consequently, it has been challenging to identify the date of *Ep.* 106, and significant questions have been raised regarding its authenticity as a letter and its purpose. Some even deny the existence of Sunnia and Fretela. These matters are all interrelated, but I will address them in two stages. First, I will speak to the issue of authenticity, which also raises the question of purpose; and second, I will suggest an answer to the question of when *Ep.* 106 was written.

6.1. The Authenticity of *Epistle* 106

In 1929, Donatien De Bruyne published an article in which he suggested that Sunnia and Fretela were fictional characters whom Jerome invented as a pretext for circulating *Ep.* 106.[70] According to De Bruyne, *Ep.* 106 is not an authentic letter. His article provoked several critical responses that dealt with the purpose of *Ep.* 106 and the historicity of Sunnia and Fretela, including essays by Arthur Allgeier and Jacques Zeiller.[71] Although I do not adhere to De Bruyne's position, I will begin my discussion with his arguments. De Bruyne brought to the surface several issues that must be addressed if we are to reach a sound perspective on the nature of *Ep.* 106.

The main objections to the authenticity of *Ep.* 106 cited by De Bruyne are as follows: (1) Jerome pretends that these two Goths wrote because they were interested in Hebrew, but he is really simply writing for a Latin audience, so he forgets Sunnia and Fretela and their supposed interest in Hebrew after the introduction. (2) It is not likely that these Goths were interested in the Hebrew text, as **1.1** claims. (3) The content of *Ep.* 106, with its long series of technical discussions, does not read like a letter. (4) When Jerome says that his work will invoke great ill will and that his erudition

---

70. Donatien De Bruyne, "La lettre de Jérôme à Sunnia et Fretela sur le Psautier," *ZNW* 28 (1929): 1–13.

71. Arthur Allgeier, "Der Brief an Sunnia und Fretela und seine Bedeutung für die Textherstellung der Vulgata," *Bib* 11 (1930): 86–107; and Jacques Zeiller, "La lettre de saint Jérôme aux Goths Sunnia et Fretela," *CRAI* 79 (1935): 238–50.

will be put on trial (**2.1**), this shows that he is writing for the Latin public, not for two Goths. (5) If evidence suggests that Goths already had a translation of the Psalter into Gothic, as Chrysostom's reference to chanting the Psalms in barbarian languages suggests, why do Sunnia and Fretela not reference this? (6) No Goths would be this interested in the Latin Bible. (7) If these particular Goths knew Greek, why does Jerome explain the meanings of Greek words in Latin? (8) We do not expect that Goths would know Latin.

For De Bruyne, these observations demonstrate that Sunnia and Fretela are not real people and that *Ep.* 106 is not a real letter. In reality, De Bruyne argues, Jerome composed this treatise for a Latin-speaking audience, and he did so for several reasons: to make corrections to the Gallican Psalter, to point out differences between the hexaplaric and popular LXX texts, to explain various scholarly points, and above all to polemicize against the revision to the Latin Bible that (De Bruyne believed) Augustine had produced (see n. 51). Against the backdrop of these objections, I will explain what I take to be the purpose of *Ep.* 106 and the likely profile of Sunnia and Fretela, and from there I can address the issue of authenticity.

The first important issue to clarify is the purpose of *Ep.* 106. As Allgeier noted, this work would look considerably different if one of its main purposes was to correct the Latin text employed by Augustine, which De Bruyne believed Augustine revised himself. This is because Augustine's *Enarrations on the Psalms* contains numerous textual peculiarities (cf. the Verona Psalter), and Jerome rarely addresses these.[72] As for other motives suggested by De Bruyne, Jerome does not give consistent attention to the hexaplaric signs, the differences between the hexaplaric and popular Greek texts, or any other general topic in such a way as to suggest that explaining these points was Jerome's main purpose. Jerome does circle back to each of these topics when they are relevant to the main goal, which is also true (*pace* De Bruyne) with regard to the Hebrew text. But the main goal itself, which gives unity to this work from start to finish, is the defense and justification of the Gallican Psalter.[73] Throughout, whether the issue is the underlying Greek text or a question of translation theory, Jerome

---

72. In fact, on at least eight occasions Augustine's Latin text matches Jerome's Gallican Psalter as defended in *Ep.* 106. See n. 66 above.

73. Kelly's statement that *Ep.* 106 "contains a thoroughgoing correction of his Gallican Psalter" is misleading (Kelly, *Jerome*, 286). The Gallican Psalter receives critical review, and sometimes Jerome corrects the faulty text of his translation that was

quotes the Gallican Psalter and reports a challenge to his translation, usually accompanied by the underlying Greek cited as evidence against his rendering. Then, Jerome explains why he translated as he did and argues in whatever way necessary that the Gallican Psalter is not incorrect and its translator is not uninformed. On the question of purpose, a single reading through this treatise along with the commentary will show not only that challenges to the Gallican Psalter are the structuring element for the whole work but also that Jerome's defense of the Gallican Psalter is his consistent mission.

As to whether or not *Ep.* 106 reports genuine criticisms of the Gallican Psalter originating from someone other than Jerome, the numerous passages in which Jerome struggles to formulate a plausible defense suggest that these criticisms are authentic. For example, at Ps 17:48 (**9.6.24**), Jerome carried over "nations" from the Vetus Latina into the Gallican Psalter (although he does not admit this) and must acknowledge that the rendering under discussion is incorrect, although he suggests the possibility that the error was due to copyists when in fact it was his own error. At Ps 55:8 (**32.2.6–7**), Jerome admits a terrible mistake that occurred "among the Latins," which he corrects without acknowledging that this erroneous translation is also found in the Gallican Psalter. At Ps 77:57 (**50.6.8–9**), Jerome appeals to the Hebrew in order to explain why the Gallican Psalter is correct, but he must subtly confess that it does not match the hexaplaric LXX. Jerome is forced to cover a mistake at Ps 114:2 (**73.1.1–2**) and offers a weak defense for his translation at Ps 114:9 (**73.2.3–4**).[74] Moreover, Jerome frequently dismisses a question as "superfluous" (see introduction, §8.5) or expresses frustration at having to take up the same issue repeatedly.[75] In many cases, of course, Jerome seems to have answered his critics to his own satisfaction. Nevertheless, *Ep.* 106 contains many examples where Jerome must manage evidence that does not support his view or else gives him no occasion to make a point. It is hard to imagine why he would have selected

---

quoted back to him, but *Ep.* 106 does not constitute a correction in the sense of a *Retractio*; rather, it is an ἀπολογητικός (see n. 26).

74. For other examples where Jerome must deal with textual data that do not put him in a positive light, see Ps 21:20 (**12.1.21–22**); Ps 24:4a (**14.1.18–19**); Ps 60:9 (**35.2.15**); Ps 61:9 (**36.1.18–19**); Ps 103:4 (**65.1.5–6**); and Ps 114:2 (**73.1.1–2**).

75. E.g., at Ps 30:5: "And so that I am not constantly repeating the same thing, you should take note that the name 'Lord' and 'God' was added quite often, but you should follow what I have emended based on the Hebrew and the Seventy translators" (**18.1**).

these texts for discussion if he had complete freedom to shape the material as he wished.[76] The best account can be given for the content of *Ep.* 106 if we postulate that Jerome composed this treatise in order to respond to genuine criticisms that had been leveled against the Gallican Psalter.

What, then, are we to make of Sunnia and Fretela and their apparent interest in the Greek, Latin, and even Hebrew texts of the Psalms? First, based on their connection with Avitus (see **2.2.25**), Sunnia and Fretela probably resided in Constantinople, where they likely served the church and perhaps operated in some administrative capacities. Just because they were Goths by background, this does not mean that they were less than fully educated and integrated into Greco-Roman society.[77] Jerome himself came from the provinces but received a first-rate primary education and completed his schooling in Rome (see introduction, §1.1). Many of De Bruyne's misconceptions about *Ep.* 106 come from his taking Jerome's comments at the beginning of this treatise too literally. To be sure, Jerome speaks of "a barbarian tongue from among the Getae" (**1.1**). But this rhetorical device of juxtaposing the curiosity of the Goths with the intellectual drowsiness of the Greeks, which may be flattering but may also be patronizing, should not lead us to conclude that Sunnia and Fretela were literally living in barbarian hinterlands asking Jerome questions so that they could translate the Psalter into Gothic. Even if they were Goths by birth, Sunnia and Fretela could have been educated in Greek and Latin and also fully engaged in ecclesiastical and biblical affairs in the empire. If they received some of their education in Rome, for example, they could be just as concerned about the Latin Bible as Jerome and Rufinus were, even when they lived in the East. If they resided in Constantinople, they naturally knew Greek. The general content of *Ep.* 106 makes better sense if we envision Sunnia and Fretela as educated Christians of Gothic background who eventually came to live in Constantinople.

As for the praise Jerome bestows on Sunnia and Fretela for their interest in Hebrew, this is somewhat puzzling, not because they were especially unlikely to be concerned about the Hebrew text, but because the challenges they made to the Gallican Psalter all presuppose the authority of the Greek, and nowhere in *Ep.* 106 does Jerome indicate that he is answering a ques-

---

76. Cf. Allgeier, "Der Brief an Sunnia und Fretela," 91.

77. Zeiller, "La lettre de saint Jérôme," 246–49. As Zeiller points out, if all Goths were known to be uneducated, Jerome would have no reason to invent Gothic names as a cover for this treatise.

tion that was based on the Hebrew. Even the words discussed at the conclusion of this treatise are Greek, not Hebrew. It is Jerome who must invoke the Hebrew in order to answer objections that were raised on the basis of the popular Greek text. In order to explain Jerome's reference to the Hebrew in **1.1**, I suggest that in the letter that probably accompanied their list of criticisms (see **2.1.17**), Sunnia and Fretela, who were aware of Jerome's interest in Hebrew, urged Jerome to explain himself if he had anything to say based on his claims to Hebrew knowledge. Jerome, in turn, took this as an opportunity to portray their challenge as a cordial exchange between learned friends with mutual respect for Hebrew. He ascribes to them an interest in Hebrew so as to further promote the Hebrew cause, even if whatever comment they made about Hebrew did not genuinely warrant this.

The pleasantries in the opening section should not be taken to imply that Sunnia and Fretela composed merely a polite inquiry into Jerome's translation of the Psalms.[78] The fact that Jerome begins this treatise with courtesy and even praise shows that he still thinks he can win over his critics, in a manner similar to his approach in *Dialogue against the Pelagians*.[79] Still, Jerome sometimes displays frustration in *Ep.* 106, and his tone can be condescending (e.g., **30.1**; **30.2**; **30.3**; **46.3**; **52.1**; **54.1**; **54.2**; **56.1**; **57.3**; **62.1**). This shows Jerome's anxiety about the reputation of his work and his public standing as a scholar. De Bruyne was correct that *Ep.* 106 is not a private correspondence. Sunnia and Fretela published a long list of criticisms of the Gallican Psalter based on detailed study of the Greek text. This list must have circulated widely enough among Latin readers that Jerome felt he needed to respond. Such a view of this work best accords with the content of *Ep.* 106, and it makes sense of Jerome's comments about his efforts invoking ill will, his erudition being put on trial, and offering himself to be judged by all (**2.1**). The words of praise at the start of this treatise do not necessarily arise out of friendship. They probably function as part of Jerome's strategy for managing this public dispute over his work.

---

78. Georg Grützmacher, *Hieronymus: Eine Biographische Studie zur Alten Kirchengeschichte*, 3 vols. (Berlin: Trowitzsch & Sohn, 1901–1908), 3:221–23, interprets the opening section of *Ep.* 106, together with the fact that the tone throughout is not more scornful, as evidence that the questions of Sunnia and Fretela were more along the lines of polite inquiry.

79. See Benoît Jeanjean, "Le *Dialogus Attici et Critobuli* de Jérôme et la Prédication Pélagienne en Palestine entre 411 et 415," in *Jerome of Stridon: His Life, Writings, and Legacy*, ed. Andrew Cain and Josef Lössl (Farnham: Ashgate, 2009), 59–71, esp. 70–71.

If the question we ask is whether *Ep.* 106 is a private letter sent from Jerome to his friends Sunnia and Fretela to help them understand the Psalms, then the answer is negative: this is not an authentic letter. *Epistle* 106 is a technical treatise written to justify the Gallican Psalter in response to a list of challenges that was circulated among Latin readers in Jerome's circle. This list was probably introduced by a polite letter, but the charges against the Gallican Psalter were substantive. Jerome responded with a treatise that begins with a cordial epistolary introduction, followed by a rigorous defense of his work. It is reasonable to conclude that Jerome's *Ep.* 106 is not authentic as a letter. But on the question of whether these criticisms were actually put to Jerome by someone else, I think it is clear that they were. As for the question of whether Sunnia and Fretela are historical persons, I see no reason to doubt it, but I can offer little evidence in favor of their historicity. Perhaps the references to Firmus (**2.2**; **46.4**), a figure known not only to Jerome but also to Augustine, suggest that Sunnia and Fretela were also real people (see **2.2.1**).

6.2. The Date of *Epistle* 106

Because the Gallican Psalter (ca. 386) is the subject of *Ep.* 106 and Jerome does not explicitly refer his readers to his IH Psalter (ca. 391), several major studies of the nineteenth century assigned *Ep.* 106 to the late 380s. In the latter half of the twentieth century, it became common to date *Ep.* 106 to the period between 404 and 410, partly because of certain convergences with the IH Psalter, but especially because of supposed connections with Augustine's *Enarrations on the Psalms*. In my view, the earlier date is more likely to be correct, although the convergences with the IH Psalter require a slight modification to the early date position. In this section I explain the reasons for the early dating, address the issue regarding Augustine, revisit the relationship between *Ep.* 106 and the IH Psalter, and then suggest an approximate date and context for this treatise.

The obvious reason for dating *Ep. 106* to the late 380s is to situate it chronologically between the Gallican Psalter and the IH Psalter. In 1876, Otto Ohrloff published a study in which he dated *Ep.* 106 to the period just before the translation of the IH Psalter.[80] If Jerome had already produced

---

80. Otto Ohrloff, "Die alttestamentlichen Bruchstücke der gotischen Bibelüber-setzung," *Zeitschrift für deutsche Philologie* 7 (1876): 282.

the IH Psalter, he would have referred Sunnia and Fretela to it when discussing the Hebrew. Therefore, based on this thinking, *Ep.* 106 predates
the IH edition. On the other end, because Sunnia and Fretela several times
quoted back to Jerome a corrupted version of the Gallican Psalter, *Ep.* 106
must have been composed long enough after the translation of the Gallican
Psalter for textual corruptions to have entered the tradition.[81] Therefore,
Ohrolff argued, if the Gallican Psalter was translated shortly after Jerome's
move to Bethlehem in around 386, *Ep.* 106 likely comes from the later 380s,
long enough after the initial translation to allow for miscopying, but prior
to the IH edition in 390 or 391. In his biographical study of Jerome, Georg
Grützmacher also favored an early date for *Ep.* 106. Grützmacher reported
that Vallarsi had dated this work to 403. According to Grützmacher, however, the language Jerome applies to his renderings from the Hebrew in *Ep.*
106 cannot refer to the IH Psalter. This makes the period early in Jerome's
stay in Bethlehem a more likely time frame.[82] Based on this thinking, it is
reasonable to conclude that *Ep.* 106 was composed between 387 and 390.

The two main reasons for assigning a later date are the convergences
that exist between *Ep.* 106 and the IH Psalter on the one hand, and the
theory that Jerome alludes to a Latin translation made by Augustine on the
other. If *Ep.* 106 presupposes the IH Psalter, this only requires a date in the
early 390s. The tendency to date this treatise to 404–410 is based entirely
on the belief that Jerome in *Ep.* 106 criticizes a translation that was made by
Augustine during this later time period. In fact, this theory about Jerome
criticizing Augustine's translation is not well founded.

The passage where Jerome purportedly criticizes Augustine's interpretation occurs at **57.3**:

> In the same (psalm): "But you rejected and looked back." In place of this
> in Greek you say that you found ἐξουδένωσας. How great an error the
> changing of one letter has caused you! For we did not translate "looked

---

81. These corruptions, however, would require only a single copying.

82. Grützmacher, *Hieronymus*, 1:85. Grützmacher was aware of four passages (Pss
30:5; 47:10; 55:10; 118:172) that had been cited in the dissertation by Johannes Mühlau
("Zur Frage nach der gotischen Psalmenübersetzung," 1904) as evidence that *Ep.* 106
presupposed the IH Psalter, but he did not regard them as conclusive. On the contrary,
Grützmacher (correctly) dismissed two of these examples as irrelevant (Ps 30:5 and
47:10), and for the other two (Ps 55:10 and 118:172) he explained that, despite the
agreement with the IH Psalter, the fact that Jerome does not mention the IH edition
explicitly shows that he had not produced it; see Grützmacher, *Hieronymus*, 3:222.

back" (*respexisti*) but "looked down on" (*despexisti*), that is, "reckoned as nothing." Although perhaps you think ἐξουδένωσας should not be translated "looked down on," but rather should be translated in accordance with the most fluent translator of this time: "nothingafy," or "nothingize," or "nullificate," or some other lexical monstrosity as can be found among the unlearned.

According to Berthold Altaner, by the phrase "the most fluent translator of this time," Jerome does not allude to Rufinus, as most had assumed, but to Augustine, who (according to De Bruyne) had made his own revision of the Latin Psalter as reflected in his *Enarrations on the Psalms*.[83] Augustine quotes Ps 88:39 in his *Enarrations on the Psalms*, in his second sermon on Ps 88. In *Ep.* 105.5.2 (ca. 403), Jerome says that he has "certain commentaries on the Psalms" (*quosdam commentariolos in psalmos*) by Augustine, and in *Ep.* 112.20.1–3 (ca. 404) Jerome references the fact that Augustine has written on the Psalms. Altaner concludes that, by the words "certain commentaries on the Psalms" in *Ep.* 105, Jerome means only Augustine's first series of expositions on the Psalms, namely, those covering Psalms 1–32 (begun ca. 392). Therefore, if in 403 Jerome only had Augustine's *Enarrations* on Psalms 1–32 and did not yet have the series that includes Ps 88, but Jerome's *Ep.* 106 refers to Augustine's *Enarrations* on Ps 88, then Jerome's *Ep.* 106 must be later than 403/404.

Altaner's argument, however, has several substantial problems. For starters, even if Augustine were the individual referenced in *Ep.* 106, there is no reason to assume that by the phrase "certain commentaries on the Psalms" in *Ep.* 105, Jerome refers only to Augustine's expositions of Psalms 1–32. Jerome could be in possession of much more of Augustine's work by 404. Moreover, Augustine's individual expositions on the Psalms are difficult to date, and apart from Pss 1–32 (and later Pss 110–117 and 119–133) they were not delivered sequentially.[84] Thus, even if one were to believe that Jerome was criticizing Augustine's *Enarrations*, there is not sufficient evidence to pinpoint a date for Augustine's treatment of Ps 88.

---

83. Berthold Altaner, "Wann Schrieb Hieronymus Seine Ep. 106 Ad Sunniam et Fretelam De Psalterio?" *VC* 4 (1950): 246–48.

84. See Michael Fiedrowicz, "General Introduction," in *Saint Augustine: Exposition of the Psalms 1–32*, trans. Maria Boulding, ed. John E. Rotelle, The Works of Saint Augustine 3.15 (Hyde Park, NY: New City, 2000), 15–16.

More importantly, the person whom Jerome calls "the most fluent translator of this time" in *Ep.* 106 is almost certainly not Augustine. First, evidence is lacking that Augustine made a revision of the Latin Psalter, and he is not known to have been a translator at all.[85] Second, in *Ep.* 106 Jerome is criticizing a translator who used the words *adnihilo*, *adnullo*, and *nullifico*. But Augustine's quotation of Ps 88:39 in his *Enarrations on the Psalms* does not use any of these words, nor does Augustine ever use these words in his preserved writings.[86] Third, several parallels between *Ep.* 106 and Augustine's *Enarrations*, where the subject of the parallel deals with the hexaplaric signs and other linguistic data that are more likely to have originated with Jerome, suggest that Augustine is using *Ep.* 106, rather than that *Ep.* 106 is responding to Augustine.[87] In sum, it is extremely unlikely that Augustine is the "unlearned" translator whom Jerome mocks in *Ep.* 106.57.3.

As for Jerome's intended target, scholars prior to Altaner tended to assume that it was Rufinus of Aquileia, and this is still the most likely view. First, in **57.3** Jerome accuses this unlearned translator of employing "lexical monstrosities" (*portenta verborum*, literally "portents of words"). In *Ruf.* 2.11 (ca. 401), in the course of mocking certain expressions in Rufinus's translation of Origen's *On First Principles*, Jerome expresses outrage that Rufinus "dared to transmit such lexical monstrosities to Rome" (*ausum ... esse haec Romam verbora portenta transmittere*). Despite Rufinus's experience as a translator, Jerome frequently jeers at his former friend's literary style (e.g., *Ruf.* 1.17, 30; 2.6, 9, 11; 3.6, 10); and as we see, Jerome even employs the phrase *verbora portenta*, "lexical monstrosities" with reference to Rufinus. Second, Jerome's sarcastic praise of this individual as "the most fluent translator of this time" is the kind of swipe we would expect Jerome to take at Rufinus, who was a prolific translator. It also reminds us of Jerome's sarcastic adulation of Rufinus elsewhere. For example, Jerome refers to Rufinus as "the Aristarchus of our day" (*Ruf.* 1.17), "a critic and a Rabbi" (*Ruf.* 1.30), "this Theophrastus" (*Ruf.* 2.9), and "one of the Seventy Translators" (*Ruf.* 3.36). Although it is impossible to be certain, Rufinus of Aquileia is the most likely candidate to be this "most fluent translator of

---

85. See the discussion at n. 51 above.

86. See G. Q. A. Meershoek, *Le latin biblique d'après saint Jérôme: Aspects linguistiques de la rencontre entre la Bible et le monde classique* (Nijmegen-Utrecht: Dekker & Van de Vegt, 1966), 49.

87. See **50.2.7–8; 67.1.20–21; 67.3.5–7; 67.3.8; 75.1.9–10; 75.7.10–11.**

this time," who produces lexical monstrosities "as can be found among the unlearned."[88]

To sum up matters so far, the primary reason for assigning a date between 404 and 410 to *Ep.* 106 is the belief that Jerome at **57.3** was criticizing Augustine's *Enarrat. Ps.* 88, which he supposedly did not see until after 403. If, however, the target of Jerome's criticism is not Augustine but Rufinus, the argument in favor of the range 404–410 does not apply. If Rufinus was the intended target of Jerome's criticism, what might this tell us about the date? Rufinus was already in Jerusalem when Jerome arrived at Bethlehem in 386. Presumably, the two were still on good terms at that time. By 392, with Epiphanius's sermon in Jerusalem against Origen, the context was established for a public rift between Rufinus and Jerome. Of course, it is possible that the feud between Jerome and Rufinus did not actually spring into existence purely as a result of the Origenist controversy but that the controversy served as the occasion for the public expression of a schism that had occurred shortly before. But, at the very least, if we were to accept Rufinus as the target of **57.3**, we would not expect *Ep.* 106 to have been written much earlier than 392.

The second piece of evidence that has been cited to show that *Ep.* 106 was composed later than Ohrloff and Grützmacher suggested is the occasional agreement between Hebrew renderings in *Ep.* 106 and the IH Psalter. Although the number of such agreements is small, at least one agreement is substantial enough to require a more precise explanation for the relationship between *Ep.* 106 and the IH edition.

As discussed above (introduction, §5.3), there are fourteen clear cases in which Jerome offers a full Latin translation for a stretch of text that is explicitly identified as a rendering of what is found "among the Hebrews,"

---

88. The editor of Codex Casinensis 557, Ambrogio M. Amelli, in trying to explain the origin of his manuscript's Vetus Latina text with hexaplaric revisions that are independent of Jerome, suggests that the revisor behind this text is none other than Rufinus. In favor of his proposal, Amelli cites certain peculiar foreign expressions common to Rufinus's writings and Codex Casinensis 557, certain characteristic readings shared between this manuscript and Rufinus's translations of Origen, and the fact that the verb *nullifico*, as ascribed to Rufinus by Jerome in *Ep.* 106.57.3 (according to Amelli), is found in this manuscript at Ps 118:118. Amelli's suggestion remains only a fascinating possibility, but it would not be surprising if Rufinus produced a revision of the Latin Psalter with input from the Greek text of Origen (cf. Jerome's *Ruf.* 2.34). See Ambrogio M. Amelli, ed., *Liber Psalmorum iuxta antiquissimam latinam versionem nunc primum ex Casinensi Cod. 557*, Collectanea Biblica Latina 1 (Rome: Pustet, 1912), xxviii–xxxiii.

where the translation is not simply a rendering of hexaplaric Greek material. What is notable about these passages is that, in nine cases, the translation that Jerome gives does not agree with what is found in the IH edition. Alongside these examples can be placed many discussions as noted above where Jerome's comments are in tension with the IH edition—for example, where he calls something an error that he uses in the IH Psalter. This substantial body of disagreements lends credibility to the theory that Jerome composed *Ep.* 106 before he decided to translate the Psalms directly from the Hebrew and that, once he turned his attention to the IH project, he gained new insights that caused him to reverse some of these former decisions.

Most of *Ep.* 106 can easily be interpreted according to this theory. It is, on the surface, not a problem that five Hebrew-based translations match the IH Psalter: Ps 54:9b (**31.2.13–14**); Ps 76:7 (**49.1.9–10**); Ps 118:136 (**75.7.10–11**); Ps 118:172 (**75.8.15–16**); and the explanation of λαξευτήριον (**86.3.18**). If *Ep.* 106 came first and the IH Psalter came later, we would expect Jerome to recollect some of the Hebraic renderings he gave in the earlier work and employ them in his IH Psalter. The complication comes at the very end of the treatise. The final words of *Ep.* 106 are as follows: "So, translating from the Hebrew we said thus: 'And now they have together cut down its carved works with axe and hewers.' Therefore, λαξευτήριον can be rendered 'hewer.' " In this last comment, which includes one of the five agreements between *Ep.* 106 and the IH edition, Jerome introduces his Hebrew rendering with the words "translating from the Hebrew we said thus." As many have noted, this past-tense reference ("we said") appears to refer to the IH Psalter.[89] The challenge, then, is to explain why the body of *Ep.* 106 proceeds as if the IH Psalter does not exist but makes an allusion to the IH Psalter at the very end.

I suggest that Jerome had not yet begun the IH Psalter when he started writing *Ep.* 106, but by the time he reached the end of *Ep.* 106 he had embarked on translating IH Psalms. In fact, based on the evolution in his thinking within this treatise on the relationship between the hexaplaric Septuagint and the original Hebrew, I propose that responding to these objections to the Gallican Psalter helped Jerome realize that the hexaplaric Septuagint was not sufficient as a representation of the Hebrew and that he

---

89. E.g., Cavallera, *Saint Jérôme*, 2:46; De Bruyne, "La lettre de Jérôme," 2; and Adam Kamesar, *Jerome, Greek Scholarship, and the Hebrew Bible*, OCM (Oxford: Clarendon, 1993), 54.

would need to produce a new version of the Psalms based directly on the Hebrew text.

Jerome's perspective on how closely the hexaplaric Septuagint and the Hebrew agree undergoes some modification in *Ep.* 106. In **2.1–4**, Jerome confidently asserts that the hexaplaric Septuagint constitutes "the Seventy themselves" and the "refuge" of the "Hebrew truth" that has been "preserved uncorrupted and unstained" such that "whatever differs from this, there is no doubt but that it also disagrees with the authority of the Hebrews." Early in the treatise, Jerome gives special attention to labeling incorrect texts as *vulgata*, "popular" or κοινή, "common" in opposition to the "genuine" hexaplaric text (**3.1**; **4.1**; **5.1**; **13.1**; once again at **57.2**). But as he works his way through each question, and especially in the latter half of *Ep.* 106, Jerome increasingly finds occasion to recognize a gap between the hexaplaric Septuagint and what the Hebrew actually says. At Ps 58:10 (**33.1**), in order to justify the Gallican Psalter's third-person construal of the sentence, he must admit that the Hebrew allows for this, whereas the (hexaplaric) Septuagint gives the second-person. In the very next passage (**33.2**), Jerome gives a rendering of the Hebrew that highlights a difference from the hexaplaric Septuagint. Shortly thereafter (**38.1**), having defended his own translation against Sunnia and Fretela, Jerome gives an alternative Hebrew meaning, saying, "It is better in Hebrew." A key moment in *Ep.* 106 occurs in the treatment of Ps 73:8 (**46.3–5**), where Jerome corrects an error that arose because someone copied into the text a marginal notation Jerome made on the meaning of the Hebrew. In correcting this mistake, Jerome must explain that what he put in the Gallican Psalter—that is, the hexaplaric Septuagint—should be sung in the churches, whereas his marginal notation was intended to explain for scholars "what the Hebrew truth contains." In this case, the "Hebrew truth" is clearly distinguished from the hexaplaric Septuagint. Such passages increase in frequency in the second half of *Ep.* 106 (e.g., **50.6**; **51.1**; **59.1**; **63.2**; **65.5**; **71.1**; **73.1**; **75.7**; **75.8**; **78.1**; **81.1**). Remarkably, on Ps 129:4 (**78.1**), Jerome appeals to the Hebrew to correct a mistake in the translation of Sunnia and Fretela–but also in his own translation–on the grounds that "we are zealous for the truth—that is, for what is in the Hebrew." It is not that Jerome's enthusiasm for the Hebrew truth developed in this treatise. Jerome was committed to the Hebrew from the start (see **1.1**; **2.3**; **7.2**; **9.5**; **11.2**; **41.6**; **46.4**; **78.1**). What changes from the beginning of *Ep.* 106 to the end is that Jerome increasingly allows for the Hebrew to differ from the hexaplaric Septuagint. He continues to defend the Gallican Psalter and promote the hexaplaric edition throughout, but by the end of the treatise, the Hebrew truth has emerged as an entity separate from the hexaplaric Septuagint.

At the start of *Ep.* 106, the hexaplaric Septuagint was seen as providing fully reliable access to the Hebrew, but by the end of this work Jerome has come to realize that the hexaplaric Septuagint often fails to capture the Hebrew truth. The most likely historical context for this treatise is therefore Bethlehem in the early 390s, when Jerome was transitioning from the hexaplaric translation to the IH translation. If *Ep.* 106 was composed at this early date, prior to his translation work on the IH edition, we would expect his Hebrew knowledge to be less than what we see in his writings after 405, when the IH edition was complete. This more modest level of Hebrew proficiency is what we see in *Ep.* 106.

Jerome does not display the Hebrew competence in *Ep.* 106 that we should expect to see if this treatise were written around 405. I am not suggesting that Jerome lacked competence to work with the Hebrew when he wrote *Ep.* 106. Jerome transcribes Hebrew words on forty-six occasions in this work.[90] These transcriptions show that Jerome normally understands how the Hebrew words match up with the Greek (which is not as simple as it seems), and that he comprehends the basic morphology of Hebrew. Jerome knows that *yod* and *vav* are distinguished by size (**78.1**), and that the Hebrew *chaialoth* (כאילות) is plural (**9.2**). Seven times he states what the Hebrew would have been if a proposed (but erroneous) Greek or Latin reading were correct. In three of these cases, the Hebrew form that Jerome provides demonstrates his grasp of Hebrew pronominal suffixes (**6.1**; **13.1**; **68.2**). Otherwise, Jerome is able to produce the words for "mouth" (**19.1**), "people" (**28.3**), "age" (**35.2**), and "you" (**37.1**), which shows that he can detach prefixes and suffixes where necessary to identify the core noun. The impression left by *Ep.* 106 is that Jerome was able to read the Hebrew text with the help of the hexaplaric versions with at least moderate comprehension of the syntax and functional knowledge of the basic vocabulary. Such competence makes sense for Jerome even in the early 390s, since he was more than ten years removed from his introduction to Hebrew and had strengthened his Hebrew skills in the mid-380s in Rome.[91]

---

90. See **4.2**; **5.1**; **6.1**; **7.1**; **9.2**; **9.3**; **13.1**; **17.2**; **19.1**; **19.2**; **23.1**; **25.2**; **25.3**; **28.2**; **28.3**; **31.2**; **32.2**; **35.2**; **37.1**; **39.2**; **40.1**; **41.4**; **41.5**; **45.5**; **46.4**; **46.6**; **46.7**; **50.1**; **50.2**; **50.3**; **50.7**; **51.1**; **57.2**; **58.1**; **63.2**; **63.4**; **64.1**; **65.3**; **65.5**; **65.5**; **65.6**; **67.1**; **68.2**; **69.2**; **75.6**; **82.1**.

91. On his process of learning Hebrew, see Graves, *Jerome's Hebrew Philology*, 76–97.

Nevertheless, in comparison with the Hebrew knowledge Jerome displays in his major prophetic commentaries completed after 401, the Hebrew learning reflected in *Ep.* 106 falls short. Unlike in his later works, in *Ep.* 106 Jerome does not spell out Hebrew words, provide different vocalization options with accompanying meanings, dissect and identify elements in composite words, explain the origins of various Greek readings by reconstructing the Hebrew text-critical and linguistic options, or discuss cogently Hebrew synonyms and points of ambiguity.[92] Frequently, in *Ep.* 106, Jerome relies on the hexaplaric Greek versions to tell him what the Hebrew means without unpacking the constituent elements of the Hebrew; for example, at Ps 77:36, Jerome transcribes two Hebrew words, יכזבו לו, "they lie to him" as one word, *icazbulo*, and he reports the meaning by giving the consensus of the hexaplaric versions without further elucidating the details of the Hebrew (**50.3**). Even for a simple addition (**49.3**), or the meaning of a common word such as טוב (**67.1**), Jerome knows what the Hebrew says because the hexaplaric versions tell him so.[93] In some passages, Jerome's explanation of the Hebrew contains an obvious flaw. Thus, Jerome claims Hebrew ambiguity based on the hexaplaric evidence when the Hebrew is not ambiguous as Jerome thinks (**17.2**); he does not seem aware that the pronoun אתה, "you" cannot be the object of the verb (**37.1**); he makes an error in matching the Greek evidence with the Hebrew (**67.3**); he translates the Hebrew word ענה ("answer" or "sing") as *loquor*, "speak" (**75.8**); and he fails to address the difference between תורא and תורה (**78.1**). In *Ep.* 106, Jerome shows less Hebrew knowledge than in his later writings, and he commits a higher number of mistakes. The Hebrew proficiency we see in *Ep.* 106 is consistent with the level we might expect from Jerome in the early 390s.

With these various factors taken into consideration, it is possible to suggest a timeframe for the writing of *Ep.* 106. If Jerome produced the Gallican Psalter early in his hexaplaric revision period (ca. 386–ca. 392), we could place this work around 387. Because of its deviations from the traditional wording of the Vetus Latina Psalter, the Gallican Psalter met with sharp criticism. A public manifestation of this criticism emerged in

---

92. On Jerome's Hebrew scholarship in his *Commentary on Jeremiah* and other exegetical writings, see Graves, *Jerome's Hebrew Philology*, 26–75, 97–127.

93. For other examples where Jerome relies on the hexaplaric versions to explain the sense of the Hebrew without unpacking the Hebrew details, see **9.2**; **9.3**; **9.6–7**; **18.2**; **24.1**; **31.2**; **41.4**; **46.3–4**; **49.3**; **50.5**; **50.6b**; **51.1**; **58.1**; **63.4**; **65.3**; **66.3**; **69.2**; **75.8**.

389 or 390 with the circulation of a list of objections to Jerome's Gallican Psalter produced by Sunnia and Fretela. This list was introduced by a letter that invited Jerome to explain why he translated as he did, with some reference to his previously announced commitment to the Hebrew. Jerome was stung by this public censure of his translation, however politely it may have been stated, and he responded in 391–392 with *Ep.* 106. This treatise defended the Gallican Psalter by explaining Jerome's individual translation choices and justifying his decision to translate from the hexaplaric Septuagint. Since Jerome was in the process of producing a complete translation of the Old Testament out of the hexaplaric Septuagint, *Ep.* 106 was initially intended to serve as a justification not only for the Gallican Psalter but also for the whole hexaplaric translation project.

In the course of writing *Ep.* 106, however, it became clear to Jerome that his Latin rendering based on the hexaplaric Septuagint did not always capture the sense of the Hebrew. Through comparing each rendering against the Hebrew directly, Jerome realized that, if he wanted to deliver the Hebrew truth to Latin ears, he would need to translate directly from the Hebrew. He could rely on the hexaplaric versions for help, but he could not follow any one Greek version consistently, not even the hexaplaric Septuagint. Thus, by the time he reached the end of *Ep.* 106 in around 392, Jerome was committed to producing new Latin translations based directly on the Hebrew. One of his first translations, perhaps his first, was the IH Psalter. In fact, he had already started on the IH Psalter by the time he completed *Ep.* 106. This is why he states "translating from the Hebrew we said thus" in **87.3**. Jerome's relationship with Rufinus was already sour by this time, which explains the disparaging allusion to Rufinus in **57.3**. By 393, the IH Psalter was completed, and the public controversy over Origen erupted between Jerome and Rufinus. This would place the composition of *Ep.* 106 in 391–392.

If this timeframe is correct, Jerome's critical work in *Ep.* 106 played a key role in his scholarly development. In this treatise, we see Jerome working through textual details on the way to deciding to embark on his complete translation of the Hebrew Bible into Latin.

7. Principles of Translation in *Epistle* 106

Many of the objections Sunnia and Fretela raise against the Gallican Psalter find their answer in Jerome's principles of translation. This is generally the case when the issue at stake is not a difference in the underlying Greek text but a difference of opinion as to how the Greek should be rendered into Latin. Because in this work Jerome offers detailed explanations for how he handles many difficult passages, *Ep.* 106 is rich in observations on the craft of translation. Two important points on this topic should be made. First, near the beginning of the treatise (**3.3**), Jerome invokes the names of Cicero ("Tullius"), Terence, Plautus, and Caecilius in defense of free translation. It is true that classical Latin writers speak about translating and adapting Greek models in a way that supports Jerome's practice of not always rendering word for word (see **3.3.4–3.3.9**). But Jerome's reason for avoiding word-for-word translation is not always the same as what one finds in authors such as Cicero. For example, whereas Cicero avoids word-for-word translation for the sake of Latin style, Jerome often deviates from word-for-word translation in order to capture the proper sense. Second, Jerome's translations of Scripture are not particularly literal in comparison with the Vetus Latina, despite Jerome's claim in *Ep.* 57.5.2 that he translates Scripture "word for word."[94] As *Ep.* 106 shows, this is intentional.[95] The comment in *Ep.* 57 should be seen primarily as a rhetorical posture taken

---

94. In *Ep.* 57.5.2, in the course of defending his free rendering of a nonbiblical book, Jerome says: *ego enim solum fateor, sed libera voce profiteor me in interpretatione Graecorum absque scripturis sanctis, ubi et verborum ordo mysterium est, non verbum e verbo, sed sensum exprimere de sensu*, "For I not only acknowledge, but I freely profess that in translating the Greeks—with the exception of the sacred scriptures, where even the order of the words is a mystery—I render not word for word, but sense for sense" (CSEL 54:508). While writing with such vigor in defense of free translation, Jerome did not want his readers to lose confidence in his biblical translations. Some have suggested that Jerome's comments in *Ep.* 57 pertain only to Greek texts, and so for Scripture this means only the Roman Psalter, the Gospels, and the hexaplaric translations; see Sebastian Weigert, *Hebraica Veritas: Übersetzungsprinzipien und Quellen der Deuteronomiumübersetzung des Hieronymus* (Stuttgart: Kohlhammer, 2016), 52. The occasion for *Ep.* 57, however, is Jerome's translation of a nonbiblical Greek work, and this probably explains the phrase "in translating the Greeks." That Jerome has more than just Greek originals in mind with his comment on Scripture is suggested by the fact that later in *Ep.* 57 he invokes the LXX and the NT as "sense for sense" translators, and when in his expositions he does appeal to the "mystery" of words, it is often in reference to Hebrew words (e.g., in his *Homilies on the Psalms*).

95. In addition to the statements in *Ep.* 106, Jerome also promotes "sense for sense" translation for Scripture in *Ep.* 112.19 and *Comm. Eph.* 1:4. Jerome regularly observed that New Testament writers quoted the Old Testament according to the sense rather than the words, e.g., *Ep.* 57.7–11; 121.2.7; *Comm. Jer.* 31:15; *Comm. Gal.* 3:8–9; 13b–14; *Comm. Matt.* 10:35–36; 27:9–10.

to address the needs of that context. The principles Jerome articulates in *Ep.* 106 better represent the ideas that guide his practice.[96]

7.1. Jerome's Statements on Translation Theory

I will begin by listing six passages from *Ep.* 106 where Jerome articulates a principle for translating Scripture. I will then derive five key concepts from these statements and offer further explanations for each concept. The six statements are as follows:

1. *Ep.* 106.3.2. Jerome rejects a proposed translation on the grounds that it displays an artificially affected style (κακοζηλία), destroys the euphony (εὐφωνία) of the text, and causes the translation to lose all seemliness (*omnem decorem*). He summarizes as follows: "This is the rule for a good translator, that he should convey the unique expressions (ἰδιώματα) of the other language in the particular idiom (*proprietate*) of his own language."

2. *Ep.* 106.26.2. Jerome criticizes a translation proposal because it would produce cacophony (κακόφωνον), and he defends his original rendering. He explains: "As it is, therefore, the elegance (*elegantia*) of the translation was preserved without losing the sense."

3. *Ep.* 106.29.2. After justifying a translation on the basis of εὐφωνία, Jerome adds: "We should not translate word for word in such a way that, while we adhere to the syllable, we lose the meaning."

4. *Ep.* 106.54.3. Jerome defends his own choice of translation against a proposed rendering that he says means essentially the same as what he translated. According to Jerome, his word makes for better Latin, as he states: "We follow this principle, that where there is no change with regard to the sense, we should maintain the elegance of Latin expression (*Latini sermonis elegantiam*)."

5. *Ep.* 106.55.1. Jerome argues that in translation we should not "contentiously scrutinize words and syllables" (*contentiose verba scrutamur et syllabas*), following the words but destroying the sequence of thought (*dum verba sequimur, sensus ordinem perdimus*). He wraps up his discussion with the general principle: "The same rule of translating should be followed here

---

96. On Jerome's principles of biblical translation, see Michael Graves, "Jerome's Principles of Biblical Translation in the Context of Classical and Sacred Ideals," in *Shifting Paradigms in the Study of Jerome*, ed. Andrew Cain, Jessica van 't Westeinde, and Matthew A. Kraus (Leuven: Peeters, forthcoming).

which we have often stated, that wherever there is no damage to the sense, the euphony (εὐφωνία) and particular idiom (*proprietas*) of the language into which we are translating should be maintained."

6. *Ep.* 106.66.1. Replying to a novel translation proposal, Jerome defends his own traditional rendering with this statement: "But in this there is no change in the sense; and so we, following the ancient translation that did no harm, did not wish to change it."

7.2. Principles of Translation

Five key concepts about translation that emerge from these statements are listed and explained below:

1. *The sense of the text should not be damaged.* For Jerome as translator of sacred Scripture, the primary aim of his translation is to communicate the content of the biblical text. This flows from the fundamental Christian belief that Scripture conveys divine teaching. Jerome is concerned about the basic Latinity of his translation, to be sure, but his overriding commitment is that he should preserve the message. This commitment manifests itself in his principle that the "sense" (*sensus*) or "meaning" (*intelligantia*) of the passage should not suffer damage, loss, or change (e.g., *damnum, perditio, immutatio*). In addition to the passages quoted above (**26.2; 29.2; 30.2; 54.3; 55.1; 66.1**), this principle finds expression in **30.2** ("when there is no loss to the sense); **54.1** ("where there is no change in the sense"); **60.1** ("there is no harm to the sense"); and in passages where Jerome evaluates possible translations on the basis of tradition or Latinity because the sense of the two options does not differ (**31.3; 45.5; 63.4; 75.8**).

It is significant that Jerome expresses this idea in the negative ("not harming the sense") rather than in the positive (e.g., "preserving the meaning"). In contrast to his statement in *Ep.* 57.5.2 about the order of scriptural words being a mystery, in *Ep.*106 Jerome assumes that the same basic content can be expressed in different ways. Jerome's focus on content reflects his Christian concern for the biblical message, but he combines this with an assumption common in classical sources that ideas can be clothed in different words.[97] Therefore, provided that the sense is not damaged, other factors can contribute to deciding how best to translate a given passage.

---

97. Cf. *Inst.* 11.1.1–3. See D. A. Russell, *Criticism in Antiquity* (London: Bristol Classical, 1995), 129–31.

2. *Traditional renderings should be retained where possible.* As noted at **66.1**, in Ps 140:3, Jerome does not wish to change the "ancient translation" (*antiquam interpretationem*) that does no harm to the sense. As long as the proper meaning is conveyed, Jerome tends to leave in place traditional renderings as hallowed by the Vetus Latina tradition, even if another option presents itself. This tendency toward conservativism certainly found useful application in translating the book of Psalms, where many passages had become widely familiar through liturgical recitation. Elsewhere in *Ep.* 106, Jerome justifies an element of the Gallican Psalter that followed the Old Latin version by pointing back to his first revision of the Psalter: "And when previously we were correcting the Psalter, wherever the sense was the same we preferred not to change the custom of the old translators, lest we deter the zeal of the reader by excessive novelty" (**12.2**). Again, at Ps 49:23, Jerome explains his rendering thus: "So, we did not wish to change what was read from early times, because the sense was the same" (**30.4**). Jerome expresses a similar commitment to preserve familiar wording when possible in the preface to his translation of the Gospels, where he says that he kept his correcting pen in check so that changes were made only where the sense was at stake (*Pref. Gos.* 2). Of course, the customary Latin version should be corrected wherever it fails to communicate the sense properly. In his IH translation, Jerome makes greater alterations to the wording because his engagement with the Hebrew brought to light greater differences in meaning between the traditional Latin version and the "true" (i.e., Hebrew) meaning. But if a novel translation proposal does not better capture the essential sense, Jerome prefers to preserve the older rendering.

3. *Each language has its own unique manner of expression that should be respected.* The term ἰδίωμα signified a specific property, characteristic, or unique feature of something. It came to be used in a linguistic sense for the distinctive, characteristic style of some corpus or mode of expression. Greek scholars applied this term both to the distinctive style of a given author and also to one dialect over against another.[98] Some authors used

---

98. Christoph Schäublin, *Untersuchungen zu Methode und Herkunft der antiochenischen Exegese* (Bonn: Hanstein, 1974), 128. For example, Dionysius of Halicarnassus references the ἰδιώματα of Thucydides in discussing this author's particular style (*2 Amm.* 1). In Pseudo-Plutarch's *On Homer*, specific forms of expression associated with Greek dialects (e.g., Doric, Ionic, Attic) are described as ἰδιώματα (*Vit. poes. Hom.* [B], 8–13).

ἰδίωμα for the distinctive idiom of one language as opposed to another.[99] The early Christian commentator Theodore of Mopsuestia explained certain linguistic peculiarities of the Septuagint, such as the use of the past tense for the future, as the product of τὸ Ἑβραϊκὸν ἰδίωμα, "the Hebraic idiom" (e.g., *Comm. Joel* 2:18).[100] In Latin, the Greek ἰδίωμα was brought into Latin as *idioma*, which Latin grammarians used to describe the difference between Latin and Greek modes of expression.[101]

Another Latin term that functioned as an equivalent for ἰδίωμα was *proprietas*, "peculiarity, particular quality." In Quintilian and other sources, *proprietas* often signified a word's "proper signification."[102] The sense of *proprietas* that is analogous to ἰδίωμα appears in Aulus Gellius, for example, when he refuses to translate Plato's Greek into Latin because no Latin speech can emulate the "distinctive properties" (*proprietates*) of Plato's words (*Noct. att.* 10.22.3). We find *proprietas* used with reference to the "particular idiom" of a given language in Rufinus's translation of Origen's *Homilies on Numbers* (*Hom. Num.* 19.3.2; 27.13.1).[103] In his commentaries

---

99. E.g., Iamblichus states, "There are certain idioms (ἰδιώματα) in every nation that are impossible to express in the language of another" (*Myst.* 7.5); see Emma C. Clarke, John M. Dillon, and Jackson P. Hershbell, eds., *Iamblichus: De mysteriis*, WGRW 4 (Atlanta: Society of Biblical Literature, 2003), 299. On each nation having its own language (φωνή ἰδία), see Let. Aris. 11; Eusebius, *Praep. ev.* 9.15.

100. See also *Comm. Os.* 12:10; *Comm. Mich.* 1:4; *Comm. Ps.* 55:7 (LXX); *Comm. Hab.* 3:4; and *Comm. Ps.* 32:7 (LXX); see Schäublin, *Untersuchungen*, 129–32. Cf. Athanasius, *C. Ar.* 2.4, τὸ τῆς γραφῆς ἰδίωμα, "the particular idiom of Scripture"; and Socrates Scholasticus, *Hist. eccl.* 2.45, τὰ τοιαῦτα τοῦ ἀποστόλου ἰδιώματα, "such particular expressions of the apostle."

101. See James E. G. Zetzel, *Critics, Compilers, and Commentators: An Introduction to Roman Philology, 200 BCE–800 CE* (New York: Oxford University Press, 2018), 115, 241–44. E.g., Charisius includes a section in his grammatical treatise *De idiomatibus*, "On Idioms," which begins: "The idioms that are in our language should be innumerable, since these are all the things that we express in our own manner and not according to that of the Greeks"; see Heinrich Keil, *Grammatici Latini*, 7 vols. (Leipzig: Teubner, 1864), 1:291.

102. E.g., *Inst.* 8.2.1–8; 5.14.34; 12.2.19. Tertullian, *Marc.* 2.9.2 refers to *proprietate verborum*, "the proper signification of the words" with regard to a Greek text.

103. In the Latin text of Origen's *Hom. Num.* 2.2.2, Rufinus uses *proprietas* for the "distinctive sense" of a word both in Paul and in Peter. It is possible, but not certain, that behind these various occurrences of *proprietas* in Rufinus's Latin stood ἰδίωμα in Origen's original Greek.

and discussions of translation, Jerome uses both the Greek ἰδίωμα and the Latin *proprietas* in the sense of "particular idiom."

In *Ep.* 106, Jerome makes reference to the "idioms" of Hebrew, Greek, and Latin in explaining his translation choices. This is clearly stated at **3.2**: "This is the rule for a good translator, that he should convey the unique expressions (ἰδιώματα) of the other language in the particular idiom (*proprietate*) of his own language." Jerome's belief that good translation comes from understanding the particular idiom of the source language and recasting it into the particular idiom of the receptor language underlies almost every translation discussion in *Ep.* 106. Passages in which Jerome articulates this thinking explicitly are **3.3** ("in the particular idioms of their own language"); **30.2** ("each language speaks in its own particular idioms"); **37.1** ("it was translated into Latin in keeping with the particular idiom of the language"); **50.4** ("Latin's own particular idiom"); **50.5** ("according to the Hebrew idiom"); **55.1** ("the euphony [εὐφωνία] and particular idiom of the language into which we are translating should be maintained"); **65.3** ("metaphorically [μεταφορικῶς] according to the particular idiom of Hebrew"); and **86.1** ("according to the particular idiom of the Latin language").

Jerome continued throughout his career appealing to the "particular idioms" of languages in his translations and explanations of Scripture.[104] He inherited the terminology and linguistic concept of ἰδίωμα/*proprietas* from the Roman grammatical tradition and Greek Christian biblical scholarship. It was Jerome's contribution to translation theory to make concern for the *proprietas* of each language a fundamental translation principle.

4. *One need not translate word for word if other principles demand a less literal translation.* Jerome inherited the phrase "word for word" from the classical Latin tradition (see **3.3.4–3.3.9**). Translations described as word for word aimed at one-for-one representation of individual elements (e.g., words, prefixes), preserving word order, refraining from adding or subtracting elements, and as much consistency as possible in using the same Latin word for a given Greek word. Naturally, any translation that respects the idiomatic usage of each language will not always be word for word. Jerome articulated this principle at **29.2**: "We should not translate word

---

104. E.g., *Ep.* 78.13.1 (the particular idiom of the Syrian language); *Ep.* 18b.17.2; 20.4.4–5.1; 57.5.2; 78.2.1; 108.26.3; 119.10.12; *Pref. Chron.*; *Jov.* 1.13; *Ruf.* 1.19; *Comm. Tit.* 3:9; *Comm. Mich.* 2:6–8; *Comm. Os.* 10:13a; *Comm. Mal.* 1:6a; *Comm. Matt.* 21:12–13; *Comm. Ezech.* 1:1; 3:9; 4:16; 8:27; 10:32.

for word in such a way that, while we adhere to the syllable, we lose the meaning."

In *Ep.* 106, Jerome consistently employs the phrase "word for word" and related terms to criticize translations proposed by Sunnia and Fretela. Latin forms based on Greek words are rejected as being "word for word" (**67.3**; cf. **57.3**). A suggested "literal" (*ad verbum*) translation is condemned as "an absurd rendering" (**17.1**). In **62.1**, Jerome denounces a word-for-word rendering: "Who would not flee from such a translation?" Anyone who favors literalistic translation is dismissed as a "contentious nitpicker of words" who is twisting himself around in "sickening explanations" (**30.2**). According to Jerome, we should not "contentiously scrutinize words and syllables" (**55.1**; cf. **63.2**; *Ep.* 57.7.4; 57.9.8). It is clear from *Ep.* 106 that Jerome did not think he had produced a literal or word-for-word translation in the Gallican Psalter and that he did not approve of corrections along these lines.

Many of Jerome's specific translation choices reflect his decision not to insist on a word-for-word approach. For example, he justifies his decision to use two Latin words to translate one Greek word, as with his rendering of ὀπωροφυλάκιον as *pomorum custodiam*. In Jerome's view, "it cannot be rendered differently than how we translated it" (**51.1**). Likewise, on ἔκστασις in Ps 30:23, he explains, "For the Latin language is not able to express ἔκστασις any other way except *mentis excessum*, 'departure of mind'" (**18.2**; cf. **50.6**; **53.1**). He acknowledges that he added *suam*, "his" at Ps 18:6 (*viam suam*, "his course") without explicit basis in the Hebrew, but his observation that "in Hebrew it is not explicitly stated" (**10.1**) makes clear his view that the pronoun, although not explicit, is implied by the passage and properly belongs in a good (i.e., not literal) Latin translation. Similarly, he asserts that the proper meaning is not conveyed unless he adds *sibi*, "themselves" at Ps 84:11a, "Mercy and truth met themselves," even though this word does not appear in the Hebrew (**55.2**). These examples illustrate Jerome's self-aware practice of translation that is not word for word.

In his negative stance toward word-for-word translation, Jerome stands in general agreement with classical Latin authors such as Cicero. It should be repeated, however, that his reason for avoiding literalistic translation was to preserve the content, defer to tradition, and conform to basic Latinity. This contrasts with the classical ideal of "translating" by adapting the original so as to create a fresh composition that might even surpass its source in style, charm, or force.

5. *The translation should reflect proper Latin in terms of basic grammatical correctness, naturalness of expression, and clarity.* In order to understand Jerome's concern for proper Latin, it is useful to consider the stylistic quality of *elegantia* within the broader category of "style" (*elocutio*). An especially relevant discussion of *elegantia* appears in the first century BCE treatise *Rhetorica ad Herennium*, according to which the three qualities of a suitable and polished style are *elegantia*, *compositio*, and *dignitas* (*Ad Her.* 4.12.17–4.13.18). *Elegantia* is that quality of speech according to which words are expressed with purity (*pure*) and clarity (*aperte*). The two basic aspects of *elegantia* are *Latinitas*, "proper Latin," and *explanatio*, "clarity of communication." *Compositio* is the manner of arranging the words (*verborum constructio*) so that the speech is smooth and polished. This covers areas of speaking such as what sounds are placed together and how words are ordered in a sentence.[105] *Dignitas* is grandeur of style that is achieved through language that is ornate and embellished with variety. The use of various figures of speech and thought fall within this sphere. A key point to observe is that *elegantia* in the sense of basic linguistic correctness is distinguished from more ambitious concerns about the arrangement of words into larger clauses or periods (*compositio*) and the embellishment of the discourse with rhetorical ornamentation (*dignitas*).[106]

Moreover, the two dimensions of *elegantia*, namely, *explanatio* (clarity) and *Latinitas* (proper Latin), receive further clarification. *Rhetorica ad Herennium* 4.12.17 states that *explanatio* is achieved by employing words that are currently in use and that properly refer to what they are meant to signify. *Latinitas* is said to keep language "pure" (*purum*) and free from every "vice" (*vitio*). Linguistic vices are two: solecism, which occurs when a word is not well accommodated to the words before it; and barbarism, which is when an utterance is expressed *vitiose*, "incorrectly."

---

105. According to Quintilian, the stylistic quality whereby words are selected that sound good together is called *vocalitas*, which is the Greek for εὐφωνία, "euphony" (*Inst.* 1.5.4).

106. This same basic distinction appears in Cicero, who says that, in training an orator to speak ornately, he will not take time to teach the basics of how to speak with proper Latin (*Latine*) and clarity (*plane*), since someone who cannot speak proper Latin cannot hope to speak ornately (*De or.* 3.10.37–38). Speaking in proper Latin and with clarity are minimal requirements for a successful orator, but no one applauds a speaker who merely avoids blunders in basic language usage and clarity; one needs ornateness and artistic composition to gain applause (*De or.* 3.14.52–53).

To sum up this point, *elegantia* does not refer to "elegance" in the sense of complex periods, rhetorical embellishments, or elaborate figures. These dimensions of language fall under *compositio* and *dignitas*. The sphere of *elegantia* is more modest. In *Ep.* 106, when Jerome says that he has translated in a certain way in order to preserve the *elegantia* of the text, he means simply that he intends to use proper grammar and natural Latin idiom while avoiding awkward-sounding expressions and obscurity.

The requirement of using proper and natural Latin often serves as the reason why Jerome deviates from word-for-word literalism. He states this explicitly on several occasions. For example, at Ps 43:15, he rejects the proposal of Sunnia and Fretela on the grounds that it would produce "cacophony" (κακόφωνον), explaining that in his own rendering "the elegance of the translation was preserved without losing the sense" (**26.2**). He says he added the pronoun "you" in his translation of Ps 93:12 because it is necessary for "euphony" (εὐφωνία) in Latin and because without this addition "it would not have literary elegance" (**60.1**). This is summed up in his comment at Ps 83:7: "We follow this principle, that where there is no change with regard to the sense, we should maintain the elegance of Latin expression" (**54.3**). Jerome shows his concern for correct Latin when he speaks of preserving εὐφωνία (e.g., **3.2**; **23.1**; **29.2**; **55.1**; **59.1**; **60.1**) and related terms such as *decor*, "seemliness" (**3.2**; cf. **12.2**). He also emphasizes the importance of avoiding stylistic faults (**30.1**; **54.2**; **60.2**). The fault κακοζηλία, "affected style" is referenced on several occasions (**3.2**; **17.1**; **50.4**).[107] Other ways Jerome describes stylistic faultiness include κακόφωνον, "cacophony" (**26.2**); *portenta verborum*, "lexical monstrosities" (**57.3**); and the judgment that a certain expression "does not sound correct in Latin" (**38.1**; **48.2**) or "does not stand in the Latin language" (**30.1**).

Jerome's concern for style in biblical translation operates at the level of *elegantia*, which deals with basic grammatical correctness, natural usage, and clarity. It does not extend to higher levels of literary refinement such as complexity of construction or verbal ornamentation. All in all, Jerome endeavors to write correct Latin, avoid stylistic faults, and use pleasing language wherever possible.

---

107. Quintilian uses the term *cacozelon* (κακοζηλία) quite broadly for anything that transgresses good style (*Inst.* 8.3.56).

7.3. Summary of Translation Principles in *Epistle* 106

Because *Ep.* 106 deals with specific passages from the Gallican Psalter, it contains a wealth of information on Jerome's thinking about translation theory. Perhaps no other work in Jerome's corpus offers so much insight into Jerome's principles of translation along with so many concrete examples. Again, the five key concepts on biblical translation in *Ep.* 106 are (1) the sense of the text should not be damaged; (2) traditional renderings should be retained where possible; (3) each language has its own unique manner of expression that should be respected; (4) one need not translate word for word, if other principles demand a less literal translation; and (5) the translation should reflect proper Latin in terms of basic grammatical correctness, naturalness of expression, and clarity.

8. Textual Criticism in *Epistle* 106

In the course of answering the objections raised by Sunnia and Fretela, Jerome discusses divergent Greek and Latin readings, manuscripts, and scribal errors. Although *Ep.* 106 is not a treatise on textual criticism in the modern sense, it contains numerous observations that are text-critical in nature. The Hebrew represents the final textual authority for Jerome, but most of the analysis takes place at the level of the Greek or Latin.

8.1. The Hebrew Truth

Just as the Greek is the final arbiter for questions about the Latin New Testament, so also the Hebrew is the final authority for questions about the Greek and Latin Old Testament texts (**2.3**). Jerome uses the image of a fount and rivulets, with the Hebrew being the fount and the various Greek and Latin copies being the rivulets. One finds the original reading by tracing variations back through the rivulets to the fount.[108] For the most part, Jerome operates with the assumption that the Hebrew text is uniform. He does not typically discuss variant readings in Hebrew manuscripts (but cf. *Comm. Gal.* 3:10; *Comm. Hab.* 2:19). In *Ep.* 106, on Ps 34:10 (Heb 35:10), he says, "There are many copies among the Hebrews that have 'Lord' not

---

108. On the metaphor of fount and rivulets, see also *Pref. Gos.* 1; *Pref. GPsal* 4; *Comm. Eccl.*, Pref.; *Ep.* 27.1.3; *Comm. Jer.*, Pref.

even once" (see **20.1.21–22**). It is likely that here he is passing on information received from a Hebrew consultant. No Hebrew manuscripts are preserved that lack the word "Lord" for this passage.

In *Ep.* 106, Jerome normally appeals to the hexaplaric versions in order to explain the meaning of the Hebrew (see introduction, §6.2). Early in this work, he says that the hexaplaric LXX Psalter is a faithful embodiment of the Hebrew (e.g., **2:4**), and he consistently supports this hexaplaric text against the popular Greek text used by Sunni and Fretela (**3.1**; **4.1**; **5.1**; **13.1**; **57.2**). In theory, the Hebrew is the ideal standard that stands behind the hexaplaric Greek. The independent role of the Hebrew emerges more clearly as *Ep.* 106 progresses (see introduction, §6.2). Jerome articulates his perspective on the Hebrew clearly at Ps 129:4 (Heb 130:4–5): "we are zealous for the truth, that is, for what is in the Hebrew" (**78.1**). In this passage, he attempts to explain the Greek versions by appealing to the difference between the Hebrew letters *vav* and *yod* (see **78.1.4–5**). In *Ep.* 106, however, explanations that make use of specific details of the Hebrew text are uncommon. In his later works, Jerome will regularly unpack the differences between Greek witnesses by spelling out Hebrew words, discussing vocalization options, identifying the shapes of various Hebrew letters, and otherwise digging deeper into the Hebrew.[109]

8.2. The Hexapla

Epistle 106 contains many important comments touching on the Hexapla and its versions.[110] The hexaplaric Greek translations played an important role in Jerome's Hebrew scholarship.[111] As early as 384, Jerome says that he was comparing the Hebrew text with the edition of Aquila (*Ep.* 32.1.2). In two other letters from this period that deal with the Psalms, Jerome references not only Aquila, Symmachus, and Theodotion but also the fifth

---

109. See Graves, *Jerome's Hebrew Philology*, 26–61; and Martin Meiser, "Hieronymus als Textkritiker," in *Die Septuaginta—Texte, Theologien, Einflüsse*, ed. Wolfgang Kraus and Martin Karrer, with Martin Meiser (Tübingen: Mohr Siebeck, 2010), 256–71, esp. 266–68. For a selection of passages that illustrate how Jerome in later years uses the Hebrew to explain the origins of divergent Greek and Latin readings, see Michael Graves, ed., *Biblical Interpretation in the Early Church*, Ad Fontes: Early Christian Sources (Minneapolis: Fortress, 2017), 171–82.

110. On Jerome and the Hexapla, see Jay, *L'exégèse de saint Jérôme*, 411–17.

111. See Kamesar, *Jerome, Greek Scholarship, and the Hebrew Bible*; and Graves, *Jerome's Hebrew Philology*.

edition (*quinta editio*) (*Ep.* 20.3.1; 34.2.1). Jerome mentions Aquila, Symmachus, and Theodotion as sources for interpreting the Hebrew in the preface to his *Commentary on Ecclesiastes* (ca. 388). Jerome's constant use of the hexaplaric versions and his regular references to the hexaplaric signs in his prophetic commentaries suggest that he was able to obtain copies of the hexaplaric translations for select books (cf. *Ruf.* 2.34). In his *Comm. Ps.* 1:4 (early 390s), Jerome says that he saw the Hexapla in Caesarea. He gives a description of the Hexapla in his *Comm. Tit.* 3:9, where he mentions not only the six standard columns, but also the fifth, sixth, and seventh editions that were added for certain poetic books.[112] I see no reason to doubt that Jerome visited Caesarea and saw the Hexapla, but given the distance between Caesarea and Bethlehem and Jerome's frequent use of the hexaplaric versions, it is probable that he worked primarily with copies of the individual texts found in the Hexapla (on Jerome and the Hexapla, see also §§5; 7.2.5–12; 7.2.12–13 above).

Several key passages occur in *Ep.* 106 where Jerome references the hexaplaric signs. The most important comment appears early in the treatise, at **7.2**:

> Wherever in the Greek something was lacking from the Hebrew truth, Origen inserted it from the translation of Theodotion and put the sign of an asterisk (that is, a star), so that, insofar as it appeared to be hidden away, he might bring it to light and publish it out in the open. Moreover, wherever something is found in the Greek codices that is not in the Hebrew, he placed before it an obelus (that is, a flat line), which we can call in Latin a "dart," by which it is shown that the text in question should be cut out and struck away, because it is not found in the authentic books. These signs are also found in the poems of the Greeks and Latins.

In addition to this explanation, Jerome mentions the asterisk eight times: **7.1** (from Theodotion); **9.1** (from the Hebrew and Theodotion); **9.5**; **19.2** (based on Hebrew, added from Theodotion); **25.1** (from the Hebrew and Theodotion); **25.3**; **65.3** (out of the Hebrew, from Theodotion); **74.1** (in the Latin codices). He refers to the obelus on another six occasions: **10.1** (under the dart); **14.1** (under the dart); **22.1** (under the dart); **36.1**; **41.6**; **55.2**. Jerome twice refers to the great errors that arise when these signs

---

112. On the fifth edition, see also Jerome's preface to his translation of Origen's homilies on the Song of Songs.

are ignored because scribes do not copy them (**22.1**; **55.2**). See **7.2.5–12**; **7.2.12–13**.[113]

In addition to the standard hexaplaric versions, Aquila, Symmachus, and Theodotion, Jerome also cites the fifth edition (*quinta editio*) and the sixth edition (*sexta editio*) in *Ep. 106*. Jerome mentions the fifth edition eight times: **19.1**; **31.2**; **41.4**; **46.4**; **49.1**; **50.2**; **63.2**; **78.1**; and the sixth edition nine times: **19.1**; **41.4**; **46.4**; **46.7**; **57.2**; **63.2**; **65.5**; **78.1**; **82.1**. Regarding these extra editions, Eusebius says that the fifth, sixth, and seventh translations (ἑρμηνεία) were "placed beside" (παραθείς) and "after" (μετά) the other editions in the Psalms (*Hist. eccl.* 6.17.3–4 [Oulton]). Little reliable information is preserved for these translations. Fragments of the fifth edition are known for the books of Kings, Job, Psalms, Song of Songs, and the Minor Prophets. The sixth edition is mentioned in various sources for a few passages in Psalms, the Song of Songs, Job, Habakkuk, and Exodus. The nature of these translations, what books they covered, and how they were accessed are unclear.[114]

One final observation on the Hexapla in *Ep. 106* is necessary in relation to how Jerome reports the hexaplaric versions. In certain instances, Jerome states that all the hexaplaric versions give a certain rendering, when in fact there is evidence to suggest that at least one of the "Three" (Aquila, Symmachus, and Theodotion) has a different reading. In each case, however, Jerome cites the hexaplaric versions in support of the Gallican Psalter against the translation suggested by Sunnia and Fretela, and in each case, despite their diversity, the hexaplaric versions favor Jerome. It appears, therefore, that occasionally when Jerome says that "all" the translators give a certain rendering, he means that each one (perhaps in its own way) provides support for how he has translated the passage. In other words, Jerome sometimes collapses the hexaplaric evidence together when it generally supports him against the proposal of Sunnia and Fretela. See **41.4.13–14**; **50.6.8–9**; **65.6.21**; **69.2.5–6**; **82.1.9–10**.

8.3. Books and Copies

Jerome uses a number of terms to refer to physical copies of the biblical text. The key terms are *exemplaria*, "copies" (**2.3**; **20.1**; **50.3**; **78.1**); *exempla*,

---

113. On the hexaplaric signs, see also *Ep.* 112.19; *Pref. GPsal.*; *Pref. Pent.*; *Pref. IH Job*; *Pref. IH Chron.*; *Pref. Josh.*; *Ep.* 134.2.

114. See Marcos, *Septuagint in Context*, 155–60.

"copies" (**46.4**); *libri*, "books" (**2.4**; **7.2**; **41.6**; **52.1**; **63.1**); and *codices*, "codices" (**2.2**; **7.2**; **18.2**; **28.1**; **29.3**; **30.3**; **41.1**; **41.4**; **46.2**; **52.1**; **56.1**; **63.1**; **70.1**; **73.1**; **74.1**). On books and copies in *Ep.* 106, see also **41.6.14**; **58.1.8–9**.

Jerome does not view all manuscripts as having equal worth. In *Ep.* 106, phrases typically used for accurate texts are applied to the hexaplaric LXX. As for "authentic books" (cf. *Comm. Tit.* 3:15), Jerome considers the hexaplaric manuscripts to be "authentic books" (**7.2**; **41.6**). In terms of "truer copies" (cf. *Comm. Os.* 1:10–11), he regards hexaplaric texts as the "true copies" (**46.4**).[115] In certain contexts, as with the Greek New Testament, Jerome holds old manuscripts in esteem (e.g., *Pref. Gos.* 2; *Comm. Gal.* 5:7). Old Latin manuscripts, however, are subject to correction (e.g., *Pref. Josh.*). In *Ep.* 106, Jerome says that old Latin codices should be corrected according to the hexaplaric text (e.g., **28.1**; **63.1**).[116]

In a few cases, Jerome makes reference to the process of critically editing or annotating manuscripts. On two occasions, Jerome says that a problematic word should be "scratched out" of the codices (**66.3**; **73.1**; see **66.3.19**). In one remarkable passage, Jerome comments on a marginal notation he made in a copy of his Gallican Psalter (**46.3–5**). As he explains, in the Gallican Psalter he followed the popular Greek and Latin tradition, but in the margin of some copy of the Gallican Psalter he gave an alternative translation, namely, the hexaplaric version. It is curious that in this case Jerome left the "popular" Greek reading in the text and only supplied the hexaplaric rendering as a marginal note. In discussing this passage in *Ep.* 106, Jerome provides a fresh translation that stays even closer to the Hebrew than the hexaplaric Septuagint does. Jerome concludes by saying that the churches should sing what the Seventy translated, whereas scholarly annotations serve to increase people's knowledge of Scripture (see **46.3.10–46.5.1–4**). This passage gives special insight into Jerome's practice of glossing his own translation.

---

115. In his *Comm. Isa.* 58:11, Jerome notes an addition that is found not only in the Alexandrian copies (*in Alexandrinis exemplaribus*) but also in the "emended and true copies of the Seventy" (*in Septuaginta emendatis et veris exemplaribus*).

116. Jerome places more confidence in copies produced or used by well-known scholars such as Origen or Pierius (*Comm. Gal.* 3:1b; *Comm. Matt.* 24:36; on Pierius, see Jerome, *Vir. Ill.* 76).

8.4. Copyists and Scribal Errors

Jerome reflects on correcting scribal errors in the preface to his translation of the Gospels: "Why not correct … things rendered badly by unreliable translators, texts emended wrongly by bold but incompetent scribes, and passages either added or changed by drowsy copyists?" (*Pref. Gos.* 1). As he says in *Ep.* 106, the goal of correcting such mistakes is to discover the author's original words: "You should therefore prefer reading things that are true, lest by accepting what was added, you thereby forsake what the prophet wrote" (**41.6**). In numerous places in *Ep.* 106, Jerome fixes errors that arose in the text of the Gallican Psalter itself, which Sunnia and Fretela quoted back to him in a corrupted form (see introduction, §3.2). Jerome was aware that his own works were subject to scribal corruption, and he occasionally asks those who copied his works to take extra care and check their copies against the original (e.g., *Ep.* 71.5; *Pref. Ezra* 1; *Pref. GPsal.* 2). In the preface to his *Gallican Psalter*, Jerome likens emending a text to ploughing a field, in which thorns (copying errors) keep sprouting up even after the field has been ploughed, so that vigilance is necessary to keep cutting down the mistakes that continue to grow back (*Pref. GPsal.* 1).

Jerome often shows surprise or frustration at the mistakes that crept into the biblical text. Sometimes this is stated ironically: "How it was corrupted in your codex I do not know" (**41.1**); "I wonder what unskilled person falsified your books" (**52.1**); "Who decided to put 'him' instead of 'to him' and thus corrupt the copies? It is not for me to determine" (**50.3**); and "How great an error the changing of one letter has caused you!" (**57.3**). In several cases, Jerome actually says, "I am astonished" (*miror*): "I am astonished at how you could blame the translator for the mistake of a drowsy copyist" (**30.3**); "I am astonished at how some heedless person, I know not who, thought he should write" (**46.3**); "I am astonished at how this was left out among the Latins by an error of the scribes" (**65.2**); "I am astonished at the one who, in emending your codex, corrupted it" (**46.2**).[117] Jerome's tone is condescending when he advises: "Add 'you,' and by correcting the mistake of your copyist you will also correct this mistake" (**56.1**).

Jerome makes many insightful observations in *Ep.* 106 about correcting scribal errors. He notes that great error and confusion arose because of the

---

117. On Jerome's awareness that scribes sometimes made intentional changes in manuscripts, see *Ep.* 71:5; *Pref. Gos.* 1; see also *Inst.* 9.4.39.

negligence of scribes who failed to copy the hexaplaric signs (**22.1**; **55.2**). He makes the following comment about a frequent addition that appears in Greek and Latin manuscripts: "So that I am not constantly repeating the same thing, you should take note that the name 'Lord' and 'God' was added quite often" (**18.1**). On Ps 107:3, Jerome recognizes that the phrase "Arise, my glory" was erroneously transferred to this passage from Ps 56:9 (**69.1**). At Ps 77:69b, he appeals to the sense of the passage according to the surrounding context to resolve a text-critical problem (**50.6b**). He offers a clever solution to a textual problem in his own translation at Ps 49:22. Where the Gallican Psalter has *et non sit, qui eripiat,* "and there is not one who rescues," Sunnia and Fretela incorrectly report the text as *et sit, qui eripiat,* "and there is one who rescues" (i.e., the *non*, "not" dropped out). Jerome proposes that someone may have copied his text with *nec*, "nor" in place of *et non*, "and not," that is, *nec sit, qui eripiat*, and the error arose because someone copied *et*, "and" instead of *nec*, "nor." In response to the many textual problems that surface in the course of *Ep.* 106, Jerome often shows insight and creativity in providing solutions.

On two occasions, Jerome delicately responds to an error in the Gallican Psalter by shifting blame to the scribes who copied his translation. See **9.6.24**; and **12.1.21–22**.

8.5. Superfluous Comments

On at least forty-three occasions, Jerome declares some element of the text suggested by Sunnia and Fretela to be superfluous (*superfluum*). In most cases, this reflects a critical judgment on Jerome's part that combines *internal* and *external* evidence. Internally, an element is deemed superfluous when it is not needed to communicate the sense of the passage. Externally, an element is deemed superfluous when it lacks support from authoritative sources, namely, the Hebrew and the hexaplaric Septuagint. In Jerome's mind, these two factors dovetail. There is a strong tendency in *Ep.* 106 to see textual elements that are absent from the proper sources as also superfluous to the sense.

In the majority of places where Jerome judges a textual element to be superfluous, it is clear that something has been added to the text (as he sees it) that should be removed.[118] In almost every case, this decision

---

118. **14.2**; **15.1**; **26.1**; **28.2**; **34.1**; **40.2**; **42.1**; **43.1**; **43.2**; **44.1**; **44.3** (*superflue*); **45.3**;

fits the context—that is, the element can be removed without harming the sense, and the Hebrew and hexaplaric Septuagint also support its removal. In at least one instance, however, he says that a word is superfluous simply because it is absent from the Gallican Psalter, even though it is present in the Hebrew and the hexaplaric Septuagint (although he does not acknowledge this; see **73.2.3–4**). In a few passages, Jerome's judgment that an element is superfluous is woven into his explanation of the sense of the passage in context (**11.1**; **28.1**; **39.1**; **53.1**; **60.2**). For example, he argues in favor of including the preposition "in" as part of the phrase "in their wickedness" at Ps 93:23, because if "their wickedness" is allowed to stand on its own as the object of the following verb (i.e., "their wickedness, he will destroy"), the object pronoun at the end of the sentence, "them," is superfluous (**60.2**).[119]

In a few cases, Jerome labels a proposed correction "superfluous," but the difference is not quantitative, but qualitative (**28.3**; **30.2**; **54.1**; **75.3**; **75.4**; **75.7**; **84.1**). In other words, the issue is not that the text suggested by Sunnia and Fretela has an additional element that is unneeded; rather, they simply give a different word. Perhaps what Jerome is saying in these cases is that their suggestion is superfluous. These passages occur in the latter part of *Ep.* 106 and may reflect Jerome's increasing sense of frustration with this long series of questions. At **75.4**, Jerome offers no response to the proposed translation ("you turned" vs. "I turned") except to say: "But this is superfluous." At **54.1**, Jerome pleads with his interlocutors: "I ask you to refrain from inept and superfluous challenges of this kind, where there is no change in the sense."

9. Interpreting the Psalms in *Epistle* 106

An important aspect of Jerome's defense of the Gallican Psalter is his endeavor to show that it makes good sense. To this end, Jerome often

---

56.2; 58.2; 61.1; 66.2; 66.3; 67.2; 67.4; 68.1; 70.2; 71.1; 72.1; 73.2; 75.1; 75.2; 75.5; 76.1; 80.1; 83.1; 83.2. At **67.4**, Jerome does not explain what was added, but simply dismisses their suggestion: "Whatever you say that you found in Greek beyond this, it is superfluous."

119. In other words, Jerome understands the passage as saying: "In their wickedness, he will destroy them." Sunnia and Fretela proposed a correction that resulted in: "their wickedness he will destroy them." If "their wickedness" serves as the object of the verb "destroy," what is the point of having "them" at the end? It is superfluous.

explains the basic linguistic meaning of the passage under discussion, with attention to the surrounding context and how his translation best suits the flow of thought. Only occasionally do theological readings come to the surface in this treatise. Even for verses that Jerome expounds theologically elsewhere, *Ep.* 106 tends to stay close to the letter of the text. This fits the main purpose of *Ep.* 106, which is to defend the Gallican Psalter as a translation. In places where Jerome alludes to theological exegesis, his primary inspiration is Origen.

9.1. Exegesis at the Basic Linguistic Level

Jerome devotes considerable attention in *Ep.* 106 to explaining what the text means at a basic level of linguistic exegesis.[120] When confronted with an alternative translation, he often finds it useful to show that the specific wording of the Gallican Psalter fits the overall sense of the passage better than what Sunnia and Fretela proposed.

Jerome states on several occasions that the immediate context is key to finding the right reading. Thus, in response to one suggested correction, he says, "the context of the passage itself shows that this is superfluous" (**28.1**). A word can have different senses *pro locorum qualitate*, "depending on the nature of the passage" (**64.1**; **79.1**). The way to identify the proper reading is to look at what comes right before and right after the disputed word or phrase (e.g., **8.1a**; **39.2**; **46.8**; **50.6b**). For example, on the phrase "let *your* eyes see equitable things" at Ps 16:2, for which Sunnia and Fretela proposed "Let *my* eyes see equitable things," Jerome explains that the psalmist just said, "Let my judgment come forth from your countenance," which shows that God is the one looking at the psalmist's deeds to see whether or not they are equitable. In grasping the basic meaning of the words, the surrounding context is the determining factor.

Several other dimensions of basic linguistic exegesis as seen in *Ep.* 106 are worth highlighting. Jerome frequently clarifies the overall sense of a passage by offering a paraphrase, introduced with phrases such as *et est breviter hic sensus*, "and briefly, this is the sense" (**75.6**; cf. **31.2**) and

---

120. In terms of the classical background of Jerome's methodology, much of basic linguistic and contextual exegesis belongs to the category of *enarratio*, "explanation," but certain aspects of this task fall within the sphere of *lectio*, "reading aloud," such as the division of words and phrases into sense units and identifying the speaker in a given passage; see Graves, *Jerome's Hebrew Philology*, 13–75.

est ordo, "this is the sequence of thought" (**32.1**; **33.5**).[121] A clear example of Jerome's commitment to linguistic coherence is his decision at Ps 103 to translate the entire passage as directed to God in the second person, against evidence from the Hebrew and hexaplaric Septuagint, because he did not think the text should jump back and forth between the second and third persons (see **6.1.5–6**). Jerome recognizes that Hebrew poetry often expresses itself through ellipsis, which helps to clarify several passages (**11.1**; **39.1**; **41.5**). For example, on the expression "You who stir up the depth of the sea, the sound of its waves" at Ps 64:8, Sunnia and Fretela recommended adding the words "Who will endure?" at the end, so that the second half reads: "The sound of its waves, who will endure?" But this is unnecessary, as Jerome explains, because the participle from the first half ("You who stir up") should be supplied in the second half, that is: "You who stir up the depth of the sea; You who stir up the sound of its waves" (see **39.1.9–10**). In short, Jerome demonstrates throughout *Ep.* 106 his desire to produce a translation that captures the text's flow of thought.

Finally, Jerome employs various technical terms in *Ep.* 106 to address issues of grammar and rhetoric in relation to straightforward exegesis.[122] On the topic of technical grammar, he discusses singular and plural grammatical number (**8.2**; **9.2**; **46.6**; **50.7**), conjunctions (**25.1**; **29.1**; **33.5**; **45.3**; **67.2**; **83.2**), syllables (**29.2**; **55.1**), the nominative and accusative cases (**41.4**), and diphthongs (**86.2**). On grammatical terms, see the commentary at **8.2.1**. As for rhetorical figures, Jerome mentions ἀπὸ κοινοῦ (**11.1**), *apostropha* (**60.1**), and metaphor (**49.2**; **65.3**).[123] For example, in justifying his inclusion of the word "in hands" in the phrase "this sea, great and spacious in hands" at Ps 103:25, he says: "And this is said metaphorically (μεταφορικῶς) according to the particular idiom of Hebrew, as if the sea holds its hands outstretched and receives all things in itself" (**65.3**).

9.2. Theological Implications of Basic Linguistic Exegesis

On a few occasions, Jerome addresses possible theological implications of his Gallican Psalter rendering. On Ps 5:9, for example, where Jerome translated "Straighten your way in my sight," Sunnia and Fretela suggested

---

121. See Graves, *Jerome's Hebrew Philology*, 51–53.

122. Graves, *Jerome's Hebrew Philology*, 45–51.

123. On Jerome's use of rhetorical figures, see John N. Hritzu, *The Style of the Letters of St. Jerome* (Washington, DC: Catholic University of America Press, 1939).

"Straighten my way in your sight" (**4.1–2**). If Jerome is correct, what does it mean for the psalmist to ask God to straighten his own way? Is this proper? Jerome likens this to the Lord's Prayer, "May your name be hallowed," in that God's name does not become hallowed because of our praying, but we are asking that God's name, which is holy in and of itself, may be hallowed in us. So also, Jerome explains, in Ps 5:9 the psalmist asks that God's way, which is straight in and of itself, may be straightened for him.

Similarly, in the Gallican Psalter at Ps 7:9, Jerome has the psalmist ask God to "judge me … according to my righteousness" as opposed to what Sunnia and Fretela propose: "according to your righteousness" (**6.1–2**). Jerome explains, "Let it not appear rash to anyone that he asks to be judged according to his own righteousness," and he proceeds to cite parallels from elsewhere in the Psalter that express the same basic idea. In passages such as these, Jerome is concerned that the basic ideas expressed by the words contain theological implications that might be problematic and therefore require explanation.

9.3. Theological Interpretation

Epistle 106 does not emphasize methods of interpretation that generate distinctively Christian theology. Jerome offers more theologically rich expositions of the Psalms in his *Homilies on the Psalms*, which follow the lead of Origen. In a few cases, *Ep.* 106 deals with a passage from a strictly linguistic standpoint, although Jerome explains the same passage elsewhere theologically (see **10.1.9–10; 57.3.26**). Still, *Ep.* 106 contains a few examples of Jerome's Christian theological reading of Scripture.

At Ps 16:13, whereas Sunnia and Fretela proposed "Forestall them and supplant them," Jerome put "Forestall him and supplant him," with the singular "him" standing for the devil (see **8.2.3–4**). Jerome interprets the sentence "The Lord makes to inhabit the deluge" in Ps 28:10 as a reference to baptism (see **17.2.16–17**). "Those not believing the Lord dwells" in Ps 67:19 are construed as people who deny the incarnation (see **41.2.2–3**), and the threefold repetition of God's name in Ps 71:18 ("the Lord God, the God of Israel") is said to represent the mystery of the Trinity (see **44.2.6**). In a particularly interesting example Jerome reconciles the Gallican Psalter's "holy (one)" with the Hebrew text's "word" by interpreting the passage as speaking about Jesus, who is both the Holy one and the Word (see **81.1.4–6**).

Such interpretations occur in *Ep.* 106, but they are not common. In my commentary I note several places where a Christian theological read-

ing was available in sources known to Jerome, but he does not make use of
them (e.g., **50.2.7–8**; **57.2.20**). At **75.6**, Jerome's reference to "how all the
ecclesiastical interpreters among the Greeks explain this passage" refers to
Origen's exegesis (see **75.6.6–7**).

TEXT, TRANSLATION, AND NOTES

EPISTULA CVI.
AD SUNNIAM ET FRETELAM DE PSALTERIO, QUAE DE LXX INTERPRETUM EDITIONE CORRUPTA SINT.

Dilectissimis fratribus Sunniae et Fretelae et ceteris, qui vobiscum
5   domino serviunt, Hieronymus.
      1.1. Vere in vobis apostolicus et propheticus sermo conpletus est:
in omnem terram exiit sonus eorum et in
fines orbis terrae verba eorum. quis hoc crederet,
ut barbara Getarum lingua Hebraicam quaereret veritatem et
10 dormitantibus, immo contendentibus Graecis ipsa Germania
spiritus sancti eloquia scrutaretur? *in veritate cognovi,*
quod non est personarum acceptor deus, sed
in omni gente, qui timet deum et operatur
dei iustitiam, acceptus est illi. 1.2. dudum callosa
248 tenendo capulo manus et digiti tractandis sagittis aptiores ad stilum
calamumque mollescunt et bellicosa pectora vertuntur in mansue-
tudinem Christianam. nunc et Esaiae vaticinium cernimus opere
conpletum: *concident gladios suos in aratra*
5 *et lanceas suas in falces et non adsumet gens*
contra gentem gladium et non discent ultra
pugnare. 1.3. rursumque in eodem: *pascetur lupus cum*
agno et pardus requiescet cum haedo et vitu-
lus et leo et taurus pascentur simul et puer
10 *parvulus ducet eos et bos et ursus in com-*
mune pascentur parvulique eorum erunt pa-

EPISTLE 106: TO SUNNIA AND FRETELA, CONCERNING PASSAGES IN THE PSALTER THAT HAVE BEEN CORRUPTED FROM THE EDITION OF THE LXX TRANSLATORS

Jerome: To my most beloved brothers, Sunnia, Fretela, and the rest who serve the Lord with you.

1.1. Truly the apostolic and prophetic word has been fulfilled in you: "Their sound has gone out into all the earth, and their words to the ends of the world."[1] Who would believe that a barbarian tongue from among the Getae would seek the Hebrew truth? Who would believe that while the Greeks sleep—or rather, I should say, while the Greeks struggle to keep up—Germany herself would investigate the declarations of the Holy Spirit? "In truth I recognize that God is no respecter of persons, but in any nation the one who fears God and does God's justice is acceptable to him."[2] **1.2.** The hand formerly callous from grasping the sword's hilt and fingers better suited to drawing arrows are becoming soft enough for the stylus and reed pen, and warlike breasts are turning towards Christian gentleness. Now also we see the prophecy of Isaiah fulfilled in deed: "They will cut their swords into ploughs and their spears into sickles; nation will not take up the sword against nation, and they will no longer learn to fight."[3] **1.3.** And again in the same place: "The wolf will graze with the lamb and the panther will lie at rest with the young goat. The calf, lion, and bull will graze together, and a young boy will lead them. The ox and the bear will graze in communion, and their young will be as equals, and the lion and ox

---

1. Rom 10:18, matches the Vulgate; cf. Ps 18:5 (Heb 19:5) according to the GPsal.
2. Acts 10:34–35 based on the Vulgate.
3. Isa 2:4 according to the OL tradition.

riter et leo et bos comedent paleas, non ut sim-
plicitas in feritatem transeat, sed ut feritas discat simplicitatem.
    2.1. Quaeritis a me rem magni operis et maioris invidiae, in qua
15 scribentis non ingenium, sed eruditio conprobetur, ut, dum ipse
cupio iudicare de ceteris, iudicandum me omnibus praebeam et in
opere Psalterii iuxta digestionem schedulae vestrae, ubicumque inter
Latinos Graecosque contentio est, quid magis Hebraeis conveniat,
significem. **2.2.** in quo illud breviter admoneo, ut sciatis aliam esse
20 editionem, quam Origenes et Caesariensis Eusebius omnesque
Graeciae tractatores κοινά – id est communem – appellant atque
vulgatam et a plerisque nunc Λουκιάνειος dicitur, aliam septuaginta
interpretum, quae et in ἑξαπλοῖς codicibus repperitur et a nobis in
Latinum sermonem fideliter versa est et Hierosolymae atque in ori-
25 entis ecclesiis decantatur. super qua re et sanctus filius meus Avitus
249 saepe quaesierat et, quia se occasio fratris nostri Firmi presbyteri dedit, qui mihi vestram epistulam tradidit a vobis, scribens in commune
respondeo et me magno amicitiae libero faenore, quod, quanto magis
solvimus, plus debemus. **2.3.** sicut autem in novo testamento, si quando
5 apud Latinos quaestio exoritur et est inter exemplaria varietas,
recurrimus ad fontem Graeci sermonis, quo novum scriptum est
instrumentum, ita et in veteri testamento, si quando inter Graecos
Latinosque diversitas est, ad Hebraicam confugimus veritatem, ut,
quicquid de fonte proficiscitur, hoc quaeramus in rivulis. **2.4.** κοινὴ
10 autem ista, hoc est communis, editio ipsa est, quae et Septuaginta.
sed hoc interest inter utramque, quod κοινὴ pro locis et tem-
poribus et pro voluntate scriptorum vetus corrupta editio est, ea
autem, quae habetur in ἑξαπλοῖς et quam nos vertimus, ipsa
est, quae in eruditorum libris incorrupta et immaculata septuaginta
15 interpretum translatio reservatur. quicquid ergo ab hac discrepat,
nulli dubium est, quin ita et ab Hebraeorum auctoritate discordet.

will eat straw."[4] The result is not that innocence is transformed into ferocity, but ferocity learns innocence.

2.1. You are requesting of me an undertaking that will involve great effort and will invoke even greater ill will, in which it is not the natural talent of the writer but his erudition that is put on trial. As a result, while I myself am presuming to adjudicate concerning everyone else, I offer myself to be judged by all—that is, where in the book of the Psalter there is disagreement among the Latin and Greek versions, I indicate what agrees more with the Hebrew, following the arrangement set out in your note. 2.2. On this topic I remind you briefly of this: you should know that there is one edition, which Origen, Eusebius of Caesarea, and all the writers of Greece call the κοινά, that is, the common and popular edition, and which nowadays is referred to by most as Lucianic (Λουκιάνειος); and there is another edition of the Seventy Translators that is found in the hexaplaric (ἑξαπλοῖς) codices, which I faithfully translated into the Latin language and which is recited both in Jerusalem and in the churches of the East. My holy son, Avitus, also inquired often into this matter, and since the opportunity now presents itself in our brother, the presbyter Firmus, who delivered to me your letter, I will respond by writing publicly and thereby free myself from a great debt of friendship, although however much I fulfill, I owe all the more. 2.3. Just as in the New Testament, whenever a question arises among the Latins and there is diversity among the copies, we have recourse to the fount of the Greek language in which the New Testament was written, so also in the Old Testament, whenever there is diversity among the Greeks and the Latins, we flee for refuge to the Hebrew truth, so that whatever originates from the fount we should look for in the rivulets. 2.4. Now, there is the κοινή, that is, common edition, and there is the edition of the Seventy themselves. There is a difference between the two. The κοινή edition has long suffered corruption in various places and times at the will of copyists. But what is found in the Hexapla (ἑξαπλοῖς), which I translated, is the edition of the Seventy themselves. This is the very translation made by the Seventy Translators, preserved uncorrupted and unstained in the books of learned men. Therefore, whatever differs from this, there is no doubt but that it also disagrees with the authority of the Hebrews.

---

4. Isa 11:6–7 according to the OL tradition.

3.1. Prima de quinto psalmo quaestio fuit: *neque habita-*
bit iuxta te malignus. pro quo habetur in Graeco: οὔτε
παροικήσει σοι πονηρὸς sive πονηρευόμενος, ut vulgata editio
20 continet. et miramini, cur παροικίαν, id est 'incolatum', Latinus
interpres non verterit, sed pro hoc posuerit 'habitationem', quae
Graece dicitur κατοικία. 3.2. quod quidem in alio loco fecisse con-
vincitur: *heu mihi, quia incolatus meus prolon-*
gatus est. et in quarto decimo psalmo rursum pro incolatu
25 habitationem posuit: *domine, quis habitabit in*
tabernaculo tuo? et sciendum, quod, si volverimus dicere:
'domine, quis incolet tabernaculum tuum?' vel illud de quinto:
250 'neque incolat iuxta te malignus', perdes εὐφωνίαν et, dum interpretationis κακοζηλίαν sequimur, omnem decorem translationis
amittimus; et hanc esse regulam boni interpretis, ut ἰδιώματα
linguae alterius suae linguae exprimat proprietate. 3.3. quod et Tullium
5 in Protagora Platonis et in Οἰκονομικῷ Xenofontis et in
Demosthenis contra Aeschinen oratione fecisse convincimus et
Plautum, Terentium Caeciliumque, eruditissimos viros, in Graecis
comoediis transferendis. nec ex eo quis Latinam linguam angustissimam putet, quod non possit verbum transferre de verbo, cum etiam
10 Graeci pleraque nostra circuitu transferant et verba Hebraica non
interpretationis fide, sed linguae suae proprietatibus nitantur
exprimere.

4.1. De eodem psalmo: *dirige in conspectu meo*
viam tuam – pro quo habetur in Graeco: κατεύθυνον ἐνώπιόν
15 σου τὴν ὁδόν μου, hoc est: *dirige in conspectu tuo*
viam meam –, quod nec Septuaginta habent nec Aquila nec
Symmachus nec Theodotio, sed sola κοινὴ editio. 4.2. denique et in Hebraeo ita scriptum repperi: 'oser laphanoi darchach', quod
omnes uoce simili transtulerunt: *dirige in conspectu meo*
20 *viam tuam,* secundum illud, quod et in oratione dominica dicitur: *pater noster, qui es in caelis, sanctificetur*
nomen tuum, non quo nobis orantibus sanctificetur, quod
251 per se sanctum est, sed quo petamus, ut, quod per naturam sui

3.1. The first question was on the Fifth Psalm: "Nor will the wicked dwell near you."[5] In place of this in the Greek it has: οὔτε παροικήσει σοι πονηρός, or πονηρευόμενος as the popular edition contains. You are amazed at why the Latin translator did not put παροικίαν, that is, "residing," but instead put "dwelling," which in Greek is κατοικία. **3.2.** In fact, it can be shown that he has done this in another passage: "Woe is me, because my residing has been prolonged."[6] Yet in the Fourteenth Psalm he again put "dwelling" instead of "residing": "Lord, who will dwell in your tabernacle?"[7] It should be known that, if we were to say, "Lord, who will *reside* in your tabernacle?" or, concerning the Fifth Psalm, "Nor will the wicked *reside* near you," it would destroy the euphony (εὐφωνίαν), and so by following this affectation (κακοζηλίαν) in our rendering, we would lose all fittingness in the translation. This is the rule for a good translator, that he should convey the unique expressions (ἰδιώματα) of the other language in the particular idiom of his own language. **3.3.** We point out that Tullius did this in translating the *Protagoras* of Plato, the Οἰκονομικός of Xenophon, and Demosthenes's oration against Aeschines. Moreover, Terence, Plautus, and Caecilius—highly learned men—did this when translating Greek comedies. From this let no one suppose that Latin is an exceptionally limited language, since it is impossible to translate word for word, as the Greeks also translated many of our works by paraphrase, and they endeavored to express Hebrew words not by fastidious translation but in the particular idioms of their own language.

4.1. Concerning the same psalm: "Straighten your way in my sight."[8] Instead of this in Greek it has: κατεύθυνον ἐνώπιόν σου τὴν ὁδόν μου, that is, "Straighten my way in your sight." Yet neither the Seventy nor Aquila nor Symmachus nor Theodotion read this way; only the κοινή edition does. **4.2.** In fact, in Hebrew we find it written thus: *oser laphanoi darchach*, which all translated using the same language: "Straighten your way in my sight." This agrees with what is said in the Lord's Prayer: "Our Father who is in the heavens, may your name be hallowed."[9] Not that it is hallowed because of our praying, since it is holy in and of itself, but we are asking that, just as it is holy by its very nature, it may also be hallowed in us. So

5. Ps 5:6 (Heb 5:5b), GPsal.
6. Ps 119:5 (Heb 120:5), GPsal.
7. Ps 14:1 (Heb 15:1), GPsal.
8. Ps 5:9 (Heb 5:9), GPsal.
9. Matt 6:9, matches the Vulgate.

sanctum est, sanctificetur in nobis. ergo et nunc propheta
postulat, ut via domini, quae per se recta est, etiam sibi recta fiat.

    5.1. De sexto psalmo: *erubescant et conturbentur*
5 *vehementer omnes inimici mei.* et dicitis in Graeco
'vehementer' non haberi. scio, sed hoc vulgata. ceterum et in
Hebraeo habet 'mod', id est 'vehementer', et omnes σφόδρα similiter transtulerunt.

    6.1. De septimo psalmo: *iudica me, domine, secun-*
10 *dum iustitiam meam.* pro quo habetur in Graeco: κατὰ
τὴν δικαιοσύνην σου, id est 'iuxta iustitiam tuam'. sed et in hoc
male; in Hebraeo enim 'sedechi' habet, quod interpretatur 'iustitia
mea', et non 'sedecach', quod 'iustitiam tuam' sonat. sed omnes
interpretes 'iustitiam meam' uoce simili transtulerunt. **6.2.** nec cuiquam
15 videatur temerarium, quod iudicari secundum iustitiam suam
postulet, cum et sequens versiculus hoc ipsum significet: *et*
secundum innocentiam meam super me et sexti
decimi psalmi hoc exordium sit: *exaudi, domine, iusti-*
tiam meam et in septimo decimo quoque dicatur: *retribuet*
20 *mihi dominus secundum iustitiam meam et*
secundum puritatem manuum mearum reddet
mihi, in vicesimo quoque quinto psalmo scriptum sit: *proba*
me, domine, et tempta me; ure renes meos et cor
meum, et in quarto dicatur: *cum invocarem, exaudi-*
25 *vit me deus iustitiae meae,* et in octogesimo quinto:
custodi animam meam, quoniam sanctus sum,
Iacob quoque loquatur in Genesi: *exaudiet me cras iusti-*
tia mea.

252   **7.1.** De octavo psalmo: *quoniam videbo caelos tuos.*
et dicitis, quod 'tuos' in Graeco non habeat. verum est, sed in
Hebraeo legitur 'samacha', quod interpretatur 'caelos tuos' et
de editione Theodotionis in septuaginta interpretibus additum est
5 sub asterisco; cuius rei breviter vobis sensum aperiam. **7.2.** ubi quid
minus habetur in Graeco ab Hebraica veritate, Origenes de trans-

also in this case, the prophet requests that the way of the Lord, which is straight in and of itself, may be made straight for him.

5.1. Concerning the Sixth Psalm: "Let all my enemies be ashamed and thoroughly confounded."[10] You say that "thoroughly" is not present in Greek..I know, but that is just the popular edition. Besides, in Hebrew it has *mod*, that is, "thoroughly," and all translated this similarly: σφόδρα.

6.1. Concerning the Seventh Psalm: "Judge me, O Lord, according to my righteousness."[11] Instead of this in Greek it has κατὰ τὴν δικαιοσύνην σου, that is, "according to your righteousness." But even in this it is mistaken. For in Hebrew it has: *sedechi*, which is translated "my righteousness," and not *sedecach*, which means "your righteousness." All the translators rendered this with the same expression, "my righteousness." 6.2. Let it not appear rash to anyone that he asks to be judged according to his own righteousness, since the following clause indicates this very thing: "and according to my innocence upon me."[12] Also, the Sixteenth Psalm begins this way: "Hear, O Lord, my righteousness."[13] And in the Seventeenth (Psalm) it is said: "The Lord will repay me according to my righteousness, and according to the purity of my hands he will restore to me."[14] Also in the Twenty-Fifth Psalm it is written: "Prove me, O Lord, and test me; burn my kidneys and my heart."[15] And in the Fourth (Psalm) it is stated: "When I called, the God of my righteousness heard me."[16] And in the Eighty-Fifth: "Guard my soul, because I am holy."[17] Moreover, Jacob says in Genesis: "My justice will hear me tomorrow."[18]

7.1. Concerning the Eighth Psalm: "Because I will see your heavens."[19] You say that it does not have "your" in Greek. This is true, but in Hebrew it says *samacha*, which is translated "your heavens," and this "your" was added in the Seventy Translators under asterisk from the edition of Theodotion. Let me briefly explain this matter to you. 7.2. Wherever in the Greek something was lacking from the Hebrew truth, Origen inserted it

---

10. Ps 6:11 (Heb 6:11), GPsal.
11. Ps 7:9 (Heb 7:9), GPsal.
12. Ps 7:9 (Heb 7:9), GPsal.
13. Ps 16:1 (Heb 17:1) GPsal.
14. Ps 17:25 (Heb 18:25), cf. GPsal.
15. Ps 25:2 (Heb 26:2), GPsal.
16. Ps 4:2 (Heb 4:2), GPsal.
17. Ps 85:2 (Heb 86:2), GPsal.
18. Gen 30:33, matches neither the OL nor the IH edition.
19. Ps 8:4 (Heb 8:4), GPsal.

latione Theodotionis addidit et signum posuit asterisci, id est
stellam, quae, quod prius absconditum videbatur, inluminet et in
medium proferat; ubi autem, quod in Hebraeo non est, in Graecis
10   codicibus invenitur, obelon, id est iacentem, praeposuit, quam nos
Latine 'ueru' possumus dicere, quo ostenditur iugulandum esse
et confodiendum, quod in authenticis libris non invenitur. quae
signa et in Graecorum Latinorumque poematibus inveniuntur.
     8.1. Sexto decimo: *oculi tui videant aequitates.*
15   pro quo in Graeco vos legisse dixistis: οἱ ὀφθαλμοί μου, id est 'oculi
mei'; sed rectius 'oculi tui', quia et supra dixerat: *de vultu tuo*
iudicium meum prodeat, ut oculi dei in propheta operante
non prava, sed recta conspiciant. **8.1b.** in ipso: *custodi me ut pu-*
pillam oculi. dicitisque in Graeco legi: *custodi me, domine,*
20   quod nec in Hebraeo nec in ullo habetur interprete. **8.2.** in eodem:
exurge, domine, praeveni eum et subplanta
eum. pro quo in Graeco sit: πρόφθασον αὐτούς, id est 'praeveni
253 eos et subplanta eos'; sed melius, si legatur numero singulari, si
quidem de inpio dictum est, de quo statim sequitur: *praeveni*
eum et subplanta eum; eripe animam meam ab
inpio. nullique dubium, quin diabolum significet.
5   **9.1.** Septimo decimo: *grando et carbones ignis.* et
quaeritis, cur Graecus istum versiculum secundum non habeat
interpositis duobus versibus. sed sciendum, quia de Hebraico et
Theodotionis editione in septuaginta interpretibus sub asterisco
additum sit. **9.2.** in eodem: *qui perfecit pedes meos tam-*
10   *quam cervorum.* pro quo scribitis in Graeco inveniri: ὡσεὶ
ἐλάφου, id est 'tamquam cervi', singularem numerum pro plurali.
sed in Hebraeo pluralis numerus positus est 'chaialoth' et omnes
interpretes pluralem numerum transtulerunt. **9.3.** in eodem: *et de-*
disti mihi protectionem salutis tuae. pro quo in

from the translation of Theodotion and put the sign of an asterisk (that is, a star), so that, insofar as it appeared to be hidden away, he might bring it to light and publish it out in the open. Moreover, wherever something is found in the Greek codices that is not in the Hebrew, he placed before it an obelus, that is, a flat line, which we can call in Latin a dart, by which it is shown that the text in question should be cut out and struck away, because it is not found in the authentic books. These signs are also found in the poems of the Greeks and Latins.

8.1. On the Sixteenth (Psalm): "Let your eyes see equitable things."[20] Instead of this in Greek you said that it reads: οἱ ὀφθαλμοί μου, that is, "my eyes." But "your eyes" is correct, since just prior to this it said: "Let my judgment come forth from your countenance,"[21] so that the eyes of God may see in the prophet's actions not crooked, but upright deeds. 8.1b. In that (psalm): "Keep me as the pupil of the eye."[22] And you say in Greek it reads: "Keep me, O Lord," but this is found neither in the Hebrew nor in any translator. 8.2. In the same (psalm): "Rise up, O Lord, forestall him and supplant him,"[23] in place of which in Greek is πρόφθασον αὐτούς, that is, "forestall them and supplant them." But it is better to read this in the singular, if in fact it was written about the wicked one, about whom it immediately follows: "Forestall him and supplant him, rescue my soul from the irreverent one."[24] There is no doubt but that this indicates the devil.

9.1. On the Seventeenth (Psalm): "Hail and coals of fire."[25] You ask: why does the Greek not have the second occurrence of this short line, two lines after the first occurrence? But it should be known that it was added under asterisk into the Seventy Translators from the Hebrew and from the edition of Theodotion. 9.2. In the same (psalm): "he who made my feet as those of stags."[26] You write that instead of this in Greek we find ὡσεὶ ἐλάφου, that is, "as those of a stag," with the singular in place of the plural. But in Hebrew it has the plural, chaialoth, and all the translators rendered the plural. 9.3. In the same (psalm): "And you gave to me the protection

20. Ps 16:2 (Heb 17:2), GPsal.
21. Ps 16:2 (Heb 17:2), GPsal.
22. Ps 16:8 (Heb 17:8), GPsal.
23. Ps 16:13 (Heb 17:13), GPsal.
24. Ps 16:13 (Heb 17:13), GPsal.
25. Ps 17:14 (Heb 18:14), GPsal.
26. Ps 17:34 (Heb 18:34), GPsal.

15 Graeco vos legisse dixistis: τῆς σωτηρίας μου, id est 'salutis meae'.
    sed in Hebraeo 'iesacha' 'salutis tuae' significat, non 'meae'; quod
    et omnes interpretes transtulerunt. **9.4.** in ipso: *subplantasti*
    insurgentes in me subtus me. pro quo in Graeco plus
    invenisse vos dicitis: *omnes insurgentes;* sed 'omnes' additum
20 est. **9.5.** in eodem: *vivit dominus et benedictus deus*
    meus. et dicitis in Graeco non haberi 'meus'. quod non sub aste-
    risco, sed ab ipsis Septuaginta de Hebraica veritate translatum
    est; et cuncti interpretes in hac parte consentiunt. **9.6.** in eodem:
    liberator meus de gentibus iracundis. pro quo in
25 Graeco invenisse vos dicitis: *ab inimicis meis fortibus* sive
    potentibus. et quia semel veritati studemus, si quid vel trans-
254 ferentis festinatione vel scribentium vitio depravatum est, simpliciter
    confiteri et emendare debemus. **9.7.** in Hebraeo nihil aliud habet: *libe-*
    rator meus ab inimicis meis. Septuaginta autem 'ira-
    cundis' addiderunt. et pro 'gentibus' tam in Hebraeo quam in
5   cunctis interpretibus 'inimici' positi sunt; et miror, quomodo pro
    'inimicis' 'gentes' mutatae sint.
        10.1. Octavo decimo: *exultauit ut gigans ad curren-*
    dam viam suam. et dicitis, quod in Graeco 'suam' non habeat;
    sed hoc nos sub veru additum repperimus et in Hebraeo non esse
10 manifestum est.
        11.1. Nono decimo: *tribuat tibi secundum cor tuum.*
    et dicitis in Graeco vos hoc versiculo additum nomen domini rep-
    perisse, quod superfluum est, quia ex superioribus ἀπὸ κοινοῦ sub-
    auditur, unde coepit et psalmus: *exaudiat te dominus in*
    die tribulationis, ut et hic sub eodem sensu dicatur:
    tribuat tibi secundum cor tuum, id est ipse dominus,
    de quo supra dictum est. **11.2.** in eodem: *et exaudi nos in die,*
    qua invocaverimus te. pro quo legisse vos dicitis: *in*

of your salvation."[27] In place of this you said that you read in Greek: τῆς σωτηρίας μου, that is, "my salvation." But in the Hebrew *iesacha* signifies "*your* salvation," not "*my* salvation." This is what all the translators rendered. **9.4.** In this very (psalm): "You subdued under me those who rose up against me."[28] In place of this in Greek you say that you have found more: "all those who rose up." But "all" was added. **9.5.** In the same (psalm): "The Lord lives, and blessed be my God."[29] And you say that there is no "my" in the Greek. Yet this is not under asterisk but was translated by the Seventy themselves based on the Hebrew truth. All the translators are in agreement on this point. **9.6.** In the same (psalm): "My deliverer from angry nations."[30] In place of this in Greek you say that you found: "from my strong"—or, "powerful"—"enemies."[31] Since we are, first of all, zealous for the truth, if anything has been distorted by the hastiness of the translator or the vice of copyists, we should simply admit this and make the correction. **9.7.** In the Hebrew it has nothing except: "My deliverer from my enemies." The Seventy, however, added "angry." Instead of "nations," both in the Hebrew and in all the translators, "enemies" is found. I am astonished at how "nations" was substituted for "enemies."

10.1. On the Eighteenth (Psalm): "He rejoices as a giant to run his course."[32] You say that in Greek it does not have "his." But we found this placed under the dart, and in Hebrew it is not explicitly stated.

11.1. On the Nineteenth (Psalm): "May he grant to you according to your heart."[33] You say that in the Greek you found the name of the Lord added to this short line, which is superfluous because it is understood ἀπὸ κοινοῦ from what is above, where the psalm begins: "May the Lord hear you in the day of tribulation."[34] Thus, also here it is said with the same sense: "May *he* grant to you according to your heart," that is, *the Lord himself*, who was mentioned above. **11.2.** In the same (psalm): "And hear us on the day in which we call on you."[35] In place of this, you say that you have read: "in

---

27. Ps 17:36 (Heb 18:36), GPsal.
28. Ps 17:40 (Heb 18:40), GPsal.
29. Ps 17:47 (Heb 18:47), GPsal.
30. Ps 17:49 (Heb 18:49), GPsal.
31. Ps 17:49 in the LXX numbering.
32. Ps 18:6 (Heb 19:6), GPsal.
33. Ps 19:5 (Heb 20:5), GPsal.
34. Ps 19:2 (Heb 20:2), GPsal.
35. Ps 19:10 (Heb 20:10), GPsal.

quocumque die; sed superius cum Hebraica veritate concordat,
20 ubi scriptum est 'biom', id est 'in die'.

    12.1. Vicesimo primo: *tu autem, domine, ne elon-*
gaveris auxilium tuum a me. pro quo dicitis invenisse
255 vos meum; quod et verum est et ita corrigendum. breve enim: si
quid scriptorum errore mutatum est, stulta credimus contentione
defendere. **12.2.** in eodem: *universum semen Iacob, magni-*
ficate eum. pro quo in Graeco scriptum sit: δοξάσατε αὐτόν,
5 id est 'glorificate eum'. sed sciendum, quod, ubicumque in Graeco
'glorificate' scriptum est, Latinus interpres 'magnificate' trans-
tulerit secundum illud, quod in Exodo dicitur: *cantemus*
domino; gloriose enim magnificatus est, pro quo in
Graeco scribitur: 'glorificatus est'; sed in Latino sermone, si trans-
10 feratur, fit indecora translatio et nos emendantes olim psalterium,
ubicumque sensus idem est, veterum interpretum consuetudinem
mutare noluimus, ne nimia novitate lectoris studium terreremus.

    13.1. Vicesimo secundo: *calix meus inebrians quam*
praeclarus est. pro quo in Graeco legisse vos dicitis: *calix*
15 *tuus*; sed hoc in κοινῇ errore obtinuit. ceterum et Septuaginta et
Hebraicum et omnes interpretes 'calix meus' habent, quod Hebraice
dicitur 'chosi'; alioquin 'calix tuus' esset 'chosach'.

    14.1. Vicesimo quarto: *confundantur omnes inique*
agentes. et dicitis, quod 'omnes' in Graeco non habeat, et bene;
20 nam nec in Hebraeo habet, sed in Septuaginta sub veru additum
est. **14.2.** in eodem: *innocentes et recti adhaeserunt*
mihi, quia sustinuite. et dicitis in Graeco vos repperisse
domine, quod superfluum est.
256   **15.1.** Vicesimo sexto: *et nunc ecce exaltavit caput*
meum. sed 'ecce' superfluum est. **15.1b.** in eodem: *exquisivit*

whatsoever day." But what is above agrees with the Hebrew truth, where it is written *biom*, that is, "on the day."

12.1. On the Twenty-First (Psalm): "But you, O Lord, do not make distant *your* help *from me*."[36] In place of this you say that you have found "*my*." This is true, and it should thus be corrected. For in brief: if anything has been altered due to an error of the copyists, we believe it to be a foolish effort to defend it. **12.2.** In the same (psalm): "All ye the seed of Jacob, magnify him!"[37] In place of this in Greek you say it is written: δοξάσατε αὐτόν, that is, "glorify him!" But it should be known that wherever in Greek "to glorify" is written, the Latin translator rendered it "to magnify," in accordance with what is said in Exodus: "Let us sing to the Lord, for he is gloriously magnified,"[38] in place of which in Greek is written: "He is glorified." But if it were translated this way in the Latin language, it would produce an unseemly translation. When previously we were correcting the Psalter, wherever the sense was the same we preferred not to change the custom of the old translators, lest we deter the zeal of the reader by excessive novelty.

13.1. On the Twenty-Second (Psalm): "My cup is remarkably intoxicating."[39] Instead of this you say that you have read in Greek: "your cup." But this is a mistake that persists in the κοινή edition. Furthermore, the Seventy, the Hebrew, and all the translators have "my cup," which in Hebrew reads *chosi*, whereas "your cup" would be *chosach*.

14.1. On the Twenty-Fourth (Psalm): "Let all those who act unjustly be confounded."[40] You say that it does not have "all" in Greek, and you are correct. For it does not have this in the Hebrew, and in the Seventy it was placed under the dart. **14.2.** In the same (psalm): "The innocent and the upright have clung to me, because I waited on you."[41] You say that you have found in the Greek "Lord," which is superfluous.

15.1. On the Twenty-Sixth (Psalm): "And now, behold, he has exalted my head."[42] But "behold" is superfluous. **15.1b.** In the same (psalm): "My

---

36. Ps 21:20 (Heb 22:20), GPsal, except GPsal lacks "from me." This is a miscopying of the GPsal text.

37. Ps 21:24 (Heb 22:24), GPsal.

38. Exod 15:1, matches both OL and IH.

39. Ps 22:5 (Heb 23:5), GPsal.

40. Ps 24:4a (Heb 25:3b), GPsal, except GPsal has "those who do unjust things" (*iniqua* for *inique*)

41. Ps 24:21 (Heb 25:21), GPsal.

42. Ps 26:6 (Heb 27:6), GPsal, except GPsal lacks "behold." This is not GPsal, but the suggested text.

facies mea. pro quo in Graeco sit positum: *quaesivit te*
facies mea. sed melius superius.

5   **16.1.** Vicesimo septimo: *exaudi vocem deprecatio-*
nis meae, pro quo vos invenisse dixistis: *exaudi, domine.*
sed et hoc additum est.

        17.1. Vicesimo octavo: *et in templo eius omnis dicet*
gloriam, pro quo in Graeco sit: πᾶς τις. quod si transferre volueri-
10   mus ad verbum 'omnis quis', in κακοζηλίαν interpretationis incurri-
mus et fit absurda translatio. **17.2.** in eodem: *dominus diluvium*
inhabitare facit, pro quo legisse vos dicitis: *dominus*
diluvium inhabitat; quorum prius ad gratiam pertinet
credentibus, secundum ad eius, in quo credunt, habitaculum. sed
15   quia 'iasaph' verbum ambiguum est et potest utrumque sonare
– nam et 'sessio' et 'habitatio' dicitur et in ipso psalmo de gratia
baptismatis dicebatur: *vox domini super aquas; domi-*
nus super aquas multas et: *vox domini praepa-*
rantis cervos et revelabit condensa et in tem-
20   *plo eius omnis dicet gloriam* –, de ipsis sentire volu-
mus, qui glorificant dominum, et interpretati sumus: *dominus*
diluvium inhabitare facit.

        18.1. Tricesimo: *quoniam tu es protector meus.* rur-
257 sum et in hoc loco additum nomen domini est; et ne eadem semper
inculcem, observare debetis nomen domini et dei saepissime additum et id vos debere sequi, quod de Hebraico et de septuaginta
interpretibus emendavimus. **18.2.** in eodem: *ego autem dixi in*
5   *excessu mentis meae.* pro quo in Latinis codicibus legebatur: *in pavore meo,* et nos iuxta Graecum transtulimus: ἐν
τῇ ἐκστάσει μου, id est 'in excessu mentis meae'; aliter enim
ἔκστασιν Latinus sermo exprimere non potest nisi 'mentis excessum'.

face sought,"[43] in place of which in Greek you say it has: "My face sought you." But the former translation is better.

16.1. On the Twenty-Seventh (Psalm): "Hear the voice of my supplication."[44] In place of this you said that you found "Hear, Lord." But this has been added.

17.1. On the Twenty-Eighth (Psalm): "And in his temple all will say, 'glory.'"[45] In place of this in Greek you say there is: πᾶς τις. But if we wanted to translate this literally "a certain all," we would rush into affectation (κακοζηλίαν) of translation, and an absurd rendering would result. **17.2.** In the same (psalm): "The Lord makes to inhabit the deluge."[46] In place of this you say that you have read: "The Lord inhabits the deluge." Of these, the first pertains to the grace given to those who believe, and the second to the habitation of him in whom they believe. In fact, it can have either meaning, because the word *iasaph* is ambiguous; for example, it can be used for both "sitting" and "inhabiting," and in this very psalm it refers to the grace of baptism: "The voice of the Lord is over the waters; the Lord is over many waters,"[47] and "The voice of the Lord who prepares deer, and he will uncover dense things, and in his temple all will say, 'glory.'"[48] We prefer to understand this as pertaining to those very ones who glorify the Lord, and so we have translated, "The Lord makes to inhabit the deluge."

18.1. On the Thirtieth (Psalm): "Because you are my protector."[49] Again also in this passage the name of the Lord has been added. So that I am not constantly repeating the same thing, you should take note that the name "Lord" and "God" was added quite often, but you should follow what I have emended based on the Hebrew and the Seventy Translators. **18.2.** In the same (psalm): "But I spoke in the departure of my mind."[50] In place of this in the Latin codices one reads: "in my alarm," but we translated according to the Greek, ἐν τῇ ἐκστάσει μου, that is, "in the departure of my mind." For the Latin language is not able to express ἔκστασις any other way except

---

43. Ps 26:8 (Heb 27:8), GPsal.
44. Ps 27:2 (Heb 28:2), GPsal.
45. Ps 28:9 (Heb 29:9), GPsal.
46. Ps 28:10 (Heb 29:10), GPsal.
47. Ps 28:3 (Heb 29:3), GPsal.
48. Ps 28:9 (Heb 29:9), GPsal.
49. Ps 30:5 (Heb 31:5), GPsal.
50. Ps 30:23 (Heb 31:23), GPsal.

aliter me in Hebraico legisse noveram: *in stupore et in*
10 *admiratione mea.*
        19.1. Tricesimo primo: *nec est in spiritu eius dolus.*
pro quo in Graeco legisse vos dicitis: ἐν τῷ στόματι αὐτοῦ, id est
in ore eius dolus, quod solus Symmachus posuit. alioquin
et septuaginta interpretes et Theodotion et Quinta et Sexta et
15 Aquila et ipsum Hebraicum *in spiritu eius* habet, quod
Hebraice dicitur 'brucho'. sin autem esset *in ore eius,* scriberetur
'baffio'. **19.2.** in eodem: *conversus sum in aerumna mea.* in
Graeco 'mea' non esse suggeritis, quod ex Hebraico et de trans-
latione Theodotionis sub asterisco additum est, et in Hebraeo
20 legitur 'lasaddi'.
        20.1. Triceismo quarto: *omnia ossa mea dicent: do-
mine.* pro quo in Graeco bis 'domine' invenisse vos dicitis. sed
sciendum, quod multa sint exemplaria apud Hebraeos, quae ne
semel quidem 'dominum' habeant.
258   **21.1.** Tricesimo sexto: *et viam eius volet.* in Graeco
volet nimis vos legisse dixistis. quod additum est nec apud
quemquam habetur interpretum.
        22.1. Tricesimo octavo: *verumtamen vane contur-
5 batur omnis homo.* et dicitis vos in Graeco non invenisse
'conturbatur'. sed et hoc sub veru in Septuaginta additum est
et hinc apud vos et apud plerosque error exoritur, quod scriptorum
neglegentia virgulis et asteriscis subtractis distinctio universa
confunditur.
10   **23.1.** Tricesimo nono: *et legem tuam in medio cordis
mei.* pro quo in Graeco repperisse vos dicitis: *in medio ventris mei,* quod et in Hebraeo scriptum est 'batthoch meai'.
sed propter euphoniam apud Latinos 'in corde' translatum est;
et tamen non debemus subtrahere, quod verum est. **23.2.** in eodem:

"departure of mind." Otherwise, I know that I have read in the Hebrew: "in my bewilderment" or "in my astonishment."

19.1. On the Thirty-First (Psalm): "Nor is there deceit in his spirit."[51] In place of this in Greek you say that you have read: ἐν τῷ στόματι αὐτοῦ, that is, there is no deceit "in his mouth," which only Symmachus put. As for the others—the Seventy Translators, Theodotion, the fifth edition (*quinta*), the sixth edition (*sexta*), Aquila, and the Hebrew itself—each one has "in his spirit," which in Hebrew reads *brucho*. If it were "in his mouth," it would be written *baffio*. **19.2.** In the same (psalm): "I was turned in my hardship."[52] You suggest that in Greek there is no "my." But this is based on the Hebrew and was added under asterisk from the translation of Theodotion. In Hebrew it reads *lasaddi*.

20.1. On the Thirty-Fourth (Psalm): "All my bones will say, 'Lord!'"[53] Instead of this you say that in Greek you have found "Lord" twice. But it should be known that there are many copies among the Hebrews that have "Lord" not even once.

21.1. On the Thirty-Sixth (Psalm): "And he shall approve his way."[54] You said that in the Greek you read: "he shall *very much* approve." But "very much" was added and is not found in any of the translators.

22.1. On the Thirty-Eighth (Psalm): "Yet every man was disquieted in vain."[55] And you say that you did not find "was disquieted" in the Greek. In fact, this was placed under the dart in the Septuagint, and here is why the error arose among you and among most people: because every distinction is confused due to the negligence of the scribes, since the signs and asterisks have been removed.

23.1. On the Thirty-Ninth (Psalm): "And your law in the midst of my heart."[56] In place of this in Greek you say that you have found: "in the midst of my belly." In Hebrew this is written *batthoch meai*. But for the sake of euphony among the Latins it was translated "in the heart." Of course, we should not remove what is true. **23.2.** In the same (psalm): "Lord, give atten-

---

51. Ps 31:2 (Heb 32:2), GPsal.
52. Ps 31:4 (Heb 32:4), GPsal.
53. Ps 34:10 (Heb 35:10), GPsal.
54. Ps 36:23 (Heb 37:23), GPsal.
55. Ps 38:12 (Heb 39:12), GPsal.
56. Ps 39:9 (Heb 40:9), GPsal.

15 *domine, in adiutorium meum respice.* pro quo in
Graeco repperisse vos dicitis: σπεῦσον, id est 'festina'. sed apud
Septuaginta πρόσσχες, id est 'respice', scriptum est.
    24.1. Quadragesimo: *et si ingrediebatur, ut videret.*
et dicitis, quod 'si' in Graeco non sit positum, cum manifestissime
20 et in Hebraeo et in cunctis interpretibus scriptum sit et Septuaginta transtulerint: καὶ εἰ εἰσεπορεύετο τοῦ ἰδεῖν.
    25.1. Quadragesimo primo: *salutare vultus mei, deus*
259 *meus.* pro quo invenisse vos dicitis: *et deus meus.* sed sciendum hoc in isto psalmo bis inveniri et in primo positum esse: *salu-*
tare vultus mei, deus meus, in secundo autem. id est in
fine ipsius psalmi: *salutare vultus mei et deus meus,*
5 ita dumtaxat, ut 'et' coniunctio de Hebraeo et de Theodotione
sub asterisco addita sit. **25.2.** in eodem: *exprobraverunt mihi,*
qui tribulant me. pro quo vos invenisse dixistis: οἱ ἐχθροί
μου, id est 'inimici mei', cum et apud Septuaginta scriptum
sit: οἱ θλίβοντές με et apud Hebraeos 'sorarai', id est 'hostes
10 mei'. **25.3.** in eodem: *spera in deum, quoniam adhuc con-*
fitebor illi. et dicitis 'adhuc' in Graeco non inveniri. quod
sub asterisco additum est; ita enim et in Hebraeo scriptum rep-
perimus 'chi od', quod significatur ὅτι ἔτι Latineque dicitur
'quoniam adhuc'. hoc ipsum etiam in quadragesimo secundo
15 intellegendum.
    26.1. Quadragesimo tertio: *et non egredieris in virtu-*
tibus nostris. pro quo in Graeco repperisse vos dicitis: *et*
non egredieris, deus. sed superfluum est. **26.2.** in ipso: *posu-*
isti nos in similitudinem gentibus, pro quo in
20 Graeco scriptum sit ἐν τοῖς ἔθνεσιν. sed, si dictum fuisset
in Latino 'in similitudinem in gentibus', κακόφωνον esset,

tion to my help."⁵⁷ In place of this in Greek you say that you have found: σπεῦσον, that is, "hasten." But in the Seventy we find written πρόσχες, that is, "pay attention."

24.1. On the Fortieth (Psalm): "And if he entered to see."⁵⁸ And you say that "if" was not put in Greek; but on the contrary, it was most clearly written both in the Hebrew and in all the translators, and the Seventy translated: καὶ εἰ εἰσεπορεύετο τοῦ ἰδεῖν.

25.1. On the Forty-First (Psalm): "The salvation of my face, my God."⁵⁹ In place of this, you say that you have found: "and my God." But it should be known that this phrase is found twice in this psalm. In the first instance it has "the salvation of my face, my God,"⁶⁰ and in the second instance, that is, at the end of this psalm, it has: "the salvation of my face, and my God,"⁶¹ and this is so simply because the conjunction "and" was added under asterisk from the Hebrew and Theodotion. **25.2.** In the same (psalm): "They who afflict me have reproached me."⁶² Instead of this you said that you found: οἱ ἐχθροί μου, that is, "my enemies." But in the Seventy it has written οἱ θλίβοντές με, and in the Hebrew *sorarai*, that is, "those hostile to me." **25.3.** In the same (psalm): "Hope in God, because yet I will confess him."⁶³ You say that "yet" is not found in the Greek. But it was added under asterisk. For thus also in Hebrew we find written *chi od*, which is represented as ὅτι ἔτι, and in Latin reads "because yet." This same thing should also be understood in the Forty-Second (Psalm).⁶⁴

26.1. On the Forty-Third (Psalm): "And you will not go out with our hosts."⁶⁵ In place of this in Greek you say that you have found: "And you will not go out, O God." But this is superfluous. **26.2.** In that very (psalm): "You have made us into an illustration to the nations."⁶⁶ In place of this in Greek you say it was written: ἐν τοῖς ἔθνεσιν. But if the phrase "into an illustration *among* the nations" had been said in Latin, it would produce

<hr>

57. Ps 39:14 (Heb 40:14). GPsal reads: *domine, ad adiuvandum me respice*; see the commentary.
58. Ps 40:7 (Heb 41:7), GPsal.
59. Ps 41:6–7 (Heb 42:6–7), GPsal.
60. Ps 41:6–7 (Heb 42:6–7), GPsal.
61. Ps 41:12 (Heb 42:12), GPsal.
62. Ps 41:11 (Heb 42:11), GPsal.
63. Ps 41:12 (Heb 42:12), GPsal.
64. Ps 42:5 (Heb 43:5), GPsal.
65. Ps 43:10 (Heb 44:10), GPsal.
66. Ps 43:15 (Heb 44:15), GPsal.

et propterea absque damno sensus interpretationis elegantia con-
servata est. alioquin in Hebraico ita scriptum repperi: *po-*
suisti nos proverbium in gentibus. 26.3. in eodem:
25 *exurge, adiuva nos.* pro quo more solito in Graeco nomen
domini additum est.
260   27.1. Quadragesimo quarto: *sagittae tuae acutae.* pro
quo in Graeco legisse vos dicitis: *acutae, potentissime.*
sed hoc male et de superiore versiculo additum est, in quo legitur:
accingere gladio tuo super femur tuum, poten-
5 *tissime.*
       28.1. Quadragesimo septimo: *quoniam ecce reges con-*
gregati sunt. pro quo in Graeco legisse vos dicitis: *quo-*
niam ecce reges eius congregati sunt. quod
superfluum esse ipse lectionis textus ostendit; et in veteribus
10 codicibus Latinorum scriptum erat *reges terrae,* quod nos
tulimus, quia nec in Hebraeo nec in Septuaginta repperitur. 28.2. in
ipso: *sicut audivimus, sic vidimus.* pro quo in
Graeco repperisse vos dicitis: *sic et vidimus,* quod superfluum est; legitur enim in Hebraeo 'chen rainu', quod interpretatur
15 οὕτως εἴδομεν, hoc est *sic vidimus.* 28.3. in eodem: *sus-*
cepimus, deus, misericordiam tuam in medio
templi tui. pro eo, quod nos de Hebraico et de septuaginta
interpretibus vertimus *templi tui,* in Graeco legisse vos dicitis
populi tui, quod superfluum est. in Hebraico scriptum est
20 'echalach', id est τοῦ ναοῦ σου, hoc est 'templi tui', et non
'ammach', quod 'populum tuum' significat.
       29.1. Quadragesimo octavo: *homo, cum in honore esset.*
pro quo in Graeco invenisse vos dicitis: *et homo, in honore*
cum esset. sed sciendum, quod iste versiculus bis in hoc psalmo
25 sit et in priori additam habeat 'et' coniunctionem, in fine non
habeat. 29.2. in eodem: *et dominabuntur eorum iusti.* pro

cacophony (κακόφωνον). As it is, therefore, the elegance of the translation was preserved without losing the sense. Alternately, it is found written thus in the Hebrew: "You have made us a proverb among the nations." (3) In the same (psalm): "Rise up, help us!"[67] Here, in the usual manner, the name of the Lord was added in Greek.

27.1. On the Forty-Fourth (Psalm): "Your arrows are sharp."[68] In place of this you say that you have read in Greek: "sharp, O most powerful one." But this was wrongly added from a previous line, in which it was said: "Gird your sword upon your thigh, O most powerful one."[69]

28.1. On the Forty-Seventh (Psalm): "For, behold, kings have been assembled."[70] In place of this you say that you have read in Greek: "For, behold, its kings have been assembled." But the context of the passage itself shows that this is superfluous. In the old codices of the Latins, "kings of the earth" was written, which we removed because it is found neither in the Hebrew nor in the Seventy. **28.2.** In this very (psalm): "As we have heard, thus we have seen."[71] In place of this in Greek you say that you have found: "thus also we have seen," which is superfluous. For in Hebrew it is read, *chen rainu*, which is translated οὕτως εἴδομεν, that is, "thus we have seen." **28.3.** In the same (psalm): "We have received, O God, your mercy in the midst of your temple."[72] In place of what we translated from the Hebrew and from the Seventy Translators as "your temple," you say that you read in Greek "your people," which is superfluous. In Hebrew it was written *echalach*; in other words, τοῦ ναοῦ σου—that is, "your temple." It is not *ammach*, which means "your people."

29.1. On the Forty-Eighth (Psalm): "Man—when he was in honor."[73] In place of this in Greek you say that you have found: "*and* man—when he was in honor." But it should be known that this short line occurs twice in this psalm: in the previous occurrence it has the conjunction "and" added,[74] but in this last occurrence it does not have it. **29.2.** In the same (psalm):

---

67. Ps 43:26 (Heb 44:27), GPsal.
68. Ps 44:6 (Heb 45:6) GPsal.
69. Ps 44:4 (Heb 45:4), GPsal.
70. Ps 47:5 (Heb 48:5), GPsal.
71. Ps 47:9 (Heb 48:9), GPsal.
72. Ps 47:10 (Heb 48:10), GPsal.
73. Ps 48:21 (Heb 49:21), GPsal.
74. Ps 48:13 (Heb 49:13), GPsal.

261 'iustis' εὐθεῖς, id est 'rectos', in Graeco legisse vos dicitis; sed
hoc propter εὐφωνίαν ita in Latinum versum est. alioquin et in eo
loco, ubi scriptum legimus: *in libro* εὐθεῖς, 'iustorum libro'
intellegimus, et non debemus sic verbum de verbo exprimere, ut,
5 dum syllabam sequimur, perdamus intellegentiam. **29.3.** in eodem: *de*
manu inferni cum liberaverit me. pro quo in
Graeco legisse vos dicitis: *cum acceperit me.* quod quidem
et nos ita de Septuaginta vertimus et miror, a quo in vestro
codice depravatum sit.
10   **30.1.** Quadragesimo nono: *sedens adversus fratrem*
tuum loquebaris. pro quo in Graeco repperisse vos dicitis:
κατὰ τοῦ ἀδελφοῦ σου κατελάλεις, et putatis non bene versum, quia
diximus: *adversus fratrem tuum loquebaris,* et
debuisse nos dicere: 'adversus fratrem tuum detrahebas'; quod
15 vitiosum esse et in nostra lingua non stare etiam stultis patet.
nec ignoramus, quod καταλαλιὰ dicatur 'detractio'; quam si
uoluerimus ponere, non possumus dicere: 'adversus fratrem
tuum detrahebas', sed: 'de fratre tuo detrahebas'. **30.2.** quod si
fecerimus, rursum contentiosus verborum calumniator inquiret,
20 quare non dixerimus: κατὰ τοῦ ἀδελφοῦ σου, hoc est 'adversus
fratrem tuum'. haec superflua sunt et non debemus in putida
nos verborum interpretatione torquere, cum damnum non sit
in sensibus, quia unaquaeque lingua, ut ante iam dixi, suis
proprietatibus loquitur. **30.3.** in ipso: *ne quando rapiat et*
25 *sit, qui eripiat.* et in Graeco repperisse vos dicitis: *et*
non sit, qui eripiat, quod et a nobis versum est et in
262 nostris codicibus sic habetur. et miror, quomodo vitium librarii
dormitantis ad culpam referatis interpretis, nisi forte fuerit hoc:
ne quando rapiat nec sit, qui eripiat, et ille pro
'nec' 'et' scripserit. **30.4.** in eodem: *sacrificium laudis*
5 *honorificabit me.* pro quo in Graeco scribitur: δοξάσει με,
id est *glorificabit me,* de quo et supra diximus. in evan-

"and the just will rule over them."[75] Instead of "the just," you say that you have read in Greek εὐθεῖς, that is, "the right." But it was translated this way into Latin for the sake of euphony (εὐφωνίαν). Elsewhere, in the passage where we read about what is written "in the book of εὐθεῖς,"[76] we understand it as "the book of the just." We should not translate word for word in such a way that, while we adhere to the syllable, we lose the meaning. **29.3.** In the same (psalm): "When from the hand of hell he shall free me."[77] Instead of this you say that you have read in Greek: "When he shall receive me." In fact, we also translated it this way from the Seventy. I am astonished at how this was corrupted in your codex.

30.1. On the Forty-Ninth (Psalm): "Sitting, you were speaking against your brother."[78] In place of this in Greek you say that you have found: κατὰ τοῦ ἀδελφοῦ σου κατελάλεις, and you think this was not well translated, because we said, "you were speaking against your brother," and we ought to have said: "you were disparaging against your brother." But it is clear even to fools that this is stylistically faulty and does not stand in the Latin language. Of course, I am not unaware that καταλαλιά means "disparaging." But if we want to use this word, we cannot say, "you were disparaging against your brother," but "you were disparaging *concerning* your brother." **30.2.** Yet if we were to do that, then some contentious nitpicker of words would ask why we did not represent κατὰ τοῦ ἀδελφοῦ σου, that is, "against your brother." These matters are superfluous, and we should not twist ourselves around in sickening explanations of words when there is no loss to the sense. As I already said before, each language speaks in its own particular idioms. **30.3.** In this very (psalm): "lest he snatch, and there is one who rescues."[79] And you say that you have found in Greek: "and there is *not* one who rescues." In fact, this is what we translated, and this is how it appears in our codices. I am astonished at how you could blame the translator for the mistake of a drowsy copyist. Perhaps it was like this: "lest he snatch, and there is not [*nec sit*] one who rescues," and he copied "*et*" instead of "*nec.*" **30.4.** In the same (psalm): "The sacrifice of praise will honor me."[80] In place of this in Greek it is written: δοξάσει με, that is, "will glorify me," which we

---

75. Ps 48:15 (Heb 49:15), GPsal.
76. See LXX 2 Sam 1:18 and the commentary.
77. Ps 48:16 (Heb 49:16). This is a miscopying of the GPsal text.
78. Ps 49:20 (Heb 50:20), GPsal.
79. Ps 49:22 (Heb 50:22). This is a miscopying of the GPsal text.
80. Ps 49:23 (Heb 50:23), GPsal.

gelio in eo loco, ubi in Graeco legimus: πάτερ, δόξασόν με τῇ
δόξῃ, ᾗ εἶχον παρὰ σοὶ πρὸ τοῦ τὸν κόσμον γενέσθαι, in Latino
legitur: *pater, clarifica me.* noluimus ergo inmutare,
10 quod ab antiquis legebatur, quia idem sensus erat.
    31.1. Quinquagesimo quarto: *expectabam eum, qui*
salvum me fecit. et dicitis vos invenisse in Graeco: *ex-*
pectabam deum, quod additum est. **31.2.** in eodem: *a pusil-*
lanimitate spiritus. et in Graeco invenisse vos dicitis:
15 ἀπὸ ὀλιγοψυχίας, quod proprie 'pusillanimitas' dicitur. sed sciendum,
quod pro ὀλιγοψυχία Aquila et Symmachus et Theodotio et
quinta editio interpretati sunt: ἀπὸ πνεύματος, id est 'a spiritu', et in Hebraeo scriptum sit 'merucha' omnisque sensus ita
apud eos legatur: *festinabo, ut salver a spiritu*
20 *tempestatis et turbinis.* **31.3.** in eodem: *quoniam, si*
inimicus maledixisset. in Graeco ὠνείδισεν, hoc est
'exprobrasset', positum est. sed inter maledicta et obprobria
sensum non discrepare perspicuum est.
263   **32.1.** Quinquagesimo quinto: *quoniam multi bel-*
lantes adversum me, ab altitudine diei ti-
mebo. et dicitis in Graeco vos invenisse: *non timebo,* quod
additum est. et est ordo: 'quoniam multi dimicant adversum me,
5 idcirco ego ab altitudine diei timebo', hoc est: 'non bellantes
adversum me, sed tuum excelsum timebo lumen'. **32.2.** in ipso: *in ira*
populos confringes. pro quo in Graeco legitur: ἐν ὀργῇ
λαοὺς κατάξεις.
et apud Latinos pro eo, quod est 'deicies', id est κατάξεις, male
10 error obtinuit κατεάξεις, id est 'confringes'; nam et in Hebraeo
'hored' habet, id est καταβίβασον, quod nos possumus dicere
'depone' et Symmachus interpretatus est κατάγαγε.
    33.1. Quinquagesimo octavo: *quia deus susceptor*
meus. pro quo in Graeco positum est: *susceptor meus es*
15 *tu.* sed sciendum in Hebraeo nec 'es' scriptum nec 'tu' et apud

discussed above.[81] In the gospel, in the passage where we read in Greek: πάτηρ, δόξασόν με τῇ δόξῃ, ᾗ εἶχον παρὰ σοὶ πρὸ τοῦ τὸν κόσμον γενέσθαι, in Latin it is read, "Father, make me illustrious."[82] So, we did not wish to change what was read from early times, because the sense was the same.

31.1. On the Fifty-Fourth (Psalm): "I was waiting on him who saved me."[83] And you say that you have found in Greek: "I was waiting on God." But this was added. **31.2.** In the same (psalm): "from faintheartedness of spirit."[84] And you say you have found in Greek: ἀπὸ ὀλιγοψυχίας, which properly means "faintheartedness." But it should be known that, in place of ὀλιγοψυχία, Aquila, Symmachus, Theodotion, and the fifth edition (*quinta*) translated ἀπὸ πνεύματος, that is, "from a spirit," and in Hebrew it is written *merucha*, and the sense of the whole passage according to them reads like this: "I will hasten, so that I may be saved from a spirit of storm and whirlwind." **31.3.** In the same (psalm): "because, if an enemy had slandered."[85] The Greek has ὠνείδισεν, that is, "had reproached." But whether it is "slandering" or "reproaching," it is clear that the sense does not differ.

32.1. On the Fifty-Fifth (Psalm): "Since many are those waging war against me, from the height of the day I will fear."[86] And you say that in Greek you found: "I will not fear." But this was added. This is the sequence of thought: "Since many contend against me, for this very reason I will fear from the height of the day," that is, "I will not fear those waging war against me, but I will fear your exalted light." **32.2.** In this very (psalm): "In anger you will break peoples."[87] In place of this in Greek it is read: ἐν ὀργῇ λαοὺς κατάξεις. But among the Latins, in place of "you will throw down," that is, κατάξεις, a terrible mistake came about: κατεάξεις, that is, "you will break." In the Hebrew, in fact, it has *hored*, that is, καταβίβασον, which we can express as "bring down" and which Symmachus translated as κατάγαγε.

33.1. On the Fifty-Eighth (Psalm): "Because God is my protector."[88] In place of this in Greek it was put: "You are my protector." But it should be known that in the Hebrew neither "are" nor "you" are written; these

---

81. See **12.2.**
82. John 17:5.
83. Ps 54:9a (Heb 55:9a), GPsal.
84. Ps 54:9b (Heb 55:9b), GPsal.
85. Ps 54:13 (Heb 55:13), GPsal.
86. Ps 55:3–4 (Heb 56:3–4), GPsal.
87. Ps 55:8 (Heb 56:8), GPsal.
88. Ps 58:10 (Heb 59:10), GPsal.

Septuaginta solos inveniri. **33.2.** in ipso: *deus meus, voluntas eius praeveniet me.* pro quo in Graeco scriptum est: τὸ ἔλεος αὐτοῦ, id est *misericordia eius,* quod et verius est. sed in Hebraeo scriptum est: *misericordia mea prae-*

20 *veniet me.* **33.3.** in eodem: *deus ostendit mihi inter ini- micos meos.* pro quo in Graeco positum est: *deus meus;* sed 'meus' additum est. **33.4.** in eodem: *ne occidas eos, ne*

264 *quando obliviscantur populi tui.* pro quo in Graeco scriptum est: *legis tuae;* sed in Septuaginta et in Hebraeo non habet 'populi tui', sed *populi mei;* et a nobis ita versum est. **33.5.** in eodem: *et scient, quia deus domi-*

5 *nator Iacob finium terrae.* pro quo in Graeco scriptum est: *et finium terrae,* sed 'et' coniunctio addita est; et ordo est: 'scient, quia deus Iacob dominator finium terrae'.

    34.1. Quinquagesimo nono: *quis deducet me usque in Idumaeam?* pro quo in Graeco habet: *aut quis de-*

10 *ducet me?* sed superfluum est.

    35.1. Sexagesimo: *quoniam tu, deus meus, exaudisti orationem meam,* pro quo legatur in Graeco: *quia tu, deus, exaudisti me.* quod non habet in Hebraeo nec in septuaginta interpretibus et in Latino additum est. **35.2.** in eodem:

15 *psallam nomini tuo in saeculum saeculi,* pro quo in Graeco sit: *in saeculum.* et in Hebraeo semel habet 'laed', id est 'in aeternum', et non 'lolam', quod est 'in saeculum'.

    36.1. Sexagesimo primo: *quia deus adiutor noster in aeternum.* pro quo in Graeco est: *deus adiutor*

20 *noster.* ergo 'in aeternum' obelus est.

    37.1. Sexagesimo secundo: *sitivit in te anima mea,* pro quo in Graeco sit: *sitivit te anima mea,* sed in Hebraeo non habet 'attha', quod significat 'te', sed 'lach', quod osten-

are found only in the Seventy. **33.2.** In this very (psalm): "My God, his goodwill shall go before me."[89] In place of this in Greek is written: τὸ ἔλεος αὐτοῦ, that is, "his mercy," which is more correct. But in Hebrew it is written: "my mercy shall go before me." **33.3.** In the same (psalm): "God shows to me among my enemies."[90] In place of this in Greek "my God" was put, but "my" was added. **33.4.** In the same (psalm): "Do not slay them, lest they ever forget your people."[91] In place of this in Greek it is written, "your law." But in the Seventy and in the Hebrew, it does not have "your people" but "my people." This is how we translated it. **33.5.** In the same (psalm): "And they will know that God is the ruler, of Jacob, of the ends of the earth."[92] In place of this in Greek it is written: "*and* of the ends of the earth," but the conjunction "and" was added. This is the sequence of thought: "They will know that the God of Jacob is the ruler of the ends of the earth."

34.1. On the Fifty-Ninth (Psalm): "Who will lead me as far as Idumea?"[93] In place of this in Greek it has: "*Or* who will lead me?" But this is superfluous.

35.1. On the Sixtieth (Psalm): "Because you, O my God, heard my prayer."[94] In place of this in Greek you say it is read: "Since you, O God, heard me." This is found neither in the Hebrew nor in the Seventy Translators but was added in the Latin. **35.2.** In the same (psalm): "I will sing to your name unto the age of the age."[95] In place of this in Greek you say is: "unto the age." In Hebrew it has just one occurrence of *laed*, that is, "unto eternity," and not *lolam*, that is, "unto the age."

36.1. On the Sixty-First (Psalm): "Because God is our helper unto eternity."[96] In place of this in Greek is: "God is our helper." Therefore "unto eternity" has an obelus.

37.1. On the Sixty-Second (Psalm): "My soul desired for you."[97] In place of this in Greek you say is: "My soul desired you." But in Hebrew it does not have *attha*, which signifies "you," but rather *lach*, which actually

---

89. Ps 58:11 (Heb 59:11), GPsal.

90. Ps 58:12a (Heb 59:11b); see the commentary.

91. Ps 58:12b (Heb 59:12a). The word "your" is a miscopying of the GPsal text.

92. Ps 58:14 (Heb 59:14), GPsal.

93. Ps 59:11 (Heb 60:11), GPsal.

94. Ps 60:6 (Heb 61:6), GPsal.

95. Ps 60:9 (Heb 61:9). This reflects the OL tradition.

96. Ps 61:9 (Heb 62:9), GPsal, with slight interference from the OL tradition.

97. Ps 62:2 (Heb 63:2), GPsal.

ditur 'tibi', quod et omnes interpretes transtulerunt. ergo secundum
25 linguae proprietatem versum est in Latinum.
265   38.1. Sexagesimo tertio: *sagittae parvulorum factae*
sunt plagae eorum. pro quo in Graeco: *sagitta parvu-*
lorum; sed, si sic dicamus, non resonat in Latino: 'sagitta
parvulorum factae sunt plagae eorum'. pro quo melius habet
5 in Hebraeo: *percutiet eos deus iaculo repentino*
et inferentur plagae eorum.
        39.1. Sexagesimo quarto: *qui conturbas profundum*
maris, sonum fluctuum eius. in Graeco additum
scribitis: *quis sustinebit?* quod superfluum est; subauditur
10 enim: 'qui conturbas profundum maris et conturbas sonum fluctuum eius'. 39.2. in eodem: *parasti cibum illorum, quo-*
niam ita est praeparatio eius. et dicitis, quod in
Graeco non sit 'eius', cum in Hebraeo 'thechina' manifeste 'prae-
parationem eius' significet; 'eius' autem, id est 'terrae', de qua
15 supra dixerat: *visitasti terram et inebriasti eam.*
        40.1. Sexagesimo quinto: *holocausta medullata of-*
feram tibi cum incensu arietum. pro quo dicitis invenisse vos: *cum incensu et arietibus,* sed male; in
Hebraeo enim scriptum est: 'em catoroth helim', quod interpre-
20 tatur: μετὰ θυμιάματος κριῶν, id est: 'cum incensu arietum'.
        40.2. in eodem: *propterea exaudivit deus.* pro quo in
Graeco invenisse vos dicitis: *exaudivit me deus,* quod
superfluum est.
        41.1. Sexagesimo septimo: *et exultent in conspectu*
25 *eius.* pro quo in Graeco invenisse vos dicitis: *et exultate in*
266 *conspectu eius.* quod ita versum est et a nobis, sed a quo
in codice vestro corruptum sit, scire non possum. 41.2. in eodem: *ete-*
nim non credunt inhabitare dominum. pro quo
in Graeco legisse vos dicitis: καὶ γὰρ ἀπειθοῦντας τοῦ κατασκηνῶ-
5 σαι. quod utrumque falsum est. nos enim transtulimus: *etenim*

represents "to you." In fact, "to you" is how all the translators rendered it. Therefore, it was translated into Latin in keeping with the particular idiom of the language.

38.1. On the Sixty-Third (Psalm): "Their blows became arrows of children."[98] In place of this in Greek: "an arrow of children." But, if we say it this way, it does not sound correct in Latin: "Their blows became an arrow of children." Instead of this, it is better in Hebrew: "God will strike them with a dart suddenly, and their blows will be inflicted."

39.1. On the Sixty-Fourth (Psalm): "You who stir up the depth of the sea, the sound of its waves."[99] You write that in Greek it has been added: "Who will endure it?" But this is superfluous, because the verb is supplied as follows: "You who stir up the depth of the sea and stir up the sound of its waves." **39.2.** In the same (psalm): "You prepared their food, for thus is its preparation."[100] And you say that in Greek there is no "its." But in Hebrew *thechina* clearly means "its preparation"—"its," that is, the preparation "of the earth," about which he had previously spoken: "You visited the earth and you watered it."[101]

40.1. On the Sixty-Fifth (Psalm): "Whole burnt offerings filled with marrow I will offer to you with the incense of rams."[102] In place of this you say that you have found: "with incense and rams." But this is wrong. For in Hebrew it is written *em catoroth helim*, which is translated μετὰ θυμιάματος κριῶν, that is, "with the incense of rams." **40.2.** In the same (psalm): "Therefore God heard."[103] In place of this in Greek you say that you found: "God heard me." But this is superfluous.

41.1. On the Sixty-Seventh (Psalm): "and they will exult in his presence."[104] In place of this in Greek you say that you have found: "and exult in his presence!" We translated it this way, too. How it was corrupted in your codex I do not know. **41.2.** In the same (psalm): "Indeed, they do not believe the Lord dwells."[105] In place of this you say that in Greek you read: καὶ γὰρ ἀπειθοῦντας τοῦ κατασκηνῶσαι. In fact, both of these are

---

98. Ps 63:8 (Heb 64:8), GPsal.

99. Ps 64:8 (Heb 65:8), GPsal.

100. Ps 64:10 (Heb 65:10), GPsal.

101. Ps 64:10 (Heb 65:10), GPsal.

102. Ps 65:15 (Heb 66:15), GPsal.

103. Ps 65:19 (Heb 66:19), GPsal.

104. Ps 67:5 (Heb 68:5). This is a miscopying of the GPsal text.

105. Ps 67:19 (Heb 68:19). This is a miscopying of the GPsal text.

non credentes inhabitare dominum, ut sit sensus
et pendeat ex superioribus: '*ascendisti in altum, cepisti
captivitatem, accepisti dona in hominibus* et
eos, qui non credebant dominum inhabitare posse mortalibus'. **41.3.** in
10 eodem: *deus benedictus dominus die cottidie.*
pro quo in Graeco invenisse vos dicitis: *dominus benedictus deus, benedictus dominus die cottidie;* sed
melius et verius, quod supra. **41.4.** in eodem: *viderunt ingressus
tui, deus,* pro quo in Graeco scriptum sit: *visi sunt ingres-
15 sus tui, deus.* in Hebraeo ita habet: 'rachua alichatach',
quod Aquila et Symmachus et Theodotio et quinta sextaque editio
interpretati sunt: *viderunt itinera tua, deus,* et, quod
sequitur: *itinera dei mei regis, qui est in sancto.*
ergo a nobis ita legendum est: *viderunt ingressus tuos,*
20 *deus,* et scriptoris vitium relinquendum, qui nominativum posuit
pro accusativo, licet in Septuaginta et in Ἑξαπλοῖς ita reppererim:
ἐθεώρησαν αἱ πορεῖαί σου, ὁ θεός, et pro eo, quod est ἐθεώρησαν,
hoc est 'viderunt', in multis codicibus habet ἐθεωρήθησαν, quod
et obtinuit consuetudo. **41.5.** in eodem: *ingressus dei mei, re-*
267 *gis mei, qui est in sancto;* subauditur: 'viderunt ingressus
dei mei, regis mei'. quod autem dicitis 'mei' in Graeco in 'rege' non
adpositum, apertissimi mendacii est; secundo enim ponitur et 'dei
mei' et 'regis mei' blandientis affectu, ut, qui omnium deus et rex
5 est, suus specialiter deus fiat et rex merito servitutis. denique in
Hebraeo scriptum habet: 'heli melchi', quod 'deum meum' et 'regem
meum' significat. **41.6.** in eodem: *regna terrae, cantate deo,
psallite domino.* et dicitis hoc in isto versiculo non esse
scriptum: *psallite domino,* quoniam statim sequatur:
10 *diapsalma. psallite deo, qui ascendit super
caelum caeli ad orientem,* cum iste versiculus magis
habere debeat iuxta Hebraicam veritatem: *cantate deo,*

incorrect. We translated: "Indeed, those not believing the Lord dwells," so that it depends on what came before, and the sense is: "You ascended on high, you captured captivity, you received gifts among people, even those who did not believe that the Lord can dwell with mortals." **41.3.** In the same (psalm): "God is blessed, the Lord day by day."[106] In place of this in Greek you say that you found: "The Lord is a blessed God, blessed is the Lord day by day." But what we said above is better and more correct. **41.4.** In the same (psalm): "They saw your processions, O God."[107] In place of this in Greek you say is written: "Your processions were seen, O God." In Hebrew it has this: *rachua alichatach*, which Aquila, Symmachus, Theodotion, the fifth edition (*quinta*), and the sixth edition (*sexta*) translated: "They saw your journeys, O God"—and what follows: "the journeys of my God, the king, who is in the sanctuary."[108] Therefore, we should read thus: "They saw your processions, O God," and we should leave behind the error of the scribe who put the nominative instead of the accusative, although in the Seventy, that is, in the Hexapla (Ἑξαπλοῖς), I found this: ἐθεώρησαν αἱ πορεῖαί σου, ὁ θεός, and in place of ἐθεώρησαν, that is, "they saw," in many codices it has ἐθεωρήθησαν, which is the reading custom that prevails. **41.5.** In the same (psalm): "the processions of my God, my king, who is in the sanctuary."[109] "They saw" is supplied, thus: "They saw the processions of my God, my king." But what you say, namely, that "my" is not found in Greek with reference to the king, is clearly false. For "my" is put twice in the spirit of one who gives praise: "my God" and "my king," so that he who is God and King of all might become specifically *his* God and King by merit of his service. Accordingly, in Hebrew it is written: *heli melchi*, which means "my God" and "my king." **41.6.** In the same (psalm): "O Kingdoms of the earth, sing to God, make music to the Lord."[110] And you say that in this short line the phrase "make music to the Lord" is not written, because what follows immediately is: "diapsalma. Make music to God, who ascends over the heaven of heaven toward the east."[111] But this short line should instead be understood according to the Hebrew truth: "Sing to God, make

---

106. Ps 67:19–20 (Heb 68:19–20), GPsal.

107. Ps 67:25a (Heb 68:25a), GPsal.

108. Ps 67:25 (Heb 68:25), the hexaplaric versions as reported by Jerome.

109. Ps 67:25b (Heb 68:25b), GPsal.

110. Ps 67:33 (Heb 68:33), GPsal.

111. Ps 67:33–34 (Heb 68:33–34), GPsal with the obelus marked as Jerome explains.

psallite domino, et illud, quod sequitur in principio versus
alterius, *psallite deo* non sit in libris authenticis, sed obelo
15 praenotatum. ergo et vos legite magis ea, quae vera sunt, ne, dum
additum suscipitis, quod a propheta scriptum est, relinquatis.

42.1. Sexagesimo octavo: *laudabo nomen dei cum
cantico.* pro quo dicitis vos repperisse in Graeco: *dei mei,*
sed 'mei' superfluum est.

20   43.1. Septuagesimo: *deus, ne elongeris a me.* quod
dicitis in Graeco positum: *deus meus,* superfluum est. 43.2. in eodem:
deus, docuisti me ex iuventute mea. et in hoc, quod
apud Graecos invenisse vos dicitis, *deus meus* superfluum est.
43.3. in eodem: *donec adnuntiem brachium tuum.* et
25 dicitis in Graeco vos repperisse: *mirabilia tua,* quod de
superiori versiculo est: *et usque nunc pronuntiabo
mirabilia tua.* bene ergo hic habet 'brachium'.

268   44.1. Septuagesimo primo: *et adorabunt eum omnes
reges.* illud, quod in Graeco invenisse vos dicitis: *reges terrae,* superfluum est. 44.2. in eodem: *benedictus dominus
deus, deus Israhel.* dicitis in Graeco bis 'deus' non haberi,
5 cum in Hebraico sit et apud Septuaginta manifestissime triplex
domini deique nuncupatio mysterium trinitatis sit. 44.3. in eodem:
*et benedictum nomen maiestatis eius in aeter-
num.* hoc ergo, quod in Gareco invenisse vos dicitis: *in aeternum et in saeculum saeculi,* superflue a Graecis sciatis
10 adpositum, quod nec Hebraeus habet nec septuaginta interpretes.

45.1. Septuagesimo secundo: *prodiet quasi ex adipe.*
et dicitis vos apud Graecos invenisse ἐξελεύσονται, id est 'pro-
dient', quod falsum est. nam et apud septuaginta interpretes ita
scriptum est: ἐξελεύσεται ὡς ἐκ στέατος ἡ ἀδικία αὐτῶν. 45.2. in eodem:

music to the Lord," and what follows at the start of the next line, "make music to God" is not present in the authentic books, but was marked with an obelus. You should therefore prefer reading things that are true, lest by accepting what was added, you thereby forsake what the prophet wrote.

42.1. On the Sixty-Eighth (Psalm): "I will praise the name of God with a song."[112] In place of which you say that you have found in Greek: "my God." But the "my" is superfluous.

43.1. On the Seventieth (Psalm): "O God, do not be far from me."[113] You say that in Greek "my God" was put, but this is superfluous. 43.2. In the same (psalm): "O God, you taught me from my youth."[114] And in this passage, what you say you found among the Greeks, "my God," is superfluous. 43.3. In the same (psalm): "until I will make known your arm."[115] And you say that you found in Greek "your wonders." But this is from the short line above: "even until now I will proclaim your wonders."[116] Therefore, it is correct here to have "arm."

44.1. On the Seventy-First (Psalm): "And all kings will worship him."[117] What you say that you found in Greek, "kings of the earth," is superfluous. 44.2. In the same (psalm): "Blessed is the Lord God, the God of Israel."[118] You say that in Greek it does not have "God" twice. Yet it is in the Hebrew, and among the Seventy the triple naming of the Lord and God is clearly the mystery of the Trinity. 44.3. In the same (psalm): "And blessed is the name of his majesty unto eternity."[119] Therefore, you should know that what you say you found in Greek, "unto eternity and unto the age of the age," was added superfluously by the Greeks. Neither the Hebrew nor the Seventy Translators have this.

45.1. On the Seventy-Second (Psalm): "It will go forth as if out of fat."[120] And you say that you found among the Greeks ἐξελεύσονται, that is, "they will go forth"; but this is incorrect. For among the Seventy Translators it is written thus: ἐξελεύσεται ὡς ἐκ στέατος ἡ ἀδικία αὐτῶν. 45.2. In the

---

112. Ps 68:31 (Heb 69:31), GPsal.
113. Ps 70:12 (Heb 71:12), GPsal.
114. Ps 70:17 (Heb 71:17), GPsal.
115. Ps 70:18 (Heb 71:18), GPsal.
116. Ps 70:17 (Heb 71:17), GPsal.
117. Ps 71:11 (Heb 72:11), GPsal.
118. Ps 71:18 (Heb 72:18), GPsal.
119. Ps 71:19 (Heb 72:19), GPsal.
120. Ps 72:7 (Heb 73:7), GPsal.

15 *quomodo scit deus*. in Graeco dicitis non esse 'deum', cum
   et apud Septuaginta scriptum sit: πῶς ἔγνω ὁ θεός, et omnes
   interpretes similiter de Hebraeo transtulerint. 45.3. in eodem: *intelle-*
   gam in novissimis eorum. pro quo in Graeco legisse vos
   dicitis: *et intellegam*; sed hic 'et' coniunctio superflua est.
20 45.4. in eodem: *defecit caro mea et cor meum*. pro quo male
   perversum ordinem quidam tenent: *defecit cor meum et*
   caro mea. 45.5. in eodem: *ut adnuntiem omnes praedi-*
   cationes tuas. pro quo vos in Graeco legisse dixistis: τὰς
   αἰνέσεις σου, id est 'laudes tuas'. et sciendum, quod in Hebraeo
25 'malochothach' scriptum habet, quod Aquila ἀγγελίας σου, id est
269 'nuntios tuos', Septuaginta τὰς ἐπαγγελίας σου, id est 'praedicationes' vel 'promissa' interpretati sunt, licet et laus et praedicatio unum utrumque significet.
       46.1. Septuagesimo tertio: *ut quid, deus, reppulisti*
 5 *in finem?* pro quo male apud Graecos legitur ordine commutato:
   ut quid reppulisti, deus? 46.2. in eodem: *quanta ma-*
   lignatus est inimicus in sancto! miror, quis in codice
   vestro emendando perverterit, ut pro 'sancto' 'sanctis' posuerit,
   cum et in nostro codice 'in sancto' inveniatur. 46.3. in eodem:
10 *incendamus omnes dies festos dei a terra*. pro
   quo in Graeco scriptum est καταπαύσωμεν et nos ita transtulimus:
   quiescere faciamus omnes dies festos dei a
   terra. et miror, quomodo e latere adnotationem nostram nescio
   quis temerarius scribendam in corpore putaverit, quam nos pro
15 eruditione legentis scripsimus hoc modo: 'non habet καταπαύσωμεν,
   ut quidam putant, sed κατακαύσωμεν, id est incendamus'. 46.4. et quia
   retulit mihi sanctus presbyter Firmus, qui huius operis exactor fuit,
   inter plurimos hinc habitam quaestionem, plenius de hoc disputan-
   dum videtur. in Hebraeo scriptum est: 'sarphu chol moedahu

same (psalm): "How does God know?"[121] You say that in Greek it does not have "God." But among the Seventy it is written: πῶς ἔγνω ὁ θεός, and all the translators translated from the Hebrew similarly. **45.3.** In the same (psalm): "I understand concerning their last ends."[122] In place of this you say that you read in Greek: "*and* I understand," but here the conjunction "and" is superfluous. **45.4.** In the same (psalm): "My flesh and my heart failed."[123] In place of this certain people incorrectly maintain a distorted order: "My heart and my flesh failed." **45.5.** In the same (psalm): "so that I might announce all your proclamations."[124] In place of this you said that you read in Greek: τὰς αἰνέσεις σου, that is, "your praises." It should be known that in Hebrew it is written: *malochothach*, which Aquila translated ἀγγελίας σου, that is, "your messages," and the Seventy translated τὰς ἐπαγγελίας σου, that is, "your proclamations" or "your promises," although both "praise" and "proclamation" indicate the same thing.

46.1. On the Seventy-Third (Psalm): "Why, O God, did you reject unto the end?"[125] In place of this among the Greeks it is read incorrectly, with the order changed: "Why did you reject, O God?" **46.2.** In the same (psalm): "How many things the enemy has done wickedly in the sanctuary!"[126] I am astonished at the one who, in emending your codex, corrupted it, so that instead of "sanctuary" he put "saints," because also in our codex it has "in the sanctuary." **46.3.** In the same (psalm): "Let us burn all the festival days of God from the land."[127] In place of this in Greek is written: καταπαύσωμεν, and thus we translated: "Let us cause to cease all the festival days of God from the land."[128] I am astonished at how some heedless person, I know not who, thought he should write in the body of the text our marginal notation, which we wrote for the instruction of the reader in this manner: "It does not have καταπαύσωμεν, as some think, but κατακαύσωμεν, that is, 'Let us burn.'" **46.4.** And because the holy presbyter Firmus, who requested that work, reported to me that many had a question about this, it seems good for me to discuss it more fully. In Hebrew it is written: *sarphu chol moedahu*

---

121. Ps 72:11 (Heb 73:11), GPsal.
122. Ps 72:17 (Heb 73:17), GPsal.
123. Ps 72:26 (Heb 73:26), GPsal.
124. Ps 72:28 (Heb 73:28), GPsal.
125. Ps 73:1 (Heb 74:1), GPsal.
126. Ps 73:3 (Heb 74:3), GPsal.
127. Ps 73:8 (Heb 74:8). This is a miscopying of the GPsal text.
128. Ps 73:8 (Heb 74:8), GPsal.

20 hel baares', quod Aquila et Symmachus verterunt: ἐνεπύρισαν πάσας
    τάς συνταγὰς τοῦ θεοῦ, id est: 'incenderunt omnes sol-
    lemnitates dei in terra', Quinta: κατέκαυσαν, id est
    'conbusserunt', Sexta: κατακαύσωμεν, id est 'conburamus',
    quod et Septuaginta iuxta exemplorum veritatem transtulisse
25 perspicuum est. Theodotion quoque ἐνεπυρίσαμεν vertit, id est
270 'succendimus'. **46.5.** ex quo perspicuum est sic psallendum, ut nos inter-
    pretati sumus, et tamen sciendum, quid Hebraica veritas habeat.
    hoc enim, quod Septuaginta transtulerunt, propter vetustatem in
    ecclesiis decantandum est et illud ab eruditis sciendum propter
5   notitiam scripturarum. unde, si quid pro studio e latere addi-
    tum est, non debet poni in corpore, ne priorem translationem pro
    scribentium voluntate conturbet. **46.6.** in eodem: *contribulasti*
    capita draconum in aquis; tu confregisti ca-
    pita draconis. sic lectionis ordo sequitur, ut in priori versu
10 'tu' non habeat, sed in secundo, et 'aquae' plurali numero
    scribantur, non singulari, sicut et Aquila verbum Hebraicum 'am-
    maim', τῶν ὑδάτων, id est 'aquarum', interpretatus est. **46.7.** in eodem:
    ne obliviscaris voces inimicorum tuorum. pro
    quo in Graeco τῶν ἰκετῶν σου, id est 'deprecantium te', scrip-
15 tum dicitis. in Hebreao 'sorarach' legitur, quod Aquila 'hostium
    tuorum', Symmachus 'bellantium contra te', Septuaginta
    et sexta editio 'inimicorum tuorum' interpretati sunt. **46.8.** et est
    sensus pendens ex superioribus: *'memor esto inpro-*
    periorum tuorum, eorum, quae ab insipiente
20 *sunt tota die; ne obliviscaris voces inimico-*
    rum tuorum, id est voces, quae te blasphemant tibique in
    populo tuo detrahunt'. unde sequitur: *superbia eorum,*
    qui te oderunt, ascendit semper, id est: 'dum tu
    differs poenas, illi proficiunt in blasphemiis'.
25   **47.1.** Septuagesimo quarto: *narrabimus mirabilia*
       tua. pro quo male apud Graecos legitur: *narrabo omnia*
       mirabilia tua.

hel baares, which Aquila and Symmachus translated: ἐνεπύρισαν πάσας τὰς συνταγὰς τοῦ θεοῦ, that is, "they burned all the solemn festivals of God in the land." The fifth edition (*quinta*) translated κατέκαυσαν, that is, "they burned." The sixth edition (*sexta*) translated κατακαύσωμεν, that is, "Let us burn," which clearly is also what the Seventy translated according to its true copies. Theodotion similarly rendered ἐνεπυρίσαμεν, that is, "we set on fire." From this it is clear that the psalm should be sung as we translated it, and nevertheless it should be known what the Hebrew truth contains. For what the Seventy translated should be sung in the churches in view of its antiquity, and what comes from scholars should be known for the sake of understanding the Scriptures. **46.5.** Therefore, if anything is added in the margin for the sake of study, it should not be put in the body of the text so that the earlier translation does not become confused at the whim of copyists. **46.6.** In the same (psalm): "you crushed the heads of dragons in the waters; you—you broke the heads of the dragon."[129] This is the correct order of the text, in that it does not have "you" in the first line but in the second; and "waters" is written not in the singular, but in the plural, even as Aquila translated the Hebrew word *amaim* as τῶν ὑδάτων, that is, "waters." **46.7.** In the same (psalm): "Do not forget the voices of your enemies."[130] In place of this in Greek you say that it is written: τῶν ἱκετῶν σου, that is, "those who entreat you." In Hebrew it reads *sorarach*, which Aquila translated "your foes," Symmachus rendered "those fighting against you," and the Seventy and the sixth edition (*sexta*) translated "your enemies." **46.8.** The sense depends on what precedes: "Remember your reproaches, which are from the fool all day; do not forget the voices of your enemies,"[131] that is, the voices that revile you and disparage you among your people. From there it continues: "the pride of those who hate you ascends always,"[132] that is, "while you defer punishment, they continue to revile."

47.1. On the Seventy-Fourth (Psalm): "We will recount your wonders."[133] In place of this it reads incorrectly among the Greeks as: "I will recount all your wonders."

129. Ps 73:13–14 (Heb 74:13–14), GPsal.
130. Ps 73:23 (Heb 74:23), GPsal.
131. Ps 73:22–23 (Heb 74:22–23), GPsal.
132. Ps 73:23 (Heb 74:23), GPsal.
133. Ps 74:2 (Heb 75:2), GPsal.

271   **48.1.** Septuagesimo quinto: *omnes viri divitiarum*
manibus suis. et non, ut vos a nescio quo depravatum legitis:
in manibus suis. **48.2.** in eodem: *terribili et ei, qui aufert*
spiritus principum. dicitis, quod 'ei' non sit scriptum in
5   Graeco; verum est, sed, nisi apposuerimus 'ei', Latinus sermo non
resonat. neque enim possumus recte dicere: 'terribili et qui
aufert spiritus principum'.
        49.1. Septuagesimo sexto: *et meditatus sum nocte*
cum corde meo et exercitabar et scopebam
10   *spiritum meum.* pro quo in Hebraeo legimus: *recorda-*
bar psalmorum meorum in nocte, cum corde
meo loquebar et scopebam spiritum meum. pro
'exercitatione' ἀδολεσχίαν, id est 'decantationem' quandam et
'meditationem' Septuaginta transtulerunt et pro eo, quod nos
15   diximus 'scopebam', illi posuerunt ἔσκαλλον, quod Symmachus
transtulit ἀνηρεύνων, id est 'perscrutabar' sive 'quaerebam' et
Quinta similiter. **49.2.** proprie autem σκαλισμὸς in agri cultura in sariendo
dicitur, id est sarculando; et, quomodo ibi quaeruntur herbae
sarculo, quae secentur, sic et iste retractatum cogitationum suarum
20   μεταφορικῶς a sarculo demonstravit. et sciendum, quod ἔσκαλον
semel, ἔσκαλλον frequenter significat. **49.3.** in eodem: *a gene-*
272 *ratione in generationem.* hoc, quod in Graeco sequens
invenisse vos dicitis: *consummavit verbum*, recte non
habet in Latino, quia et in nullo habetur interpretum.
        50.1. Septuagesimo septimo: *et narrabunt filiis suis.*
5   pro quo in Graeco habet ἀναγγελοῦσιν, quod est 'adnuntiabunt'.
sed sciendum, quod in Hebraeo 'iasaphpheru' scriptum est, quod
Aquila et Symmachus 'narrabunt' transtulerunt. **50.2.** in eodem: *et*
occidit pingues eorum. sic habet et in Hebraeo, hoc est
'bamasmnehem', quod Aquila interpretatus est ἐν λιπαροῖς αὐτῶν,
10   Symmachus τοὺς λιπαρωτέρους αὐτῶν, Septuaginta et Theodotion
et Quinta ἐν τοῖς πίοσιν αὐτῶν. quod quidam non intellegentes pro

48.1. On the Seventy-Fifth (Psalm): "All the men of wealth with their hands."[134] —and not the text, distorted by someone or other, as you read: "in their hands." **48.2.** In the same (psalm): "To the terrifying one, and to him who removes the spirits of rulers."[135] You say that in Greek, "to him" is not written. This is true, but unless we add "to him," it does not sound correct in the Latin language. For we cannot rightly say, "To the terrifying one, and who removes the spirits of rulers."

49.1. On the Seventy-Sixth (Psalm): "And I meditated at night with my heart, and I was vexed, and I searched my spirit."[136] In place of this in Hebrew we read: "I remembered my songs in the night, with my heart I spoke, and I searched my spirit." For "vexing," the Seventy translated ἀδολεσχίαν, that is, a kind of repetition or meditation. For what we rendered as "I searched," the Seventy put ἔσκαλλον, Symmachus translated ἀνηρεύνων—that is, "I sought" or "I examined"—and the fifth edition (*quinta*) translated similarly. **49.2.** Properly speaking, in fact, σκαλισμός refers to "stirring up" in the cultivation of a field, that is, "hoeing." Just as in the case of a field, plants are "examined" with a hoe so that they may be separated out, thus he describes going over his own thoughts metaphorically (μεταφορικῶς) with a hoe. It should be known that ἔσκαλον means examining once, ἔσκαλλον frequently. **49.3.** In the same (psalm): "From generation to generation."[137] That which you say you found after this in Greek, "he has completed the word," is not correctly present in the Latin, because it is not present in any of the translators.

50.1. On the Seventy-Seventh (Psalm): "and they will recount to their sons."[138] In place of this in Greek it has: ἀναγγελοῦσιν, that is, "they will announce." But it should be known that in Hebrew it is written *iasaphpheru*, which Aquila and Symmachus translated "they will recount." **50.2.** In the same (psalm): "And he killed their fat ones."[139] It has this also in the Hebrew, that is, *bamasmnehem*, which Aquila translated ἐν λιπαροῖς αὐτῶν, Symmachus rendered τοὺς λιπαρωτέρους αὐτῶν, and the Seventy, Theodotion, and the fifth edition (*quinta*) translated ἐν τοῖς πίοσιν αὐτῶν. Certain people, not understanding this, thought that πλείοσιν was written instead

---

134. Ps 75:6 (Heb 76:6), GPsal.
135. Ps 75:12–13 (Heb 76:12–13), GPsal.
136. Ps 76:7 (Heb 77:7), GPsal.
137. Ps 76:9 (Heb 77:9), GPsal.
138. Ps 77:6 (Heb 78:6), GPsal.
139. Ps 77:31 (Heb 78:31), GPsal.

πίοσιν putaverunt scriptum πλείοσιν. 50.3. in eodem: *dilexerunt*
eum in ore suo et lingua sua mentiti sunt ei. et
in Hebraeo ita scriptum est: 'icazbulo', et omnes voce simili trans-
15 tulerunt: ἐψεύσαντο αὐτῷ, id est 'mentiti sunt ei'. quis autem voluerit
pro 'ei' ponere 'eum' et vitiare exemplaria, non est mei iudicii.
50.4. in eodem: *et propitius fiet peccatis eorum et*
non disperdet eos. dicitis, quod 'eos' in Graeco non habeat,
quod et verum est; sed nos, ne sententia pendeat, Latinum ser-
20 monem sua proprietate conplevimus. si quis autem putat διαφθερεῖ
non 'perditionem' sonare, sed 'corruptionem', recordetur illius
tituli, in quo scribitur: εἰς τὸ τέλος μὴ διαφθείρῃς, hoc est: *in*
finem ne disperdas et non, ut plerique κακοζήλως inter-
273 pretantur, *ne corrumpas.* **50.5.** in eodem: *et induxit eos*
in montem sanctificationis suae, montem, quem
adquisivit dextera eius. pro quo apud Septuaginta legitur: ὄρος τοῦτο, ὃ ἐκτήσατο ἡ δεξιὰ αὐτοῦ – et non, ut vos
5 ponitis, ὃ ἐκτήσατο –, hoc est: *quem adquisivit*
dextera eius. ergo secundum Hebraicam proprietatem interpretatus est Symmachus: *montem, quem adquisivit*
dextera eius. **50.6.** in eodem: *et averterunt se et non*
servaverunt pactum, quemadmodum patres
10 *eorum.* scio, quod 'pactum' non habeat in Hebraeo, sed,
quando omnes voce simili transtulerunt ἠσυνθέτησαν et apud
Graecos συνθήκη 'pactum' dicitur, ex uno verbo significatur:
non servaverunt pactum, licet Septuaginta ἠθέτησαν
posuerint. **50.6b.** in eodem: *in terra, quam fundavit in*
15 *saecula.* pro quo scriptum invenisse vos dicitis: *in terra*
fundavit eam in saecula. in Hebraeo ita scriptum est,
ut vertit et Symmachus: εἰς τὴν γῆν, ἣν ἐθεμελίωσεν εἰς τὸν αἰῶνα.
si autem non de terra dicitur, quod fundata sit, sed de alia,
quae fundata videatur in terra, probent ex prioribus et sequenti-
20 bus, quis sensus sit, ut nescio quid, quod non dicitur, fundatum
videatur in terra. sin autem sanctificium in terra fundatum

of πίοσιν. 50.3. In the same (psalm): "They loved him with their mouth, and with their tongue they lied to him."[140] And in Hebrew it is written thus: *icazbulo*, and all with similar voice translated ἐψεύσαντο αὐτῷ, that is, "they lied to him." Who decided to put "him" instead of "to him" and thus corrupt the copies? It is not for me to determine. 50.4. In the same (psalm): "And he will make atonement for their sins and will not destroy them."[141] You say that in Greek it does not have "them." This is true. But we filled out the Latin expression according to Latin's own particular idiom, so that the thought is not left hanging. If anyone thinks that διαφθερεῖ does not mean "destruction," but "corruption," let him remember the title that is written: εἰς τὸ τέλος μὴ διαφθείρῃς, that is, "Unto the end. Do not destroy,"[142] and not as most translate using an affected manner (κακοζήλως): "Do not corrupt." 50.5. In the same (psalm): "And he led them to the mountain of his holiness, the mountain that his right hand acquired."[143] Among the Seventy this reads: ὄρος τοῦτο ὃ ἐκτήσατο ἡ δεξιὰ αὐτοῦ, and not as you put: ὃ ἐκτήσατο, that is, "which his right hand acquired."[144] And so Symmachus translated according to the Hebrew idiom: "the mountain that his right hand acquired." 50.6. In the same (psalm): "They turned themselves away and they did not maintain the covenant, just like their fathers."[145] I know that "covenant" is not present in Hebrew, but since all with similar voice translated ἠσυνθέτησαν, and among the Greeks συνθήκη means "covenant," by this one word it signifies: "they did not maintain the covenant." Yet the Seventy put ἠθέτησαν. 50.6b. In the same (psalm): "in the land that he founded unto the ages."[146] In place of this you say that you have found written: "In the land, he founded it (*eam*) unto the ages." In Hebrew it is written thus, as Symmachus rendered: εἰς τὴν γῆν, ἣν ἐθεμελίωσεν εἰς τὸν αἰῶνα. But if it is not speaking about the land being founded, but about something else that was supposedly founded in the land, then let them show from the preceding or following context what the sense is, because I cannot tell what unstated thing was supposedly founded in the land. If they think the

---

140. Ps 77:36 (Heb 78:36), GPsal.

141. Ps 77:38 (Heb 78:38), GPsal.

142. Ps 74:1; also Pss 56:1; 57:1; 58:1.

143. Ps 77:54 (Heb 78:54), GPsal.

144. On this text, see the commentary.

145. Ps 77:57 (Heb 78:57), GPsal.

146. Ps 77:69b (Heb 78:69b), GPsal.

putant, debuit scribi: *in terra fundavit illud in sae-*
cula. 50.7. in eodem: *et in intellectibus manuum*
suarum deduxit eos. non habet ἐν τῇ συνέσει, ut scribitis,
25 numero singulari, sed ἐν ταῖς συνέσεσιν, quod 'intellegentias' sonat,
sicut habetur et in Hebraeo 'bathabunoth', quod est 'intellectibus'.
    51.1. Septuagesimo octavo: *posuerunt Hierusalem in*
274 *pomorum custodiam.* quod Graece εἰς ὀπωροφυλάκιον
dicitur nec aliter potest verti, quam a nobis translatum est; significat autem speculam, quam custodes agrorum et pomorum habere
consuerunt, ut de amplissima urbe parvum tuguriunculum vix
5 remanserit. hoc secundum Graecos. ceterum in Hebraeo 'lichin'
scriptum habet, quod Aquila vertit λιθάριον, id est 'acervum et
cumulum lapidum', quibus vineae et agri purgari solent.
    52.1. Septuagesimo nono: *et plantasti radices eius*
hinc. et dicitis, quod in Graeco 'hinc' non habeat; et bene, nam
10 et in nostris codicibus non habetur; et miror, quis inperitorum vestros
libros falsaverit.
    53.1. Octogesimo secundo: *hereditate possideamus*
sanctuarium dei. et dicitis, quod in Graeco sit scriptum
κληρονομήσωμεν ἑαυτοῖς, id est 'possideamus nobis'. quae
15 superflua quaestio est; quando enim dicitur 'possideamus', intellegitur et 'nobis'.
    54.1. Octogesimo tertio: *cor meum et caro mea exul-*
tavit in deum vivum. pro quo in Graeco scriptum dicitis
exultaverunt. in hoc nulla contentio est; si enim legimus
20 'exultavit', intellegitur 'cor meum exultavit et caro mea
exultavit'; sin autem 'exultaverunt', duo pariter exultaverunt, id
est cor et caro. et quaeso vos, ut huius modi ineptias et super-
fluas contentiones, ubi nulla est sensus inmutatio, declinetis. 54.2. in

sanctuary is what was founded in the land,[147] then it should have been written: "In the land, he founded it (*illud*) unto the ages."[148] 50.7. In the same (psalm): "And by the comprehensions of his hands he guided them."[149] It does not have, as you write, ἐν τῇ συνέσει with the singular, but ἐν ταῖς συνέσεσιν, which means "comprehendings," just as it has in the Hebrew, *bathabunoth*, which is "comprehensions."

51.1. On the Seventy-Eighth (Psalm): "They made Jerusalem into a keep of fruits."[150] In Greek this reads εἰς ὀπωροφυλάκιον, and it cannot be rendered differently than how we translated it. It refers to a watchtower typically set up by those who keep fields and orchards. This suggests that, even in this large city, hardly a small hut remains standing. This is according to the Greeks. Otherwise, the Hebrew has *lichin*, which Aquila translated λιθαόριον, that is, a heap and pile of stones such as are normally cleared away from vineyards and fields.

52.1. On the Seventy-Ninth (Psalm): "And you planted its roots here."[151] And you say that in Greek it does not have "here"; and you say this correctly, because it is also not found in our codices. I wonder what unskilled person falsified your books.

53.1. On the Eighty-Second (Psalm): "Let us possess by inheritance the sanctuary of God."[152] You say that in Greek it is written: κληρονομήσωμεν ἑαυτοῖς, that is, "Let us inherit for ourselves." This is a superfluous point of discussion, because when someone says, "let us inherit," "for ourselves" is implied.

54.1. On the Eighty-Third (Psalm): "My heart and my flesh has rejoiced in the living God."[153] In place of this in Greek you say it is written: "have rejoiced." There is no conflict in this. For if we read "has rejoiced," it is understood as "my heart has rejoiced, and my flesh has rejoiced." But if we read "have rejoiced," then the two have rejoiced in unison, that is, the heart and the flesh. I ask you to refrain from inept and superfluous challenges of this kind, where there is no change in the sense. 54.2. In the same

---

147. See Ps 77:69a (Heb 78:69a).
148. Ps 77:69b (Heb 78:69b), GPsal.
149. Ps 77:72 (Heb 78:72), GPsal.
150. Ps 78:1 (Heb 79:1), GPsal.
151. Ps 79:10 (Heb 80:10). This is a miscopying of the GPsal text.
152. Ps 82:13 (Heb 83:13), GPsal.
153. Ps 83:3 (Heb 84:3), GPsal.

eodem: *beatus vir, cuius est auxilium abs te.* in
25 Graeco invenisse vos dicitis: *cui est auxilium eius abs*
275 *te;* quod quia nos in Latina interpretatione vitavimus, ut dicitis, re-
prehendimur. cui enim non pateat, quod, si dicere voluerimus: *cui*
est auxilium eius, apertissimum vitium sit et, quando
praecesserit 'cui', sequi non debeat 'eius'? nisi forte vitii arguimur,
5 quod vitavimus vitium. **54.3.** in eodem: *in valle lacrimarum.*
pro quo dicitis in Graeco scriptum esse κλαυθμῶνος, id est 'plorationis', sed, sive ploratum sive planctum sive fletum sive lacri-
mas dixerimus, unus est sensus. et nos hoc sequimur, ut, ubi nulla
de sensu est inmutatio, Latini sermonis elegantiam conservemus.
10   **55.1.** Octogesimo quarto: *benedixisti, domine, ter-*
ram tuam. pro eo, quod est 'benedixisti', in Graeco scriptum
dicitis εὐδόκησας. et quaeritis, quomodo hoc verbum exprimi debeat
in Latinum. si contentiose verba scrutamur et syllabas, possumus
dicere: 'bene placuit, domine, terra tua' et, dum verba
15 sequimur, sensus ordinem perdimus. aut certe addendum est
aliquid, ut eloquii ordo servetur, et dicendum: 'conplacuit
tibi, domine, terra tua'. quod si fecerimus, rursum a nobis
quaeritur, quare addiderimus 'tibi', cum nec in Graeco sit nec in
Hebraeo. eadem igitur interpretandi sequenda est regula, quam saepe
20 diximus, ut, ubi non fit damnum in sensu, linguae, in quam transferimus, εὐφωνία et proprietas conservetur. **55.2.** in eodem: *miseri-*
cordia et veritas obviaverunt sibi. et dicitis, quod
in Graeco 'sibi' non habeat. nec in Hebraeo habet et apud Septuaginta obelo praenotatum est, quae signa dum per scriptorum
25 neglegentiam a plerisque quasi superflua relinquuntur, magnus in
legendo error exoritur. sin autem non fuerit additum 'sibi', misericordia et veritas non sibi, sed alii occurrisse credentur nec iustitia
et pax sibi dedisse osculum, sed alteri.
276   **56.1.** Octogesimo quinto: *et non proposuerunt te in*
conspectu suo. et dicitis, quod in vestro codice 'te' non habeat.

(psalm): "Blessed is the man whose help is from you."[154] In Greek you say that you have found: "to whom his help is from you." Because, as you point out, we avoided this in our Latin translation, we are rebuked! To whom is it not obvious that, if we tried to say: "to whom his help is," it is a clear stylistic fault? When "to whom" comes before a word, "his" should not come after it. We should not be charged with a fault because we avoided a fault. **54.3.** In the same (psalm): "In the valley of tears."[155] In place of this you say in Greek it is written: κλαυθμῶνος, that is, "of weeping." But whether we say: "of weeping," "of wailing," "of crying," or "of tears," the sense is the same. We follow this principle, that where there is no change with regard to the sense, we should maintain the elegance of Latin expression.

55.1. On the Eighty-Fourth (Psalm): "You blessed, O Lord, your land."[156] In place of "you blessed," you say that the Greek has εὐδόκησας, and you ask how this word should be expressed in Latin. If we contentiously scrutinize words and syllables, we can say: "It was well pleasing, O Lord, your land," and while we are following the words, we destroy the sequence of thought. Or, at least, something should be added that preserves proper style, such as to say: "It was pleasing *to you*, O Lord, your land." But if we did this, we would again be interrogated as to why we added "to you," when this is neither in the Greek nor in the Hebrew. Therefore, the same rule of translating should be followed here that we have often stated, that wherever there is no damage to the sense, the euphony (εὐφωνία) and particular idiom of the language into which we are translating should be maintained. **55.2.** In the same (psalm): "Mercy and truth met themselves."[157] You say that it does not have "themselves" in the Greek. In fact, it is not present in the Hebrew, and it was marked with an obelus among the Seventy. When these signs are ignored by the majority as superfluous as a result of scribal negligence, great error arises in the reading. But if "themselves" is not added, mercy and truth will not be thought to encounter "themselves" but someone else, nor will justice and peace kiss "themselves" but another.[158]

56.1. On the Eighty-Fifth (Psalm): "And they did not set you in their sight."[159] You say that in your codex it does not have "you." Add "you," and

---

154. Ps 83:6 (Heb 84:6), GPsal.
155. Ps 83:7 (Heb 84:7), GPsal.
156. Ps 84:2 (Heb 85:2), GPsal.
157. Ps 84:11a (Heb 85:11a), GPsal.
158. See Ps 84:11b (Heb 85:11b), GPsal.
159. Ps 85:14 (Heb 86:14), GPsal.

addite 'te' et emendato errore librarii vestrum quoque errorem
emendabitis. **56.2.** in eodem: *et tu, domine deus, miserator et*
5 *misericors.* in Graeco invenisse vos dicitis: *et tu, domine*
deus meus, quod superfluum est; 'meus' enim nec in Hebraeo
habetur nec in Septuaginta.

   57.1. Octogesimo octavo: *magnus et horrendus.* pro
quo in Graeco invenisse vos dicitis φοβερός, quod significat 'ter-
10 ribilis', 'timendus', 'formidandus'. ego puto in id ipsum significari et
'horrendum' – non, ut vulgus existimat, despiciendum et squali-
dum – secundum illud:
mihi frigidus horror
membra quatit
15 et:
horror ubique animo, simul ipsa silentia terrent
et:
monstrum horrendum, ingens
et multa his similia. **57.2.** in eodem: *tunc locutus es in*
20 *visione sanctis tuis.* pro quo in Graeco *filiis tuis*
invenisse vos dicitis. sed sciendum, quod in Hebraeo 'laasidach'
habet, quod omnes τοῖς ὁσίοις σου, id est 'sanctis tuis',
transtulerunt et sola sexta editio *prophetis tuis*
interpretata est sensum magis quam verbum exprimens; et
25 in κοινῇ tantum pro 'sanctis' 'filios' repperi. **57.3.** in eodem: *tu*
vero reppulisti et respexisti. pro quo in Graeco
ἐξουδένωσας invenisse vos dicitis. unius litterae mutatio quantum
277 vobis fecit errorem! non enim 'respexisti', sed 'despexisti' et 'pro
nihilo duxisti' interpretati sumus. nisi forte ἐξουδένωσας non
putatis transferendum 'despexisti', sed secundum disertissimum
istius temporis interpretem 'adnihilasti' vel 'adnullasti' vel 'nulli-
5 ficasti' et si qua alia possunt inveniri apud inperitos portenta verborum.

   58.1. Octogesimo nono: *a saeculo et usque in saecu-*
lum tu es, deus. et dicitis, quod in Graeco non sit 'deus'. quod
apud eos deesse manifestum est. nam est in Hebraico et omnes alii
10 interpretes et Septuaginta similiter transtulerunt: ἀπὸ τοῦ αἰῶνος
καὶ ἕως τοῦ αἰῶνος σὺ εἶ, ὁ θεός, quod Hebraice dicitur:
'meolam ad olam ath hel'. **58.2.** in eodem: *quoniam super-*

by correcting the mistake of your copyist you will also correct this mistake. **56.2.** In the same (psalm): "And you, O Lord God, are compassionate and merciful."[160] And you say that in Greek you found: "And you, my Lord God." But this is superfluous. For "my" is present neither in the Hebrew nor in the Greek.

57.1. On the Eighty-Eighth (Psalm): "Great and horrible."[161] In place of this in Greek you say that you found φοβερός, which means "terrible," "fearful," "dreadful." But I think this is precisely what is signified by "horrible"— not as commonly understood, "filthy" and "despised"—but in this sense: "a cold horror shook my limbs"; "everywhere, the horror in my soul and the silence itself terrify"; and "a horrible monster, enormous," and many passages similar to these.[162] **57.2.** In the same (psalm): "Then you spoke in a vision to your saints."[163] In place of this in Greek you say that you found: "to your sons." But it should be known that the Hebrew has *laasidach*, which all translated as τοῖς ὁσίοις σου, that is, "to your saints," with only the sixth edition (*sexta*) rendering it as "to your prophets," expressing the sense rather than the word. Only in the κοινή edition does one find "sons" instead of "saints." **57.3.** In the same (psalm): "But you rejected and looked back."[164] In place of this in Greek you say that you found ἐξουδένωσας. How great an error the changing of one letter has caused you! For we did not translate "looked back" (*respexisti*) but "looked down on" (*despexisti*), that is, "reckoned as nothing." Although perhaps you think ἐξουδένωσας should not be translated "looked down on," but rather should be translated in accordance with the most fluent translator of this time: "nothingafy," or "nothingize," or "nullificate," or some other lexical monstrosity as can be found among the unlearned.

58.1. On the Eighty-Ninth (Psalm): "From age unto age you are, O God."[165] You say that "O God" is not in the Greek. But it is clear that this was left out in their copies. For it is in the Hebrew, and all the translators and the Seventy rendered similarly: ἀπὸ τοῦ αἰῶνος καὶ ἕως τοῦ αἰῶνος σὺ εἶ, ὁ θεός. In Hebrew this reads: *meolam ad olam ath hel*. **58.2.** In the same

---

160. Ps 85:15 (Heb 86:15), GPsal.

161. Ps 88:8 (Heb 89:8), GPsal.

162. Virgil, *Aen.* 3.29–30, 658; 2.755.

163. Ps 88:20 (Heb 89:20), GPsal.

164. Ps 88:39 (Heb 89:39). This is a miscopying of the GPsal text.

165. Ps 89:2 (Heb 90:2), GPsal.

venit mansuetudo et corripiemur. in Graeco
vos dicitis invenisse: *mansuetudo super nos.* sed et
15 hoc superfluum est.

59.1. Nonagesimo: *dicet domino: susceptor meus*
es tu. et dicitis, quod in Graeco 'es' non habeat. ego vobis amplius
dicam, quod apud Hebraeos nec 'es' habeat nec 'tu', sed apud
Septuaginta et apud Latinos pro εὐφωνίᾳ et verborum consequentia
20 positum sit.

60.1. Nonagesimo tertio: *beatus homo, quem tu eru-*
dieris, domine. dicitis in Graeco non esse 'tu'. et verum est,
sed apud Latinos propter εὐφωνίαν positum. si enim dicamus:
'beatus homo, quem erudieris, domine', conpositionis ele-
25 gantiam non habebit. et quando dicitur 'domine' et apostrofa fit
278 ad dominum, nihil nocet sensui, si ponatur et 'tu'. **60.2.** in eodem: *et*
in malitia eorum disperdet eos. in Graeco dicitis non
esse praepositionem 'in', sed legi: *malitiam eorum disper-*
det. sciendum autem, quod et in Hebraeo et in cunctis inter-
5 pretibus positum sit: *in malitia eorum disperdet eos.*
si autem voluerimus legere: *malitiam eorum disperdet,*
id, quod in Septuaginta sequitur in fine versiculi 'eos', et superfluum
erit et vitiosum.

61.1. Nonagesimo septimo: *recordatus est miseri-*
10 *cordiae suae.* pro quo in Graeco invenisse vos dicitis: *miseri-*
cordiae suae Iacob; sed hic 'Iacob' nomen superfluum est.

62.1. Centesimo: *oculi mei ad fideles terrae, ut se-*
derent me cum. pro quo in Graeco invenisse vos dicitis: τοῦ
συγκαθῆσθαι αὐτοὺς μετ' ἐμοῦ. quis non talem fugiat interpreta-
15 tionem, ut verbum ad verbum exprimens dicat: 'ut consederent ipsi mecum'?

63.1. Centesimo primo: *vigilavi et factus sum sicut*
passer solitarius in tecto. et dicitis vos in Graeco inve-

(psalm): "Because gentleness came upon, and we shall be corrected."[166] You say that you have found in Greek: "gentleness ... upon us," but this is super-fluous.

59.1. On the Ninetieth (Psalm): "he will say to the Lord, 'you are my protector.'"[167] You say that in Greek it does not have "are." Let me explain to you more fully that among the Hebrews it has neither "are" nor "you," but among the Seventy and among the Latins these were added for the sake of euphony (εὐφωνία) and verbal flow.

60.1. On the Ninety-Third (Psalm): "Blessed is the man whom you instruct, O Lord."[168] You say that in Greek there is no "you." This is true, but among the Latins it was added for the sake of euphony (εὐφωνία). For if we were to say, "Blessed is the man whom (you) instruct, O Lord," it would not have literary elegance. When it says: "O Lord," and an *apostrofa* is made toward the Lord, there is no harm to the sense if "you" is added. **60.2.** In the same (psalm): "And in their wickedness he will destroy them."[169] You say that in Greek there is no preposition "in," but it should read: "he will destroy their wickedness." But it should be known that both the Hebrew and all the translators have: "in their wickedness he will destroy them." Furthermore, if we were to read: "he will destroy their wickedness," then what follows in the Seventy at the end of this short line, "them," would be superfluous and faulty.

61.1. On the Ninety-Seventh (Psalm): "He has remembered his mercy."[170] In place of this in Greek you say that you have found: "his mercy toward Jacob." But here the name "Jacob" is superfluous.

62.1. On the One Hundredth (Psalm): "My eyes are on the faithful of the land, that they may dwell with me."[171] In place of this in Greek you say that you found: τοῦ συγκαθῆσθαι αὐτοὺς μετ' ἐμοῦ. Who would not flee from such a translation, which, expressing word for word, says: "that they themselves may co-dwell with me"?

63.1. On the One Hundred and First (Psalm): "I watched, and I became as a lonely sparrow on the roof."[172] You say that in Greek you found ἐπὶ

---

166. Ps 89:10 (Heb 90:10), GPsal.
167. Ps 90:2 (Heb 91:2), GPsal.
168. Ps 93:12 (Heb 94:12), GPsal.
169. Ps 93:23 (Heb 94:23), GPsal.
170. Ps 97:3 (Heb 98:3), GPsal.
171. Ps 100:6 (Heb 101:6), GPsal.
172. Ps 101:8 (Heb 102:8), GPsal.

20 nisse ἐπὶ δώματι, quod antiqui codices Latinorum interpretati sunt 'in
aedificio'. δῶμα in orientalibus provinciis ipsum dicitur, quod
apud nos 'tectum'; in Palaestina enim et Aegypto, ubi vel scripti
sunt divini libri vel interpretati, non habent in tectis culmina, sed
δώματα, quae Romae vel solaria vel Maeniana vocant, id est plana
tecta, quae transversis trabibus sustentantur. denique et Petrus
279 in Actibus apostolorum, quando ascendit in δῶμα, in tectum aedi-
ficii ascendisse credendus est et, quando praecipitur nobis, ut
faciamus δώματι nostro coronam, hoc praecipitur, ut in tecto faciamus per circuitum quasdam eminentias, ne facilis in praeceps lapsus
5 sit. et in evangelio: *quae*, inquit, *auditis in aure, dicite*
super δώματα, id est *super tecta.* et in Esaia: *quid*
vobis est, quod omnes ascendistis in tecta
vana? et multa istius modi. **63.2.** in eodem: *factus sum sicut*
νυκτικόραξ *in domicilio.* quod similiter habetur in Graeco;
10 et quaeritis, quid significet νυκτικόραξ apud Latinos. in Hebraeo
pro nycticorace verbum 'bos' scriptum est, quod Aquila et Septuaginta et Theodotio et quinta editio 'nycticoracem' interpretati
sunt, Symmachus 'upupam', sexta editio 'noctuam', quod et nos
magis sequimur. denique, ubi apud nostros et Graecos legitur:
15 *factus sum sicut* νυκτικόραξ *in domicilio*, apud
Hebraeos dicitur: *factus sum sicut noctua in rui-*
nosis. plerique 'bubonem' contentiose significari putant. **63.3.** in
eodem: *a facie irae et indignationis tuae.* pro
quo in Graeco invenisse vos dicitis: *a facie irae tuae,*
20 cum manifestissimum sit, quod et apud Hebraeos et apud
septuaginta interpretes sic habet: ἀπὸ προσώπου τῆς ὀργῆς σου
καὶ τοῦ θυμοῦ σου. **63.4.** in eodem: *quoniam placuerunt*
servis tuis lapides eius et terrae eius
miserebuntur. pro terra in Hebraeo 'afar' positum est,
25 quod omnes χοῦν transtulerunt; et potest tam 'pulvis' quam
'humus', id est 'terra', interpretari.

δώματι, which the ancient codices of the Latins translated "on a building." In the eastern provinces δῶμα is the very word used for what we would say as "roof." For in Palestine and in Egypt, where the divine books were either written or translated, they do not have tops on their roofs, but δώματα, which the Romans call "terraces" or "balconies," that is, level roofs that are supported by crossing beams. So, in the Acts of the Apostles when Peter went up to the δῶμα, it should be understood that he went up to the "roof" of the building.[173] Moreover, when we are commanded to make a parapet for our δῶμα, this is a command to make elevated sections on the "roof" going all around so that someone does not easily fall off the edge.[174] In the gospel it says: "What you hear in the ear, speak on the δώματα," that is, "on the roofs," and in Isaiah, "What is wrong with you, that you all have gone up to vain roofs?"[175] There are many passages of this kind. **63.2.** In the same (psalm): "I became like a νυκτικόραξ in a house."[176] This is precisely what it has in Greek, and you ask what νυκτικόραξ means among the Latins. In Hebrew the word for *nycticorax* is written *bos*, which Aquila, the Seventy, Theodotion, and the fifth (*quinta*) edition rendered as *nycticorax*, whereas Symmachus translated it as "hoopoe," and the sixth (*sexta*) edition used "night owl," which we are more inclined to follow. So, where the Greeks and I put: "I became like a νυκτικόραξ in a house," among the Hebrews it says: "I became like a night owl among ruins." Most who interpret this stringently think that the "horned owl" is meant. **63.3.** In the same (psalm): "from the face of your anger and wrath."[177] In place of this in Greek you say that you found: "from the face of your anger." But it is entirely clear both among the Hebrews and among the Seventy Translators that it has as follows: ἀπὸ προσώπου τῆς ὀργῆς σου καὶ τοῦ θυμοῦ σου. **63.4.** In the same (psalm): "Because its stones were pleasing to your servants, and they will have mercy on its land."[178] In place of "land," in Hebrew it has *afar*, which all rendered as χοῦν. This can be translated both as "dust" and as "ground," that is, "land."

---

173. Acts 10:9.

174. Deut 22:8.

175. Matt 10:27; Isa 22:1 according to the OL tradition.

176. Ps 101:7 (Heb 102:7), GPsal, except GPsal transliterates the Greek into Latin: *nycticorax*.

177. Ps 101:11 (Heb 102:11), GPsal.

178. Ps 101:15 (Heb 102:15), GPsal.

280   **64.1.** Centesimo secundo: *non in perpetuo irascetur.*
pro quo in Graeco invenisse vos dicitis: *non in finem.* sed
verbum Hebraicum 'nese' et 'perpetuum' et 'finis' et 'victoria' pro
locorum intellegitur qualitate.

5   **65.1.** Centesimo tertio: *qui facis angelos tuos spiri-*
tus. pro quo in Graeco invenisse vos dicitis: ὁ ποιῶν τοὺς ἀγγέλους
αὐτοῦ, id est: *qui facit angelos suos.* a quibus breviter
quaerite, quomodo, cum ad deum sermo sit, quasi ad alium loquens
propheta repente mutetur. maxime cum sic incipiat: *domine,*

10   *deus meus, magnificatus es vehementer; con-*
fessionem et decorem induisti, et: *qui tegis in*
aquis superiora eius – id est caeli –, *qui ponis nubem*
ascensum tuum, qui ambulas super pennas
ventorum. et statim sequitur: *qui facis angelos tuos*

15   *spiritus et ministros tuos ignem urentem. qui*
fundasti terram super stabilitatem suam. et
post paululum: *ab increpatione tua fugient, a voce*
tonitrui tui formidabunt. et: *in loco, quem fun-*
dasti eis. qui emittis fontes in convallibus. et

20   illud: *ut educas panem de terra.* si ergo omnia ad se-
cundam personam sunt, id est ad deum, quomodo in uno versiculo tertia persona subito et extra ordinem introducitur? **65.2.** in
eodem: *a voce tonitrui tui formidabunt.* habet et in
Hebraeo *tonitrui tui*; et miror, quomodo apud Latinos

25   scriptorum errore subtractum sit. **65.3.** in eodem: *hoc mare ma-*
gnum et spatiosum manibus. dicitis in Graeco 'manibus'

281 non haberi. et ego novi, sed ex Hebraico et de Theodotionis editione in Septuaginta sub asterisco additum est. denique et in Hebraeo
ita scriptum est: 'ze haiam gadol uarab idaim', quod
Aquila sic interpretatus est: αὐλὴ καὶ πλατεῖα χερσὶν et omnes

5   interpretes: αὕτη ἡ θάλασσα ἡ μεγάλη καὶ εὐρύχωρος χερσίν. et hoc

64.1. On the One Hundred and Second (Psalm): "Not forever will he be angry."[179] In place of this in Greek you say that you found: "Not to the end." But the Hebrew word *nese* can have the sense "forever," "end," and "victory" depending on the nature of the passage.

65.1. On the One Hundred and Third (Psalm): "You who make your angels spirits."[180] In place of this in Greek you say that you found: ὁ ποιῶν τοὺς ἀγγέλους αὐτοῦ, that is, "he who makes his angels." On this matter, ask yourself briefly: Since the discourse is directed toward God, why would the prophet suddenly switch around, as if he were speaking to someone else? This is especially clear when we observe how he begins: "Lord, my God, you are exceedingly magnified; you have put on praise and beauty;" and: "you who cover with water the upper parts of it"—that is, "of heaven"— "you who make the cloud your ascent, you who walk upon the wings of the winds."[181] And then immediately follows: "You who make your angels spirits, and your ministers a flaming fire; you who founded the earth upon its firmness."[182] And after a little while: "At your rebuke they will flee, at the sound of your thunder they will be afraid;" and, "in the place that you founded for them;" "you who send forth springs in the valleys;" and this: "so that you might bring out bread from the earth."[183] If, then, all these passages are directed unto the second person, that is, unto God, why in a single verse would the third person be introduced suddenly and out of sequence? **65.2.** In the same (psalm): "At the sound of your thunder they will be afraid."[184] The Hebrew also has "of your thunder." I am astonished at how this was left out among the Latins by an error of the scribes! **65.3.** In the same (psalm): "this sea, great and spacious in hands."[185] You say that in Greek it does not have "in hands." I am aware of this, but it was added in the Septuagint under asterisk out of the Hebrew from the edition of Theodotion. In fact, in Hebrew it is written as: *ze haiam gadol uarab idaim.* Aquila translated it like this: αὐλὴ καὶ πλατεῖα χερσίν, and all the other translators: αὕτη ἡ θάλασσα ἡ μεγάλη καὶ εὐρύχωρος χερσίν. This is

---

179. Ps 102:9 (Heb 103:9), GPsal, except GPsal has *perpetuum* instead of *perpetuo.*
180. Ps 103:4 (Heb 104:4), GPsal.
181. Ps 103:1, 3 (Heb 104:1, 3), GPsal, except GPsal has *pinnas* instead of *pennas.*
182. Ps 103:4–5a (Heb 104:4–5a), GPsal.
183. Ps 103:7, 8, 10, 14 (Heb 104:7, 8, 10, 14), GPsal, except GPsal has *locum* instead of *loco.*
184. Ps 103:7 (Heb 104:7), GPsal.
185. Ps 103:25 (Heb 104:25), GPsal.

secundum Hebraicam dicitur proprietatem μεταφορικῶς, quod
quasi expansas manus habeat et in se cuncta suscipiat. **65.4.** in eodem:
ut educas panem de terra. pro quo invenisse vos dicitis:
ut educat; sed non potest aliud ad ipsum, aliud de ipso dici.

10 aut omnia quasi ad deum loquebatur propheta aut omnia ad alium
de eo referebat. cum autem pleraque ad ipsum dirigantur, et ea, quae
ambigua sunt, ad ipsius personam dirigenda sunt. **65.5.** in eodem:
herodii domus dux est eorum. pro herodio, quod in
Hebraeo dicitur 'asida', Symmachus ἰκτῖνα, id est 'milvum', interpre-

15 tatus est. denique et nos ita vertimus in Latinum: *ibi aves nidificabunt; milvi abies domus est,* quod scilicet semper in
excelsis et arduis arboribus nidos facere consueverit. unde et sexta
editio manifestius interpretata est: *milvo cupressi ad nidifi-
candum.* pro abietibus autem et cupressis in Hebraeo ponitur

20 'barusim', quod magis abietes quam κυπαρίσσους significat. **65.6.** in
eodem: *petra refugium erinaciis.* pro quo in Hebraeo
positum est 'sphannim' et omnes τοῖς χοιρογρυλλίοις uoce simili

282 transtulerunt exceptis Septuaginta, qui 'lepores' interpretati sunt.
sciendum autem animal esse non maius ericio, habens similitudinem
muris et ursi, unde et in Palaestina ἀρκόμυς dicitur. et magna
est in istis regionibus huius generis abundantia semperque in

5 cavernis petrarum et terrae foveis habitare consuerunt.
    66.1. Centesimo quarto: *dedit terra eorum ranas.* pro
quo in Graeco ἐξῆρψεν vos legisse dixistis. quod potest ita interpretari: 'ebullivit terra eorum ranas'; sed et in hoc nulla est in
sensu mutatio et nos antiquam interpretationem sequentes, quod

10 non nocebat, mutare noluimus. **66.2.** in eodem: *et contrivit lignum finium eorum.* pro quo in Graeco invenisse vos dicitis
omne lignum. sed et hoc additum est et superfluum. **66.3.** in eodem:
quoniam memor fuit verbi sancti sui, quod

said metaphorically (μεταφορικῶς) according to the particular idiom of Hebrew, as if the sea holds its hands outstretched and receives all things in itself. **65.4.** In the same (psalm): "so that you might bring out bread from the earth."[186] In place of this you say that you found: "so that he might bring out." But it is not possible to have one thing said *to* a person and then to have something else said *about* that person. Either the prophet said everything as if to God, or else he addressed everything to someone else about God. So, since most of these things are directed to him, the statements that are ambiguous should also be understood as directed to his person. **65.5.** In the same (psalm): "The house of the heron is their leader."[187] In place of "heron," which in Hebrew reads *asida*, Symmachus translated ἰκτῖνα, that is, "kite." In fact, we also translate into Latin thus: "There the birds will build their nests; the house of the kite is the silver fir," evidently because it is their custom always to build their nests in high and lofty trees. On this basis, the sixth edition (*sexta editio*) translated more clearly: "for the kite, cypress trees are for building nests." However, in place of "silver firs" or "cypress trees," in Hebrew it has *barusim*, which means "silver firs," rather than κυπαρίσσους. **65.6.** In the same (psalm): "The rock is a refuge for hedgehogs."[188] In place of this the Hebrew has *sphannim*, and all translated with a similar voice τοῖς χοιρογρυλλίοις, except for the Seventy, who translated "hares." Now, it should be known that this animal is no larger than a hedgehog, bearing some resemblance to a rat and a bear. From this it is called ἀρκόμυς in Palestine. There is a great number of this species in those regions, where they habitually dwell in rocky caves and in holes in the ground.

66.1. On the One Hundred and Fourth (Psalm): "Their land gave frogs."[189] In place of this in Greek you said that you read: ἐξῆρψεν, which can be translated thus: "their land brought forth frogs." But in this there is no change in the sense; and so we, following the ancient translation that did no harm, did not wish to change it. **66.2.** In the same (psalm): "And he broke the tree of their borders."[190] In place of this in Greek you say that you found: "every tree." But this was added and is superfluous. **66.3.** In the same (psalm): "Because he was mindful of his holy word, which he had

---

186. Ps 103:14 (Heb 104:14), GPsal.
187. Ps 103:17 (Heb 104:17), GPsal, except GPsal has *erodii* instead of *herodii*.
188. Ps 103:18 (Heb 104:18), GPsal.
189. Ps 104:30 (Heb 105:30), GPsal.
190. Ps 104:33 (Heb 105:33), GPsal.

habuit ad Abraham, puerum suum. pro quo in Graeco

15 legisse vos dicitis ὅν διέθετο, id est: *quod disposuit.* ita enim
et in Hebraeo et apud septuaginta habetur interpretes: ὅτι ἐμνήσθη
τοῦ λόγου τοῦ ἁγίου αὐτοῦ, τοῦ πρὸς Ἀβραὰμ τὸν δοῦλον αὐτοῦ.
ergo, quod in Graeco dicitur ὅν διέθετο, in hoc loco et superfluum
est et radendum.

20   **67.1.** Centesimo quinto: *confitemini domino, quo-*
niam bonus. pro quo in Graeco legisse vos dicitis: *quoniam*
χρηστός, id est *suavis.* sed sciendum, quod χρηστός et in 'bonum'
et in 'suave' verti potest. denique et in Hebraeo ita scriptum est:

283 'chi tob', quod omnes voce simili transtulerunt: *quia bonus.* ex
quo perspicuum est, quod et χρηστὸς 'bonus' intellegatur. **67.2.** in eodem:
non fuerunt memores multitudinis misericor-
diae tuae. dicitis, quod in Graeco inveneritis: *et non fue-*

5 *runt memores.* 'et' coniunctio superflua est. **67.3.** in eodem: *et in-*
ritaverunt ascendentes in mare, Mare Ru-
brum. pro quo in Graeco invenisse vos dicitis; καὶ παρεπίκραναν,
et putatis verbum e verbo debere transferri: 'et amaricaverunt'. sed et haec interpretatio 'adnullationi' consimilis est sive 'ad-

10 nihilationi'. legite Ezechiel et invenietis παραπικρασμὸς 'inritationem
et exacerbationem' semper expressum, ubi dicitur: οἶκος παραπικραίνων, id est 'domus exasperans'. **67.4.** in eodem: *et vidit,*
cum tribularentur, et audivit orationem
eorum. quidquid extra hoc in Graeco invenisse vos dixistis,

15 superfluum est.

        68.1. Centesimo sexto: *et statuit procellam eius*
in auram et silverunt fluctus eius. hoc ergo, quod
pro isto in Graeco invenisse vos dicitis: καὶ ἐπετίμησεν τῇ καταιγίδι
αὐτῆς καὶ ἔστη εἰς αὔραν, superfluum est. **68.2.** in eodem: *et deduxit*

20 *eos in portum voluntatis eorum.* pro quo in-

unto Abraham his servant."[191] In place of this in Greek you say that you read: ὃν διέθετο, that is, "which he set forth." But this is what is found both in the Hebrew and among the Seventy Translators: ὅτι ἐμνήσθη τοῦ λόγου τοῦ ἁγίου αὐτοῦ, τοῦ πρὸς Αβρααμ τὸν δοῦλον αὐτοῦ. Therefore, what is read in the Greek, ὃν διέθετο, in this passage is superfluous and should be scratched out.

67.1. On the One Hundred and Fifth (Psalm): "Give thanks to the Lord, because he is good."[192] In place of this in Greek you say that you read: "because he is χρηστός," that is, "pleasant." But it should be known that χρηστός can be translated both as "pleasant" and as "good." In fact, in Hebrew it is written thus: *chi tob*, which all translated with similar voice: "for he is good." From this it is clear that χρηστός may also be understood as "good." 67.2. In the same (psalm): "They were not mindful of the multitude of your mercy."[193] You say that in Greek you found: "And they were not mindful." But the conjunction "and" is superfluous. 67.3. In the same (psalm): "And they provoked, going up into the sea, the Red Sea."[194] In place of this in Greek you say that you found: καὶ παρεπίκραναν, and you think this should be translated word for word, "And they embitterized." But this translation is quite similar to "nothingization" or "nothingafication."[195] Read Ezekiel, and you will find that παραπικρασμός is always rendered as "provocation" and "exasperation," where it says: οἶκος παραπικραίνων, that is, "a vexing house."[196] 67.4. In the same (psalm): "And he saw when they were afflicted, and he heard their prayer."[197] Whatever you say that you found in Greek beyond this, it is superfluous.

68.1. On the One Hundred and Sixth (Psalm): "And he settled its tempest into a breeze; and its waves were silent."[198] Therefore, what you say that you found instead of this in Greek: καὶ ἐπετίμησεν τῇ καταιγίδι αὐτῆς καὶ ἔστη εἰς αὔραν, is superfluous. 68.2. In the same (psalm): "And he led them into the haven of their wish."[199] In place of this you say that you found:

---

191. Ps 104:42 (Heb 105:42), GPsal.
192. Ps 105:1 (Heb 106:1), GPsal.
193. Ps 105:7a (Heb 106:7a), GPsal.
194. Ps 105:7b (Heb 106:7b), GPsal.
195. Cf. *Ep.* 106.57.3.
196. See Ezek 2:5–8; 3:9, 26–27; 12:2–3, 9, 25, 27; 17:12; 24:3; 44:6.
197. Ps 105:44 (Heb 106:44), GPsal, except GPsal has *audiret* instead of *audivit*.
198. Ps 106:29 (Heb 107:29), GPsal.
199. Ps 106:30 (Heb 107:30), GPsal.

venisse vos dicitis: *in portum voluntatis suae.* sed in
Hebraeo non habet 'ephsau', quod 'voluntatis suae' significat,
sed 'ephsam', quod 'voluntatis eorum' sonat.

284   **69.1.** Centesimo septimo: *exurge, gloria mea.* quod dicitis in
Latino non esse, recte in isto psalmo non habet, quia nec apud
Hebraeos nec apud ullum interpretum repperitur, sed habetur in
quinquagesimo sexto psalmo, de quo mihi videtur a quodam in istum
5   locum esse translatum. **69.2.** in eodem: *mihi alienigenae amici
facti sunt.* pro quo in Graeco invenisse vos dicitis ὑπετάγησαν,
hoc est 'subditi sunt'. sed hoc in quinquagesimo nono psalmo
scriptum est; in praesenti autem ita apud omnes invenimus trans-
latores: ἐμοὶ ἀλλόφυλοι ἐφιλίασαν, id est *amici facti sunt,*
10   quod Hebraice dicitur 'ethrobe'.

        70.1. Centesimo nono: *virgam virtutis tuae emittet
dominus ex Sion.* dicitis vos in Graecis codicibus non
legisse 'virtutis tuae', quod manifeste et in Herbaeo et in septuaginta interpretibus habet. **70.2.** in eodem: *dominare in medio
15   inimicorum tuorum.* dicitis in Graeco legi: *et dominare.* sed hoc nec in Hebraeo habetur nec apud Septuaginta
et superfluum est.

        71.1. Centesimo decimo: *confitebor tibi, domine, in
toto corde.* in Graeco invenisse vos dicitis: *in toto corde
20   meo.* sed et hoc hic superfluum est.

        72.1. Centesimo tertio decimo: *deus autem noster in
caelo.* pro quo in Graeco legisse vos dicitis: *in caelo et in
terra.* sed et hoc hic superfluum est.

285   **73.1.** Centesimo quarto decimo: *et in diebus meis invocabo te.* dicitis, quod in Graeco non sit 'te', et bene; e vestris
quoque codicibus eradendum est. **73.2.** in ipso: *placebo domino*

"into the haven of his wish." But in Hebrew, it does not have *ephsau*, which means "his wish," but rather *ephsam*, which means "their wish."

69.1. On the One Hundred and Seventh (Psalm): "Arise, my glory."[200] You say that this is not in the Latin—that is correct, it is not found in this psalm, since it appears neither among the Hebrews nor in any translator. But it does appear in the Fifty-Sixth Psalm.[201] It seems to me that someone transferred it from that passage to this one. **69.2.** In the same (psalm): "Foreign tribes have become friends to me."[202] In place of this, you say that in Greek you found: ὑπετάγησαν, that is, "were subjected." But this is what was written in the Fifty-Ninth Psalm.[203] In the present passage, however, we find in all the translators the following: ἐμοὶ ἀλλόφυλοι ἐφιλίασαν, that is, "became friends," which in Hebrew reads *ethrohe*.

70.1. On the One Hundred and Ninth (Psalm): "The Lord will send forth the staff of your strength out of Zion."[204] You say that you did not read "of your strength" in the Greek codices; but this is clearly in the Hebrew and in the Seventy Translators. **70.2.** In the same (psalm): "Rule in the midst of your enemies!"[205] You say that in Greek it reads, "And rule." But this is found neither in the Hebrew nor among the Seventy, and it is superfluous.

71.1. On the One Hundred and Tenth (Psalm): "I will confess to you, O Lord, with all heart."[206] In Greek you say that you found: "with all my heart." But here this is superfluous.

72.1. On the One Hundred and Thirteenth (Psalm): "But our God is in the heaven."[207] In place of this you say that in Greek you read: "in the heaven and on the earth." But this also is superfluous.

73.1. On the One Hundred and Fourteenth (Psalm): "And in my days I will call on you."[208] You say that in Greek it does not have "you," and you are correct. This should be scratched out from your codices, too. **73.2.** In this very (psalm): "I will be pleasing to the Lord in the land of the living."[209]

---

200. Ps 107:3 (Heb 108:3). This is a miscopying of the GPsal text.
201. Ps 56:9 (Heb 57:9).
202. Ps 107:10 (Heb 108:10), GPsal.
203. Ps 59:10 (Heb 60:10).
204. Ps 109:2a (Heb 110:2a), GPsal.
205. Ps 109:2b (Heb 110:2b), GPsal.
206. Ps 110:1 (Heb 111:1). GPsal gives the text with *meo: in toto corde meo*, "with all my heart."
207. Ps 113:11 (Heb 115:3), GPsal.
208. Ps 114:2 (Heb 116:2), GPsal.
209. Ps 114:9 (Heb 116:9), GPsal.

in regione vivorum. pro quo in Graeco legisse vos dicitis:
5 *placebo in conspectu domini.* sed hoc superfluum est.

　　　74.1. Centesimo septimo decimo: *et in nomine domini,*
quia ultus sum in eos. dicitis 'quia' in Graecis codicibus
non inveniri; sed et in Latinis sub asterisco legendum est.

　　　75.1. Centesimo octavo decimo: *et meditabar in man-*
10 *datis tuis, quae dilexi.* in Graeco *vehementer* additum legisse vos dicitis; sed hoc superfluum est. 75.2. in eodem: *le-*
vavi manus meas ad mandata tua, quae dilexi.
　in Graeco legisse vos dicitis: *ad mandata tua, <quae dilexi*
vehementer,> sed hoc superfluum est. 75.3. in eodem: *cogitavi*
15 *vias meas.* in Graeco *vias tuas* legisse vos dicitis, sed
hoc superfluum est et rectius 'meas' legitur. 75.4. in eodem: *et averti*
pedes meos in testimonia tua. in Graeco legisse vos
dicitis: *et avertisti.* sed et hoc superfluum est. 75.5. in eodem: *ego*
autem in toto corde scrutabor mandata tua.
20 in Graeco *in toto corde meo* legisse vos dicitis; sed hic 'meo'
286 superfluum est. 75.6. in eodem: *anima mea in manibus meis*
semper; et legem tuam non sum oblitus. pro quo in
Graeco legisse vos dicitis: *anima mea in manibus tuis*
semper. sed sciendum et apud Hebraeos et apud Septuaginta
5 et omnes alios interpretes scriptum esse 'in manibus meis', et
non 'in manibus tuis', quod Hebraice dicitur 'bachaffi'; et omnes
apud Graecos ecclesiastici interpretes istum locum sic edisserunt
et est breviter hic sensus: 'cottidie periclitor et quasi in manibus
meis sanguinem meum porto et tamen legem tuam non obliviscor'.
10 75.7. in eodem: *exitus aquarum deduxerunt oculi mei,*
quia non custodierunt legem tuam. pro quo in
Graeco legisse vos dicitis, *quia non custodivi legem*
tuam. sed hoc superfluum est, quia et in Hebraeo legitur: *rivi*

In place of this you say that you read in Greek: "I will be pleasing in the sight of the Lord." But this is superfluous.

74.1. On the One Hundred and Seventeenth (Psalm): "and in the name of the Lord, because I have taken vengeance on them."[210] You say that in the Greek codices "because" is not found, but also in the Latin codices it should be read under asterisk.

75.1. On the One Hundred and Eighteenth (Psalm): "And I meditated on your commandments, which I loved."[211] You say that you read in Greek that "intensely" is added, but this is superfluous. **75.2.** In the same (psalm): "I lifted up my hands unto your commandments, which I loved."[212] You say that you read in Greek: "unto your commandments, which I loved intensely." But this is superfluous. **75.3.** In the same (psalm): "I have contemplated my ways."[213] In Greek you say that you read: "your ways," but this is superfluous. The correct reading is "my." **75.4.** In the same (psalm): "And I turned my feet unto your testimonies."[214] You say that in Greek you read: "you turned." But this is also superfluous. **75.5.** In the same psalm: "But I will search out your commands with all heart."[215] You say that you read in Greek: "with all my heart." But this "my" is superfluous. **75.6.** In the same (psalm): "My life is in my hands always, and I have not forgotten your law."[216] In place of this in Greek you say that you read: "My life is in your hands always." But it should be known that among the Hebrews and among the Seventy and all other translators it is written, "in my hands," which in Hebrew reads *bachaffi*, and not "in your hands." Furthermore, this is how all the ecclesiastical interpreters among the Greeks explain this passage. Briefly, this is the sense: "Every day I am exposed to danger as if carrying my blood in my hands, and in spite of this I do not forget your law." **75.7.** In the same (psalm): "My eyes let down issues of water, because they did not keep your law."[217] In place of this in Greek you say that you read: "because I did not keep your law." But this is superfluous, because in the

---

210. Ps 117:10 (Heb 118:10), GPsal.

211. Ps 118:47 (Heb 119:47), GPsal.

212. Ps 118:48 (Heb 119:48), GPsal. On the GPsal text, see the commentary.

213. Ps 118:59a (Heb 119:59a), GPsal.

214. Ps 118:59b (Heb 119:59b). The texts of GPsal and *Epist.* 106 are uncertain; see the commentary.

215. Ps 118:69 (Heb 119:69), GPsal.

216. Ps 118:109 (Heb 119:109), GPsal.

217. Ps 118:136 (Heb 119:136), GPsal.

aquarum fluebant de oculis meis, quia non cu-
15 *stodierunt legem tuam.* 75.8. in eodem: *pronuntiabit*
lingua mea eloquium tuum. pro 'pronuntiabit' in
Graeco φθέγξεται vos legisse dixistis, quod verbum, sive dicas
'pronuntiabit' sive 'effabitur' sive 'loquetur', id ipsum significat.
denique et nos de Hebraeo ita vertimus: *loquetur lingua*
20 *mea sermonem tuum.*

    76.1. Centesimo nono decimo: *domine, libera ani-*
mam meam a labiis iniquis, a lingua dolosa. in
Graeco legisse vos dicitis: *et a lingua dolosa.* 'et' superfluum est.

25   77.1. Centesimo vicesimo sexto: *beatus vir, qui inplebit*
287 *desiderium suum ex ipsis.* in Graeco dicitis 'vir' non
haberi, quod manifestissime et in Hebraeo et in septuaginta
interpretibus continetur.

    78.1. Centesimo vicesimo nono: *propter legem tuam*
5 *sustinuite, domine.* dicitis vos in Graeco invenisse: *prop-*
ter nomen tuum, et nos confitemur plura sic exemplaria
repperiri. sed quia veritati studemus, quid in Hebraeo sit, simpliciter debemus dicere: pro 'nomine' sive 'lege' apud eos legitur
'thira', quod Aquila interpretatus est φόβον, hoc est 'timorem',
10 Symmachus et Theodotion νόμον, id est 'legem', putantes 'thora'
propter litterarum similitudinem iod et vav, quae tantum magni-
tudine distinguntur. quinta editio 'terrorem' interpretata est,
sexta 'verbum'.

    79.1. Centesimo tricesimo primo: *sicut iuravit domino,*
15 *votom vovit deo Iacob.* pro eo, quod nos interpretati
sumus 'votum vovit', in Graeco ηὔξατο legisse vos dicitis et putatis
interpretari debuisse 'oravit', sed hoc male; εὐχὴ enim pro
locorum qualitate et orationem et votum significat secundum
illud: *redde deo vota tua,* id est τὰς εὐχάς σου.

20   80.1. Centesimo tricesimo quinto: *qui fecit luminaria*
magna. dicitis, quia in Graeco inveneritis: *magna solus;*
sed hoc de superiori versiculo est, ubi legimus: *qui fecit*

Hebrew it reads: "Streams of water flowed from my eyes, because they did not keep your law." 75.8. In the same (psalm): "My tongue will announce your declaration."[218] In place of "announce," you said that in Greek you read: φθέγξεται. But this word, whether you say, "announce," "utter," or "speak," means the same thing. In fact, we translate thus from the Hebrew: "My tongue will speak your word."

76.1. On the One Hundred and Nineteenth (Psalm): "O Lord, free my soul from unjust lips, from a deceitful tongue."[219] In Greek you say that you read: "and from a deceitful tongue." The "and" is superfluous.

77.1. On the One Hundred and Twenty-Sixth (Psalm): "Blessed is the man who will fulfill his desire with them."[220] In Greek you say that it does not have "man," but it clearly is contained in both the Hebrew and in the Seventy Translators.

78.1. On the One Hundred and Twenty-Ninth (Psalm): "For the sake of your law, I wait on you, O Lord."[221] You say that you found in Greek: "For the sake of your name." We acknowledge that many such copies are found. But because we are zealous for the truth, that is, for what is in the Hebrew, we must plainly say: In place of "name" or "law" among the Hebrews it reads *thira*, which Aquila translated as φόβον, that is, "fear," but which Symmachus and Theodotion translated as νόμον, that is, "law," thinking that it was *thora* due to the similarity of the letters *iod* and *uau*, which are distinguished only by size. The fifth edition (*quinta*) translated "terror," and the sixth edition (*sexta*) translated "word."

79.1. On the One Hundred and Thirty-First (Psalm): "Just as he swore to the Lord; he vowed a vow to the God of Jacob."[222] In place of what we translated as "he vowed a vow," you say that you read in Greek ηὔξατο, and you think that it should be translated, "he prayed." But that is incorrect. For depending on the nature of the passage εὐχή can mean both "prayer" and "vow," as in this phrase: "Render to God your vows," that is, τὰς εὐχάς σου.

80.1. On the One Hundred and Thirty-Fifth (Psalm): "who made the great lights."[223] You say that in Greek you found: "(who) alone (made the) great (lights)." But this is from the above verse, where we read: "who alone

218. Ps 118:172 (Heb 119:172), GPsal.
219. Ps 119:2 (Heb 120:2), GPsal.
220. Ps 126:5 (Heb 127:5), GPsal.
221. Ps 129:4 (Heb 130:4–5), GPsal.
222. Ps 131:2 (Heb 132:2), GPsal.
223. Ps 135:7 (Heb 136:7), GPsal.

mirabilia magna solus. ibi ergo legendum est et hic
quasi superfluum non scribendum.

25   **81.1.** Centesimo tricesimo septimo: *quoniam magni-*
288 *ficasti super omne nomen sanctum tuum.* in
Graeco repperisse vos dicitis: *super omnes.* sed in Septuaginta
ita legitur: ὅτι ἐμεγάλυνας ἐπὶ πᾶν τὸ ὄνομα τὸ ἅγιόν σου, sicuti
et nos in Latinum vertimus. ceterum apud Hebraeos ita esse
5   cognoscite: *quia magnificasti super omne nomen*
tuum verbum tuum. iuxta editionem autem Latinam hic
sensus est: 'quoniam magnificasti super omne nomen, hoc
est, quod in caelo et in terra dici potest sanctum, filium tuum'.

          82.1. Centesimo tricesimo octavo: *quia non est sermo in*
10 *lingua mea.* pro quo in Graeco legisse vos dicitis: *quia non*
est dolus in lingua mea, quod solum sexta editio interpretata est. ceterum et apud Septuaginta et apud omnes interpretes
et ipsum Hebraicum vel λαλιὰν vel λόγον, id est 'eloquium' et 'verbum', scriptum habet. denique Hebraice 'mala' dicitur.

15   **83.1.** Centesimo tricesimo nono: *funes extenderunt in*
laqueum. pro quo in Graeco invenisse vos dicitis: *funes ex-*
tenderunt laqueum pedibus meis. sed hoc in hoc loco
superfluum est. **83.2.** in eodem pro eo, quod est: *habitabunt*
recti cum vultu tuo, in Graeco repperisse vos dicitis:
20 *et habitabunt;* sed hic 'et' coniunctio superflua est.

          84.1. Centesimo quadragesimo: *dissipata sunt ossa*
nostra secus infernum. pro quo in Graeco legisse vos
dicitis: *ossa eorum.* sed et hoc superfluum est.

289   **85.1.** Centesimo quadragesimo sexto: *nec in tibiis viri*
bene placitum erit ei. pro 'ei' 'domino' legisse vos dicitis,
quod non habetur.

          86.1. Ideo autem, quod et vos in fine scedulae quaeritis et sanc-
5   tus filius meus Avitus frequenter efflagitat, quomodo Graeca inter-
pretanda sunt verba, breviter adnotavi. νεομηνία mensis

did great wonders."[224] Therefore, it should be read there, but here it should not be written since it is superfluous.

81.1. On the One Hundred and Thirty-Seventh (Psalm): "Because you magnified your Holy (one) above every name."[225] In Greek you say that you found: "above all (people)." But in the Seventy it reads thus: ὅτι ἐμεγάλυνας ἐπὶ πᾶν τὸ ὄνομα τὸ ἅγιόν σου, just as we translated into Latin. Besides, you should know that among the Hebrews it is thus: "Because you magnified your Word above all your name." But according to the Latin edition, this is the sense: "Because you magnified your holy Son above every name, that is, (above every name) that can be spoken in heaven and on earth."

82.1. On the One Hundred and Thirty-Eighth (Psalm): "because there is no discourse on my tongue."[226] In place of this in Greek you say that you read: "because there is no deceit on my tongue," which only the sixth edition (*sexta editio*) translated. Otherwise, among the Seventy, among all (other) translators, and in the Hebrew itself it has written λαλιάν or λόγον, that is, "speech" or "word." In fact, in Hebrew it reads *mala*.

83.1. On the One Hundred and Thirty-Ninth (Psalm): "They stretched out cords as a snare."[227] In place of this in Greek you say that you found: "They stretched out cords, a snare for my feet." But in this passage, this is superfluous. **83.2.** In the same (psalm), in place of: "The upright will dwell with your countenance," in Greek you say that you found: "And (the upright) will dwell."[228] But here the conjunction "and" is superfluous.

84.1. On the One Hundred and Fortieth (Psalm): "Our bones were scattered by the side of the inferno."[229] In place of this in Greek you say that you read: "their bones." But this is also superfluous.

85.1. On the One Hundred and Forty-Sixth (Psalm): "Nor will he take pleasure in the legs of a man."[230] In place of "He," you say that you read: "the Lord." But it does not have this.

86.1. Finally, because you request it at the end of your note, and because my holy brother Avitus frequently demands it, I will briefly comment on how certain Greek words should be translated. νεομηνία is the

---

224. Ps 135:4 (LXX).
225. Ps 137:2 (Heb 138:2), GPsal.
226. Ps 138:4 (Heb 139:4), GPsal.
227. Ps 139:6 (Heb 140:6), GPsal.
228. Ps 139:14 (Heb 140:14), GPsal.
229. Ps 140:7 (Heb 141:7), GPsal.
230. Ps 146:10 (Heb 147:10), GPsal.

exordium est, quod nos secundum Latinae linguae proprietatem
kalendas possumus dicere. verum quia apud Hebraeos mensis
secundum lunae cursum supputatur et apud Graecos μήνη luna
10 dicitur, νεομηνία quasi nova luna appellatur. **86.2.** ἔρημος autem desertum vel solitudinem significat, θρόνος sedem vel solium, νυκτικόραξ,
ut diximus, noctuam. κυνόμυια non, ut Latini interpretati sunt,
'musca canina' dicitur per υ Graecam litteram, sed iuxta Hebraicam intellegentiam per δίφθογγον debet scribi οι, ut sit κοινόμυια,
15 id est 'omne muscarum genus', quod Aquila πάνμικτον, id est 'omnimodam muscam', interpretatus est. **86.3.** λαξευτήριον autem, pro quo
Latinus 'asciam' vertit, nos genus ferramenti interpretamur, quo
lapides dolantur. denique ex Hebraeo vertentes ita diximus: *et*
nunc sculpturas eius pariter bipinne et do-
20 *latoriis deraserunt;* λαξευτήριον ergo dolatorium dici
potest.

beginning of the month. We, according to the particular idiom of the Latin language, can express this as "Kalends." But because among the Hebrews the month is calculated according to the course of the moon, and because among the Greeks the word for "moon" is μήνη, νεομηνία means, as it were, "new moon." **86.2.** Furthermore, ἔρημος means "desert" or "solitude," θρόνος means "seat" or "throne," and νυκτικόραξ, as we said, means "night owl." κυνόμυια does not mean "dog-fly," as the Latins translate it, as if written with the Greek letter υ. Rather, in keeping with the Hebrew understanding it should be written with the diphthong (δίφθογγον) οι, so that it is κοινόμυια, that is, "every species of flies." Aquila translated this as πάνμικτον, that is, "fly of every kind." **86.3.** And as for λαξευτήριον, in place of which the Latin rendered "hatchet," we interpret it to be a type of iron tool with which stones are hewed. So, translating from the Hebrew we said thus: "And now they have together cut down its carved works with axe and hewers."[231] Therefore, λαξευτήριον can be rendered "hewer."

---

231. Ps 73:6 (Heb 74:6).

COMMENTARY

1.1.9. *barbara Getarum lingua*, "a barbarian tongue from among the Getae." The Getae were a Thracian tribe on the Lower Danube river who were depicted in early Greek sources as brave and just among the Thracians. Down to Roman imperial times they proved difficult to subjugate, eventually coming under Roman control in the first century CE. By late antiquity, the Getae had been absorbed into other tribal identities such as Germanic and Slavic.[1] Jerome is invoking the rustic image associated with this identity as an ironic contrast with the supposed sophistication of the Greeks, who (he says) have shown less interest in the Hebrew truth than have Sunnia and Fretela.

1.1.9. *Hebraicam ... veritatem*. On the "Hebrew truth" (*hebraica veritas*), see also **2.3**; **7.2**; **9.5**; **11.2**; **41.6**; **46.4**; **78.1**; introduction, §8.1. Jerome began his study of Hebrew while living in the desert of Chalcis in the mid-370s, but he became more serious about learning it after he relocated to Rome around 382. By the early 390s, he began using the phrase *hebraica veritas* to represent the Hebrew text as the standard for correcting Greek and Latin copies.[2] For example, see *Comm. Eccl.* 8:13 (*iuxta sensus Hebraici veritatem*); *Qu. hebr. Gen.* Pref.; 13:1–4; *Pref. IH Ps.* 2; *Pref. Kings* 3; and many other passages in his letters and commentaries.[3]

---

1. Iris von Bredow, "Getae," in *Brill's New Pauly: Encyclopaedia of the Ancient World*, ed. Hubert Cancik and Helmuth Schneider (Leiden: Brill, 2004), 842–43.

2. Kamesar, *Jerome*, 42–43. See also Jay, *L'exégèse de saint Jérôme*, 89–102; and Monika Ozóg, "Saint Jerome and *Veritas Hebraica* on the Basis of the Correspondence with Saint Augustine," *Vox Patrum* 30 (2010): 511–19.

3. E.g., *Ep.* 49.19.1; 53.3.6; 57.7.4; 57.9.7; 65.9.3; 71.5.3; 72.2.1; 78.2.2; 78.17.3; 78.35.2; 109.1.3; 121.2.5; 121.2.6; 122.2.1; *Comm. Os.* 8:1–4; 11:1–2; 13:3; *Comm. Joel*, Pref.; 3:1–3; *Comm. Am.* 5:7–9; *Comm. Obad.* 20–21; *Comm. Mich.*, Pref.; 2:9–10; 6:10–16; *Comm. Soph.*. 2:3–4; *Comm. Agg.* 1:6; *Comm. Mal.*, Pref.; 1:9–10; *Comm. Dan.* 3:91a; 4:5a; 10:21b; *Comm. Isa.* 2:13; 6:2–3; 7:17; 9:3–5; 22:15–25; 15:3–9; 24:14–15; 25:1–5; 42:1–4; 52:7–8; 60:15–16; *Comm. Ezech.* 9:6b–7a; 11:2b–12; 11:24–25; 16:13d;

When Jerome asks, "Who would believe that a barbarian tongue from among the Getae would seek the Hebrew truth?" he should not be taken to imply that Sunnia and Fretela accepted the authority of the Hebrew as he himself does. In fact, the challenges to the Gallican Psalter that Sunnia and Fretela make according to *Ep.* 106 imply that they do not operate with any sense of the authority of the Hebrew. It is possible that, in listing their objections to Jerome's translations, they inquired about the possible Hebrew basis for the peculiar form of Jerome's translation. If so, Jerome would have taken the opportunity to praise them for seeking the Hebrew truth, whether or not their inquiry into the Hebrew was sincere. See introduction, §6.1.

1.1.11–14. *in veritate … acceptus est illi,* "in truth … is acceptable to Him." Acts 10:34–35. This quotation is close to the Vulgate version, but here Jerome uses *cognovi quod,* "I recognize that" (Vulgate: *conperi quoniam,* "I ascertain that"), and makes "God" more explicit: "the one who fears God and does God's justice" (Vulgate: "the one who fears him and does justice," which matches the Greek).

1.2.4–7. *concident gladios suos … pugnare,* "They will cut their swords … to fight." Isaiah 2:4 according to the OL tradition.[4] Jerome's citation has some distinctive features, such as *lanceas,* "spears," in place of *zibynas* = ζιβύνας, "spears," and *pugnare,* "to fight," instead of *bellare* or *belligerare,* "to wage war." Jerome is likely quoting from memory, and he may be recollecting the Greek text and making his own ad hoc translation into Latin.

1.3.7–12. *pascetur lupus … bos comedent paleas,* "the wolf will graze … ox will eat straw." Isaiah 11:6–7 according to the OL tradition.[5] Jerome offers a few distinctive verbal forms (e.g., *requiescet* instead of *conquiescet,* "lie at rest"), and he also gives "lion, and bull" (= a few LXX manuscripts = MT) in place of other OL witnesses that have "bull, and lion" (= most LXX manuscripts).

2.1.14. *rem … maioris invidiae,* "an undertaking that will involve … even greater ill will." In the prefaces he wrote for his translations and treatises, Jerome often gave little attention to introducing the content of the work at hand. Instead, he devoted his efforts to explaining the importance

---

40:14–16; 40:35–43; 40:44–49; 41:22b–26; 42:1–12; 45:13–14; *Comm. Jer.* 2:23c–24; 22:13–17; 27:18–22; 28:3b–4; 28:12–14; 31:31–34; 31:38–40.

4. Roger Gryson, *Esaias 1–39,* VL 12.1 (Freiburg: Herder, 1987–1993), 97–98.

5. Gryson, *Esaias 1–39,* 354–57.

of the work, justifying his methodology, criticizing adversaries, and anticipating criticisms so that he might respond in advance.[6]

2.1.15–16. *eruditio conprobetur … iudicandum me omnibus praebeam,* "his erudition that is put on trial … I offer myself to be judged by all." Throughout his career, Jerome showed deep concern for his reputation as a Christian scholar, investing significant energy in prefaces and letters through which he crafted his persona as an advocate for asceticism and learned Christian culture.[7]

2.1.17. *iuxta digestionem schedulae vestrae,* "following the arrangement set out in your note." Sunnia and Fretela sent Jerome a list of corrections to the Gallican Psalter. He states that he will respond to what they set forth in their *schedula,* "sheet" or "note." Jerome often uses *scedula/schedula* in the plural for the "sheets" of a larger composition.[8] In the singular, this word typically refers to a letter, even just a short note.[9] By *schedulae vestrae,* "your note," Jerome probably refers to the letter that accompanied their list of corrections. This familiar phrase ("your note") gives the feel of a personal exchange between friends, as if Sunnia and Fretela wrote their learned friend Jerome a letter, and now he is cordially writing back to help them with their questions. In fact, the content of *Ep.* 106 suggests that their criticisms were sharp, and Jerome's replies are often pugnacious. The reality is that he is writing publicly to defend his reputation as a scholar.

---

6. See Andrew Cain, "Apology and Polemic in Jerome's Prefaces to His Biblical Scholarship," in *Hieronymus als Exeget und Theologe: Interdisziplinäre Zugänge zum Koheletkommentar des Hieronymus,* ed. Elisabeth Birnbaum and Ludger Schwienhorst-Schönberger (Leuven: Peeters, 2014), 107–28; and Canellis, *Jérôme: Préfaces aux livres de la Bible,* 174–79.

7. See Cain, *The Letters of Jerome*; Megan H. Williams, *The Monk and the Book: Jerome and the Making of Christian Scholarship* (Chicago: University of Chicago Press, 2006); and Mark Vessey, "Jerome's Origen: The Making of a Christian Literary Persona," *StPatr* 28 (1993): 135–45.

8. E.g., *Comm. Matt.,* Pref.; *Comm. Isa.* 13, Pref.; *Ep.* 84.1.1; *Ruf.* 3.4, 5, 18, 20, 26, 33, 34. In *Ep.* 60.11.3, Jerome mentions someone who spurns gold and instead desires *scedulas,* "sheets," i.e., "books." In the preface to IH Job, Jerome uses the plural form to refer to "poor sheets" (*pauperes scidulas*) as opposed to books on purple parchment or beautiful codices. On Jerome's writing materials in general, see Paulo E. Arns, *La technique du livre d'après saint Jérôme* (Paris: Boccard, 1953), 13–35.

9. E.g., *Ep.* 8.3.1; 9.1.1; 71.1.1; 71.4.3; see also *Ep.* 72.1.1; *Ruf.* 3.22. In *Ep.* 59.5.1, Jerome uses *extrema schedula,* "this final page" for the final segment of a longer letter. In *Vit. Hil.* 26, *schedula* is employed for a "sheet" containing a list.

The stakes are higher than is apparent based on the polite introduction to this treatise.

Jerome says that he plans to answer their objections in the order in which they asked them. For the most part, he works through passages in the book of Psalms in canonical order (see introduction, §3.2), so we may assume that the challenges raised by Sunnia and Fretela proceeded in this way. See also **86.1.4.**

2.1.18–19. *quid magis Hebraeis conveniat significem,* "I indicate what agrees more with the Hebrew." In the early sections of *Ep.* 106, Jerome speaks of the hexaplaric LXX Psalter as if it were a fully accurate and perfectly preserved representation of the Hebrew, such that if one understood the meaning of this Greek text, one would understand the proper sense of the Hebrew.[10] Although Jerome does not abandon his high regard for the hexaplaric LXX Psalter in *Ep.* 106, as this treatise progresses, he moderates his position on how closely aligned the hexaplaric edition is with the Hebrew. See introduction, §6.2.

2.2.22. Λουκιάνειος. Jerome calls the "popular" Septuagint text upon which Sunnia and Fretela base their questions "Lucianic."[11] The term comes from the presbyter Lucian of Antioch (ca. 250–312), a biblical scholar associated with the school of Antioch. He spent some portion of his life excommunicated from the church at Antioch and then died a martyr. A critical recension of Scripture that came to circulate widely in the region of Antioch was associated with his name by the fourth and fifth centuries. In modern research on the Greek Bible, biblical quotations in the commentaries of Theodoret of Cyrus and John Chrysostom have played a key role in identifying the type of biblical text that was current in Antioch and its environs in late antiquity. This text can be called Antiochene, and it has frequently also been labeled Lucianic, as Jerome does, although it is uncertain how this text type might be connected to the historical Lucian. Although Jerome considers the Lucianic Septuagint to be a corrupted text vis-à-vis the hexaplaric edition, in fact, the Lucianic (or Antiochene) text

---

10. Cf. Guillaume Bady, "La 'vérité hébraïque' ou la 'vérité des Hexaples' chez Jérôme d'après un passage de la *Lettre 106*," in *L'exégèse de saint Jérôme,* ed. Élie Ayroulet and Aline Canellis (Saint-Étienne: Publications de l'Université de Saint-Étienne, 2018), 91–99.

11. See also **2.4** (κοινή, i.e., *communis editio,* "common edition"); **3.1** (*vulgata editio,* "popular edition"); **4.1** (κοινή *editio*); **5.1** (*vulgata*); **13.1** (κοινή); **57.2** (κοινή). See introduction, §5.

preserves many early readings that may represent the original Old Greek translation.[12]

2.2.23. ἐξαπλοῖς *codicibus.* The hexaplaric edition was the text of the LXX based on the fifth column of Origen's Hexapla. In places where the Greek text was lacking material in relation to the Hebrew, Origen supplied the missing words from another Greek version, usually Theodotion. These words were marked with an asterisk. Wherever the Greek text had material that was absent from the Hebrew, Origen marked this with an obelus.[13] Copies of the Greek Old Testament based on Origen's edition were thus closer to the contemporary Hebrew text.[14]

2.2.24–25. *et Hierosolymae atque in orientis ecclesiis decantatur,* "both in Jerusalem and in the churches of the East." Elsewhere Jerome speaks of a "threefold diversity" (*trifaria varietas*) of usages, with Egypt favoring the textual recension of Hesychius, Constantinople to Antioch favoring the Lucianic edition, and Palestine reading Origen's hexaplaric LXX (*Pref. IH Chron.* 2). See also Jerome's *Pref. Gos.* 1 for the distinction between codices associated with Hesychius and Lucian. See introduction, §5.

2.2.25. *sanctus filius meus Avitus,* "my holy son, Avitus." Avitus is also mentioned at §86.1, where Jerome refers to him as "my holy brother Avitus" (*sanctus filius meus Avitus*) and says that he requested from Jerome the explanation of certain Greek words. Jerome references "my son Avitus" (*filio meo Avito*) in *Ep.* 79.1 as part of his explanation for why he presumes to write a letter of consolation to the noblewoman Salvina at the death of her husband Nebridius even though he has not met Salvina. He expresses concern lest anyone think that he writes to Salvina merely to seek the friendship of powerful people. On Jerome's account, his reasons for writing are three: because he loves all Christians, because of his intimate bond with Nebridius' father (there is no way to assess this claim), and because Avitus requested that he write. Based on the connection between Avitus

---

12. On the "Lucianic" recension in modern scholarship, see Tov, *Textual Criticism of the Hebrew Bible,* 145–47; Marcos, *The Septuagint in Context,* 223–38; and introduction, §§4.2; 5.1.

13. Cf. 2.4; 7.1–2; 10.1; 14.1; 22.1; 25.3; 36.1; 41.4; 41.6; 55.2; 65.3; 74.1. See introduction. §§2.2; 5; 8.2.

14. On the Hexapla and the hexaplaric LXX text, see Peter J. Gentry, "1.3.1.2 Pre-Hexaplaric Translations, Hexapla, Post-Hexaplaric Translations," in *Overview Articles,* vol. 1 A of *Textual History of the Bible: The Hebrew Bible,* ed. Armin Lange and Emanuel Tov (Leiden: Brill, 2016), 211–35; and Marcos, *The Septuagint in Context,* 204–22.

and Nebridius and also the content of *Ep.* 79, it is logical to assume that Avitus belonged to the same ascetic circle as Nebridius and Salvina at the imperial court of Constantinople.[15]

In *Ep.* 124.1, Jerome identifies "my dear Avitus" (*Avite carissime*) as the one who requested a copy of Jerome's translation of Origen's *On First Principles*. J. N. D. Kelly doubts that the Avitus of *Ep.* 124.1 is the same person as the Avitus of *Ep.* 79.1, since the latter Avitus apparently resided in Constantinople. Kelly prefers to connect the Avitus of *Ep.* 124.1 to Avitus the Spanish presbyter mentioned by Gennadius in *Vir. ill.* 48.[16] In Kelly's view, there are two persons named Avitus: (1) the friend of Nebridius and Salvina who resided in Constantinople (*Ep.* 79.1; 106.2, 86) and (2) Avitus the Spanish presbyter (*Ep.* 124.1; Gennadius, *Vir. ill.* 48). Since we do not know that Avitus of Constantinople was not a Spaniard, and we cannot pinpoint the geography of the events referenced in *Ep.* 124, it is possible that all of these passages refer to the same individual. In the end, however, it is impossible to be certain.[17]

If we are correct to identify Avitus of *Ep.* 106 with Avitus of Constantinople, then we may also suggest that the Gothic priests Sunnia and Fretela reside in Constantinople and are connected with ecclesial and possibly governmental affairs in the imperial capital. If so, then we should take Jerome's comments in **1.1–3** with a grain of salt when he speaks of the Germanic barbarians learning how to be civilized. Even if Sunnia and Fretela were ethnic Goths (as their names suggest), this says nothing about their levels of education, travels, or connections. They may have been educated privately in their hometown and then (like Jerome) sent to Rome or another major city for more advanced instruction, at which point they may have entered the circles of the cultured elite in the Roman empire. If they truly had such interest in the Greek Psalter as *Ep.* 106 suggests, Sunnia and Fretela must have been well educated. See introduction, §6.1.

2.2.1. *fratris nostri Firmi presbyteri,* "our brother, the presbyter Firmus." Jerome says that Firmus is the one who delivered the letter (*epistula*) of Sunnia and Fretela to him. The criticisms of the Gallican Psalter that Sunnia and Fretela produced may have been framed as a letter to Jerome, or else the two Goths may have sent a letter of explanation along with their list of objections. Firmus is mentioned here and also at **46.4.17**, where Jerome

---

15. Fürst, *Hieronymus*, 162.
16. Kelly, *Jerome*, 303.
17. Fürst, *Hieronymus*, 162.

says that Firmus requested a copy of his Gallican Psalter with annotations in the margin. Firmus served as a transmitter of letters between Jerome and Augustine (e.g., Jerome's *Ep.* 115.1; 116.1; 134.2) and of Augustine's letters generally (e.g., Augustine's *Ep.* 191.1; 194.1; 200.1).[18] In other words, Firmus is a known figure from Jerome's time. The fact that Jerome mentions him in this treatise contributes to the impression that *Ep.* 106 reflects a genuine historical exchange of ideas between Jerome and his critics.

2.2.2–3. *scribens in commune respondeo*, "I will respond by writing publicly." At the level of *Ep.* 106 as a reply to Sunnia and Fretela, Jerome is "responding" to their questions. The true purpose of this treatise, however, is not to conciliate Sunnia and Fretela but to make public his defense for the translations that the two Goths criticized. It seems that Sunnia and Fretela circulated their objections publicly, or at least Jerome believes that they have or will, so Jerome must respond by issuing a public defense. See introduction, §6.1.

2.3.4–6. *sicut autem in novo testamento … recurrimus ad fontem Graeci sermonis*, "Just as in the New Testament … we have recourse to the fount of the Greek language." In translating the gospels, Jerome explained that part of his task was to decide, when the Latin readings disagreed, which were in agreement with the "Greek truth" (*ut … illa quae cum Graeca consentiant veritate decernam; Pref. Gos.* 1). Just as the original Greek serves as the court of appeal for the New Testament, the Hebrew is the final arbiter for disputes about the Old Testament (cf. *Ep.* 71.5; 112.20).

2.3.4–7. *novo testamento … novum … instrumentum … in veteri testamento*, "in the New Testament … the New Testament … in the Old Testament." Jerome uses the term *testamentum* for the Old Testament, and he uses both *testamentum* and *instrumentum* for the New Testament. In the late second century CE, Christians writing in Greek began to associate the idea of "testament" (διαθήκη) with the writings that came to make up the New Testament. Tertullian indicates that *testamentum* was the common Latin equivalent (e.g., *Marc.* 4.1), which matches the Greek in referring primarily to a last will and testament. Yet Tertullian himself more often employs the term *instrumentum*, which can be used for a legal document.[19] Erasmus cites Jerome in defending his use of the term *instrumentum* for

---

18. Fürst, *Hieronymus*, 179.

19. Harry Y. Gamble, *The New Testament Canon: Its Making and Meaning* (Minneapolis: Fortress, 1985), 21; and Adolf Harnack, *The Origin of the New Testament*, trans. John R. Wilkinson (London: Williams & Norgate, 1925), 209–17.

the New Testament, suggesting that *instrumentum* more naturally refers to books, whereas *testamentum* is used properly for wills.[20] For the idea of "covenant," Jerome usually translates the Greek διαθήκη as *testamentum*, whereas for the Hebrew בְּרִית, "covenant," he favors *pactum* (e.g., *Comm Jer.* 11:1–3a; 31:31–34).

2.3.8. *Hebraicam … veritatem*, "the Hebrew truth." See **1.1.9**.

2.4.9. *quicquid de fonte proficiscitur, hoc quaeramus in rivulis*, "Whatever originates from the fount we should look for in the rivulets." Jerome often speaks of the relationship between copies or translations of a text and their presumed original through the analogy of rivulets and their fountainhead (e.g., *Pref. Gos.* 1; *Pref. GPsal* 4; *Comm. Eccl.*, Pref.; *Ep.* 27.1.3; *Comm. Jer.*, Pref.). See introduction, §8.1.

2.4.14–15. *quae in eruditorum libris incorrupta et inmaculata septuaginta interpretum translatio reservatur*, "this is the very translation made by the Seventy Translators, preserved uncorrupted and unstained in the books of learned men." In this passage, Jerome says that the original LXX was preserved uncorrupted in the hexaplaric codices and that one can expect this original LXX to agree with the Hebrew. In other words, when Origen corrected the Greek text to match the Hebrew, he restored the original LXX. It should be emphasized that this is not the view of modern scholarship. Today, for example, scholars consider most of the additions made in the LXX from Theodotion to be corruptions of the earlier Greek text.[21] Therefore, what Jerome regards as the genuine LXX, that is, the "Seventy themselves," scholars today will typically see as a correction of the Old Greek toward the Hebrew.

Jerome's views on the LXX as expressed throughout his career were complex. On the one hand, he sometimes charged the LXX with concealing christological passages (e.g., *Qu. hebr. Gen.*, Pref.; *Pref. Pent.*; *Pref. Isa.*) or making translation errors (frequently in his commentaries). On the other hand, he sometimes denied that his Hebrew scholarship was meant to criticize the LXX (e.g., *Ruf.* 2.24; *Pref. Pent.*), and he continued to speak positively about the LXX well after he began his IH translation in 390 (e.g., *Pref. IH Chron.*, 397 CE). Especially later in his career, Jerome's rhetoric affirming the LXX reflects a defensive posture deemed necessary because

---

20. Nelson H. Minnich, ed., *Collected Works of Erasmus, Volume 84: Controversies*, trans. Daniel Sheerin (Toronto: University of Toronto Press, 2005), 56–57.

21. On the Hexapla, see Kreuzer, "Origins and Transmission of the Septuagint," 35–37; and introduction, §8.2.

of criticisms against him for undercutting the Septuagint's authority. In addition, there is good reason to think that he always favored the hexaplaric LXX as the best version of the Greek Bible due to its being closest to the Hebrew.[22] In *Ep*. 106.2, he articulates a naive conception of the perfect preservation of the hexaplaric LXX and its full harmony with the Hebrew. This conception fits the context of his hexaplaric LXX translation project on which he worked starting around 386 (see introduction, §2.2). In the course of *Ep*. 106, Jerome finds occasion to question and even adjust this viewpoint. By the end of this treatise, he seems to have reached a more nuanced view on the relationship between the Hebrew and Greek texts (see introduction, §6.2).

3.1.18–20. *neque habitabit iuxta te malignus*, "Nor will the wicked dwell near you." Ps 5:6 (Heb 5:5b), GPsal. The preserved LXX reads: οὐδὲ (for οὔτε) παροικήσει σοι πονηρευόμενος, "nor will the one acting wickedly dwell with you" (Rahlfs 85). For Jerome, this is merely the *vulgata editio*, "the popular edition." His first option for the final word, πονηρός, is a correction toward the Hebrew (רַע) that matches Aquila (Field 2:92). This was likely the reading in the hexaplaric LXX Psalter.

Jerome notes the surprise (*et miramini*, "and you are amazed") of Sunnia and Fretela at his translation. He will later express astonishment at their errors (see introduction, §8.4). Apparently, Sunnia and Fretela wondered why the Latin translator (i.e., Jerome) used *habitabit*, "dwell," which strictly speaking (they argued) should render the κατοικία word group, when the Greek verb here is related to παροικία, that is, *incolo*, "reside." According to Sunnia and Fretela, Jerome should have translated παροικήσει as "reside" (*incolet*), rather than as "dwell" (*habitabit*).

Jerome responds by illustrating his intentional variation in translation practice. On the one hand, in Ps 119:5 he rendered the Greek παροικία with the Latin *incolatus*, "residing," in keeping with what Sunnia and Fretela suggested. On the other hand, in Ps 14:1 (as in Ps 5:6) he chose to render the Greek παροικήσει with *habitabit*, "dwell." These two examples

---

22. Kamesar, *Jerome, Greek Scholarship, and the Hebrew Bible*, 55–58. E.g., see *Comm. Isa.*, Bk. 16, Pref., where Jerome favors the (true, in his view) LXX translators (i.e., the hexaplaric LXX) rather than the common (κοινή) edition; and *Comm. Isa.* 58:11, where Jerome favors the hexaplaric LXX as the authentic and corrected version. For Jerome criticizing the hexaplaric LXX in comparison with the Hebrew, see *Ep*. 112.19. In this passage, Jerome states that the hexaplaric insertions corrupt the original LXX.

(Ps 119:5 and Ps 14:1) are meant to show that Jerome knew precisely what he was doing when he translated the Gallican Psalter. It is not that Jerome is unaware that παροιϰία often corresponds to the Latin *incolatus*. Rather, as he explains, the word has a range of nuances and idiomatic contexts. Sometimes he chose to translate the word in one way, and sometimes he chose to translate it in another way, depending on the context. As for his specific reason for using *habitabit* (and not *incolet*) in his translation of Ps 5:6, this is what he goes on to explain.

3.2.1. εὐφωνίαν. On euphony in Jerome's translation theory, see introduction, §7.2.

3.2.2. ϰαϰοζηλίαν. The term ϰαϰόζηλον was used for an affected, overly ornate style that strove excessively for artistic expression.[23] Jerome condemns ϰαϰοζηλία as a stylistic fault when discussing Latin translations of Greek classical works in *Ep.* 57.5. See introduction, §7.2.

3.2.3. ἰδιώματα, "idioms" or "unique expressions." See introduction, §7.2.

3.3.4. *suae linguae … proprietate*, "in the particular idiom of his own language." The word *proprietas* came to be used as an equivalent in Latin for the Greek ἰδίωμα; see introduction, §7.2.

3.3.4. *Tullium.* Jerome regarded Cicero (Marcus Tullius Cicero) as a model for best practice in translation, citing this same basic combination of Latin translations in *Epist* 57.5.2–5. See also *Ep.* 121.6.6 (Cicero as translator of Xenophon; cf. Cicero, *Off.* 2.24.87; *Inst.* 10.5.2); *Pref. Chron.* (Cicero as translator of Xenophon, Aratus, and Plato); *Ruf.* 2.25; *Pref. Pent.* (Cicero as translator of Xenophon, Demosthenes, and Plato); *Comm. Isa.* bk. 12, Pref.; *Comm. Am.* 5:3 (Cicero as translator of Plato).[24] Jerome typically knows Latin authors firsthand, but most of his references to Greek writers come secondhand through his Latin sources.[25]

---

23. Heinrich Lausberg, *Handbook of Literary Rhetoric*, ed. David E. Orton and R. Dean Anderson, trans. Matthew T. Bliss, Annemick Jansen, and David E. Orton (Leiden: Brill, 1998), §1073.

24. See G. J. M. Bartelink, *Hieronymus: Liber de optimo genere interpretandi (Epistula 57). Ein Kommentar* (Leiden: Brill, 1980), 47–51.

25. Pierre Courcelle, *Late Latin Writers and their Greek Sources*, trans. Harry E. Wedeck (Cambridge: Harvard University Press, 1969), 59–89; and Harald Hagendahl, *Latin Fathers and the Classics: A Study on the Apologists, Jerome and Other Christian Writers* (Göteborg: Almquist & Wiksell, 1958), 93–94.

3.3.7–8. *Plautum, Terentium Caeciliumque, eruditissimos viros, in Graecis comoediis transferendis,* "Terence, Plautus, and Caecilius—highly learned men—did this when translating Greek comedies." Plautus (ca. 254–184 BCE) and Terence (ca. 185–159 BCE) were important early Latin authors whose comic plays were based closely on Greek models. Caecilius Statius (fl. 190 BCE) was a comic poet whose works were likewise derived from Greek sources.[26] Of these three early Latin "translators," or better, "adaptors," of Greek originals, Caecilius was held in lowest esteem, and fewer of his writings are preserved. In *Att.* 7.3.10, Cicero compares the usage of Caecilius, whose *Latinitas* is poor, with that of Terence, whose work exhibits *elegantia*.

3.3.8–9. *nec ex eo quis Latinam linguam angustissimam putet,* "From this let no one suppose that Latin is an exceptionally limited language." The idea that Latin was poor in vocabulary or mode of expression in comparison with Greek was common among Latin writers. For example, Quintilian explains that one reason why Greek excels Latin in charm is because of the richer vocabulary found in Greek (*Inst.* 12.10.34). In a brief letter to a friend, Pliny politely states that his Latin rendering of his friend's Greek epigrams has not succeeded in matching the quality of the originals, partly due to his own limitations, and partly due to the poverty of the Latin language, citing Lucretius 1.832 (Pliny, *Ep.* 4.18). Nevertheless, Cicero argues that Latin, far from having a poor vocabulary as many suppose, is actually richer than Greek (*Fin.* 1.3.10; cf. 3.2.5; *Nat. d.* 1.4.8). Jerome can appeal to the poverty of Latin as a trope to deflect possible criticism of his style and to invite the reader's admiration for his efforts; for example, writing to bishop Theophilus about one of the bishop's letters that Jerome translated from Greek into Latin, Jerome says, "For your sake I wished to find a match for Greek eloquence out of the poverty of the Latin language" (*latinae linguae … paupertate*).[27] In other cases, however, Jerome will defend the Latin language as he does here, explaining that the problem is not simply the poverty of Latin vis-à-vis Greek, but the difficulty of translation in gen-

26. See Siobhán McElduff, *Roman Theories of Translation: Surpassing the Source*, Routledge Monographs in Classical Studies (New York: Routledge, 2013), 61–95; and Jorma Kaimio, *The Romans and the Greek Language*, Commentationes Humanorum Litterarum 64 (Helsinki: Societas Scientiarum Fennica, 1979), 271–94.

27. *Ep.* 114.3.1 (CSEL 55:395). Cf. *Comm. Eph.* 1:4; *Comm. Phlm.* 20; *Jov.* 1.13. See Tim Denecker, *Ideas on Language in Early Christianity: From Tertullian to Isidore of Seville* (Leiden: Brill 2017), 250–51.

eral, since the Greeks likewise could not capture the nuances of Hebrew by strict translation. In his *Comm. Isa.* 40:12–17, Jerome refers to the poverty of Greek and Latin in comparison with Hebrew.

3.3.9. *quod non possit verbum transferre de verbo*, "since it is impossible to translate word for word." The expression *verbum de verbo*, "word for word," first appears in Terence, who says that he "brought forth" (*extulit*) a passage from his Greek model *verbum de verbo*, "word for word," in contrast to Plautus, who omitted the scene altogether (*Ad.* Pref. [Barsby]).[28] Cicero employs the expression "word for word" often in discussing the act of translating or adapting Greek sources. For example, in one passage he discourages translation "word for word" and prefers paraphrase or adaptation of one's Greek model, the goal being to develop one's own voice as a speaker rather than simply convey content (*Opt. gen.* 5.14–15; cf. 7.23). Elsewhere, Cicero claims that he will not express everything "word for word" (*verbum e verbo*), as is the practice of "unskilled translators" (*interpretes indiserti*), when there is a suitable Latin word in regular usage that communicates the same idea (*Fin.* 3.4.15 [Rackham]). In *Art of Poetry*, Horace discourages writers from translating "word for word" (*verbo verbum*) as a "faithful translator" (*fidus interpres*), advising them instead to take up popular themes and appropriate them in their own way (*Ars* 133–134 [Fairclough]). Jerome's negative appraisal of word-for-word translation in *Ep.* 106 fits into the classical stream of thought. This runs counter to Jerome's statement in *Ep.* 57.5.2 that he translates Scripture "word for word." See introduction, §7.2.

3.3.9–10. *cum etiam Graeci pleraque nostra circuitu transferant*, "as the Greeks also translated many of our works by paraphrase." By the fourth century, a substantial number of Latin literary works had been translated into Greek, such as Virgil's *Aeneid* and *Fourth Eclogue*, Sallust's *Histories*, and Tertullian's *Apology*.[29] In *Vir ill.* 134, Jerome states that a certain Sophronius translated some of his own (Jerome's) works into Greek, including his *Life of Hilarion* and his Hebrew-based translations of the Psalms and Prophets. Exegetical parallels between Jerome and Cyril of Alexandria sug-

---

28. On the formula *verbum de verbo*, see Heinrich Marti, *Übersetzer der Augustin-Zeit* (Munich: Fink, 1974), 64–72.

29. Elizabeth Fisher, "Greek Translations of Latin Literature in the Fourth Century A.D.," in *Later Greek Literature*, ed. John J. Winkler and Gordon Williams, YCS 27 (Cambridge: Cambridge University Press, 1982), 173–215.

gest that a Greek translation or exegetical source based on Jerome's IH edition and commentaries existed already in the fifth century.[30]

3.3.10, 11. *circuitu*, "by paraphrase." *interpretationis fide*, "by fastidious translation." *proprietatibus*, "in the particular idioms." Jerome praises Symmachus in particular for translating the sense of the Hebrew rather than merely the words; for instance, in his *Comm. Am.* 3:11, he describes Symmachus as a translator "who does not normally follow the affectation (κακοζηλίαν) of the words but the order of the sense" (see also *Pref. Job*; Pref. Eusebius' *Chronicon*; and often in commentaries, e.g., *Comm. Eccl.* 1:10; 3:22; 6:9; 7:2; 7:12–13; 7:28–30; 8:14; 9:1; 9:3–4a; 10:4). In the case of Symmachus and the Bible, the "affectation" that Symmachus avoids is the stylistic fault of imitating Hebraic idiom too closely.[31] At **57.2**, Jerome describes the Sixth edition (*sexta*) as "expressing the sense rather than the word."

4.1.13–14. *dirige in conspectu meo viam tuam*, "Sraighten your way in my sight." Ps 5:9 (Heb 5:9), GPsal. Sunnia and Fretela challenged the Gallican Psalter on the grounds that the Greek reads κατεύθυνον ἐνώπιόν σου τὴν ὁδόν μου, "straighten my way in your sight." Jerome responds that this Greek text is merely the "popular" (κοινή) edition of the LXX, not the true LXX (= the hexaplaric LXX Psalter). The reading suggested by Sunnia and Fretela is found in Codex Vaticanus, Codex Alexandrinus, MS 55 Rome, most Lucianic manuscripts, Theodoret's *Commentary**, the Syro-Hexapla, the Verona Psalter (Greek and Latin), and in Latin witnesses such as Codex Sangermanensis and Codex Casinensis 557. The Greek text favored by Jerome is supported by Codex Sinaiticus, Papyrus 2008, the Sahidic Coptic version, a few Lucianic manuscripts, and all the hexaplaric versions, and it matches the MT (Rahlfs 85; Amelli 5; Field 2:92). This is also the text Jerome gives in the *Commentaries on the Psalms* (CC 72:186).

Jerome offers a transliteration of the Hebrew: *oser laphanoi darachach*, in MT: הושר לפני דרכך. According to the Leningrad Codex, Jerome's trans-

---

30. Jean-Dominique Barthélemy, "Quinta ou Version selon les Hébreux?" *TZ* 16 (1960): 342–53; Alexander Kerrigan, *St. Cyril of Alexandria: Interpreter of the Old Testament* (Rome: Pontifical Biblical Institute, 1952), 254–65; and F.-M. Abel, "Parallélisme exégétique entre S. Jérôme et S. Cyrille d'Alexandrie," *Vivre et Penser* 1 (1941): 94–119, 212–30.

31. On Symmachus and Jerome, see Matthew A. Kraus, *Jewish, Christian, and Classical Exegetical Traditions in Jerome's Translation of the Book of Exodus*, VCSup 141 (Leiden: Brill, 2017), 111–12; and Field 1:xxx–xxxv.

literation matches the *ketiv* (הושר) rather than the *qere* (הישר), although the Qere is represented in a Cairo Genizah manuscript and over twenty medieval Hebrew manuscripts (BHS 1089; Kennicott 2:309).

4.2.21–22. *pater noster, qui es in caelis, sanctificetur nomen tuum*, "Our Father who is in the heavens, may your name be hallowed." Matt 6:9. This quotation essentially matches the preserved Vulgate NT. Here Jerome gives *qui es in caelis*, which is also found in Codex Sangermanensis and Codex Amiatinus. Other Vulgate manuscripts read *qui in caelis es*, which is the reading favored by Weber-Gryson (WG 1533).

5.1.6. *erubescant et conturbentur vehementer omnes inimici mei*, "Let all my enemies be ashamed and thoroughly confounded." Ps 6:11 (Heb 6:11), GPsal. The Greek text consulted by Sunnia and Fretela lacked σφόδρα, "thoroughly," which is supported by the Greek text of the Verona Psalter, the Lucianic manuscripts, Theodoret's *Commentary**, the Syro-Hexapla, MS 55 Rome, and in the OL tradition by the Verona Psalter and Augustine's *Enarrations* (Rahlfs 86–87; CC 38:33). Jerome counters that their reading is merely the *vulgata*, the "popular" edition; in other words, it is not the text of the hexaplaric LXX Psalter. In defense of the hexaplaric edition, Jerome explains that the Hebrew contains the word *mod*, (מאד, "exceedingly"), and he states, *omnes σφόδρα similiter transtulerunt*, "all translated this similarly: σφόδρα."[32] By "all" Jerome means all the hexaplaric versions. In fact, the Gallican Psalter is supported in its inclusion of σφόδρα by major Greek witnesses such as Codex Vaticanus, Codex Sinaiticus, Codex Alexandrinus, MS 1220 (fourth century), and the Bohairic and Sahidic Coptic versions.

6.1.9–10. *iudica me, domine, secundum iustitiam meam*, "Judge me, O Lord, according to my righteousness." Ps 7:9 (Heb 7:9), GPsal. Sunnia and Fretela reported the Greek reading κατὰ τὴν δικαιοσύνην σου, "according to your righteousness," in order to correct the Gallican Psalter. When Jerome says *pro quo in habetur in Graeco*, "instead of this in Greek it has," it appears at first that he accepts this as the true Greek reading; but his next words, *sed et in hoc male*, "but even in this it is mistaken," show that he does not regard this to be what the Greek truly contains. Once Jerome develops a pattern for this treatise, he typically introduces the Greek text

---

32. In the *Commentaries on the Psalms*, Jerome quotes this text as *convertantur et erubescant valde velociter*, "let them be converted and very quickly ashamed," where *valde velociter*, "very quickly" stands for σφόδρα; but in his explanation, he says the wicked will be ashamed *non leviter, sed vehemnter*, "not lightly, but thoroughly" (CC 72:188).

that was quoted to him by Sunnia and Fretela with words such as *dicitis …
non habeat*, "you say … does not have" (**7.1**); *invenisse vos dicitis*, "you say
that you have found" (**9.4**); and *legisse vos dicitis*, "you say that you have
read" (**13.1**).

The Greek text proposed by Sunnia and Fretela is found in Papyrus
2025, Hesychius of Jerusalem, a few Lucianic manuscripts, and MS 55
Rome (Rahlfs 87). Otherwise, most Greek witnesses have "my righteousness," although the key for Jerome is that *omnes interpretes 'iustitiam meam'
voce simili transtulerunt*, "all the translators [i.e., the hexaplaric versions
and presumably the hexaplaric LXX] rendered this with the same expression, 'my righteousness.'"

As Jerome points out, the Hebrew gives *sedechi* (צדקי) "my righteousness," whereas "your righteousness" would be *sedecach* (צדקך). In explaining the origins of various Greek and Latin readings, Jerome sometimes
supplies what the Hebrew would have been if a proposed Greek or Latin
translation were correct. On Jerome's knowledge of Hebrew as seen in *Ep.*
106, see introduction, §6.2.

6.2.18–19. *exaudi, domine, iustitiam meam*, "Hear, O Lord, my righteousness." Ps 16:1 (Heb 17:1) GPsal. Jerome uses *exaudi*, "Hear," (with the
prefix *ex-*) to imitate the Greek εἰσάκουσον (with the prefix εἰσ-). The LXX
(μου), followed by the Gallican Psalter (*meam*), adds "my" ("my righteousness"), which is implied by the context but is not explicitly stated in the
Hebrew.

6.2.19–22. *et in septimo decimo … reddet mihi*, "and in the Seventeenth
(Psalm) … he will restore to me." Ps 17:25 (Heb 18:25). This matches the
Gallican Psalter, except that the words at the end of the quotation, "he will
restore to me" (*reddet mihi*), are absent from the Gallican Psalter. This
phrase, however, is found in the Greek (ἀνταποδώσει μοι) according to
Codex Alexandrinus and the Greek text of the Verona Psalter, and it is
represented in OL witnesses such as the Verona Psalter, Codex Sangermanensis, and the Sinai Psalter (Sabatier 35; Rahlfs 103; Thibaut 37; cf. v.
21). The fact that Jerome includes these words suggests that he is quoting
from memory.

6.2.22–24. *in vicesimo quoque quinta psalmo … cor meum*, "also in the
Twenty-Fifth Psalm … my heart." Ps 25:2 (Heb 26:2), GPsal. The Hebrew
verb צרף, "refine, smelt," can convey the sense "test, prove." It was rendered
here by the LXX as πύρωσον, "burn," followed by the Latin (*ure*).

6.2.24–25. *et in quarto dicatur … exaudivit me deus iustitiae meae*,
"and in the Fourth (Psalm) … the God of my righteousness heard me." Ps

4:2 (Heb 4:2), GPsal. The perfect verb *exaudivit*, "heard me," matches the LXX (εἰσήκουσεν) and not the vocalization according to the MT, עֲנֵנִי (= the imperative: "hear me!").

6.2.27–28. *Exaudiet me cras iustitia mea*, "My justice will hear me tomorrow." Gen 30:33. This does not match IH Genesis: *respondebitque mihi cras iustitia mea*, "and my justice will respond to me tomorrow," or the most common OL translation: *et obaudiet me iustitia mea*, "and my justice will obey me."[33] The LXX has ἐπακούσεται, which means "hear, obey, answer."

7.1.1. *quoniam videbo caelos tuos*, "because I will see your heavens." Ps 8:4 (Heb 8:4), GPsal. Sunnia and Fretela objected to the presence of *tuos*, "your," in the Gallican Psalter on the grounds that it is absent from the Greek. The absence of "your" is confirmed uniformly by LXX witnesses (Rahlfs 89). Jerome concedes that this is true (*verum est*), by which he means that the commonly known Greek text lacks "your."[34] Yet from Jerome's perspective, "your" is present in the genuine LXX because σου, "your," was supplied under asterisk (*sub asterisco*) from Theodotion on the basis of the Hebrew, *samacha* (שמיך) (see Field 2:96).

It is important to grasp what Jerome means when he says *ubi quid minus habetur in Graeco ab Hebraica veritate*, "Wherever in the Greek something was lacking from the Hebrew truth." I do not think he intends to say that something was lacking in the original LXX that needed to be supplied from Theodotion. To be sure, later discussions in *Ep.* 106 open up the possibility that the original LXX could be brought into stricter conformity to the Hebrew (see introduction, §6.2). But based on Jerome's confident assertion at the beginning of this treatise that the hexaplaric LXX corresponds to the Hebrew (**2.2–3**), at this juncture in *Ep.* 106 we may assume that he intends to say that when Origen inserted σου, "your," in the Seventy Translators he was restoring the LXX to its original state.

7.2.5–12. *ubi quid minus habetur in Graeco ab Hebraica veritate …* *quod in authenticis libris non invenitur*, "wherever in the Greek something

---

33. Bonifatius Fischer, ed., *Genesis*, VL 2 (Freiburg: Herder, 1951), 324.

34. Ps 8:4 as quoted by Jerome in the *Commentaries on the Psalms* lacks *tuos* (CC 72:191). This probably reflects the LXX text Origen inherited when he produced the Hexapla. As Jerome says in his preface to the *Commentaries*, Origen was his main source for this work; see Siegfried Risse, trans. and intro., *Hieronymus. Commentarioli in Psalmos: Anmerkungen zum Psalter*, Fontes Christiani 79 (Turnhout: Brepols, 2005), 29–30.

was lacking from the Hebrew truth ... because it is not found in the authentic books." On "authentic books," see introduction, §8.3. On the hexaplaric signs, see also Jerome's *Pref. GPsal* 3:

> Let each person observe for himself where there is either a flat line or a radiant sign, that is, either an obelus or an asterisk. Wherever he sees a "small rod" (*virgula*, cf. *Inst.* 1.4.3) preceding some text, from there up to two points that I have made, let him know that there is a "plus" in the Seventy Translators. But where he observes the likeness of a star, from there likewise up to two points, let him know that this text has been added from the Hebrew scrolls, at least according to the edition of Theodotion, who in simplicity of expression does not differ from the Seventy Translators. (SC 592:408)

Jerome explains the meanings of these critical signs on numerous occasions (e.g., *Ep.* 112.19; 134.2; *Pref. Pent.* 2; *Pref. IH Job* 1; *Pref. IH Chron.* 2; *Pref. Josh.* 2). Moreover, in his commentaries he often discusses passages that are under asterisk (e.g., *Comm. Isa.* 2:22; 13:19–14:1a; 23:12c–13; 40:6–8; 56:10–12; 60:13) or marked with an obelus (e.g., *Comm. Isa.* 8:5–8; 8:11–15; 13:4c–5; 13:10; 26:17–18b; 29:22–24; 40:1–2; 51:9–11; 52:1; 60:13). He notes that many errors crept into Greek and Latin manuscripts because scribes failed to record these critical signs (see **22.1**; **55.2**). See introduction, §§8.2, 4.

7.2.12–13. *quae signa ... inveniuntur.* Critical signs (σημεῖα) were employed in editions (ἐκδόσεις) of classical texts, above all Homer, by scholars at the library of Alexandria in the third and second centuries BCE. Zenodotus of Ephesus (b. ca. 325 BCE) and Aristophanes of Byzantium (ca. 257–180) used the obelus (—) to indicate a line suspected of being inauthentic, and they used the asterisk (※) to mark lines that were repeated elsewhere in the work. Aristarchus of Samothrace (ca. 216–144) employed these signs and others as well, some of which linked to textual discussions found in his accompanying commentaries (ὑπομνήματα).[35] Jerome was

35. On the use of critical signs in classical Alexandrian scholarship, see Rudolf Pfeiffer, *History of Classical Scholarship: From the Beginning to the End of the Hellenistic Age* (Oxford: Oxford University Press, 1968), 105–14, 171–78, 216–18; Francesca Schironi, "The Ambiguity of Signs: Critical ΣHMEIA from Zenodotus to Origen," in *Homer and the Bible in the Eyes of Ancient Interpreters*, ed. Maren R. Niehoff (Leiden: Brill 2012), 87–112; and Schironi, *The Best of the Grammarians: Aristarchus of Samothrace on the Iliad* (Ann Arbor: University of Michigan Press, 2018), 49–62.

aware of the classical background of these critical signs and their application to the Bible by Origen.[36]

In his hexaplaric edition of the LXX, Origen apparently marked elements present in the Greek but absent in the Hebrew (and thus "inauthentic" from the vantage point of the Hebrew) with an obelus. For elements lacking in the Greek but present in the Hebrew, Origen supplied the missing elements from Aquila, Symmachus, or Theodotion (typically Theodotion) and marked these with an asterisk.[37] Origen's use of the obelus is similar to its function in Alexandrian Homeric criticism, although Origen did not intend for readers to delete passages marked with an obelus, as is clear from his discussion in the *Epistle to Africanus* and his many exegetical works based on the Greek.[38] Origen's use of the asterisk is innovative, although one could say that the material added in Origen's edition under asterisk was repeated from Theodotion (or whatever the source).

8.1.14. *oculi tui videant aequitates,* "Let your eyes see equitable things." Ps 16:2 (Heb 17:2), GPsal. Most LXX witnesses read οἱ ὀφθαλμοί μου, "my eyes," as Sunnia and Fretela propose (Rahlfs 99). Field cites Codex Vat. 754 (tenth century) as reporting that "the Three" (οἱ Γ´) read ὁμοίως, "similarly" (Field 2:107). We might conclude from this that the hexaplaric versions also had οἱ ὀφθαλμοί μου, "my eyes," so that the hexaplaric LXX likely had "my eyes" as well. If this were so, Jerome's *oculi tui,* "your eyes," originated simply from his understanding of the flow of thought; in fact, this is precisely how he justifies his rendering. This is one possible explanation, namely, that "the Three" and the hexaplaric LXX had οἱ ὀφθαλμοί μου, "my eyes," and Jerome put *oculi tui,* "your eyes," in the Gallican Psalter because it made better sense in context.

---

36. Graves, *Jerome's Hebrew Philology,* 24; and Karl K. Hulley, "Light Cast by St. Jerome on Certain Palaeographical Points," *HSCP* 54 (1943), 83–92, esp. 91–92.

37. See *Ep. Afr.* 3–7; *Comm. Matt.* 15:14; cf. *Comm. John* 28.16.137. See also Eusebius of Caesarea, *Ecclesiastical History* 6.16.1–4. For issues in scholarship on the Hexapla, see Marcos, *The Septuagint in Context,* 206–22. See also introduction, §§5; 8.2. On Origen's use of critical signs, see Bernhard Neuschäfer, *Origenes als Philologe,* 2 vols. (Basel: Reinhardt, 1987), 1:86–103, 122–38; and Schironi, "The Ambiguity of Signs," 100–109.

38. On Origen's motives in compiling the Hexapla, see Kamesar, *Jerome,* 4–28. According to Ronald E. Heine, *Origen: Scholarship in the Service of the Church* (Oxford: Oxford University Press, 2010), 73–76, Origen compiled the Hexapla as a tool for establishing an accurate text of Scripture for the sake of exegesis and theology in a school setting.

On the other hand, it is significant that the preserved Hebrew text gives the second-person: עֵינֶיךָ, "your eyes." Another possible explanation, therefore, is that at least one of the hexaplaric versions put οἱ ὀφθαλμοί σου, "your eyes" (contra Codex Vat. 754), and Jerome followed this when he produced the Gallican Psalter. Given the second-person pronoun in the Hebrew and the vague testimony for the hexaplaric versions (ὁμοίως, "similarly"), I favor this latter explanation. I suspect that Jerome's understanding of the sense started from linguistic information he received from the Hexapla, rather than that he worked out the flow of thought in contradiction to all the hexaplaric versions and the Old Latin (Sabatier 30; Weber 27; Thibaut 35). If this second explanation is correct, why does Jerome not cite a Greek version in his defense? Perhaps the hexaplaric versions were divided between the first-person (μου, "my") and the second-person (σου, "your"), and whereas Jerome picked the second-person for the Gallican Psalter (*oculi tui*, "your eyes"), the hexaplaric LXX actually gave the first-person: οἱ ὀφθαλμοί μου, "my eyes." In such a case, Jerome would not wish to bring up the fact that he is not in accord with the hexaplaric LXX.

8.1.15. *pro quo in Graeco*, "instead of this in Greek." These words are found in some manuscripts in their present position, and in other manuscripts they appear after οἱ ὀφθαλμοί μου. Hilberg placed them in brackets [*pro quo in Graeco*], suspecting that they may have been a marginal reading in the text underlying all preserved manuscripts and that they were subsequently integrated into the text in different places (Hilberg 252). Because they fit the highly formulaic style of this letter, I think these words are probably original. We may suppose that an early copyist accidentally omitted them, realized the mistake immediately, and then added them back in by writing them in the margin. Some later copyist, however, reintegrated the phrase in the incorrect place. Hilberg has placed them in the correct position. The Benedictine edition prints these words in this position without brackets (Gasquet 12). This is how the text is presented here.

8.1b.18–19. *custodi me ut pupillam oculi*, "Keep me as the pupil of the eye." Ps 16:8 (Heb 17:8), GPsal. Sunnia and Fretela propose that the vocative κύριε, "Lord," should be part of this text: *custodi me, domine*, "keep me, O Lord." The addition of κύριε is supported by a number of Lucianic manuscripts, Theodoret's *Commentary**, the Syro-Hexapla, the Bohairic Coptic version, and in the OL tradition by witnesses such as Codex Sangermanensis, Augustine's *Enarrations*, and the Roman Psalter (Rahlfs 99; Sabatier 31; Weber 27; Thibaut 35; CC 38:93).

As Jerome notes, the word "Lord" is lacking in the Hebrew and is absent from the majority of LXX manuscripts. When Jerome says *nec in ullo … interprete*, "nor in any translator," he means that κύριε is lacking in the Greek hexaplaric versions and also in the hexaplaric LXX.

8.2.21–22. *exurge domine, praeveni eum et subplanta eum*, "Rise up, O Lord, forestall him and supplant him." Ps 16:13 (Heb 17:13), GPsal. When Jerome says *pro quo in Graeco sit*, "in place of which in Greek is," his use of the subjunctive (*sit*) indicates that he is reporting what Sunnia and Fretela *say* the LXX contains without necessarily committing himself to the view that this is truly the original LXX. For this proposed reading, Jerome quotes the Greek only for the first verb and object (πρόφθασον αὐτούς), but his translation makes clear that the Greek text reported to him had the plural object pronoun in place of the singular in both cases.

The LXX as preserved uses plural pronouns: πρόφθασον αὐτούς καὶ ὑποσκέλισον αὐτούς, "forestall them and trip them."[39] Jerome's use of singular object pronouns in the Gallican Psalter matches Aquila and Symmachus (Field 2:108), who follow the Hebrew: קדמה פניו הכריעהו, literally, "Get ahead of his face, subdue him." However, both Aquila and Symmachus rendered פניו literally, τὸ πρόσωπον αὐτοῦ, "his face," whereas Jerome in the Gallican Psalter kept the LXX's idiomatic rendering of this phrase ("forestall them"), merely changing the pronoun into the singular ("forestall him"). This illustrates how hexaplaric evidence (and the Hebrew, indirectly) might influence the Gallican Psalter without totally replacing the base translation already found in the LXX. We may suppose that the hexaplaric LXX made the pronoun singular (αὐτόν) but refrained from adding τὸ πρόσωπον, "face," and this explains Jerome's choice in the Gallican Psalter. In the IH edition, Jerome will render the Hebrew more literally (*faciem eius*, "his face").

8.2.1. *numero singulari*, "in the singular"; literally, "in the singular number." Comments touching on grammatical number appear elsewhere in this work (**8.2; 9.2; 46.6; 50.7**), and they are not uncommon in Jerome's commentaries; for example, see *Qu. hebr. Gen.* 6:2; *Comm. Os.* 11:1–2; *Comm. Isa.* 26:2; *Comm. Jer.* 2:12; 9:13; 31:22. The category of grammatical number was clearly defined by ancient grammarians; for example, the *Ars grammatica* of Aelius Donatus, Jerome's former teacher, states *Numeri sunt*

---

39. Rahlfs does not indicate any Greek variants (Rahlfs 99). In Latin, Codex Casinensis 557 gives *praeveni faciem eius*, "forestall his face," but this probably reflects a correction towards the Hebrew through a Greek source.

duo, singularis et pluralis: singularis, ut hic sapiens, pluralis, ut hi sapientes,
"There are two numbers, singular and plural: the singular, as in 'This one is wise,' and the plural, as in 'These are wise.'"[40]

In his commentaries, Jerome shows that he knows that *-im* is the masculine plural ending in Hebrew and that *-oth* is the feminine plural (e.g., *Comm. Isa.* 1:2; *Comm. Ezech.* 9:2–3; on the topic of grammatical gender, see *Comm. Isa.* 40:9–11; *Qu. hebr. Gen.* 4:6–7; *Ep.* 18b.1). In terms of Hebrew morphology in the prophetic commentaries, Jerome observes that the letter ו can signify *u* or *o* (*Comm. Obad.* 1), that *u* in Hebrew means "and" (*Comm. Isa.* 37:8–13), and that *o* written with the letter ו signifies "his" (*Comm. Am.* 4:12–13). Specific details about Hebrew grammar of this sort are generally lacking in *Ep.* 106, but Jerome makes a brief remark on the singular and plural of a Hebrew word below at **9.2**. On grammatical terms in *Ep.* 106, see introduction, §9.1.

8.2.3–4. *eripe animam meam ab inpio ... diabolum significet,* "rescue my soul from the irreverent one.... This indicates the devil." Jerome identifies the "irreverent one" as the devil, supported by the singular object pronouns (forestall *him* and supplant *him*) and the singular "irreverent one" (*inpio*). In *Comm. Ps.* 16:13, Jerome interprets "rescue my soul from the irreverent one" by explaining that God gives power to our enemies for a time so as to punish us for our sins, and he likens this to Paul delivering the wayward over to Satan to teach them not to blaspheme (see 1 Tim 1:20; CC 72:195). In agreement with Jerome, Cassiodorus, *Exp.* 16:13 offers an interpretation of the "irreverent one" as the devil (CC 97:148). In contrast to this, following the LXX's plural object pronouns ("forestall *them* and trip *them*"), Latin witnesses such as Codex Casinensis 557, the Verona Psalter, and Augustine's *Enarrations* give the plural *impiis,* "irreverent ones" (Rahlfs 99; Amelli 12; Sabatier 31; CC 38:93). The plural "enemies" (ἐχθρῶν; OL = *inimicorum*) in the following line is also significant for understanding why some texts construe the adversaries in this passage as plural. In a catena fragment probably going back to Origen, the plural Greek pronouns and "enemies" are interpreted as demons who oppose God's will.[41] It is possible

40. Keil, *Grammatici Latini,* 4:376. On technical grammar and Jerome's exegesis, see Graves, *Jerome's Hebrew Philology,* 45–47. Jerome refers to Donatus on three occasions as *praeceptor meus,* "my teacher" (*Chron.* 354; *Ruf.* 1.16; *Comm. Eccl.* 1:9). See Graves, *Jerome's Hebrew Philology,* 14–16.
41. Jean B. Pitra, ed., "Origenes in Psalmos," *Analecta sacra spicilegio Solesmensi parata* (Paris: Tusculum, 1884), 2:470 (see also PG 12:1221). The preserved exegesis of

that Jerome was aware of such an interpretation, but in light of the singular pronouns in his version he changed the "demons" into the "devil."

9.1.6–7. *grando et carbones ignis*, "hail and coals of fire." Ps 17:14 (Heb 18:14), GPsal. According to Jerome, Sunnia and Fretela asked: *cur Graecus istum versiculum secundum non habeat interpositis duobus versibus*, "Why does the Greek not have the second occurrence of this short line, two lines after the first occurrence?" The short line (*versiculum*) "hail and coals of fire" first occurs in v. 13, two Latin lines prior to the second occurrence of the phrase in v. 14 (*interpositis duobus versibus*, "two lines having been interposed"). Obviously, this short line was not present for v. 14 in Sunnia and Fretela's copy of the LXX and in fact is absent from most LXX witnesses (Rahlfs 101–2). Jerome reports that it was supplied from Theodotion in the hexaplaric LXX, which agrees with the Hebrew text as preserved in the Leningrad Codex and Aleppo Codex. It should be noted, however, that the short line "hail and coals of fire" is absent from v. 14 in at least four medieval Hebrew manuscripts (Kennicott 2:318; De-Rossi 4:11; cf. 2 Sam 22:14).

9.2.9–10. *qui perfecit pedes meos tamquam cervorum*, "He who made my feet as those of stags." Ps 17:34 (Heb 18:34), GPsal. The Hebrew, כאילות, "as stags," is plural. Jerome does not directly dispute the claim that the LXX contains the singular, but he cites the Hebrew and "all the translators" (including the LXX?) in defense of the Gallican Psalter's plural translation: *tamquam cervorum*, "as those of stags." Most LXX witnesses read ἐλάφου, (as those) "of a stag" (singular), as do most OL witnesses (Sabatier 35; Thibaut 38). As exceptions, Codex Alexandrinus offers the plural ἐλάφους, (as) "stags," and in Latin Codex Casinensis 557 gives the plural: *sicut cervos*, "as stags" (Amelli 13), but these are either idiomatic corrections to match the plural "feet" or else (more likely) corrections toward the Hebrew. The genitive plural (ἐλάφων) occurs in London Brit. Mus. Papyrus 37, the Sahidic Coptic version, and the LXX column of the tenth-century MS 1098, but in each case the text probably transmits the reading of the hexaplaric LXX Psalter (Rahlfs 103).[42] In all likelihood, therefore, the pre-

---

Didymus of Alexandria on Ps 16:13 makes no connection to demons or the devil; see Ekkehard Mühlenberg, *Psalmenkommentare aus der Katenenüberlieferung*, 2 vols., PTS 15–16 (Berlin: de Gruyter, 1975–1977), 1:185–86.

42. See Giovanni Mercati, *Psalterii Hexapli Reliquiae, Pars Prima: Codex Rescriptus Bybliothecae Ambrosianae O 39 SVP* (Rome: Vatican Library, 1958), 5. On the genitive plural ἐλάφων as the reading of the hexaplaric versions, see Mercati, *Psalterii Hexapli Reliquiae, Pars Prima: 'Osservazioni,' Commento Critico al Testo dei Frammenti*

hexaplaric Greek Psalter gave the singular as Sunnia and Fretela proposed. Jerome cites the Hebrew text and the agreement of the (hexaplaric) Greek versions in defense of the plural.

9.2.11–12. *singularem numerum pro plurali. sed in Hebraeo pluralis numerus*, "with the singular (number) in place of the plural. But in Hebrew it has the plural." See **8.2.1.**

9.3.13–14. *et dedisti mihi protectionem salutis tuae*, "And you gave to me the protection of your salvation." Ps 17:36 (Heb 18:36), GPsal. The preserved Hebrew has יִשְׁעֶךָ, "your salvation" ("my salvation" would be יִשְׁעִי). Jerome's testimony that all three hexaplaric versions read "your salvation" is supported by two manuscripts cited by Montfaucon (Field 2:112). This Hebraizing correction ("your salvation") is also present in MS 55 Rome. On the other hand, column d (Sym) and column e (LXX) in MS 1098 contain σ(ωτη)ρίας μου, "my salvation."[43] One might suppose that Jerome preserved *salutis tuae*, "your salvation," from the Roman Psalter (Weber 34) rather than follow the LXX or the hexaplaric versions (Caloz 114–5). It is difficult to imagine, however, that Jerome would have written *salutis tuae*, "your salvation," in the Gallican Psalter and defended his translation here with such confidence if the hexaplaric LXX and Symmachus had the first-person. It seems more likely that at least column e (LXX) in MS 1098 is mistaken, in which case Jerome's claim that "all the translators" had "your" is incorrect as regards Symmachus, or else both column d (Sym) and column e (LXX) reflect miscopying. To be sure, there are occasions in *Ep.* 106 where Jerome simplifies the hexaplaric evidence (see introduction, §8.2), but in these cases all the versions could at least be interpreted as generally supporting his position. The broader textual evidence supports the idea that the Gallican Psalter gave the hexaplaric correction toward the Hebrew, whereas Sunnia and Fretela's text ("my salvation") was the standard Greek reading (Rahlfs 104).

9.4.17–18. *subplantasti insurgentes in me subtus me*, "You subdued under me those who rose up against me." Ps 17:40 (Heb 18:40), GPsal. Since the word "all" is lacking in the Hebrew, it was likely absent from the hexaplaric LXX (thus Caloz 56), as indirectly supported by a preserved Aquila reading that omits "all" (Field 2:112). Because Jerome considered the hexaplaric LXX to be the original text, he believed the presence of "all"

Esaplari (Rome: Vatican Library, 1965), 11. As Mercati observes, the form ἔλαφον in column c (perhaps Aquila) is probably a miscopying for ἐλάφων.

43. Mercati, *Psalterii Hexapli Reliquiae* (1958), 5.

(πάντας) was secondary—that is, it had been erroneously added into the Greek text used by Sunnia and Fretela. In reality, the Old Greek Psalter may well have contained πάντας, since it is present in most LXX manuscripts and many OL witnesses (Weber 34; Thibaut 38). The absence of πάντας from Codex Sinaiticus can be explained as a Hebraizing correction (Rahlfs 104). Of the Latin witnesses that lack *omnes*, "all," some may have been influenced by revised Greek texts such as Codex Sinaiticus, for example Codex Sangermanensis and Augustine's *Enarrations* (Sabatier 36; CC 38:100). Of special note, Codex Casinensis 557 gives a Latin text that lacks *omnes* but also appears to be independent of other Latin versions: *subiecisti resurgentes mi(c)hi sub me*, "You subjected below me those arising (in opposition) to me" (Amelli 13).

9.5.21–22. *et benedictus deus meus*, "And blessed be my God." Ps 17:47 (Heb 18:47), GPsal. As Jerome notes, the first-person pronoun "my" is not only present in the Hebrew but is also found in almost all Greek and Latin witnesses. Consequently, there was no need for "my" to be supplied under asterisk in the hexaplaric LXX. Jerome's use of the phrase *ab ipsis Septuaginta*, "by the Seventy themselves" to mean "in the Greek text as unaltered by hexaplaric revision" is surprising. What I think he means is that, in this case, the popular text actually contains the correct reading, that is, the reading of the Seventy themselves, and therefore it already stands in pristine harmony with the Hebrew truth. This textual dispute did not arise because of a difference between the popular and hexaplaric recensions; rather, the particular copy of the Psalter consulted by Sunnia and Fretela was corrupt. There is a seventh-century Greek manuscript that agrees with Sunnia and Fretela's text in lacking "my" (Rahlfs 105), and in Latin, Codex Casinensis 557 has simply: *potentissimus*, "Most Powerful One" (Amelli 13).

Further, one should note that the Hebrew underlying "my God" (ὁ θεός μου, *deus meus*) is צוּרִי, "my rock." The translation of "rock" as "God" when applied metaphorically to the Deity is common in the LXX, OL tradition, and Gallican Psalter.[44] Even in the IH Psalter Jerome tends to avoid this metaphor, whether he renders צוּר as *Deus* (e.g., Deut 32:4, 15, 18, 30; 32:31; 2 Sam 22:47; Ps 17:47) or handles it in some other way (Deut 32:37; 1 Sam 2:2; 2 Sam 22:3, 32; 23:3; Isa 17:10; 26:4; 30:29; 44:8; Pss 17:3, 32; 18:15; 27:1; 61:3, 7, 8; 77:35; 88:27; 91:16; 143:1). In a few cases in the IH edition,

---

44. On this translation equivalency in the LXX, see Staffan Olofsson, *God is My Rock: A Study of Translation Technique and Theological Exegesis in the Septuagint* (Stockholm: Almqvist & Wiksell, 1990), 35–42.

however, Jerome allows God to be likened to a rock (Pss 17:3; 93:22; 94:1). In passages where Jerome renders "rock" literally with reference to God, he is following the consistent practice of Aquila, who typically rendered צוּר in connection to God with a literal equivalent such as πέτρα.[45] Therefore, the hexaplaric reading reported by Field for Ps 17:47, καὶ πάντες: καὶ εὐλογητὸς ὁ θεός μου (Field 2:113), is probably incorrect, at least for Aquila.[46] As for the literal sense of צוּר, Jerome discusses this word in his commentaries (e.g., *Comm. Am.* 3:11; *Comm. Isa.* 10:24–27; *Comm. Jer.* 21:13–14).

9.5.22. *de Hebraica veritate.* On the "Hebrew truth," see **1.1.9**.

9.6.24. *liberator meus de gentibus iracundis,* "my deliverer from angry nations." Ps 17:48 (Heb 18:49), GPsal. The textual history of this passage is complicated. The Hebrew text as it appears in the Leningrad Codex is as follows: מְפַלְּטִי מֵאֹיְבָי אַף מִן קָמַי תְּרוֹמְמֵנִי. The meaning of אַף is a matter of uncertainty. If אַף is taken to be אַף I, "also," then these lines read: "My deliverer from my enemies, also above those rising against me you lift me up." If, however, one interprets this as אַף II, "anger," and reads it with the preceding words, one might arrive at something like: "My deliverer from my angry enemies; above those rising against me you lift me up." Interestingly, the word אַף is lacking in three medieval Hebrew manuscripts (Kennicott 2:320) and in the parallel at 2 Sam 22:49.[47]

The evidence for the LXX overall suggests reading the first half as: ὁ ῥύστης μου ἐξ ἐχθρῶν μου ὀργίλων, "My deliverer from my angry enemies" (Rahlfs 105).[48] The reading that Sunnia and Fretela sent to Jerome was apparently something like: ὁ ῥύστης μου ἐξ ἐχθρῶν μου δυνατῶν, "My deliverer from my strong (or "powerful") enemies" (cf. Ps 17:18, LXX). Jerome does not address the issue of "strong" in place of "angry," but that this reading existed in Greek is suggested by the presence of *dominus/domine*, "Lord" (perhaps δυνατός) in the OL tradition (Sabatier 37). According to this hypothesis, δυνατῶν entered v. 49 by way of harmonization with v. 18, and then δυνατῶν was translated as if δυνατός (i.e., *dominus/domine*) in some branch of the OL tradition.

As for "nations" instead of "enemies," I have seen no Greek LXX evidence for "nations," but *de gentibus iracundis,* "from angry nations" is found in Codex Sangermanensis, the Sinai Psalter, and other OL witnesses (Saba-

---

45. Joseph Reider, *An Index to Aquila*, rev. Nigel Turner (Brill, Leiden, 1966), 305.

46. Mercati, *Psalterii Hexapli Reliquiae* (1965), 33.

47. See *HALOT*, s.v. "אַף"; "אַף II."

48. See also P.Bod. 24: ὁ ῥύστης μου ἐξ ἐχ(θ)ρῶν μου ὀργίλων (KT 46).

tier 37; Weber 35; Thibaut 38; CC 97:167; cf. λαούς, *populos* in the previous line). Codex Casinensis 557 has *Qui liberat me ab inimicis meis*, "who
delivers me from my enemies" (Amelli 13), which is closer to the Hebrew
(*et* is used for Hebrew אף, "also," to begin the next clause), and it resembles
Jerome's IH translation without matching it precisely (see below).

In the Gallican Psalter, Jerome apparently carried over the rendering
"nations" from the *Vetus Latina*. Since he does not refer to the hexaplaric
edition, we may assume that it agreed with the Hebrew against Jerome's
"nations." Jerome acknowledges that a correction needs to be made, perhaps admitting his mistake, and yet he leaves open the possibility that the
error was caused by "the vice of copyists" (i.e., the scribes who produced
Sunnia and Fretela's copy of the Gallican Psalter) rather than "the hastiness
of the translator" (i.e., Jerome himself). In any case, if Jerome was mistaken (as he explains), the error was due to hastiness, not incompetence.
In his final comment, "I am astonished at how 'nations' was substituted
for 'enemies,'" he falls short of taking responsibility for the mistranslation.
Moreover, at this stage of his Hebrew knowledge he is unable to sort out the
distinction between אף, "anger," and אף, "also," so he cannot explain why
the LXX added "angry."

Sunnia and Fretela's question brings to light a genuine problem in the
Gallican Psalter that Jerome is not truly able to resolve. On the topic of
whether or not the inquiries presented in *Ep.* 106 are genuine questions
put to Jerome, this discussion of Ps 17:48 does not seem like something
he would invent in order to display his linguistic skills. In his IH edition,
Jerome will translate this passage as *qui servas me ab inimicis meis*, "you
who rescue me from my enemies," thus correcting the problem.

10.1.7–8. *exultavit ut gigans ad currendam viam suam*, "He rejoices as
a giant to run his course." Ps 18:6 (Heb 19:6), GPsal. In this case, Sunnia
and Fretela rightly point out that Jerome has included the LXX's "his"
(αὐτοῦ) in his translation, despite the fact that it was marked with an obelus
(*sub veru*, "under the dart," see **7.14.22**) in the hexaplaric LXX. This runs
counter to Jerome's claim that in the Gallican Psalter he gave a Latin version according to Origen's recension. Jerome does not deny or renounce
his translation, but he insists that he did see that the word was placed under
obelus to mark it as absent from the Hebrew. His decision to include *suam*,
"his," had to do with Latin idiom rather than textual exactitude.

10.1.9–10. *in Hebraeo non esse manifestum est.* In justifying his translation, Jerome concedes that the pronoun is absent from the Hebrew, but
he is careful to say that it is not "explicitly stated" (*manifestum*). In other

words, although the word "his" is not formally expressed, it is implied by the context and suits Latin idiom. Presumably this is why he chose to render it in the Gallican Psalter, despite its absence from the hexaplaric LXX and the Hebrew.

The pronoun is absent from the text as quoted in Jerome's *Commentaries on the Psalms* (*exsultavit ut gigans ad currendam viam*), where he comments: *per solem mystice de Xpisto intellegitur*, "By 'sun' it is understood mystically to be about Christ" (CC 72:196). A fragment of Origen's exegesis is preserved that says: ὁ κύριος ἡμῶν ὁ ἥλιος τῆς δικαιοσύνης ἐστὶν, ἐν αὐτῷ δὲ κατασκηνοῖ ὁ πατήρ, κατὰ το ἐγω ἐν τῷ πατρὶ καὶ ὁ πατὴρ ἐν ἐμοί. καὶ πάλιν: ὁ πατὴρ ἐν ἐμοὶ μένων αὐτὸς ποιεῖ τὰ ἔργα. καὶ ὁ ἀπόστολος: θεὸς ἦν ἐν τῷ Χριστῷ κόσμον καταλλάσσων ἑαυτῷ, "Our Lord is the Sun of righteousness (Mal 3:20 LXX), and in him the Father dwells (John 1:14), as in 'I am in the Father and the Father is in me' (John 14:11), and again: 'the Father abiding in me, He does the works' (John 14:10), and the Apostle: 'God was in Christ reconciling the world to himself' (2 Cor 5:19)" (PG 12:1241). Didymus of Alexandria on this passage likewise refers to Christ as the "Sun of righteousness."[49]

Jerome will omit the pronoun in the IH edition: *exultavit ut fortis ad currendam viam*.

11.1.11. *tribuat tibi secundum cortuum*, "May He grant to you according to your heart." Ps 19:5 (Heb 20:5), GPsal. The name of the Lord, κύριος (i.e., "May the Lord grant to you"), was present in this verse according to the copy of the LXX consulted by Sunnia and Fretela. Evidence for this reading is found in the Bohairic Coptic version and also in the OL tradition as witnessed by the Verona Psalter, Codex Sangermanensis, the Sinai Psalter, and Augustine's *Enarrations* (Rahlfs 107; Sabatier 40; Thibaut 40; CC 38:113).

11.1.13. ἀπὸ κοινοῦ, "in common." Jerome is referring to a figure of speech whereby two or more clauses share a single word or phrase in common (cf. Jerome's *Comm. Jer.* 21:11–12; 25:34–35). This figure was described by ancient grammarians as ζεῦγμα ("joining") or ἀπὸ κοινοῦ.[50] Quintilian discussed this figure of speech, ἐπεζευγμένον, "joined together" as one type of "figure by subtraction" (*figura per detractionem*) that aimed at brevity and novelty (*Inst.* 9.3.58–62). Jerome is suggesting that the psalmist

---

49. Mühlenberg, *Psalmenkommentare aus der Katenenüberlieferung*, 1:211.
50. Lausberg, *Handbook of Literary Rhetoric*, §§697–704.

meant for the reader to assume "the Lord" as the subject of the verbs in vv. 3–5 based on the identification of the "Lord" in v. 2. Thus, the word "Lord" is shared in common between all these lines. This is certainly the proper interpretation of the passage as a whole. It is uncertain whether presuming the same subject for a series of verbs in this manner constitutes ζεῦγμα or ἀπὸ κοινοῦ according to classical usage.

11.2.18–19. *in die,* "on the day." Ps 19:10 (Heb 20:10), GPsal. The LXX renders this idiom ἐν ᾗ ἂν ἡμέρᾳ (subjunctive plus ἄν), "in whatsoever day," which communicates a sense of indefiniteness that is not self-evident in the Hebrew ביום (Jerome's *biom*). Some OL witnesses render this phrase along the lines of what Sunnia and Fretela propose; for example, Codex Sangermanensis has *in quacunque die,* "in whatsoever day" (Sabatier 40).

In the *Commentaries on the Psalms,* Jerome gives the text with *quacumque,* as in Codex Sangermanensis: *Domine, salvum fac regem, et exaudi nos in quacumque die invocaverimus te,* "O Lord, save the king, and hear us in whatsoever day we call on you." Then he offers another translation based on the Hebrew: *In hebraeo ita scriptum est: Domine, salvum fac regem, qui exaudiet nos in quacumque die invocaverimus eum,* "In Hebrew it is written thus: 'O Lord, save the king, who will hear us in whatsoever day we call on him.'" (CC 72:197). In the *Commentaries,* Jerome's Hebrew-based rendering changes the imperative *exaudi,* "hear" into the future *exaudiet,* "will hear," and in keeping with this change he also switches the final object pronoun from *te,* "you" to *eum,* "him." Indeed, the Hebrew supports the future (יענגו, "he will hear us"), as was clear in Aquila and Symmachus (Field 2:116). But the addition of the relative pronoun (*qui*) is not strictly grounded in the Hebrew, and the final pronoun (*te* or *eum*) is not formally represented in the Hebrew at all (ביום קראנו, "in the day of our calling"). Moreover, in the *Commentaries* Jerome pays no attention to the translation of ביום as "on the day" rather than "in whatsoever day." It is noteworthy that the Gallican Psalter has the imperative *exaudi* and the final object pronoun *te* from the LXX. If the *Commentaries* was written first, it is odd that Jerome did not follow the future (*exaudiet*) and the third-person pronoun (*eum*) in the Gallican Psalter. If the Gallican Psalter came first, however, it is odd that in the *Commentaries* he stays with *in quacumque die* rather than simply *in die.*

The most likely scenario is that Jerome translated the Gallican Psalter before composing the *Commentaries on the Psalms*; therefore, when he produced the Gallican Psalter, Jerome had not yet been alerted by his sources for the *Commentaries* (especially Origen) about the future indicative *exaudiet*. Later, when Jerome wrote the *Commentaries*, he used *in quacumque die* for the Greek ἐν ᾗ ἂν ἡμέρᾳ without paying attention to the difference between this rendering and the Gallican Psalter's *in die qua*, because they are nearly equivalent. It was only when Sunnia and Fretela challenged the Gallican Psalter that Jerome replied in *Ep.* 106 that *quacumque* is not in the Hebrew. According to this way of thinking, the order of the works was the Gallican Psalter first, then the *Commentaries on the Psalms*, and lastly *Ep.* 106.

11.2.19. *cum Hebraica veritate*. On the "Hebrew truth," see **1.1.9**.

12.1.21–22. *tu autem, domine, ne elongaveris auxilium tuum a me*, "But you, O Lord, do not make distant *your* help *from me*." Ps 21:20 (Heb 22:20), GPsal. According to Jerome, "in place of this" (*pro quo*) Sunnia and Fretela suggested *meum*, "my." A key question regarding this passage is what exactly Sunnia and Fretela sought to correct. Did the two Gothic clergymen recommend *auxilium meum*, "my help" instead of *auxilium tuum*, "your help"? Or was *auxilium meum* meant to replace the entire phrase *auxilium tuum a me*, "your help from me"?

To begin, manuscripts of the Gallican Psalter uniformly lack *a me*, "from me" (WG 792), although these words are attested in some OL witnesses, for example, the Roman Psalter, the Verona Psalter, the Sinai Psalter, and Augustine's *Enarrations* (Sabatier 44; Weber 42; Thibaut 42; CC 38:119). Greek texts that support this addition include London Brit. Mus. Papyrus 37, the Greek text of the Verona Psalter, MS 1219 Washington, the Lucianic manuscripts, the Syro-Hexapla, and Theodoret's *Commentary** (Rahlfs 111). We may assume that a scribe wrongly added *a me* in the copy of Jerome's translation consulted by Sunnia and Fretela based on its widespread attestation elsewhere. When Jerome says: *quod et verum est et ita corrigendum*, "This is true, and it should thus be corrected," he probably means to include this wrong addition of *a me*. In other words, Jerome agrees that *a me*, "from me," should be removed from the translation. This was not his mistake. These words were mistakenly added *scriptorum errore*, "due to an error of the copyists."

Nevertheless, there is a second issue in this passage. What about the suggestion of *auxilium meum*, "my help," in place of *auxilium tuum*, "your help"? The text of the Gallican Psalter as Sunnia and Fretela quoted it back to Jerome (*auxilium tuum*) does in fact represent the attested Gallican Psalter reading, which follows many OL witnesses and agrees with Codex Sinaiticus. By contrast, the reading proposed by Sunnia and Fretela (*auxilium meum*) matches most Greek witnesses (τὴν βοήθειάν μου) and also the Hebrew, which presents the verse somewhat differently: "And you, O Lord, do not be distant; my strength, hasten to my help (לעזרתי)."

I think it likely that the hexaplaric LXX read τὴν βοήθειάν μου, "my help," in agreement with the Hebrew. The correction proposed by Sunnia and Fretela (*auxilium meum*) agreed with the hexaplaric LXX against Jerome's Gallican Psalter. Jerome recognized that his own rendering (*auxilium tuum*) was indefensible based on the hexaplaric LXX, so he rolled this mistranslation in with the wrongful addition of *a me*, attributing both (*tuum a me*) to scribal error introduced by someone who miscopied his text. The only true scribal mistake was the addition of *a me*, but Jerome leaves the impression that his *tuum* (= GPsal) instead of *meum* (= the hexaplaric LXX) is also the product of a later copyist.

The expanded text as found in Sunnia and Fretela's copy of Jerome's translation (*auxilium tuum a me*) was adopted in the Sixto-Clementine Vulgate (Van Ess 46). As for Jerome's later thinking, in the IH Psalter he construes the verse in a different sense that more closely matches the Hebrew: *tu autem domine ne longe fias, fortitudo mea in auxilium meum festina*, "But you, O Lord, do not become distant; my strength, hasten to my help."

12.1.1–2. *si quid scriptorum errore mutatum est, stulta credimus contentione defendere*, "If anything has been altered due to an error of the copyists, we believe it to be a foolish effort to defend it." On Jerome's practice of textual criticism in *Ep.* 106, see introduction, §8.

12.2.3–4. *universum semen Iacob, magnificate eum*, "All ye the seed of Jacob, magnify him!" Ps 21:24 (Heb 22:24), GPsal. The issue at hand is not the reading of the text but the proper Latin translation of the Greek word δοξάζω. See also **30.4**.

12.2.10. *fit indecora translatio*, "It would produce an inelegant translation." On Jerome's concern for the Latinity of his translation, see introduction, §7.2.

12.2.10. *et nos emendantes olim psalterium*, "And when previously we were correcting the Psalter." Jerome's previous corrections to the Psalter include his modestly revised version of the *Vetus Latina* Psalter produced around 384 at Rome and the Gallican Psalter under discussion here. See introduction, §2.1.

12.2.11–12. *ubicumque sensus idem est, veterum interpretum consuetudinem mutare noluimus*, "Wherever the sense is the same we preferred not to change the custom of the old translators." Jerome expresses this same basic principle elsewhere with respect to the Septuagint. For example: *In hoc loco Septuaginta interpretationem secuti sumus, quia non multum* *ab hebraico distat in sensu*, "In this passage we follow the translation of the Seventy, because it does not differ much from the Hebrew in sense" (*Comm. Isa.* 22:3a); *In eo loco, ubi nos iuxta Septuaginta interpretati sumus, ne quid innovare videremur, quia vulgatum est testimonium*, "In this passage, where we translated according to the Seventy, so that we do not appear to be making any innovations, seeing that it is the popular witness" (*Comm. Isa.* 58:12). On the principle of preserving traditional renderings where possible, see introduction, §7.2.

13.1.13–14. *calix meus inebrians quam praeclarus est*, "My cup is remarkably intoxicating." Ps 22:5 (Heb 23:5), GPsal. The reading "your cup" (τὸ ποτήριόν σου), which Jerome labels an error in the κοινή edition, is the standard reading for the majority of LXX witnesses. Jerome's reading "my cup" matches the Hebrew as well as a few Lucianic manuscripts and a copy of the Sahidic Coptic Psalter dating from around 400 (Rahlfs 112). He supports his rendering by appealing to "all the translators" (i.e., Aquila, Symmachus, and Theodotion) and the "Seventy," by which he means the "original" Greek version as found in the hexaplaric LXX, even though in reality the text cited by Sunnia and Fretela is probably the original Greek reading and Jerome's "my" is a correction toward the Hebrew.

13.1.17. *chosi ... chosach.* Jerome gives the Hebrew reading for "my cup" as *chosi* (i.e., כוסי), and he also supplies what the Hebrew would have been if "your cup" were correct, *chosach* (i.e., כוסך). See also **6.1.9–10**. It is interesting that Jerome does not comment on the phrase *quam praeclarus*, "remarkably," which corresponds to the Greek ὡς κράτιστον but does not directly represent anything in the Hebrew and does not appear in the IH edition.

14.1.18–19. *confundantur omnes inique agentes*, "Let all those who act unjustly be confounded." Ps 24:4a (Heb 25:3b), GPsal.[51] The word "all" (πάντες; LXX 24:3b) appears in Codex Alexandrinus, in a corrected hand in Codex Vaticanus, and in the Greek text of the Verona Psalter (Rahlfs

---

51. The preserved Gallican Psalter reads *iniqua agentes*, "those who do unjust things," as does at least one eleventh-century manuscript of *Ep.* 106 (see Gasquet 15 and Hilberg 255), but the majority of witnesses to *Ep.* 106 offer the reading *inique agentes*, "those who act unjustly." We may assume that *iniqua* in the *Ep.* 106 manuscript is a correction towards the Gallican Psalter, and that *inique* is the earliest recoverable reading for *Ep.* 106. It is unclear whether this was a fault in the text as quoted by Sunnia and Fretela which Jerome failed to notice, or if *inique* came about as an early scribal error in the transmission of *Ep.* 106.

114). There is a single Hebrew manuscript listed by Kennicott (2:324) that adds "all" and has no connection to the Greek evidence. In both the Greek tradition and the Hebrew manuscript, "all" was carried over into this sentence from the previous one (כל קויך; πάντες οἱ ὑπομένοντές σε). Evidence for "all" at 24:4a in the OL tradition is lacking.

We may suppose that Jerome included this occurrence of "all" in the Gallican Psalter because when he was translating out of the hexaplaric LXX his eye slipped over the obelus ("under the dart") and he neglected to remove it. Perhaps Jerome marked this text with an obelus in the Gallican Psalter, but if so it is surprising that he does not complain about the confusion caused by those who failed to copy his critical signs (see introduction, §8.2). All he does in this case is acknowledge that the text proposed by Sunnia and Fretela is correct based on his stated principles and assure his readers that he is aware of the evidence, namely, that the Hebrew lacks "all" and the hexaplaric LXX marked it with in obelus.

14.2.23. *quia sustinui te*, "because I waited on you." Ps 24:21 (Heb 25:21), GPsal. The text used by Sunnia and Fretela apparently added κύριε, "Lord," to the end of this line: "because I waited on you, O Lord." In fact, κύριε appears in most LXX witnesses and was a common OL reading (Sabatier 50; Weber 48; Thibaut 46; CC 38:140; CC 97:228). On the other hand, the word "Lord" is lacking in Greek witnesses such as P.Bod. 24 and Codex Sinaiticus and in Latin texts such as Codex Casinensis 557 and Codex Sangermanensis (Rahlfs 116; KT 58; Amelli 18). There is no word for "Lord" in the preserved Hebrew text. Jerome did not include *domine* in the Gallican Psalter, probably because it was absent from the hexaplaric LXX. Here he dismisses its proposed addition as *superfluum*, "superfluous," because it is absent from the authoritative texts and because it is obvious that the psalmist waited on God (see introduction, §8.5).

Hans Bardtke in BHS commends the restoration of יהוה at the end of the verse on the grounds that the second hemistich is too short vis-à-vis the first ("metrum"; BHS 1107).

15.1.1. *et nunc ecce*, "And now, behold" Ps 26:6 (Heb 27:6). The word "behold" (*ecce*) is not present in the Gallican Psalter. The text with which Jerome begins his discussion is not his own translation but the text that Sunnia and Fretela suggested to him, which includes *ecce*, "behold"; it is found in Latin texts such as the Verona Psalter, the Coislin Psalter, the Lyon Psalter, the Ambrosian Psalter, the Sinai Psalter, and Augustine's *Enarrations* (Weber 51; Thibaut 47; CC 38:152). As for Greek evidence, ἰδού, "behold" is widely attested in the LXX (Rahlfs 118). Sunnia and Fretela must have questioned Jerome as to why he did not include "behold" in the Gallican Psalter. In fact, "behold" is absent from the Hebrew and from the hexaplaric versions (Field 2:125). It must also have been omitted from the hexaplaric LXX (cf. Caloz 141). In answer to their question, Jerome briefly notes that *ecce* is "superfluous," that is, unnecessary for the meaning and unsupported by the Hexapla and Hebrew (see introduction, §8.5).

15.1b.2–3. *exquisivit facies mea*, "My face sought." Ps 26:8 (Heb 27:8), GPsal. The Masoretic Text reads בַּקְּשׁוּ פָנָי, "Seek (pl.) my face." But the sense of this clause is difficult. Why "my" face? Does the psalmist imagine the voice of God addressing him? And if the psalmist is speaking in the singular, why is the verb plural? Some scholars emend the Hebrew text to read "Seek (sing.) his face" (BHS 1109). The Greek evidence is diverse. For example, Codex Vaticanus and Codex Alexandrinus give ἐξεζήτησα τὸ πρόσωπόν σου, "I sought your face," whereas in Codex Sinaiticus, the scribe apparently took the word "face" (plural in form) to be the subject of the verb (בקשו), which was construed as a perfect: ἐζήτησεν τὸ πρόσωπόν μου, "my face sought" (or else "he sought my face"). Further variations in the Greek exist (see Rahlfs 118). The OL tradition shows some variation, but the best attested construal is: "I sought your face," either *quaesivi faciem tuam* as in Codex Sangermanensis or else *quaesivi vultum tuum* as in the Verona Psalter, Codex Casinensis 557, the Sinai Psalter, and Augustine's *Enarrations* (Sabatier 53; Amelli 19; Thibaut 47; CC 38:153).

As for the Gallican Psalter, Jerome's translation is illuminated by the hexaplaric versions. Aquila translated literally, ἐξεζήτησαν πρόσωπά μου, "my face (pl.) sought," and Symmachus translated more idiomatically, σὲ ἐζήτει τὸ πρόσωπόν μου, "my face sought you" (Field 2:126).[52] In the Gallican Psalter, Jerome seems to have followed Aquila, producing a translation close to the Hebrew but unclear in meaning. The translation suggested by Sunnia and Fretela follows the same basic interpretation but clarifies the sense by adding the object "you" in accordance with Symmachus. Perhaps Jerome realizes that their proposed translation is clearer, and he likely knows that it is supported by Symmachus, so he does not reject it outright but merely affirms that his original rendering is "better." In the version of

---

52. On Aquila and Symmachus, see MS Ottobonianus Graecus 398, and for Symmachus see also the Syro-Hexapla: *lk b'' hw' prṣwpy*; see Adrian Schenker, *Psalmen in den Hexapla: Erste kritische und vollständige Ausgabe der hexaplarischen Fragmente auf dem Rande der Handschrift Ottobonianus Graecus 398 zu den Ps 24–32*, StT 295 (Vatican: Biblioteca Apostolica Vaticana, 1982), 143–45.

the Gallican Psalter produced by Alcuin and later in the Sixto-Clementine edition, "you" is included: *exquisivit te facies mea* (see WG 798; Van Ess 48).

16.1.6–7. *'exaudi, domine.' sed et hoc additum est,* " 'Hear, Lord.' But this has been added." Ps 27:2 (Heb 28:2), GPsal. Jerome omitted "Lord" in the Gallican Psalter in agreement with Aquila and Symmachus (Field 2:127) and perhaps also the hexaplaric LXX. This matches the preserved Hebrew text. Here Jerome insists that *domine*, "Lord," has been incorrectly added.

As for other evidence, the word "Lord" appears in this passage according to various witnesses, including not only the Lucianic manuscripts, Theodoret's *Commentary**, the Syro-Hexapla, and MS 55 Rome but also the Arabic version and Jerome's IH edition (Rahlfs 119; BHS 1109).[53] One must keep open the possibility that a Hebrew text circulated in late antiquity that included the word "Lord," which perhaps influenced the Lucianic manuscript tradition and served as the basis for Jerome's IH Psalter.

17.1.9–10. πᾶς τις … *omnis quis.* Ps 28:9 (Heb 29:9), GPsal. The Hebrew has כֻּלּוֹ, literally "all of it." The LXX rendered each constituent element, כל = πᾶς, and ו = τις, producing a collocation that meant something like "every single" (cf. LXX Gen 6:5) or "any single" (cf. LXX 2 Sam 3:35).[54] Examples of how this might be expressed in Latin can be found in Augustine's *Enarrations*, which translates πᾶς τις as *unusquisque*, "each one individually" (CC 38:171), and in the Sinai Psalter, which gives *omnis quisque* (Thibaut 49). Jerome does not dispute that the Greek text contains πᾶς τις, but he insists that a truly literal translation is absurd, and that a simpler translation is better in this instance.

17.1.10. *ad verbum*, "literally." See introduction, §7.2.

17.1.10. κακοζηλίαν, "affectation." See introduction, §7.2.

17.2.11–12. *dominus diluvium inhabitare facit*, "The Lord makes to inhabit the deluge." Ps 28:10 (Heb 29:10), GPsal. The Masoretic Text has: יְהוָה לַמַּבּוּל יָשָׁב, "the LORD sat at the deluge." In most LXX witnesses, we find: κύριος τὸν κατακλυσμὸν κατοικιεῖ, "The Lord will settle the deluge." The translation proposed by Sunnia and Fretela, *dominus diluvium inhabitat*,

---

53. In Latin, *domine* is present in Lucifer of Calgliari (CC 8:173), Cassiodorus's *Explanation* (CC 97:244), and some copies of Augustine's *Enarrations* (CC 38:168).

54. Didymus of Alexandria explains πᾶς τις as follows: οὐχ ὁ μὲν ὁ δὲ ἀλλὰ πᾶς τις, "Not just this one or that one, but every single one"; see Lincoln H. Blumell, with Thomas W. Mackay and Gregg W. Schwendner, eds., *Didymus the Blind's Commentary on Psalms 26:10–29:2 and 36:1–3*, P.BYU 1 (Turnhout: Brepols, 2019), 45.

"The Lord inhabits the deluge," is supported by the OL tradition (Sabatier 56; Thibaut 49), the Bohairic Coptic, and the Syro-Hexapla (Rahlfs 121).[55]

17.2.15. *iasaph.* Hebrew: יֹשֵׁב. Jerome's transliteration *iasaph* deserves comment. First, although Jerome recognizes differences between שׁ, ס, and צ (see *Nom. Hebr.*; CC 72:72; *Comm. Isa.* 11:1–3) and even knows two pronunciations of שׁ (i.e., שׂ and שׁ; *Qu. hebr. Gen.* 21:30–31), he typically represents Hebrew sibilants simply with Latin *s*. Second, the transcription of ב as *ph* is unusual. Jerome normally represents ב as *b*, even at the end of words, as illustrated by his treatment of names such as *Iacob, Iob,* and *Moab* in *Book of Hebrew Names* (cf. his discussion of *beth* at *Comm. Jer.* 9:22).

Jerome's explanation of the ambiguity of *iasaph* probably reflects his dependence on the hexaplaric versions. To be sure, the verb יָשַׁב can refer either to "sitting" or "inhabiting," but the difference between "inhabit" (יָשַׁב, *qal*) and "make (someone) to inhabit" (הוֹשִׁיב, *hiphil*) is not a question of ambiguity in the word's lexical meaning but of a difference in grammatical form. The Syro-Hexapla gives *ytb* (cf. Hebrew: יֹשֵׁב) for Aquila and Symmachus, for which Field postulated the Greek ἐκάθισεν (Field 2:130).[56] If Jerome based his interpretation of the Hebrew on the possible usages of ἐκάθισεν, it is clear why he thought the Hebrew could mean either "sit/inhabit" or "cause to sit/inhabit."[57] In fact, the Hebrew יֹשֵׁב means simply "sits" or "inhabits."

In the IH edition, Jerome will translate *dominus diluvium inhabitat,* "The Lord inhabits the deluge," that is, the very translation suggested by Sunnia and Fretela and one that better matches the Hebrew.

17.2.16–17. *de gratia baptismatis,* "the grace of baptism." As Jerome explains this psalm, those who are said to glorify the Lord in v. 9 (i.e., who say, "glory") are made to inhabit the flood (i.e., the grace of baptism) in v. 10.

18.1.1. *quoniam tu es protector meus,* "Because You are my Protector." Ps 30:5 (Heb 31:5), GPsal. The word "Lord" (χύριε) appears in the Lucianic manuscripts, Theodoret's *Commentary**, the Syro-Hexapla, Codex Alexandrinus, MS 55 Rome, the Roman Psalter, and a few other OL witnesses

---

55. This is likewise the reading given in the *Commentaries on the Psalms* (CC 72:203). For this passage, Codex Casinensis 557 gives the reading of the Gallican Psalter (Amelli 20). Cf. χατοιχεῖ, "inhabit" in P.Bod. 24 (KT 63).

56. Cf. ἐκάθησεν in MS Ottobonianus Graecus 398 (Schenker, *Psalmen in den Hexapla,* 210–11).

57. LSJ, s.v. "χαθίζω."

(Rahlfs 123; Weber 57). Similarly, the abbreviation for "Lord" (χε) is found in the LXX column of MS 1098.[58] Jerome's testimony in *Ep.* 106, however, suggests that it was not present in the hexaplaric LXX.[59] Here Jerome observes: *rursum et in hoc loco additum nomen domini est,* "Again also in this passage the name of the Lord has been added." He just commented on the addition of the word "Lord" at **16.1.**

18.2.4–5. *ego autem dixi in excessu mentis meae,* "But I spoke in the departure of my mind." Ps 30:23 (Heb 31:23), GPsal. Apparently Sunnia and Fretela questioned Jerome's translation by citing the standard OL rendering, *in pavore meo,* "in my alarm." In this case, Jerome's defense is not to say that they have cited the wrong Greek text, but instead he explains that the proper sense of the underlying Greek cannot be expressed otherwise than through his roundabout translation. Thus, the word ἔκστασις, "displacement," "movement outwards," or more fully "distraction of mind, from terror, astonishment, anger" should be translated into Latin as *excessus mentis* ("departure of mind"), not simply as *pavor* ("alarm, fear").[60] Jerome might have been thinking of the Latin version of Acts 11:5, which translates ἐν ἐκστάσει as *in excessu mentis.*

18.2.9. *aliter me Hebraico legisse noveram,* "Otherwise, I know that I have read in the Hebrew." The Hebrew has בחפזי, "in my haste (in fear)."[61] The two Hebrew options that Jerome offers are Aquila and Symmachus: Aquila: ἐν θαμβήσει μου = Jerome's *in stupore (meo),* "in my bewilderment"; and Symmachus: ἐν τῇ ἐκπλήξει μου = Jerome's *in admiratione mea,* "in my astonishment" (Field 2:134).[62] In the IH edition, Jerome follows Aquila: *in stupore meo.*

19.1.11. *nec est in spiritu eius dolus,* "Nor is there deceit in his spirit." Ps 31:2 (Heb 32:2), GPsal. The LXX and Symmachus have στόματι "mouth," and all the other translations give πνεύματι, "spirit," which matches the Hebrew: וברוח.[63] When Jerome includes "the Seventy" among those who translate "spirit," he means by this the hexaplaric LXX.

---

58. See Mercati, *Psalterii Hexapli Reliquiae* (1958), 31.

59. Caloz 36 suggests that χε, i.e., κύριε, "Lord" was not originally part of the LXX column of MS 1098 but entered the text as a variant LXX reading registered as a gloss in between the columns.

60. LSJ, s.v. "ἔκστασις."

61. *HALOT*, s.v. "חפז."

62. See also Schenker, *Psalmen in den Hexapla,* 309.

63. Marginal readings in MS Ottobonianus Graecus 398 testify to the readings of

19.1.16–17. *brucho … baffio.* Jerome gives both the Hebrew as it is (i.e., ברוחו, "in his spirit") and the Hebrew as it would need to be if the other option were correct (i.e., בפיו, "in his mouth"). See **6.1.9–10.**

19.2.17. *conversus sum in aerumna mea,* "I was turned in my hardship." Ps 31:4 (Heb 32:4), GPsal. The MT gives the verb in the third-person and contains a word, לשדי, whose meaning is not fully clear. The noun לשד occurs in Num 11:8 with the apparent meaning "cake," but this makes little sense in context.[64] Another avenue of interpretation involves reading לְשׁנִי, "my tongue," which produces something like "Changed was my tongue."[65] The Syriac Peshitta reads *bḥdyy,* "in my breast," as if from ב, "in" and שדי, "breast" (Pesh 31). One medieval Hebrew manuscript, by a slip of the pen or editorial desperation, changes the text to נהפך לבי, "my heart was changed" (Kennicott 2:330). There is no obvious solution to the problem of the original Hebrew text for this passage.

The LXX (ἐστράφην εἰς ταλαιπωρίαν, "I was turned into hardship") gives the first-person verb and takes לשדי to be a form of שׁד II, "oppression, devastation."[66] This would allow for the initial ל to be the preposition "to, into," which collocates well with the verb, "to turn into" something.[67] If this were correct, however, what does one make of the final *yod?* The obvious answer is to interpret this as the first-person singular suffix, "my." Jerome understands the Hebrew this way and he testifies that "my" (μου) was present in the hexaplaric LXX under asterisk, added from Theodotion.[68]

19.2.20. *lasaddi.* The manuscripts of *Ep.* 106 repeat the Hebrew word *lasaddi* (spelled variously) without further comment. According to Hilberg (25) and Gasquet (16), this indicates a lacuna in the manuscripts, in which Jerome offered some specific discussion of the Hebrew word. This is

---

Aquila and Quinta (πνεύματι), and Symmachus (στόματι); see Schenker, *Psalmen in den Hexapla,* 326–27.

64. See *HALOT,* s.v. "לשד." Hayim b. Y. Tawil, *An Akkadian Lexical Companion for Biblical Hebrew* (Jersey City, NJ: Ktav, 2009), 193 notes an Akkadian cognate for לשד with the meaning "cream."

65. E.g., Hans-Joachim Kraus, *Psalms 1–59: A Continental Commentary* (Minneapolis: Fortress, 1993), 366–67.

66. *HALOT,* s.v. "שׁד II."

67. *DCH,* s.v. "הפך."

68. The evidence for the hexaplaric versions is not fully clear (cf. Field 2:135; Rahlfs 126), but overall the evidence supports Jerome's report that Theodotion included the first-person suffix μου; see Schenker, *Psalmen in den Hexapla,* 334–35.

certainly possible, and if so, it is regrettable that Jerome's final comments
were lost. It should be noted, however, that he does occasionally end his
treatment of a biblical lemma by simply stating how the Hebrew word is
said (e.g., *Comm. Jer.* 10:12–16). If Jerome's final comment was simply "In
Hebrew it is said *lasaddi*," then the repetition of the Hebrew in the text of
Ep. 106 might have arisen at an early stage of transmission out of uncertainty as to the proper spelling of the Hebrew word and the desire to preserve both spellings known to the copyist. I think this latter explanation
is probably correct, so the text printed in this edition deletes the second
occurrence *lasaddi*.

20.1.21–22. *omnia ossa mea dicent: domine*, "All my bones will say,
'Lord!'" Ps 34:10 (Heb 35:10), GPsal. The Hebrew text has יהוה (Greek:
κύριε; Latin: *domine*) written once. In the Greek tradition, Codex Alexandrinus, the Lucianic manuscripts, Theodoret's *Commentary**, and Theodore of Mopsuestia give κύριε twice (Rahlfs 132; Hill 358). This reflects
the Hebrew אדני יהוה. Sunnia and Fretela apparently had a Latin text that
read *domine, domine*, in imitation of the Greek witnesses that contain the
repetition.

Jerome's comment that "many copies" (*multa ... exemplaria*) among
the Hebrews do not even have the word "Lord" once is surprising. There
are no preserved Hebrew manuscripts that lack יהוה in this passage. One
wonders what basis he has for this statement. Has he consulted various
copies of the Hebrew text? On rare occasions Jerome mentions multiple
Hebrew manuscripts (e.g., *Ep.* 32.1; 36.1) or refers to variations between
different copies of the Hebrew (e.g., *Comm. Hab.* 2:19; *Comm. Gal.* 3:10),
but I am skeptical that he was making use of "many copies" of the Hebrew
Psalter while working on this treatise. It is likely that he is passing on information from a Hebrew scholar, a Jew or Jewish convert to Christianity,
whom he consulted on this question. The source of that individual's information is unknown.

21.1.1–2. *in Graeco 'volet nimis' vos legisse dixistis*, "You said that in the
Greek you read: 'he shall *very much* approve.'" Ps 36:23 (Heb 37:23), GPsal.
Codex Alexandrinus, the Lucianic manuscripts, the Syro-Hexapla, Theodoret's *Commentary**, and Theodore of Mopsuestia add the word σφόδρα,
"very much" (Rahlfs 137; Hill 430). This appears as *nimis* in Latin witnesses
such as the Roman Psalter and the Sinai Psalter (Weber 77; Thibaut 60).
Sunnia and Fretela reported to Jerome a Greek text that includes the word
σφόδρα. Jerome corrects this addition by noting the absence of σφόδρα
from all the hexaplaric versions.

22.1.4–5. *verumtamen vane conturbatur omnis homo,* "Yet every man was disquieted in vain." Ps 38:12 (Heb 39:12), GPsal. Many LXX witnesses have ταράσσεται, "is troubled," which stands behind the Gallican Psalter's *conturbatur,* "was disquieted." The word is not present in the Hebrew and is lacking in Greek witnesses such as Codex Alexandrinus and Codex Sinaiticus and in Latin texts such as Codex Casinensis 557, the Roman Psalter, and the Sinai Psalter (Rahlfs 142; Amelli 28; Weber 85; Thibaut 63). Apparently, the copy of the Psalms used by Sunnia and Fretela lacked ταράσσεται.

22.1.6. *sub veru,* "under the dart." This means the word was marked with an obelus in the hexaplaric LXX. See introduction, §8.2.

22.1.7. *et hinc apud vos et apud plerosque error exoritur,* "And here is why the error arose among you and among most people." Jerome's explanation for how this "error" arose is somewhat peculiar at first sight. One might argue that the manuscript consulted by Sunnia and Fretela was right to omit ταράσσεται, since it had been placed "under the dart" (i.e., under obelus) in the hexaplaric LXX. From Jerome's perspective, however, the proper way to handle the critical text is not to delete the material under obelus but to preserve it along with the critical sign that marks it as suspect. But if so, the error in the Greek text used by Sunnia and Fretela came about not simply because someone deleted the signs but because someone deleted a word marked with an obelus. Therefore, in terms of what is found in the Greek, Jerome should be lamenting copyists who delete words in accordance with critical signs rather than those who simply do not copy the signs.

In reality, the error with which Jerome is most concerned is the one that occurred in the copying of his own Gallican Psalter. He had included *conturbatur* in his translation marked with an obelus to show that it was not part of the authentic text. This obelus had been omitted from the copy of the Gallican Psalter consulted by Sunnia and Fretela. Thus the error they wrongly ascribed to Jerome had actually been caused by the negligence of the scribes (*scriptorum neglegentia*) who copied his work.

In the IH edition, Jerome will remove the intrusive word: *verumtamen vanitas omnis homo,* "yet every man is vanity."

22.1.8. *virgulis,* "signs," from *virgula,* literally "a small twig." The word is defined as "a critical mark, as a sign of spuriousness (i. q. obelus)."[69] See

---

69. LD, s.v. "virgula."

Inst. 1.4.3. Thus, by *vergulis et asteriscis*, "signs and asterisks," Jerome refers to the obelus and asterisk. See introduction, §8.2.

22.1.8. *distinctio*, "distinction." In a textual discussion of this sort, one would expect *distinctio* to mean "punctuation." But Jerome is saying not that the punctuation of the text has become confused but that distinctions have become confused between inauthentic but perhaps traditional texts under obelus and authentic texts supplied from Theodotion under asterisk because scribes have not been careful in coping the critical signs.

23.1.10–11. *et legem tuam in medio cordis mei*, "and your law in the midst of my heart." Ps 39:9 (Heb 40:9), GPsal. The Latin *cordis*, "heart" was the standard OL translation, which Jerome preserved in the Gallican Psalter (Sabatier 81; Weber 86).[70] In place of *cordis*, the LXX has κοιλίας, "belly," which followed the Hebrew idiom בתוך מעי, "in the midst of my belly." Jerome transliterates this as *batthoch meai*, although the manuscripts of *Ep.* 106 show considerable variation for this transliteration (Hilberg 258).

23.1.13. *propter euphoniam*, "for the sake of euphony." Jerome places a restriction on his freedom to translate for the sake of style by saying *non debemus subtrahere, quod verum est*, "We should not remove what is true." In other words, in recasting the literal wording to improve how the expression strikes the ear we must preserve the true sense. On Jerome's approach to translation, see introduction, §7.2.

23.2.15. *domine, in adiutorium meum respice*, "Lord, give attention to my help." Ps 39:14 (Heb 40:14). The preserved Gallican Psalter reads *domine, ad adiuvandum me respice*, "Lord, give attention to helping me." The text that Sunnia and Fretela quoted back to Jerome as his own does not precisely match Jerome's translation as preserved; that is, they give *in adiutorium meum*, "to my help," instead of Jerome's *ad adiuvandum me*, "to helping me." A common OL reading is *in auxilium meum*, "to my aid," which is similar to their wording. It is possible that Sunnia and Fretela quoted the text to him in a corrupted form, but the wording was close enough to his own version and the traditional Latin Psalter that Jerome did not notice.

Many LXX witnesses, including P.Bod. 24, the Leipzig papyrus (MS 2013), Codex Vaticanus, and Codex Sinaiticus give the verb πρόσχες, "give attention" (Rahlfs 144; KT 87).[71] In many OL witnesses this became *respice*,

---

70. The Ambrosian Psalter, however, has *ventris*, "belly."
71. Hilberg prints πρόσσχες, but the standard spelling is given by Gasquet 17.

"give attention" (Sabatier 82; Weber 87), which Jerome preserved in the Gallican Psalter, probably because the hexaplaric LXX kept it. If, in fact, the hexaplaric LXX retained πρόσχες, that is why Jerome tells Sunnia and Fretela that this is the reading of the Seventy.

On a different track, the preserved Hebrew text has חושה, "hasten," which generated the rendering σπεῦσον, "hasten," found in Greek witnesses such as Codex Alexandrinus, the Zürich Greek Psalter, and numerous Lucianic manuscripts (Rahlfs 144).[72] In Latin, this interpretation appears in Codex Casinensis 557, which gives *propera*, "hasten" (Amelli 29), and also in the Sinai Psalter, which has *festina*, "hasten" (Thibaut 65). As for preserved hexaplaric evidence, it appears that Aquila rendered חושה as σπεῦσον (Field 2:151). Thus in this case Sunnia and Fretela suggested a translation that better accords with the Hebrew and was actually used by Aquila. In *Ep.* 106 Jerome simply refers his audience back to the hexaplaric LXX, which presumably read πρόσχες. But in the IH edition, Jerome will follow the Hebrew text and Aquila, translating *festina*, "hasten," which is the interpretation Sunnia and Fretela suggested.

24.1.18. *et si ingrediebatur, ut videret*, "And if he entered to see." Ps 40:7 (Heb 41:7), GPsal. The Hebrew text contains "And if" (ואם), and the "if" is retained in most Greek manuscripts, although Codex Alexandrinus lacks "if" (εἰ), probably, as Rahlfs suggested, due to a slip of the eye involving the εἰ- at the start of the following word: εἰ εἰσεπορεύετο (Rahlfs 146). The word *si*, "if," is absent from many OL sources, for example, Codex Sangermanensis, the Verona Psalter, the Sinai Psalter, Augustine's *Enarrations*, and Cassiodorus's *Explanation* (Sabatier 83; Weber 89; Thibaut 65; CC 38:454; CC 97:375), although we find *si* in Codex Casinensis 557: *et si ingrediebar intus vidire* (read: *videre*), "And if I entered within to see" (Amelli 30). Sunnia and Fretela consulted a Greek text that lacked εἰ, "if," and Jerome responds by affirming the presence of "if" in the Hebrew and all the hexaplaric versions (but see Field 2:153 on Symmachus, for whom there is some uncertainty).

25.1.22-1. *deus meus*, "my God." Ps 41:6-7 (Heb 42:6-7), GPsal. Jerome reports that Sunnia and Fretela claimed to have found *et deus meus*, "and my God." The Hebrew text of this psalm is difficult on the phrase in question. In its first occurrence at the end of v. 6 and the beginning of v. 7,

---

72. In the text of Theodore of Mopsuestia's *Commentary on the Psalms*, the biblical lemma has πρόσχες, but in his comments Theodore says ταχεῖάν σου καὶ ἐσπουδασμένην ποίησον τὴν βοήθειαν, "make your help quick and hastened" (Hill 504).

the Leningrad Codex has יְשׁוּעֹת פָּנָיו אֱלֹהָי, "the deliverances of his face, my God," although at least two medieval Hebrew manuscripts have פני ואלהי, "my face and my God" (Kennicott 2:341; De-Rossi 4:29), the issue being whether the *vav* belongs to what precedes it (i.e., "his face") or what follows it (i.e., "and his God"). Similarly, in v. 12, where the Leningrad Codex has יְשׁוּעֹת פָּנַי וֵאלֹהָי, "the deliverances of my face and my God," three medieval Hebrew manuscripts have פניו אלהי, "his face, my God," with one manuscript giving "his face, and my God," and a few other variations (Kennicott 2:342; De-Rossi 4:29–30). Given the lack of clarity surrounding the sense of the passage and the possibilities for graphical confusion, it is not surprising that we also find various renditions of these words in the ancient versions.

In many LXX witnesses, καί, "and," appears in neither passage. In the first instance we find σωτήριον τοῦ προσώπου μου ὁ θεός μου, "salvation of my face, my God" (v. 6), and in the second instance we find ἡ σωτηρία τοῦ προσώπου μου ὁ θεός μου, "the salvation of my face, my God" (v. 12). Evidence for καί in v. 6 is found in Codex Alexandrinus, the Greek text of the Verona Psalter, the Lucianic manuscripts, Theodoret's *Commentary**, and the Syro-Hexapla, and also in much of the OL tradition (Rahlfs 147; Sabatier 86; Weber 91). The evidence for καί in v. 12 is similar. Jerome holds that the commonly known text of the Septuagint lacked καί in both verses but that καί had been added in v. 12 in the hexaplaric LXX under asterisk from Theodotion.

25.1.5. *'et' coniunctio*, "the conjunction 'and.'" According to Donatus's *Ars grammatica* (see **8.2.1**), *Coniunctio est pars orationis adnectens ordinansque sententiam*, "A conjunction is a part of speech connecting and ordering a sentence."[73] The grammarian Diomedes begins his discussion of *coniunctio* as follows: *Coniunctio est pars orationis indeclinabilis copulans sermonem et coniugens vim et ordinem partium orationis*, "A conjunction is an indeclinable part of speech joining a stretch of language and connecting the import and sequence of parts of speech."[74] On *coniunctio*, see also **29.1**; **33.5**; **45.3**; **67.2**; **83.2**.

---

73. Keil, *Grammatici Latini*, 4:388–89.

74. Diomedes, *Art. Gram.*, Bk. 1, *De coniunctione*; see Keil, *Grammatici Latini*, 1:415. On the standardization of grammatical definitions among late antique grammarians, see Anneli Luhtala, "On Definitions in Ancient Grammar," in *Grammatical Theory and Philosophy of Language in Antiquity*, ed. Pierre Swiggers and Alfons Wouters, Orbis Supplementa 19 (Leuven: Peeters, 2002), 257–86, esp. 272.

25.2.6–7. *exprobaverunt mihi, qui tribulant me,* "They who afflict me have reproached me." Ps 41:11 (Heb 42:11), GPsal. For *qui tribulant me,* "they who afflict me," what Jerome reports for the LXX, οἱ θλίβοντές με, "those afflicting me" has the widest attestation, whereas the reading put forward by Sunnia and Fretela, οἱ ἐχθροί μου, "my enemies" is found in Codex Alexandrinus, MS 1219 Washington, the Lucianic manuscripts, the Syro-Hexapla, Theodoret's *Commentary**, and Theodore of Mopsuestia (Rahlfs 148; Hill 530). In Latin, *inimici mei,* "my enemies," is given in Codex Casinensis 557, the Ambrosian Psalter, Psalterium Augiense 2, and a correction in the Lyon Psalter (Amelli 31; Weber 93). Jerome's rendering in the Gallican Psalter reflects οἱ θλίβοντές με, but in *Ep.* 106 he also justifies his translation by appealing to the Hebrew *sorarai,* that is, צוררי, "those treating me with hostility," for which he gives the Latin rendering *hostes mei,* "those hostile to me," that is, opponents in war or political foes, rather than *inimici,* "personal enemies."[75]

25.3.10–11. *spera in deum, quoniam adhuc confitebor illi,* "Hope in God, because yet I will confess him." Ps 41:12 (Heb 42:12), GPsal. Most LXX witnesses lack anything to correspond to the Latin *adhuc,* "yet" (Rahlfs 148).[76] As Jerome reports, the Hebrew says: "Hope in God, because yet (כי עוד) I will confess him." Jerome transliterates כי עוד as *chi od,* and he states that עוד, that is *adhuc,* "yet" was supplied as ἔτι in the hexaplaric LXX from Theodotion. Based on Jerome's perspective as expressed at the beginning of *Ep.* 106, we may assume that he regards this "addition" from Theodotion to be a restoration of the original LXX. As Jerome notes, the same issue is at play at Ps 42:5 (Heb 43:5).

26.1.16–17. *et non egredieris in virtutibus nostris,* "And you will not go out with our hosts." Ps 43:10 (Heb 44:10), GPsal. The Leningrad Codex at Heb Ps 44:10 reads וְלֹא תֵצֵא בְּצִבְאוֹתֵינוּ, "And you will not go out with our hosts." The same basic sentence appears in Heb Ps 60:12, except that אֱלֹהִים,

---

75. *HALOT,* s.v. "צורר"; LD, s.v. "inimicus."

76. The word "yet" is represented in the Syro-Hexapla: *mṭl dtwb 'wd' lh,* "For yet *(twb)* I will praise him," according to Antonio M. Ceriani, *Codex Syro-Hexaplaris Ambrosianus: Photolithographice editus* (1874; repr., Piscataway, NJ: Gorgias, 2013). According to the edition of Kasser and Testuz, P.Bod. 24 also contains this word: ἔτι ἐξομολογήσομαι, "yet (ἔτι) I will confess" (KT 91); but Albert Pietersma correctly observes that the most likely reconstruction of this line is: ἐπὶ τὸν θν ὅτι ἐ]ξομ[ολογ] ήσο[μαι, i.e., without ἔτι; see Albert Pietersma, "The Edited Text of P. Bodmer XXIV," *BASP* 17 (1980): 67–79, esp. 73.

"God," appears after וְלֹא תֵצֵא, thus producing "And you will not go out, O God." At least six medieval Hebrew manuscripts also have "God" at Heb Ps 44:10 (Kennicott 2:342).

In Greek, the following witnesses include "God" at Ps 43:10, as it was quoted by Sunnia and Fretela: Codex Alexandrinus, MS 1219 Washington, the Lucianic manuscripts, some copies of Theodoret's *Commentary**, and the Greek text of the Verona Psalter (Rahlfs 150). In Latin, "God" appears in the Latin text of the Verona Psalter, the Sinai Psalter, Augustine's *Enarrations*, Cassiodorus's *Explanation*, the Roman Psalter, and the Sixto-Clementine edition of the Vulgate (Weber 96; Thibaut 68; CC 38:485; CC 97:395; and Van Ess 60). I suspect the word "God" (θεός) did not appear in the hexaplaric LXX even under obelus, since Jerome simply dismisses it as "superfluous" (see introduction, §8.5). The word "God" (*Deus*) is absent from the text as quoted in the *Commentaries on the Psalms* (CC 72:209).

26.2.18–19. *posuisti nos in similitudinem gentibus*, "You have made us into an illustration to the nations." Ps 43:15 (Heb 44:15), GPsal. At issue is the difference between Greek and Latin idiom. The LXX translated this phrase ἔθου ἡμᾶς εἰς παραβολήν ἐν τοῖς ἔθνεσιν, literally, "you made us into a parable among (ἐν) the nations." Sunnia and Fretela challenged Jerome as to why his translation reads *similitudinem gentibus*, "illustration to the nations," which construes *similitudinem* with the dative *gentibus* ("*to* the nations"), rather than following *similtudinem* with a prepositional phrase (in + ablative: "among" the nations) as in the Greek. Jerome responds with a translation principle: *interpretationis elegantia*, "the elegance of the translation," should be preserved as much as possible, but without harm to the sense (*absque damno sensus*). In Jerome's view, even if *similitudinem in gentibus* is closer to the Greek, nevertheless it sounds bad in Latin and therefore should be avoided. On κακόφωνον, "cacophony," and translation theory, see introduction, §7.2.

Finally, Jerome offers a translation that represents the Hebrew: תשימנו משל בגוים, *posuisti nos proverbium in gentibus*, "You made us a parable among the nations." Here Jerome actually uses the prepositional phrase, *in gentibus*, presumably because the prepositional phrase sounds acceptable after *proverbium*, whereas it sounds unacceptable after *similitudinem*. This raises the question: Why did Jerome not simply translate the Greek παραβολή with *proverbium* in the first place? The answer: *similitudo* was used in the OL, and Jerome wanted to keep the traditional wording as much as possible (Sabatier 89; Thibaut 68).

Ironically, in his IH edition Jerome will employ a translation close to the one he calls κακόφωνον here: *posuisti nos similitudinem in gentibus*, "You have made us an illustration among the nations" (rather than *in similitudinem*, "into" an illustration).

26.3.25. *exsurge, adiuva nos*, "Rise up, help us!" Ps 43:26 (Heb 44:27), GPsal. The word "Lord" is present in this verse (ἀνάστα, κύριε, βοήθησον ἡμῖν) in most LXX and OL witnesses (Rahlfs 152; Sabatier 90; Weber 98) but is not found in the Hebrew and was omitted from the Gallican Psalter.[77]

27.1.1. *sagittae tuae acutae*, "Your arrows are sharp." Ps 44:6 (Heb 45:6) GPsal. Most LXX manuscripts contain τὰ βέλη σου ἠκονημένα, δυνατέ, "Your arrows are sharp, O powerful one" (Rahlfs 152).[78] The recently discovered P.Oxy. 5101, however, offers a pre-Origenian Greek text that lacks δυνατέ, "O powerful one" (CH 5), in agreement with the Hebrew and Gallican Psalter. As for the Latin tradition, the presence of "O most powerful one" (*potentissime*) is supported by Codex Sangermanensis, the Roman Psalter, and other sources, whereas *sagittae tuae acutae potentissimae*, "your most powerful sharp arrows" is the reading found in the Verona Psalter, Augustine's *Enarrations*, and Cassiodorus's *Explanation* (Rahlfs 152; Sabatier 91–92; Weber 99; CC 38:504; CC 97:406).[79]

As noted above, there is no evidence in Hebrew for the word "powerful" at v. 6, but, as Jerome observes, v. 4 in Hebrew has גִּבּוֹר, "O powerful one." Jerome suspects that δυνατέ was wrongly added in v. 6 under the influence of v. 4. Jerome's Gallican Psalter translation, which omits "O powerful one" at v. 6, looks like a straightforward Hebraizing revision based on the hexaplaric LXX, which either omitted the word or placed it under obelus (cf. Caloz 143). In light of the absence of δυνατέ in P.Oxy.

---

77. The word *domine*, "Lord," is absent from the unrevised text of the Lyon Psalter, probably under the influence of the Gallican Psalter, and it is also absent from Codex Casinensis 557 as part of a different translation tradition: *exurge auxiliare nobis*, "Rise up, assist us!" (Amelli 32). This same basic translation appears in the Sinai Psalter, but with "Lord": *exurge domine auxiliare nobis*, "Rise up, O Lord, assist us!" (Thibaut 69).

78. See also the Didymus of Alexandria fragment in Carmelo Curti, *La Catena Palestinese sui Salmi Graduali* (Catania: Centro Di Studi Sull'Antico Cristianesimo, 2003), 117.

79. Codex Casinensis 557 omits this verse. The Sinai Psalter contains: *Sagitte tue acute potentissime* (Thibaut 69). Given the common alternation in Latin manuscripts between *ae* and *e*, we may assume the first three words are *sagittae tuae acutae*. Whether the final word was intended as *potentissime* or *potentissimae* is not clear.

5101, it is possible that Origen's base text for the hexaplaric LXX already lacked this word such that no obelus was necessary.[80]

28.1.6–7. *quoniam ecce reges congregati sunt,* "For, behold, kings have been assembled." Ps 47:5 (Heb 48:5), GPsal. The Greek text consulted by Sunnia and Fretela apparently had βασιλεῖς αὐτῆς, "its kings," (i.e., the kings of the earth; cf. v. 3), as witnessed by the Leipzig papyrus (Rahlfs MS 2013) and the Bohairic Coptic version (Rahlfs 157). This reading appears in Latin (*reges eius,* "its kings") in the Ambrosian Psalter (Weber 104). Jerome regards it as "superfluous," that is, unneeded and without sufficient textual basis (see introduction, §8.5).

28.1.9. *ipse lectionis textus,* "the context of the passage itself." Literally, "the context (*textus*) itself of the passage (*lectio*)." See introduction, §9.1.

28.1.9–10. *in veteribus codicibus Latinorum,* "in the old codices of the Latins." As Jerome states, *reges terrae,* "the kings *of the earth,*" is the main-stream OL reading (Sabatier 96; Thibaut 72).[81] Moreover, the added *terrae* appears in two important Gallican Psalter manuscripts and ultimately found its way into the Sixto-Clementine Vulgate (WG 826; Van Ess 62). Greek texts that contain "of the earth" (τῆς γῆς) include P.Bod. 24, Codex Alexandrinus, the Greek text of the Verona Psalter, MS 1219 Washington, the Lucianic manuscripts, and Theodoret's *Commentary** (Rahlfs 157; KT 100). When Jerome says τῆς γῆς is absent from the LXX, he means that it was not found in the hexaplaric LXX. It is probable that "of the earth" was added in Ps 47:5 under influence from Ps 2:2. There is no evidence for the addition "of the earth" (ארץ) in any Hebrew manuscripts, including 4QPsⁱ, frg. 1 (Ulrich 643).

One does not get the impression that Sunnia and Fretela asked about *terrae.* It seems they asked only about *eius,* but Jerome thought *terrae* was the more important variant to discuss.

28.2.12. *sicut audivimus, sic vidimus,* "As we have heard, thus we have seen." Ps 47:9 (Heb 48:9), GPsal. Sunnia and Fretela report the Greek reading οὕτως καὶ εἴδομεν, in other words, *sic et vidimus,* "thus *also* we have seen." Greek texts that give καί ("also") as cited by Sunnia and Fretela include the

---

80. Jannes Smith suggests that δυνατέ was not present in the original Greek translation of the Psalter but was added in the course of transmission by a Greek scribe or commentator; see "The Text-Critical Significance of P.Oxy. 5101 (RA 2227) for the Old Greek Psalter," *JSCS* 45 (2012): 5–22, esp. 11–12.

81. But Codex Casinensis 557 has *regimonia,* "rulerships," without *eius* or *terrae* (Amelli 34).

Leipzig papyrus (Rahlfs MS 2013), the Greek text of the Verona Psalter, the Lucianic manuscripts, Theodoret's *Commentary**, the Syro-Hexapla, and MS 55 Rome (Rahlfs 157). The "also" (*et*) in Latin appears in witnesses such as the Roman Psalter, the Sinai Psalter, and Augustine's *Enarrations* (Weber 105; Thibaut 72; CC 38:543). Hebrew evidence for the conjunction is lacking, and Jerome dismisses the addition as superfluous (see introduction, §8.5). Jerome offers *chen rainu* as a transliteration for the Hebrew: כן ראינו.

28.3.17. *templi tui*, "your temple." Ps 47:10 (Heb 48:10), GPsal. Instead of this, Sunnia and Fretela suggested *populi tui*, "your people." Most LXX witnesses read τοῦ λαοῦ σου, "your people" (see Rahlfs 158; cf. Ps 26:4), and this carried over into some OL witnesses, such as Codex Sangermanensis (*plebis tui*), and also the Verona Psalter, the Saint-Gall Psalter, and Augustine's *Enarrations* (*populi tui*) (Sabatier 97; Weber 105; CC 38:546). Jerome reports a Greek reading τοῦ ναοῦ σου, "your temple," which matches the Hebrew text (היכלך) and agrees with the hexaplaric versions (Field 2:168). This reading also found its way into the OL tradition in various forms, for example, *templi tui* in the Roman Psalter, the Sinai Psalter, and Cassiodorus's *Explanation*; *templo tuo* in Codex Casinensis 557, Saint Zenon of Verona's Psalter, and one of the chief witnesses to the Mozarabic Psalter; and *in templo sancto tuo* in the Corbie Psalter (Weber 105; Thibaut 72; CC 97:428; Amelli 34). When Jerome says of this reading, "we translated from the Hebrew and from the Seventy Translators," this indicates that the hexaplaric LXX gave τοῦ ναοῦ σου as its text.

Three points of interest in this discussion may be noted: first, Jerome gives a transliteration of the Hebrew היכלך, *echalach*, and he explains that it means "your temple." This can be compared with the transliteration that appears in John Chrysostom's *Exposition of the Psalms*: ἠχαλάχ δεμμηνοῦ, which probably represents the Hebrew דמינו ... היכלך, "we ponder ... your temple" (but in reverse order), although Chrysostom actually interprets the Greek as "people" rather than "temple." (PG 55:219). Jerome's treatment, although rudimentary, is less confused. Second, Jerome provides what the Hebrew would have been if the erroneous reading "your people" had been correct: *ammach*, עמך (cf. **6.1.9–10**). This shows basic Hebrew knowledge beyond what one finds in most Greek and Latin writers of his time. Third, Jerome once again dismisses a reading as "superfluous" (see introduction, §8.5). Presumably, in addition to the fact that the Hebrew lacks the superfluous element, Jerome means that it is unnecessary for the people to say in the first-person: "We (i.e., your people) have received your mercy in the midst of your people."

29.1.22. *homo, cum in honore esset,* "Man—when he was in honor." Ps 48:21 (Heb 49:21), GPsal.[82] The LXX at Ps 48:13 contains: καὶ ἄνθρωπος ἐν τιμῇ ὢν οὐ συνῆκεν, "and man, being in honor, does not understand." The same line occurs in LXX Ps 48:21, except that manuscripts vary as to whether or not v. 21 begins with καί. The Greek Psalter consulted by Sunnia and Fretela apparently had καί at v. 21, which is supported by a number of important Greek witnesses, including Codex Sinaiticus, Codex Alexandrinus, MS 1219 Washington, the Greek text of the Verona Psalter, the Lucianic manuscripts, Theodoret's *Commentary**, the Syro-Hexapla, and MS 55 Rome (Rahlfs 160). Jerome's Gallican Psalter has *et* in v. 13 but omits it in v. 21. This matches MT and also P.Oxy. 5101 (CH 7).[83] Because Jerome based the Gallican Psalter on the hexaplaric LXX, it is reasonable to assume that the hexaplaric LXX signaled the absence of καί at the start of v. 21. The existence of an early Greek text (P.Oxy. 5101) that lacks καί at v. 21 suggests that Origen may have had a manuscript at hand when producing the hexaplaric LXX that gave v. 21 without the initial καί (cf. **27.1.1**). Otherwise, καί could have been marked with an obelus.

Regarding v. 13, in place of what the Greek and Latin texts have as "does not understand," the Hebrew reads בל ילין, "does not reside," whereas in v. 21 it reads ולא יבין, "and does not understand."[84] The Syro-Hexapla preserves a reading for Symmachus at v. 13: *l' nbwt* (i.e., "does not reside") that matches the Hebrew (Field 2:171). In the Gallican Psalter, Jerome has *non intellexit,* "does not understand" for v. 13 (= the Greek). In the IH Psalter at v. 13, Jerome will translate *non commorabitur,* "will not reside," agreeing with the Hebrew and Symmachus.

29.1.25. *'et' coniunctionem,* "the conjunction 'and.'" See **25.1.5**.

---

82. There are variations in both the manuscripts of *Ep.* 106 and in the manuscripts of the Gallican Psalter at Ps 48:21 as to whether this phrase should read: *homo, cum in honore esset,* or else: *homo, in honore cum esset.* Hilberg 260 gives the text: *homo, cum in honore esset,* which agrees with the wording of v. 13, whereas Gasquet 18 gives: *homo, in honore cum esset,* which is also Weber-Gryson's text at Ps 48:21 (see WG 828). Because (1) the GPsal text of Ps 48:13 seems clearly to have *homo, cum in honore esset,* and (2) because Jerome's discussion of v. 21 in *Ep.* 106 assumes that the wording of v. 13 and the wording of v. 21 (apart from the *et* in v. 13) are identical, I am following Hilberg in reading *homo, cum in honore esset* here at *Ep.* 106.29, and I also favor this as the reading of the Gallican Psalter at Ps 48:21.

83. Kennicott (2:347) lists four Hebrew manuscripts that include "and" in v. 21, which reflects harmonization to v. 13.

84. A few Hebrew manuscripts read ילין at v. 21 as well (De-Rossi 4:35).

29.2.26. *et dominabuntur eorum iusti*, "and the just will rule over them." Ps 48:15 (Heb 49:15), GPsal. As Sunnia and Fretela pointed out and Jerome agrees, the Greek has εὐθεῖς, "straight." In Hebrew, this is ישרים, "straight, right." Sunnia and Fretela suggested that *rectus*, "straight, right" is a closer semantic representation of the Greek εὐθεῖς than Jerome's *iustus*, "just, upright" as found in the Gallican Psalter.

29.2.2. εὐφωνίαν. On euphony in Jerome's translation theory, see introduction, §7.2. Jerome does not dispute that the Greek text says εὐθεῖς, but he is saying that to translate *rectus* here would sound bad in Latin, which is unnecessary, because Latin can communicate the same meaning in language that sounds more pleasing by using *iustus*.

29.2.3. Jerome is referring to the "Book of Jashar" (ספר הישר), which is mentioned in the Hebrew Bible at Josh 10:13 and 2 Sam 1:18. In the LXX, this book is referenced in 2 Sam 1:18 as βιβλίου τοῦ εὐθοῦς, and although LXX Josh 10:12–13 does not refer to the Book of Jashar, one Greek witness to Josh 10:12 mentions βιβλίον τὸ εὐθές.[85] Based on Jerome's statement, we may assume that the OL translated τοῦ εὐθοῦς in 2 Sam 1:18 as *iustorum*. In the Gallican Psalter at Ps 48:15, Jerome followed this same practice and translated οἱ εὐθεῖς as *iusti*, and he defends his decision in *Ep.* 106 by explaining his translation philosophy. In the IH edition, Jerome will reverse himself and render ישרים as *recti*, as Sunnia and Fretela suggested.

29.2.4. *non debemus ... verbum de verbo exprimere*, "We should not translate word for word." On word-for-word translation in *Ep.* 106, see introduction, §7.2.

29.2.5. *syllabam*, "syllable." On Jerome's training in technical grammar and use of grammatical terminology, see **8.2.1.** Donatus begins the section *De syllaba* of his *Ars grammatica* with the following definition: *Syllaba est conprehensio litterarum vel unius vocalis enuntiatio temporum capax. Syllabarum aliae sunt breves, aliae longae, aliae communes*, "A syllable is the combining of letters or the enunciation of a single vowel, consisting of quantity. Some syllables are short, some are long, and some are common."[86] On long and short syllables, see *Inst.* 9.4.84–86.[87]

---

85. Alan E. Brooke, Norman McLean, and Henry St. J. Thackeray, eds., *The Old Testament in Greek according to the Text of Codex Vaticanus* (Cambridge: Cambridge University Press, 1906–1940), 2:712. Moreover, the Greek text of 1 Kgs 8:53 cites βιβλίῳ τῆς ᾠδῆς, "Book of the Song," i.e., ספר השיר, which is likely a corrupted form of ספר הישר.

86. Keil, *Grammatici Latini*, 4:368.

87. On the syllable in Latin antiquity, see Giovanna Marotta, "Syllable and Prosody

29.3.5–6. *de manu inferni cum liberaverit me,* "When from the hand of hell he shall free me."[88] Ps 48:16 (Heb 49:16). The Hebrew, Greek, and Latin texts are not appreciably different in this instance. The Gallican Psalter reads: *Deus redimet animam meam de manu inferi cum acceperit me,* "God will redeem my soul, from the hand of hell, when he shall receive me." It is possible that some confusion arose as to whether *de manu inferi* is connected to what comes before ("God will redeem my soul from the hand of hell") or with what comes after ("when he shall receive me from the hand of hell"). It is noteworthy that Jerome takes it with what follows. Perhaps this confusion led some scribe to reproduce a variation on *redimet* (Greek: λυτρώσεται) in the second half of the verse, changing Jerome's original *acceperit* into *liberaverit* ("free," similar to "redeem"). In this instance, what Sunnia and Fretela thought was a fault in Jerome's Gallican Psalter is really a scribal error in their copy of his text, and the alternative translation they propose is Jerome's own rendering.

30.1.10–11. *sedens adversus fratrem tuum loquebaris,* "Sitting, you were speaking against your brother." Ps 49:20 (Heb 50:20), GPsal. The Greek word in question, κατελάλεις, can be understood as a combination of the elements κατά, "against" and λαλέω, "speak," with the meaning "to speak against," as frequently in the LXX and in Jas 4:11; 1 Pet 2:12; 3:16. The LXX uses this verb, κατελάλεις, together with a prepositional phrase starting with κατά, "against": κατὰ τοῦ ἀδελφοῦ σου, "against your brother." The OL as represented by Codex Sangermanensis and the Sinai Psalter translated this sentence as *Sedens adversus fratrem tuum detrahebas,* "Sitting, you were disparaging against your brother" (Sabatier 102; Thibaut 75), preserving the "contrary" element in both the verb (*detrahebas,* "you were disparaging") and in the prepositional phrase (*adversus,* "against"), as in the Greek. This is what Sunnia and Fretela thought Jerome should have done.

30.1.15. *vitiosum,* "faulty," in this case, "stylistically faulty." On Jerome's avoidance of stylistic faults in translation, see introduction, §7.2.

30.1.18. *de fratre tuo detrahebas,* "you were disparaging *concerning* your brother." As Jerome makes clear, the traditional Latin rendering they

---

in Latin Grammarians," in *The Notion of Syllable Across History: Theories and Analysis,* ed. Dominico Russo (Newcastle upon Tyne: Cambridge Scholars Publishing, 2015), 55–86.

88. The Gallican Psalter as preserved has *inferi* (the older form) for *inferni* ("mostly poet. And post-Aug."; LD, s.v. "*inferi*"). At least two manuscripts of *Ep.* 106 also read *inferi* (Hilberg 261).

propose (*detrahebas … adversus*) sounds stylistically redundant in Latin, in a way that is not a problem for Greek idiom. In his view, proper Latin idiom requires either *loquebaris … adversus*, "you were speaking against," or *detrahebas … de*, "you were disparaging." By way of comparison, Codex Casinensis 557 has: *Sedens de fratre tuo insusurrabas*, "Sitting, you were insinuating concerning your brother" (Amelli 36).

30.2.21. *haec superflua sunt*, "These matters are superfluous." See introduction, §8.5.

30.2.23–24. *quia unaquaeque lingua, ut ante iam dixi, suis proprietatibus loquitur*, "As I already said before, each language speaks in its own particular idioms." On Jerome's concern for the idioms of each language in translation, see introduction, §7.2.

30.3.24–25. *ne quando rapiat et sit, qui eripiat*, "lest he snatch, and there is one who rescues." Ps 49:22 (Heb 50:22). The text Sunnia and Fretela proposed, with *non*, is in fact the Gallican Psalter text: *ne quando rapiat et non sit, qui eripiat*, "lest he snatch, and there is not one who rescues." As elsewhere in *Ep.* 106, Jerome must point out that the erroneous text quoted to him is not really his translation but arose through *vitium librarii dormitantis*, "the mistake of a drowsy copyist" (see introduction, §8.4). In this instance, he offers an explanation for how the error arose: perhaps the text had been written with *nec* instead of *non*: *nec sit, qui eripiat*, "nor is there one who rescues," and from there a scribe accidentally wrote *et* in place of *nec*.

30.4.5. *honorificabit*, "will honor." Ps 49:23 (Heb 50:23), GPsal. In Ps 49:23, Jerome translates δοξάζω, "glorify" with *honorifico*, "honor." Sunnia and Fretela probably asked why he did not use the Latin *glorifico*.

Jerome refers to an earlier discussion (*de quo et supra diximus*; see **12.2**) where he states that Latin normally renders δοξάζω with *magnifico*, "magnify." In both places (**12.2** and **30.4**), he acknowledges that δοξάζω can be translated into Latin as *glorifico*. But he is by no means ready to concede that δοξάζω simply means *glorifico* or that *glorifico* is always the best way to translate δοξάζω. To add support to his position, Jerome cites John 17:5, where δοξάζω had been traditionally rendered into Latin with *clarifico*, "make illustrious," to illustrate that a Greek word may legitimately be translated into Latin in a variety of ways depending on the passage.[89] He

---

89. The version of John 17:5 quoted by Jerome in Greek is close to the Greek text found in the original hand of the uncial D (fifth century) and in Epiphanius, and it is reflected in the Latin text of Irenaeus (NA[28] 359). On Jerome and New Testament

sums up this discussion with one of his basic principles: provided that the sense remains the same, other factors such as style or convention can and should be considered. See introduction, §7.2.

31.1.11–12. *expectabam eum, qui salvum fecit,* "I was waiting on him who saved me." Ps 54:9a (Heb 55:9a), GPsal. The word "God" (τὸν θεόν) is added before "him who saved me" (τὸν σῴζοντά με) in MS 1219 Washington, the Lucianic manuscripts, Theodoret's *Commentary**, and the Syro-Hexapla (Rahlfs 168). The word "God" is not present in the Hebrew and was probably lacking in the hexaplaric LXX.

31.2.13–14. *a pusillanimitate spiritus,* "from faintheartedness of spirit." Ps 54:9b (Heb 55:9b), GPsal. The Hebrew text for this verse is challenging. As vocalized in the Leningrad Codex it reads אָחִישָׁה מִפְלָט לִי מֵרוּחַ סֹעָה מִסָּעַר, "I will hurry to a refuge for myself from a rushing wind, from a storm." A key difficulty in this verse is סֹעָה, which occurs only here in the Hebrew Bible. One suggestion interprets this word as related to the Arabic *s'y*, "go quickly," so that רוּחַ סֹעָה is a "rushing wind."[90] Another suggestion is to read מֵרוּחַ סְעָרָה, "from the wind of a storm," with סעה being the result of dittography (cf. BHS 1136).

The LXX reads: προσεδεχόμην τὸν σῴζοντά (i.e., מִפַלֵּט) με ἀπὸ ὀλιγοψυχίας καὶ καταιγίδος, "I was waiting on him who saves me from faintheartedness and storm." As for the primary expression in question, מרוח סעה, "from the wind/soul of סעה," this was rendered in the LXX as ἀπὸ ὀλιγοψυχίας, "from faintheartedness" (literally, "from small life/soul"). This expression appeared in the OL typically as: *a pusillanimitate*, "from faintheartedness," or else *a pusillo animo*, "from small mind/soul" (Sabatier 109; Weber 121; Thibaut 78; CC 61:146). In Codex Casinensis 557, we find a rendering that looks like a reflection of the Hebrew independent of the standard LXX, probably through a Greek intermediary: *a spiritu procellarum*, "from a spirit of rushing winds" (Amelli 38).

In the Gallican Psalter, Jerome kept the Old Latin rendering *a pusillanimitate*, but he added the word *spiritus*, "spirit," presumably based on his understanding of the hexaplaric LXX, which probably had ἀπὸ πνεύματος

---

textual criticism, see Bruce M. Metzger, "St. Jerome's Explicit References to Variant Readings in Manuscripts of the New Testament," in *New Testament Studies: Philological, Versional, and Patristic* (Leiden: Brill, 1980), 199–210.

90. ʾĀmôs Hakham, *Sefer Tehillim,* 2 vols., Daʿat Miqra (Jerusalem: Mossad Harav Kook, 1979), 1:319. Cf. Edward W. Lane, *Arabic-English Lexicon,* 8 vols. (Edinburgh: Williams & Norgate, 1872), 4:1366.

in keeping with all the hexaplaric versions that he cites (see Field 2:178–79). At first glance, Jerome's choice to add the word *spiritus* to match πνεύματος (רוח) seems straightforward. Upon closer reflection, however, it becomes evident that the word ὀλιγοψυχίας (*pusillanimitate*) already represents the word "spirit" in the form of -ψυχίας (-*animitate*). This makes his addition of the word *spiritus* redundant. Strictly speaking, if he wanted to render πνεύματος (רוח) separately as *spiritus*, he should not have used *pusillanimitate*, because this includes "spirit" within it.

I suspect that Jerome understands these linguistic issues better when writing *Ep.* 106 than when he first translated the Gallican Psalter. So, in order to show his current grasp of the verse's meaning, he concludes by summing up the sense in keeping with all these versions, specifically their rendering of מרוח (*merucha*) as ἀπὸ πνεύματος: *festinabo, ut salver a spiritu tempestatis et turbinis*, "I will hasten, so that I may be saved from a spirit of storm and whirlwind." This is precisely the translation he will use when he produces his IH Psalter.

31.3.20–21. *quoniam, si inimicus maledixisset*, "because, if an enemy had slandered." Ps 54:13 (Heb 55:13), GPsal. The only point of dispute in this passage is the proper Latin translation of the Greek ὠνείδισεν. Jerome's *maledixisset* preserved a common OL rendering (Sabatier 110; Thibaut 79), but the translation proposed by Sunnia and Fretela, *exprobrasset*, also appears in Augustine's *Enarrations* (CSEL 94.1:159).[91] In defense of his translation, Jerome states simply that the sense does not differ either way. The unstated piece of his argument is that he is preserving what he understands to be the traditional wording, which he tends to do whenever there is no significant difference in meaning (see introduction, §7.2).

32.1.3. *ab altitudine diei timebo*, "From the height of the day I will fear." Ps 55:3–4 (Heb 56:3–4), GPsal. According to Jerome, Sunnia and Fretela said they found in Greek *non timebo*, "I will not fear." But Jerome says the negative (οὐ, *non*) was added. In the main LXX witnesses, v. 4 contains φοβηθήσομαι, "I will fear," whereas in v. 5 and v. 12 it has οὐ φοβηθήσομαι, "I will not fear." Apparently, in the copy of the LXX used by Sunnia and Fretela, οὐ φοβηθήσομαι is also the reading in v. 4. The addition of the negative particle in v. 4 is supported by the Leipzig papyrus (Rahlfs MS 2013), the

---

91. Cf. Codex Casinensis 557: *inproperavit*, "taunted" (Amelli 38); and Hilary, *Tractatus* 54.13: *improperasset* (CC 61:148).

Lucianic manuscripts, the Syro-Hexapla, Theodoret's *Commentary**, Theodore of Mopsuestia, and MS 55 Rome (Rahlfs 171; Hill 724).

32.1.4. *est ordo*, "This is the sequence of thought." On Jerome's contextual exegesis, see introduction, §9.1.

32.2.6–7. *in ira populos confringes*, "In anger you will break peoples."[92]
Ps 55:8 (Heb 56:8), GPsal. In this instance, Jerome explains a translation error that occurred in the OL tradition. The LXX has κατάξεις, from
κατάγω, "bring down." Jerome says that a better translation for this word
would have been *deicies*, from *deicio*, "throw down." As Jerome explains,
however, the Old Latin version read the Greek as if it were κατεάξεις, from
κατάγνυμι, "break" (see Matt 12:20) and so gave the erroneous translation
confringes, "you will break." Jerome supports his explanation by appealing
to the Hebrew, *hored*, הורד (*hiphil* of ירד, "bring down"), which he interprets using two Greek words, κατάγαγε (from κατάγω, "carry/bring down")
of Symmachus, and καταβίβασον (from καταβιβάζω, "bring down"), which
is Aquila (see Field 2:182).

What is especially noteworthy about Jerome's discussion is that he
makes no attempt to defend his Gallican Psalter translation. In the Gallican Psalter, Jerome gave *confringes*, "you will break," in keeping with the
OL tradition he inherited (Sabatier 112).[93] Presumably, Jerome sees no
way that he can justify his translation, so he chooses simply to correct it,
although without drawing attention to the mistake. Rather than introducing the proposed reading by saying *dicitis in Graeco vos invenisse*, "You

---

92. The manuscripts of *Ep.* 106 read: *pro quo in Graeco legitur:* ἐν ὀργῇ λαοὺς
κατάξεις, *id est 'confringes.'* "In place of this in Greek it is read ἐν ὀργῇ λαοὺς κατάξεις,
that is, 'you will break.'" But this is an unlikely text, because Jerome's point is to explain
that κατάξεις does not mean "you will break." It is not in keeping with Jerome's usage
to follow the word κατάξεις immediately with *id est* and then the mistaken meaning.
Hilberg 263 resolves the difficulty by adding to the text as follows: *pro quo in Graeco
legitur:* ἐν ὀργῇ λαοὺς κατάξεις, <*id est 'deicies,' non* κατεάξεις,> *id est 'confringes.'* "In
place of this in Greek it is read ἐν ὀργῇ λαοὺς κατάξεις, <that is, 'you will throw down,'
not κατεάξεις,> that is, 'you will break.'" Hilberg's emendation offers a sensible text
and assumes omission by *parablepsis* (κατάξεις, *id est* ... κατεάξεις, *id est*). The editors
of the Benedictine edition simply omit *id est, confringes* (Gasquet 20). Because Jerome
proceeds to offer a Latin rendering for each Greek verb, I have cautiously followed the
Benedictine text.

93. Alternatively, the text given in the Sinai Psalter, Hilary's *Tractatus*, and Augustine's *Enarrations* is *deduces*, "lead down" or "lead forth" (Thibaut 80; CC 61:157; CC
39:687). Codex Casinensis 557 gives *inmisisti*, "cast in" (Amelli 39).

say that in Greek you found," and then explaining the true state of affairs, Jerome begins simply: *pro quo in Graeco scriptum est*, "In place of this in Greek it is written." There is no doubt as to what the Greek should be. The question arose because of a mistake that occurred *apud Latinos*, "among the Latins." Jerome explains the origin of the error and provides the proper translation, but he does not explicitly acknowledge that this error "among the Latins" also appears in his own Gallican Psalter. In the IH edition, he will translate this word as *detrahet*, "take down" or "lead away."

33.1.13–14. *quia deus susceptor meus*, "Because God is my protector." Ps 58:10 (Heb 59:10), GPsal. The issue addressed in this passage arose because the Hebrew text is terse, and the versions needed to be more expansive for the sake of clarity. Verse 9 addresses God in the second-person, and then in v. 10 there is some confusion as to the speaker and addressee, with reference made to "his strength" (the Leningrad Codex and many medieval Hebrew manuscripts) or else "my strength" (the LXX; the Targum [עושני]; at least eleven medieval Hebrew manuscripts) at the start of v. 10 (BHS 1140; De-Rossi 4:39; White II, 247). The second half of v. 10 in Hebrew continues thus: כי אלהים משגבי, "because God is my refuge." The LXX followed the second-person discourse in v. 9 when translating this phrase in v. 10: ὅτι ὁ θεὸς ἀντιλήμπτωρ μου εἶ, "because, O God, you are my protector." Moreover, in the Lucianic manuscripts, some copies of Theodoret's *Commentary**, and MS 55 Rome, the pronoun σύ, "you" is added before ὁ θεός (Rahlfs 175).

Evidence for the Old Latin tradition is not consistent. For example, Codex Sangermanensis and Hilary's *Tractatus* read *quia deus susceptor meus est*, "because God is my protector" (Sabatier 117; CC 61:178), which is similar to the Gallican Psalter except that Jerome dropped *est*. On the other hand, the Roman Psalter has *quia tu deus susceptor meus es*, "because you, O God, are my protector" (Weber 131), which follows the LXX according to the Lucianic tradition with the addition of *tu/σύ*. The Sinai Psalter gives this second-person reading, but without the pronoun: *quia deus susceptor meus es* (Thibaut 82). In Codex Casinensis 557 we find a slightly different approach: *quoniam deus protectio mea*, "because God is my protection" (Amelli 41).

Jerome's response to this question reveals a perspective on the Hebrew and LXX that is more nuanced than what is articulated in the preface. When Jerome produced the Gallican Psalter, he preserved the third-person construal of the passage as found in his OL text. The Hebrew will bear this interpretation, and in fact Jerome omitted *est*, for which there is no matching element in the Hebrew. But the LXX construed this passage in the second-person, adding εἶ and in some witnesses σύ. This is the text cited by Sunnia and Fretela. Jerome justifies his Gallican Psalter translation by pointing out that the second-person pronoun and verb are interpretive additions made by the LXX that are absent from the Hebrew. He does not claim that the original LXX lacked these elements but acknowledges that the LXX added these words, and because the Hebrew lacks them, his third-person reading is also justified. In this case, Jerome subtly invokes the Hebrew to defend his Gallican Psalter translation against the LXX.

Two noteworthy observations should be made about the IH edition. First, in addition to its meaning "refuge," the Hebrew word משגב has the basic sense "high point," which explains why Jerome renders it as *elevator*, "one who raises up" in his Hebrew Psalter (hexaplaric evidence is lacking).[94] Second, in the IH edition, Jerome will switch over to the second-person construal by adding *tu*, thus producing: *quoniam tu deus elevator meus*.

33.2.16–17. *deus meus, voluntas eius praeveniet me*, "My God, his goodwill shall go before me." Ps 58:11 (Heb 59:11), GPsal. The Hebrew word in question is חסד, translated by the LXX as τὸ ἔλεος, "mercy," which the standard OL rendered *misericordia*, "mercy, compassion" (Sabatier 117; Weber 131; Thibaut 83).[95] The precise signification of the word חסד is notoriously difficult to pin down, with potential English glosses including "joint obligation," "loyalty," "faithfulness," "goodness," "graciousness," "godly action," and "proofs of mercy."[96] In the Gallican Psalter, Jerome chose to break from tradition and translated this word as *voluntas*, "will" or "good will." But when confronted with the Greek τὸ ἔλεος, Jerome concedes that the best rendering is, in fact, *misericordia*. This is what Jerome will use in the IH edition. As for *Ep.* 106, he does not say that his Gallican Psalter translation is wrong, only that the rendering proposed by Sunnia and Fretela is *verius*, "truer, more correct."

33.2.19–20. *sed in Hebraeo scriptum est: misericordia mea praeveniet me*, "But in Hebrew it is written: 'my mercy will go before me.' " Having acknowledged that his Gallican Psalter translation was not as precise as it could be, Jerome moves on to cite the Hebrew text, perhaps to illustrate that no translation, not even the LXX, captures every nuance—and so his

---

94. *HALOT*, s.v. "משגב."

95. *Deus meus miserere mei*, "My God, have mercy on me" in Codex Casinensis 557 (Amelli 41).

96. *HALOT*, s.v. "חסד."

questionable rendering of τὸ ἔλεος should be overlooked. The Hebrew, according to Jerome, says "my mercy" rather than "his mercy." In the Leningrad Codex, Jerome's "my mercy" (חסדי) represents the *qere*, whereas "his mercy" (חסדו) is the *ketiv*. In fact, over thirty medieval Hebrew manuscripts and the Targum (טובי) agree with Jerome and the *qere* (De-Rossi 4:39–40; White II, 248). Evidence for the hexaplaric versions is lacking, so it is not possible to explore Jerome's relationship to his Greek sources. Particularly significant in this discussion is Jerome's willingness to recognize that neither the Gallican Psalter nor the Greek text, which is tacitly acknowledged to be the genuine LXX, represents the Hebrew with complete accuracy.

In the IH edition, Jerome will give a slightly different translation for this verse, construing the Hebrew אלהי not as nominative (*deus meus*, "my God") but as genitive: *dei mei misericordia praeveniet me*, "The mercy of my God will go before me."

33.3.20–21. *deus ostendit mihi inter inimicos meos*, "God shows to me among my enemies." Ps 58:12a (Heb 59:11b). The Latin text as quoted here matches the OL as found in Codex Sangermanensis (Sabatier 117). The preserved Gallican Psalter reads: *deus ostendet* (or *ostendit*) *super inimicos meos* (WG 840). For the preposition, the form of the text in *Ep.* 106 (*inter*) is closer to the underlying Greek (ἐν τοῖς ἐχθροῖς μου) than what we find in the Gallican Psalter (*super*). It may be an error in the transmission or in the original composition of the treatise, but in this case the text that Jerome accepts as his own in *Ep.* 106 differs slightly from what is attested for the Gallican Psalter.

33.3.22. *sed 'meus' additum est*, "but 'my' was added." The addition of "my" (μου, *meus*) to this phrase (cf. ὁ θεός μου at 58:11a LXX) is attested in Codex Vaticanus, Codex Sinaiticus, the Greek and Latin (*deus meus*) texts of the Verona Psalter, MS 55 Rome, the Roman Psalter, the Sinai Psalter, Hilary's *Tractatus*, Augustine's *Enarrations*, and Cassiodorus's *Explanation*, (Rahlfs 176; Weber 131; Thibaut 83; CC 61:178; CSEL 94.1:351; CC 97:525).

33.4.1–2. *populi tui*, "your people." Ps 58:12b (Heb 59:12a). Jerome has two points to make on this text: (1) his reading *populi*, "people" is correct, and the word they suggested, *legis*, "law" is incorrect; and (2) his version actually gave *populi mei*, "my people," not *populi tui*, "your people," as they quoted it to him. Once again, the Gallican Psalter text used by Sunnia and Fretela was faulty (see introduction, §3.2).

The Greek text proposed by Sunnia and Fretela, τοῦ νόμου σου, "your law," is supported by various witnesses: P.Bod. 24, Codex Vaticanus, Codex

Sinaiticus, the Lucianic manuscripts, Theodoret's *Commentary**, the Greek text of the Verona Psalter, MS 55 Rome, the Bohairic Coptic; and in Latin: the Verona Psalter, Codex Sangermanensis, the Roman Psalter, the Sinai Psalter, Hilary's *Tractatus*, Augustine's *Enarrations*, and Cassiodorus's *Explanation* (Rahlfs 176; KT 116; Sabatier 117; Weber 131; Thibaut 83; CC 61:179; CSEL 94.1:352; CC 97:525). This reading follows the wording of LXX Ps 118:61, 109, 153.

But as Jerome explains, *in Septuaginta et in Hebraeo non habet 'populi tui,' sed 'populi mei,'* "in the Seventy and in the Hebrew, it does not have 'your people,' but 'my people.'" The Hebrew text has עמי, "my people," which is the reading of Codex Alexandrinus (τοῦ λαοῦ μου) and is attested for Aquila and Theodotion (Rahlfs 176; Field 2:187). Jerome followed this text in his Gallican Psalter: *populi mei*. When Jerome invokes the *Septuaginta*, he means the "true" LXX as reflected in the hexaplaric Psalter, which accords with the Hebrew.

33.5.5–6. *et scient, quia deus dominator Iacob finium terrae*,[97] "and they will know that God is the ruler, of Jacob, of the ends of the earth." Ps 58:14 (Heb 59:14), GPsal. The punctuation I have given reflects the text's lack of clarity among its earliest readers. In what is probably the original Greek text, the passage reads: καὶ γνώσονται ὅτι ὁ θεὸς δεσπόζει τοῦ Ιακωβ, τῶν περάτων τῆς γῆς, "And they will know that God rules over Jacob, over the ends of the earth." In harmony with the Greek text consulted by Sunnia and Fretela, numerous witnesses add "and" after "Jacob" (i.e., "over Jacob and over the ends of the earth"); for example, the Greek text of the Verona Psalter, the Lucianic manuscripts, Theodoret's *Commentary**, the Syro-Hexapla, and Theodore of Mopsuestia (Rahlfs 176). In Latin, not only do many OL witnesses add "and" (Sabatier 118; Thibaut 83), but this addition also appears in the Sixto-Clementine Vulgate (Van Ess 68).[98] Alternatively,

---

97. There is variation among the manuscripts both for *Ep.* 106 and for the Gallican Psalter involving *dominator*, "ruler" (Hilberg's text for *Epist* 106); *dominatur*, "rules" (Weber-Gryson's text for GPsal and the Benedictine edition's text for *Epist* 106); and *dominabitur*, "will rule" (e.g., the Sixto-Clementine edition). I think it probable, whatever the case, that the reading was originally the same in both places. Jerome concludes his discussion with a clarifying paraphrase that follows the word in question with a genitive (*finium terrae*). On the grounds that the noun *dominator* more naturally takes a genitive than the verb does (the verb expects the ablative), I am following Hilberg's *dominator*, "ruler," and positing tentatively that this is also the correct reading of the Gallican Psalter.

98. Hilary's *Tractatus* gives: *et scient, quoniam deus dominatur Iacob finium terrae,*

other sources (e.g., P.Bod. 24; Codex Vaticanus) rearrange the text so that τοῦ Ιαχωβ follows right after ὁ θεός (i.e., "the God of Jacob").[99] This is Jerome's solution as he explains the passage in *Ep.* 106.

33.5.6. '*et*' *coniunctio*, "the conjunction 'and.'" See **25.1.5.**

33.5.6–7. *ordo est*, "This is the sequence of thought." See introduction, §9.1. Here Jerome clarifies the sense by reordering the words, placing *Iacob* right after *deus* (i.e., "the God of Jacob"; see the Greek evidence above). The hexaplaric versions are lacking for this passage. The Hebrew has וידעו כי אלהים משל ביעקב לאפסי הארץ, "And they will know that God rules over Jacob to the ends of the earth." In the IH edition, Jerome will translate: *et sciant quoniam deus dominatur Iacob in finibus terrae*, "And (so that) they may know that God rules over Jacob to the ends of the earth."

34.1.8–9. *quis deducet me usque in Idumaeam*, "Who will lead me as far as Idumea?" Ps 59:11 (Heb 60:11), GPsal. The word "or" (ἤ) is added before this question in P.Bod. 24, the Greek text of the Verona Psalter, MS 1219 Washington, the Lucianic manuscripts, and Theodoret's *Commentary** (Rahlfs 178; KT 118; see also Codex Alexandrinus at LXX Ps 107:11). In Latin, the Roman Psalter and the Sinai Psalter contain "or" (*aut*) at Ps 59:11 (Weber 134; Thibaut 84).

35.1.11–12. *quoniam tu, deus meus, exaudisti orationem meam*, "because you, O my God, heard my prayer." Ps 60:6 (Heb 61:6), GPsal. In terms of significant differences, the alternative text cited by Sunnia and Fretela lacks *meus*, "my," and replaces *orationem meam*, "my prayer," with *me*, "me." Jerome's comment that "this was added in the Latin" is unclear, perhaps intentionally so.

"And they will know that God rules over Jacob, over the ends of the earth" (close to the LXX), which he paraphrases as (that) *Deus Iacob dominetur finium terrae*, "the God of Jacob rules over the ends of the earth" (CC 61:179–80). This paraphrase is similar to Jerome's *ordo est* explanation. As for Codex Casinensis 557, this manuscript includes *et*, "and," and like Saint Zenon of Verona's Psalter adds *omnium*, "all": *et omnium finium terrae*, "and over all the ends of the earth" (Weber 132; Amelli 41).

99. P.Bod. 24: ὁ θς τοῦ ϊαχωμ᾽ δεσπόζει τῶν περάτων [τῆς γῆς] (KT 116). This passage is cited four times in Eusebius's exegesis on the Psalms. In two instances, the quotations match what I suggested above as the original Greek text. In one instance, τοῦ Ἰαχώβ is omitted. In the fourth instance, the phrase "the God of Jacob" is taken as a whole and moved to the end: καὶ γνώσονται ὅτι δεσπόζει τῶν περάτων τῆς γῆς ὁ θεὸς τοῦ Ιαχωβ; see Carmelo Curti, *Eusebiana I: Commentarii in Psalmos*, 2nd ed. (Catania: Centro Di Studi Sull'Antico Cristianesimo, 1989), 163–64.

On the one hand, there is no basis in the Hebrew or in the Greek for translating "me" instead of "my prayer," so Jerome can justly say that this proposed reading is found neither in the Hebrew nor in the LXX but exists only in the Latin text that Sunnia and Fretela quoted.[100] On the other hand, Jerome in the Gallican Psalter added *meus* (*deus meus*, "O my God") with no apparent basis in the Hebrew, Greek, or OL. So, Jerome's *meus* may also be regarded as an addition that occurs neither in the Hebrew nor in the LXX but only in Latin, that is, Jerome's own Latin. Although Jerome does not specify which issue he has in mind, we may assume that he wants to focus attention on the change from *orationem meam*, "my prayer" to *me*, "me" (i.e., the baseless rendering made by Sunnia and Fretela). As for Jerome's baseless addition of *meus*, "my," in the IH edition he will omit *meus*.

35.2.15. *psallam nomini tuo in saeculum saeculi*, "I will sing to your name unto the age of the age." Ps 60:9 (Heb 61:9). This translation matches the LXX: ψαλῶ τῷ ὀνόματί σου εἰς τὸν αἰῶνα τοῦ αἰῶνος. The text Jerome cites is essentially the OL, except that most OL witnesses add *deus* after *nomini tuo* (Sabatier 121; Thibaut 84; CC 61:196). The Gallican Psalter has *psalmum dicam nomini tuo in saeculum saeculi*, "I will recite a psalm to your name unto the age of the age." How is it that Sunnia and Fretela quote the OL to Jerome as if it were his own, and yet he does not correct their mistaken citation? The translation issue in question occurs at the end of the sentence, *in saeculum saeculi*. This is where Jerome's attention is focused. The copy of Jerome's translation owned by Sunnia and Fretela must have contained an error at this point (i.e., *psallam* for *psalmum dicam*), in this case a correction toward the OL that Jerome failed to notice. This is not surprising, given Jerome's intimate familiarity with the language of the Old Latin Psalter.

Sunnia and Fretela claim that the Greek does not have two words for "age," *in saeculum saeculi*, but only one word, *in saeculum*. Perhaps the Greek source used by Sunnia and Fretela contained what is preserved in the Lucianic manuscripts, Theodoret's *Commentary**, and MS 55 Rome: τοὺς αἰῶνας (Rahlfs 179). The Hebrew has לעד, which Jerome transliterates as *laed*. Apparently, he recognizes that the rendering he borrowed from the OL and used in the Gallican Psalter, *in saeculum saeculi*, is not defensible

---

100. It should be noted, however, that, whereas the singular τῆς προσευχῆς, "prayer" (= GPsal) is found in Codex Sinaiticus and the Sahidic Coptic version, most LXX witnesses have the plural, ἐυχῶν or προσευχῶν (Rahlfs 179).

based on the Hebrew. Consequently, although he acknowledges that the Hebrew has only one occurrence of the word in question, he shifts the topic to a discussion of which Hebrew word is used. As he notes, the Hebrew has לעד, which he glosses as *in aeternum*, "unto eternity," rather than *lolam* (i.e., לעולם), which he glosses as *in saeculum*, "unto the age." Thus, even if Jerome's *in saeculum saeculi* is not strictly correct, neither is *in saeculum* as proposed by Sunnia and Fretela, if one goes back to the Hebrew. In this instance, Jerome has left both the Gallican Psalter and the LXX behind to take shelter in the Hebrew. When he produces the IH Psalter, Jerome translates לעד as *iugiter*, "continually."

36.1.18–19. *quia deus adiutor noster in aeternum*, "because God is our helper unto eternity." Ps 61:9 (Heb 62:9), GPsal. This is the Gallican Psalter translation, except that *quia* has been included from the OL tradition (Sabatier 122; Weber 137). At the end of this clause in Hebrew we find the poetic particle סלה, which is represented as διάψαλμα in the LXX and is omitted in most OL witnesses. In Aquila, סלה regularly becomes ἀεί, "always."[101] Although Aquila is not preserved for this specific passage, Jerome's *in aeternum* in the Gallican Psalter clearly goes back to Aquila's interpretation of this word (see Jerome's *Ep.* 28.2, ca. 384 CE).

Interestingly, when challenged on his inclusion of *in aeternum*, Jerome simply acknowledges its suspect status, saying *obelus est*, literally, "there is an obelus" (see introduction, §8.2). Two questions arise. First, was there an obelus on διάψαλμα in the hexaplaric LXX of Ps 61:9? Since it is present in the Hebrew and Theodotion is known to have preserved διάψαλμα (e.g., Pss 3:3; 4:5; 19:4; 38:6; 58:14; 74:4), there is no reason why the hexaplaric LXX would have an obelus on this word. Perhaps Jerome is simply agreeing to delete *in aeternum*, and he expresses this by saying *obelus est*, by which he means "Yes, delete this," rather than literally: "this word has an obelus in the hexaplaric LXX." Second, if Jerome initially gave *in aeternum* as a rendering of Aquila's ἀεί that stands for the Hebrew סלה, why does he not explain any of this here? Perhaps when he translated this passage in the Gallican Psalter he was following Aquila's interpretation of סלה, but since then he has changed his mind. Jerome now sees this as a mistake and is eager to move on to the next question. This would explain the brevity of this entry.

---

101. Reider, *Index to Aquila*, 5.

37.1.21. *sitivit in te anima mea*, "My soul desired for you."[102] Ps 62:2 (Heb 63:2), GPsal. I have translated *sitivit* ("thirsted") as "desired" because this better allows me to convey in English the linguistic difficulties Jerome faced in this passage. I understand the flow of thought as follows.

In the Gallican Psalter, Jerome translated: "My soul desired for you (*in te*)." This was comprehensible but awkward in Latin. Sunnia and Fretela suggest that the Greek has "My soul desired you (*te*)," which matches the Greek (ἐδίψησέν σοι) in that no preposition is added (as with *in te*), even though the Greek verb takes the dative case (σοι), whereas their Latin suggestion involves the accusative (*te*) since *sitivit* naturally takes the accusative case.

Jerome's response is that the Hebrew does not transfer into Latin as "you" in the accusative (*te*). This would be *attha* (אתה). Jerome is either unaware or uninterested in the fact that the independent personal pronoun אתה can only be used as a subject, not an object. His point is that the Hebrew, *lach* (לך), has a specific preposition (ל) attached to the word "you," which, strictly speaking, should be translated *tibi*, "to you" (dative). This (σοι, dative) is how all the Greek versions translated. If one wanted to be precise according to the Hebrew and Greek, one should translate the Latin as *sitivit tibi anima mea*, "My soul desired to you (*tibi*)." In Jerome's ears, however, this was so unidiomatic as to be out of the question. Still, to give the most natural Latin rendering (i.e., the accusative: *te*) would be to ignore the surface grammar completely, which is unacceptable. Therefore, Jerome's compromise was to use *in te* ("desired *for you*"), which gives some representation to the formal grammar of the Hebrew and Greek (ל, dative) but is more idiomatic than *tibi* and thus shows at least some basic concern for the particular idiom of Latin.

In the IH edition, Jerome will give up his concern for the surface grammar of the original and just give the fully idiomatic Latin accusative: *sitivit te anima mea*, "my soul desired you."

37.1.24–25. *secundum linguae proprietatem*, "in keeping with the particular idiom of the language." On Jerome's concern for the particular idioms of each language in translation, see introduction, §7.2.

---

102. The manuscripts of *Ep.* 106 read: *sitivit tibi anima mea*, which is the text given by Hilberg (Hilberg 264). What is given here, however, is the text reconstructed by the Benedictine edition (Gasquet 22), which agrees with the Gallican Psalter, and which follows the logic of the passage as explained by Donatien De Bruyne, "La reconstitution du Psautier hexaplaire in Latin," *Revue bénédictine* 41 (1929): 307–8. The text in the *Commentaries on the Psalms* also has *in te* (CC 72:213).

38.1.1–2. *sagittae parvulorum factae sunt plagae eorum*, "Their blows became arrows of children." Ps 63:8 (Heb 64:8), GPsal. As noted by Sunnia and Fretela, the LXX has the singular βέλος, "arrow, dart," instead of the plural (Rahlfs 183; CH 10). In the Gallican Psalter, Jerome preserved the OL plural *sagittae*, "arrows" (Sabatier 125; CC 61:219).

38.1.3. *non resonat in Latino*, "it does not sound correct in Latin." Jerome concedes that the original Greek has the singular. His choice to retain the plural was based on stylistic concerns. See introduction, §7.2.

38.1.5–6. *percutiet eos deus iaculo repentino et inferentur plagae eorum*, "God will strike them with a dart suddenly, and their blows will be inflicted." The key change in Jerome's Hebrew-based paraphrase is from "children" (νηπίων, *parvulorum*) to "suddenly" (*repentino*). The Hebrew text has פתאום, "suddenly." The LXX understood this word to be a form of פתי, "young, naïve person," and thus translated it as νήπιος (see LXX Pss 18:8; 114:6; 118:130; Prov 1:32; and many manuscripts at Ezek 45:20). Jerome could have learned this interpretation of the Hebrew from Aquila (παραχρῆμα) or Symmachus (αἰφνίδιον), although only Symmachus gives the singular for "dart" as Jerome does (Field 2:195). The Hebrew-based paraphrase that Jerome gives in *Ep.* 106 is similar to, but not the same as, what he will translate in the IH edition: *sagittabit ergo eos deus iaculo repentino enferentur plagae eorum*, "Therefore God will shoot them with a dart suddenly, their blows will be inflicted."

39.1.7–8. *qui conturbas profundum maris, sonum fluctuum eius*, "You who stir up the depth of the sea, the sound of its waves." Ps 64:8 (Heb 65:8), GPsal. The ambiguity in this passage involves the final expression, *sonum fluctuum eius*, "the sound of its waves." What is the sense of these words? In some witnesses to the LXX (e.g., MS 1219 Washington, the Lucianic manuscripts, Theodoret's *Commentary**, and the Syro-Hexapla), the sense is filled out by the addition of τίς ὑποστήσεται, "Who will endure?" These words produce a separate sentence: "Who will endure the sound of its waves?" (Rahlfs 184; cf. LXX Pss 129:3; 147:6). This addition (*quis sustinebit*) appears in many OL witnesses (Sabatier 126; Weber 142).

39.1.9–10. *quod superfluum est; subauditur enim*, "But this is superfluous, because the verb is supplied as follows." Literally: "which is superfluous, because it is supplied." By *subauditur*, Jerome means that the verb *conturbas*, "you stir up," from the first half of the line is to be supplied in the second half of the line, as Jerome explains by his paraphrase. This illustrates Jerome's awareness of one basic element of Hebrew poetic parallelism: ellipsis, specifically verb gapping.[103] Given this understanding of the line, to add a new verb for these final words is superfluous. On Jerome's identification of superfluous elements in the text, see introduction, §8.5.

39.2.11–12. *parasti cibum illorum, quoniam ita est praeparatio eius*, "You prepared their food, for thus is its preparation." Ps 64:10 (Heb 65:10), GPsal. Most LXX witnesses read ἡ ἑτοιμασία σου, "your preparation," but P.Bod. 24, the Lucianic manuscripts, and Theodoret's *Commentary** attest the omission of the pronoun, as in the Greek text consulted by Sunnia and Fretela (Rahlfs 184; KT 124). Most OL texts likewise have *tua*, "your" (Sabatier 126; Thibaut 87; CC 61:230). Jerome's *eius*, "its," corresponds to the Hebrew and probably the hexaplaric LXX (see below). Codex Casinensis 557 likewise has *eius* but with a different noun: *paratura eius*, "its preparing" (Amelli 44).

39.2.13. *thechina*. The MT has תְּכִינֶהָ, "you establish it." The Hebrew root כון can mean "establish" or "prepare."[104] If this word were miscopied or misinterpreted as the related noun תכונה, it could produce "preparation" or perhaps "its preparation."[105] But the expected form of the noun with the third-person feminine suffix would be תכונתה. Of the hexaplaric versions, only Symmachus is preserved, who essentially follows the MT: ἥδρασας αὐτήν, "you readied it" (Field 2:196; see also Theodoret's *Commentary*). We may suppose that the hexaplaric LXX preserved the traditional Greek noun ἑτοιμασία, "preparation" (as opposed to the verb). Perhaps the hexaplaric LXX added the third-person feminine suffix ("its"), possibly on the basis of Theodotion, and Jerome followed this in the Gallican Psalter. Alternatively, the fact that Jerome mentions only the Hebrew and not the Greek versions to justify his translation might suggest that the hexaplaric LXX lacked the pronoun "its" (cf. Caloz 361–2).

In the IH Psalter, Jerome will follow the Hebrew more closely: *praeparabis frumentum eorum quia sic fundasti eam*, "you will prepare their grain (Heb דגנם; contra Symmachus: αὐτῆς, "its" grain), because thus you established it."

---

103. See Robert Alter, *The Art of Biblical Poetry* (New York: Basic Books, 1985), 23–26; and Wilfred G. E. Watson, *Classical Hebrew Poetry*, JSOTSup 26 (Sheffield: JSOT Press, 1986), 48.

104. *HALOT*, s.v. "כון."

105. There is a single medieval Hebrew manuscript that gives the miscopied form תבונה (Kennicott 2:359).

40.1.17. *cum incensu arietum*, "with the incense of rams." Ps 65:15 (Heb 66:15), GPsal. The text proposed by Sunnia and Fretela, *cum incensu et arietibus*, "with incense and rams," is the preserved LXX reading: μετὰ θυμιάματος καὶ κριῶν.[106] Jerome's translation in the Gallican Psalter agrees with the Hebrew, עם קטרת אילים, which Jerome transliterates: *em catoroth helim*. In explaining the Hebrew, Jerome first gives the Greek translation, and then the Latin. This suggests that μετὰ θυμιάματος κριῶν was the reading that Jerome followed in the hexaplaric LXX (cf. Caloz 153). Jerome does not say that καί was under obelus; he simply quotes the text without καί.

40.2.21. *propterea exaudivit deus*, "Therefore God heard." Ps 65:19 (Heb 66:19), GPsal. The preserved LXX includes the word μου, "me," in support of Sunnia and Fretela. The Gallican Psalter omits μου in agreement with the MT, the hexaplaric versions (Field 2:199), and probably the text of the hexaplaric LXX. Because the sense of the passage is clear without μου and the authoritative sources lack it, Jerome says it is *superfluum*; see introduction, §8.5.

41.1.24–25. *et exultent in conspectu eius*, "and they will exult in his presence." Ps 67:5 (Heb 68:5). This is the reading found in Codex Sangermanensis (Sabatier 130–31).[107] The copy of Jerome's translation owned by Sunnia and Fretela must have contained a scribal error at this point caused by interference from the OL. The imperative, as Jerome actually translated in the Gallican Psalter, matches the Hebrew and LXX. The imperative (*exsultate*) is also witnessed in Latin by Codex Casinensis 557, the Sinai Psalter, Hilary's *Tractatus*, Augustine's *Enarrations*, Cassiodorus's *Explanation*, and (*gaudete*) the Roman Psalter (Weber 148; Amelli 45; Thibaut 90; CC 61:263; CC 39:871; CC 97:587).

41.2.2–3. *etenim non credunt inhabitare dominum*, "Indeed, they do not believe the Lord dwells." Ps 67:19 (Heb 68:19). The Hebrew text for this verse involves several difficulties that generate complications in the Greek tradition. I will briefly explain the issues relevant to Jerome's comments.

In the LXX according to most witnesses, the first part of the verse, ἔλαβες δόματα ἐν ἀνθρώπῳ, "you received gifts among people," is followed by the phrase καὶ γὰρ ἀπειθοῦντες τοῦ κατασκηνῶσαι, "indeed, they were

---

106. Like the Gallican Psalter and agreeing with the MT, P.Bod. 24 and the Sahidic Coptic version omit the conjunction (KT 126; Rahlfs 186).

107. Cyprian, *Test.* 2.6 (CC 3:36–37) cites the beginning of Ps 67:5 but stops just short of this phrase.

disobeying (= nominative) to dwell," which is followed by χύριος ὁ θεὸς εὐλογητός, "the Lord God is blessed." It is not clear how χαὶ γὰρ ἀπειθοῦντες τοῦ χατασχηνῶσαι is connected to what surrounds it. One solution is to read ἀπειθοῦντας (= accusative), so that the meaning is: "You received gifts among people, indeed those disobeying to dwell." In other words, ἀπειθοῦντας is an object of ἔλαβες, "you received." This reading is found in the Greek text of the Verona Psalter, the Lucianic manuscripts, the Syro-Hexapla, and Theodoret's *Commentary** (Rahlfs 190). This Lucianic reading is the Greek text recommended by Sunnia and Fretela.

As for Latin sources, Codex Sangermanensis has *etenim non credunt inhabitare. dominus*, "Indeed, they do not believe to dwell. The Lord" (Sabatier 133). Augustine, *Enarrations* quotes this text with the relative *qui* added (*qui ... credunt*) to convey the sense of the Greek participle: *etenim qui non credunt inhabitare*, "Indeed, those who do not believe to dwell."[108] Augustine is also aware of another reading (*vel quod nonnulli codices habent*): *etenim non credentes inhabitare*, "indeed, those not believing to dwell," which uses the Latin participle and could be nominative or accusative (CC 39:889). Augustine's alternative reading is found in Hilary's *Tractatus* (CC 61:274). All these Latin renderings take the following word, *dominus*, "Lord," as nominative and therefore belonging to what follows ("the Lord God is blessed").[109] Jerome, on the other hand, understands "Lord" (*dominum*) as the accusative subject of the infinitive *inhabitare*, and he gives the participle like Hilary and Augustine's alternative rendering, thus producing: *etenim non credentes inhabitare dominum*, "Indeed, those not believing (that) the Lord dwells." This is the actual Gallican Psalter version, which Jerome provides (*nos enim transtulimus*). Apparently, Jerome's translation had been corrupted under the influence of an OL text such as one finds in Codex Sangermanensis (*etenim non credunt inhabitare*), but with Jerome's interpretation of "Lord" as accusative (*dominum*) retained. This corrupted text is what Sunnia and Fretela quoted back to Jerome as his own.

Jerome's response is to say that neither the corrupted Latin text (which has *credunt* instead of *credentes*) nor the Greek text cited (which fails to include "Lord") is correct. He makes clear the correctness of his own ver-

---

108. This is also the reading of the Sinai Psalter (Thibaut 90–91).

109. Alternately, Codex Casinensis 557 takes "Lord" as dative: *nam non obedientes inhabitare domino deo*, "Because those not obedient to the Lord God dwell" (Amelli 46).

sion by offering a paraphrase that contains theological elaboration: When God ascended on high, he received gifts even among those who did not believe that the Lord can dwell with mortals, that is, who did not believe in the incarnation.

The *Commentaries on the Psalms* also gives the text as Jerome explains it, with a similar explanation: *Et his hominibus, id est, ex gentibus populo largitus est Xpistus, qui non credebant Deum inhabitare posse mortalibus,* "And Christ gave lavishly 'from these men,' that is, from the gentiles who did not believe that God can dwell with mortals" (CC 72:215). In other words, God gave bountifully to his people out of the riches gained from the "nations" who do not believe in the possibility of the incarnation. The interpretation in Jerome's *Homilies on the Psalms* follows the same trajectory: *Etenim non credentes inhabitare Dominum: Et hos saluasti, qui non credebant quod possible est Deum habitare in homine, hoc est, Salvatorem accipere carnem,* "Indeed, they do not believe the Lord dwells: And you saved those who did not believe that it is possible for God to dwell in a man, that is, that the Savior took on flesh." (CC 78:44). This theological reading likely goes back to Origen.

41.3.10. *deus benedictus dominus die cottidie,* "God is blessed, the Lord day by day." Ps 67:19–20 (Heb 68:19–20), GPsal. Because Jerome took the LXX's κύριος (Heb יה) in v. 19 as accusative (*dominum*) and connected it with what precedes (see above), the next sentence in the Gallican Psalter begins with ὁ θεός (Heb אלהים). The words in Hebrew that correspond to Jerome's translation are אלהים ברוך אדני יום יום, in vv. 19–20. What Sunnia and Fretela propose as the Greek text is the best preserved LXX (Rahlfs 190), with the initial κύριος of v. 19 included, and also a repetition of the word εὐλογητός at the start of v. 20. Jerome's translation presupposes his prior decision about *dominum* (*sed melius et verius, quod supra*) and also the elimination of the extra εὐλογητός, which likely follows the hexaplaric LXX.

41.4.13–14. *viderunt ingressus tui, deus,* "They saw your processions, O God." Ps 67:25a (Heb 68:25a), GPsal. The Hebrew text has ראו הליכותיך, "they saw your processions," for which Jerome gives the striking transliteration *rachua alichatach*. Especially notable are *ch* for א, and the final *a* at the end of *rachua*/ראו. The LXX presents this passage with the verb in the passive voice and the noun "processions" as the nominative subject: ἐθεωρήθησαν αἱ πορεῖαί σου, "your processions were seen." In the Gallican Psalter, Jerome gave a translation that agrees with the Hebrew: *viderunt ingressus tui,* "they saw your processions," with *ingressus* being accusative plural and *tui* being genitive singular, the genitive of the personal pronoun standing for the possessive (*tuos*) as is common in later Latin.[110] Sunnia and Fretela challenge Jerome's translation by citing the text of the LXX.

Jerome's response is to give a transliteration of the Hebrew and then justify his interpretation of the Hebrew by appealing to all the hexaplaric versions, each of which (he says) translate with the active voice and an accusative direct object: *viderunt itinera tua*, "They saw your journeys," which Field reconstructs as ἐθεώρησαν τὰς πορείας σου, "They saw your processions" (2:203).[111] Jerome unpacks the sense further by showing how these other Greek versions understand the rest of the verse. When he restates his own interpretation ("Therefore, we should read thus"), he alters his Latin rendering slightly by giving the more idiomatic *tuos* (agreeing with the accusative plural *ingressus*) rather than the genitive singular *tui* (as in the Gallican Psalter).

According to Jerome, the confusion in this passage arose because a Greek scribe mistakenly wrote the nominative αἱ πορεῖαί instead of the accusative τὰς πορείας. We can imagine that, once the nominative had crept in erroneously, some later scribe attempted to straighten out the sense by converting the verb from active (ἐθεώρησαν) to passive (ἐθεωρήθησαν). Jerome states that the text he found in the Hexapla, which he identifies as the LXX (*in Septuaginta et in* Ἐξαπλοῖς), was: ἐθεώρησαν αἱ πορεῖαί σου, ὁ θεός, "your processions saw, O God," which reflects the scribal error of changing the nominative into the accusative but not the subsequent correction from active to passive. This results in a text that makes little sense. Presumably Jerome mentions not only the LXX but also the Hexapla to suggest that this is a copyist error in the transmission of the hexaplaric text rather than a flaw in the original LXX. The reading custom that Jerome says prevailed in many codices, ἐθεωρήθησαν αἱ πορεῖαί σου, ὁ θεός, "your processions were seen, O God," is preserved in virtually all LXX witnesses today.

---

110. Albert Blaise, *A Handbook of Christian Latin: Style, Morphology, and Syntax*, trans. Grant C. Roti (Washington, DC: Georgetown University Press, 1994), §§80, 81, 169.

111. Field offers an alternative reconstruction of Symmachus based on the Syro-Hexapla: *ḥzyn hww l'wrḥtk*, which in Greek he renders as ἐθεώρουν τὰς ὁδούς σου, "They were seeing your journeys" (imperfect verb to match the active participle plus enclitic *hw'*, and ὁδός for *'wrḥ'*). Reconstructions based on the Latin and Syriac can never be certain. But it is not implausible that, e.g., Symmachus read ἐθεώρουν and Aquila read ἐθεώρησαν and yet Jerome summarized both with the rendering *viderunt*, because they both support his position on the central issue—namely, that the verb is active and takes an accusative object.

41.4.20–21. *qui nominativum posuit pro accusativo*, "who put the nominative instead of the accusative." The six cases: *nominativus, genitivus, dativus, accusativus, vocativus,* and *ablativus* were discussed in detail by Roman grammarians, for instance, Donatus, *Ars grammatica*, and Diomedes, *Artis Grammaticae*.[112] See also Varro, *Ling.* 9.52–53, 75–80, 89–91, 102–3; 10 (e.g., 10.7, 62).

41.5.1–2. *ingressus dei mei, regis mei, qui est in sancto*, "the processions of my God, my king, who is in the sanctuary." Ps 67:25b (Heb 68:25b), GPsal. As Jerome just explained (**41.4**), the verb *viderunt* from the beginning of the verse should be understood as the verb governing the second half of the verse as well. On *subauditur*, see also **39.1**. Sunnia and Fretela asserted that the pronoun "my" (μου) is used with reference to God ("my God"), but not with reference to "king." The pronoun μου is indeed lacking from τοῦ βασιλέως, "the king," in virtually all LXX witnesses; other than the Gallican Psalter, the only other evidence cited by Rahlfs for μου after τοῦ βασιλέως is a corrector to Codex Sinaiticus (Rahlfs 191). The preserved Hebrew text has "my" after both nouns: אלי מלכי בקדש, "my God, my king in the sanctuary." Jerome justifies his translation *regis mei*, "my king," by appealing to the Hebrew (see below).

41.5.6–7. *heli melchi, quod deum meum et regem meum significat*, "*heli melchi*, which means 'my God' and 'my king.'"[113] It is interesting that Jerome asserts the presence of "my" after "king" so confidently, since the Latin rendering he gave above (**41.4**) for all the hexaplaric versions (*itinera dei mei regis, qui est in sancto*) lacks the pronoun "my" (*mei*) after "king" (*regis*). Furthermore, "my" is absent from "king" in Symmachus according to the Syro-Hexapla: *'wrḥt' d'lhy mlk' qdyš'*, "the ways of my God, the holy king" (Field 2:203).

Is it possible that the hexaplaric LXX had "my king" (τοῦ βασιλέως μου) even though all the hexaplaric versions lacked it? This is unlikely,

---

112. See Keil, *Grammatici Latini*, 1:301–3; 4:377–79. See also Daniel J. Taylor, "Latin Declensions and Conjugations: From Varro to Priscian," *Histoire Épistémologie Langage* 13 (1991): 85–109 (esp. 93–107).

113. When Jerome says: *quod 'deum meum' et 'regem meum' significat*, the conjunction (*et*) is not part of the quotation. He simply means that the text says both "my God" and also "my king." Thus I have followed the interpretation given in the Benedictine edition, *deum meum* et *regem meum* (Gasquet 23), rather than Hilberg: '*deum meum et regem meum*' (Hilberg 267). There is a single medieval Hebrew manuscript that reads ומלכי, "and my king" (Kennicott 2:363), which I take to be simply an idiomatic adjustment.

especially in view of the presence of "my" in the Hebrew. A better explanation is that Jerome's Latin rendering of all the hexaplaric versions at **41.4** was imprecise on this detail; perhaps only Symmachus lacked "my" after "king." In all probability, Theodotion or Aquila (or both) gave τοῦ βασιλέως μου, "my king," and this was the reading of the hexaplaric LXX that Jerome followed when he produced the Gallican Psalter.

41.6.7–8. *regna terrae, cantate deo, psallite domino*, "O Kingdoms of the earth, sing to God, make music to the Lord." Ps 67:33 (Heb 68:33), GPsal. This passage involves a textual confusion that can best be explained by laying out the Hebrew text as follows:

(33) (a) ממלכות הארץ (b) שירו לאלהים (c) זמרו אדני (d) סלה

(34) (a) לרכב בשמי שמי קדם

In other words:

(33) (a) O Kingdoms of the earth, (b) sing to God, (c) make music to the Lord, (d) selah

(34) (a) to the One who rides on the heavens of the heavens, eastward (or, "from old")

Some important LXX witnesses translate v. 33a, b, and c in a straightforward fashion and represent v. 33d סלה as διάψαλμα. After 33d and before 34a, these LXX texts contain an additional phrase: ψάλατε τῷ θεῷ, "make music to God." Directly after this addition comes v. 34a. This is the text given by Codex Vaticanus, MS 1220 (fourth century), the Bohairic and Sahidic Coptic versions, and in Latin by Codex Sangermanensis (Rahlfs 192; Sabatier 134–35).

The Greek text consulted by Sunnia and Fretela contains the added phrase (ψάλατε τῷ θεῷ) between 33d and 34a, but it lacks 33c (ψάλατε τῷ κυρίῳ). Jerome does not accept this Greek text as authentic, but neither does he support the fully expanded LXX text; instead, he says the verse should be read according to the *hebraica veritas* (see **1.1.9**). Jerome's *hebraica veritas* text contains 33c and lacks the LXX's additional phrase between 33d and 34a in keeping with the preserved Hebrew, P.Bod. 24, Codex Sinaiticus, the Lucianic manuscripts, Theodoret's *Commentary**, the Syro-Hexapla, and MS 55 Rome (Rahlfs 191–92; KT 132).[114] Whereas Jerome's

---

114. Jerome, however, makes no reference to סלה/διάψαλμα.

Hebrew-based translation for זמרו אדני (33c) here is *psallite domini,* in the IH Psalter he renders this phrase *canite domino.*

41.6.14–15. *'psallite deo' non sit in libris authenticis, sed obelo praeno-tatum,* "'Make music to God' is not present in the authentic books but was marked with an obelus." Jerome notes that the LXX's additional phrase, ψάλατε τῷ θεῷ (= *psallite deo*), is marked with an obelus—presumably in the Gallican Psalter, no doubt because it was marked with an obelus in the hexaplaric LXX. On the obelus, see introduction, §8.2. This phrase (*psallite deo*) was included in the Sixto-Clementine edition without critical marking (Van Ess 73).

41.6.14. *in libris authenticis,* "in the authentic books." On "authentic books," see introduction, §8.3. Elsewhere Jerome refers to *veriora exemplaria,* "truer copies" (*Comm. Os.* 1:10) and *emendatis et veris exemplaribus,* "emended and true copies" (*Comm. Isa.* 58:11).

41.6.15. *ergo et vos legite magis ea, quae vera sunt,* "You should therefore prefer reading things that are true." As Jerome states in another place, manuscripts should be valued more for their accuracy than for their outward beauty (*Pref. IH Job*).

41.6.15–16. *ne, dum additum suscipitis, quod a propheta scriptum est, relinquatis,* "lest by accepting what was added you thereby forsake what the prophet wrote." Jerome's statement illustrates his notion that the goal of textual criticism is to restore the text to its original form as it left the prophetic author's pen.

42.1.17–18. *laudabo nomen dei cum cantico,* "I will praise the name of God with a song." Ps 68:31 (Heb 69:31), GPsal. The text quoted by Sunnia and Fretela with the addition of "my" (τοῦ θεοῦ μου) agrees with the Lucianic manuscripts, Theodoret's *Commentary**, and MS 55 Rome in Greek, and with the Roman Psalter (*dei mei*) in Latin (Rahlfs 195; Weber 159). On *superfluum est,* see introduction, §8.5.

43.1.20. *deus, ne elongeris a me,* "O God, do not be far from me." Ps 70:12 (Heb 71:12), GPsal. The text with "my" (ὁ θεός μου) quoted by Sunnia and Fretela is supported by P.Bod. 24, the Greek text of the Verona Psalter, MS 1219 Washington, the Lucianic manuscripts, Theodoret's *Commentary**, the Syro-Hexapla, the Bohairic and Sahidic Coptic texts, the Latin text of the Verona Psalter, and (*domine deus meus*) Augustine's *Enarrationes* (Rahlfs 198; KT 138; Sabatier 141; CC 39:949). On *superfluum est,* see introduction, §8.5.

43.2.22. *deus, docuisti me ex iuventute mea,* "O God, you taught me from my youth." Ps 70:17 (Heb 71:17), GPsal. As at **42.1** and **43.1**, Jerome addresses the addition of "my" (ὁ θεός μου, "my God"). The text with "my" quoted by Sunnia and Fretela matches the Lucianic manuscripts, Theodoret's *Commentary**, and the Syro-Hexapla (Rahlfs 198). On *superfluum est*, see introduction, §8.5.

43.3.24. *donec adnuntiem brachium tuum*, "until I will make known your arm." Ps 70:18 (Heb 71:18), GPsal. The Hebrew text has עד אגיד זרועך, "until I will make known your arm/strength." This is also the reading of the Greek and Latin versions. As Jerome points out, the text proposed by Sunnia and Fretela has mistakenly put *mirabilia* (θαυμάσια) in place of *brachium* (βραχίονα), borrowing from v. 17. This probably occurred because it was not clear to some copyist what it would mean to "make known" the Lord's arm.

44.1.1–2. *et adorabunt eum omnes reges*, "And all kings will worship him." Ps 71:11 (Heb 72:11), GPsal. Sunnia and Fretela quote a text that reads οἱ βασιλεῖς τῆς γῆς, "the kings of the earth." The addition of τῆς γῆς, "of the earth," is supported by Greek witnesses such as P.Bod. 24, Codex Sinaiticus, MS 1219 Washington, the Greek text of the Verona Psalter, the Lucianic manuscripts, and Theodoret's *Commentary**. In Latin, this addition (*terrae*) appears in witnesses such as Codex Sangermanensis, the Verona Psalter, the Roman Psalter, the Sinai Psalter, Codex Casinensis 557, and Augustine's *Enarrations* (Rahlfs 200; KT 141; Sabatier 143; Weber 166; Thibaut 97; Amelli 49; CC 39:981). The Sixto-Clementine Vulgate included the addition in its text: *omnes reges terrae* (Van Ess 76). On *superfluum est*, see introduction, §8.5.

44.2.3–4. *benedictus dominus deus, deus Israhel*, "Blessed is the Lord God, the God of Israel." Ps 71:18 (Heb 72:18), GPsal. The Leningrad Codex reads: ברוך יהוה אלהים אלהי ישראל, "Blessed is the LORD God, the God of Israel," which matches the Gallican Psalter. The text proposed by Sunnia and Fretela lacks אלהים, "God." In this case, almost all LXX and OL witnesses agree with Sunnia and Fretela,[115] as do three medieval Hebrew manuscripts (Kennicott 2:368). Based on evidence for the hexaplaric versions (see Field 2:212), it is likely that both occurrences of "God" were represented in the hexaplaric LXX, so Jerome translated both of them in

---

115. In Latin, Codex Casinensis 557 does represent both *deus* (אלהים) and *deus Israhel* (אלהי ישראל). The Sixto-Clementine Vulgate (*Benedictus Dominus Deus Israël*) printed the shorter text of Sunnia and Fretela rather than Jerome's Gallican Psalter text (Van Ess 76).

the Gallican Psalter in keeping with "the Hebrew" and "the Seventy," that is, the "true" Seventy as found in the hexaplaric LXX.

44.2.6. *mysterium trinitatis*, "the mystery of the Trinity." Didymus of Alexandria interpreted this passage in light of God as Father and Son, appealing to John 5:19 to explain why God is said to act "alone" (μόνος).[116] Jerome takes the triple naming of God (*dominus deus, deus*) to represent the Trinity. He first affirms that the third reference to God appears in the Hebrew (*cum in Hebraico sit*), and then he adds, "and among the Seventy the triple meaning of the Lord and God is clearly the mystery of the Trinity." Jerome associates the trinitarian interpretation particularly with the Septuagint. This accords with a general tendency he shows elsewhere to connect Christian spiritual or theological interpretation to the LXX as the church's traditional text.[117] In some instances, Jerome employs the Hebrew to correct theological readings held by Christians whose religious views he accepts but whose spiritual interpretation of a certain passage he ascribes to "pious error" grounded in a Greek mistranslation (e.g., see *Comm. Isa.* 63:1; *Comm. Am.* 4:12–13; *Comm. Jer* 13:18–19; 17:9–10; 23:18). Still, the Hebrew can be productive for Christian theological reading; for example, at *Comm. Jer.* 23:36b–40, Jerome makes the point that only the Hebrew gives three names for God (*dei viventis, domini exercituum, dei nostri*), signifying the Trinity: "It should be noted that the Greek and Latin codices do not have the words 'of the living God, the Lord of Hosts, our God.' Let the Hebrews (i.e., the Jews) read this against themselves in their own scrolls, because this properly signifies the mystery of the Trinity."[118]

44.3.7–8. *et benedictum nomen maiestatis eius in aeternum*, "And blessed is the name of his majesty unto eternity." Ps 71:19 (Heb 72:19), GPsal. The text quoted by Sunnia and Fretela, which adds *et in saeculum saeculi* (καὶ εἰς τὸν αἰῶνα τοῦ αἰῶνος), "and unto the age of the age," is the reading of the preserved LXX and appears in Latin in Codex Sangermanensis, the Roman Psalter, and the Sinai Psalter (Rahlfs 201; Sabatier 144; Weber 168; Thibaut 98). Jerome omitted these words in the Gallican Psalter in agreement with the Hebrew, no doubt following the hexaplaric LXX: *quod nec Hebraeus habet nec septuaginta interpretes* (cf. Caloz 161). On Jerome's removal of "superfluous" material, see introduction, §8.5.

---

116. Mühlenberg, *Psalmenkommentare aus der Katenenüberlieferung*, 2:103–4.

117. Graves, *Jerome's Hebrew Philology*, 189–91. Hebrew proper name etymologies, however, are regularly incorporated into spiritual exegesis by Jerome.

118. Graves, *Jerome: Commentary on Jeremiah*, 148.

45.1.11. *prodiet quasi ex adipe*, "It will go forth as if out of fat." Ps 72:7 (Heb 73:7), GPsal. The Hebrew text (Leningrad Codex) for this passage reads יָצָא מֵחֵלֶב עֵינֵמוֹ, which may be taken as a poetic way to express יָצָא מֵחֵלֶב עֵינַם, "their eye goes forth from fat." It is not clear what this would mean. As Jerome notes, the LXX translates ἐξελεύσεται ὡς ἐκ στέατος ἡ ἀδικία αὐτῶν, "their misdeed will go forth as if out of fat." This presupposes the Hebrew עֲוֺנָמוֹ (from עָוֺן, "misdeed") instead of עֵינֵמוֹ (from עַיִן, "eye").[119] The Syriac Peshitta and Gallican Psalter also translate "misdeed" instead of "eye" (Rahlfs 202; Pesh 82; WG 858). Jerome appeals to the LXX in order to justify his singular rendering of the verb: the verb should be singular (ἐξελεύσεται), not plural (ἐξελεύσονται), because the subject is ἡ ἀδικία (*iniquitas*).

From where did Sunnia and Fretela get their plural verb? Both Aquila and Symmachus interpreted עינמו as "their eyes" and so translated it as plural ὀφθαλμοὶ αὐτῶν (Field 2:213). This requires that the Greek verb be plural. Sunnia and Fretela must have had a Greek text that had been corrected along the lines of Aquila and Symmachus at this point.

Although in *Ep.* 106 Jerome says that the plural Greek verb is wrong (*quod falsum est*), in the IH Psalter he will follow the interpretation of Aquila and Symmachus: *processerunt a pinguidine oculi eorum*, "their eyes came forth from fat." By giving the plural verb and "eyes" instead of "misdeed" in the IH edition, he corrects the Gallican Psalter and ends up agreeing with the text quoted by Sunnia and Fretela.

45.2.15. *quomodo scit deus*, "How does God know?" Ps 72:11 (Heb 73:11), GPsal. Preserved witnesses to the LXX support Jerome's claim that the "Seventy" include the word θεός, "God" (Rahlfs 202). The underlying Hebrew, however, is not אלהים, "God," but the shorter form אל, "God" or "power." Both Aquila and Symmachus translated the word as ἰσχυρός, "strength" (Field 2:214). The fact that Aquila and Symmachus did not use θεός explains why Jerome says all the translators translated "similarly" (*similiter*), that is, they did not all use θεός. But despite their differences, all the translators testify to the presence of the word. Apparently, Sunnia and Fretela consulted a Greek text that omitted אל altogether.

45.3.17–18. *intellegam in novissimis eorum*, "I understand concerning their last ends." Ps 72:17 (Heb 73:17), GPsal. Sunnia and Fretela quote a

---

119. Five medieval Hebrew manuscripts read עינמו, perhaps interpreting this word as עָוֺן (De-Rossi 4:51).

Greek text that adds "and" (καί) to the start of this half line. This is the preserved LXX reading (Rahlfs 203). There is no conjunction in Hebrew, and
Eusebius's *Commentary on the Psalms* has a quotation of this text that lacks
καί (PG 23:844). Given these two pieces of evidence, and because this is a
minor detail unlikely to send Jerome searching in other versions, I assume
that Jerome in the Gallican Psalter omitted the conjunction "and" because
it was lacking in the hexaplaric LXX (cf. Caloz 366). Despite its absence
from the Gallican Psalter, the conjunction was included in the Sixto-Clementine Vulgate (Van Ess 77). On *superflua est*, see introduction, §8.5.

45.3.19. *'et' coniunctio*, "the conjunction 'and.'" See **25.1.5.**

45.4.20. *defecit caro mea et cor meum*, "My flesh and my heart failed."
Ps 72:26 (Heb 73:26), GPsal. The "distorted order" (*perversum ordinem*)
suggested apparently by Sunnia and Fretela (*quidam tenent*, "certain people
maintain") is the preserved LXX: ἐξέλιπεν ἡ καρδία μου καὶ ἡ σάρξ μου
(Rahlfs 204). The word order followed by Jerome in the Gallican Psalter
matches the Hebrew and probably depends on the hexaplaric LXX.

45.5.22–23. *praedicationes tuas*, "your proclamations." Ps 72:28 (Heb
73:28), GPsal. The Hebrew word as found in the MT is מַלְאֲכוֹתֶיךָ, vocalized as if from the lexeme מְלָאכָה, "work, deed." Jerome transliterates this
word as *malochothach*. A similar phrase occurs at Ps 9:15: למען אספרה כל
תהלתיך, "so that I might announce all your praises," which the LXX rendered with αἰνέσεις, "praises" (for תהלה), just as here. Perhaps the Hebrew
text underlying the LXX had תהלתיך instead of מלאכותיך, or else the LXX
translator was reminded of Ps 9:15.[120] In any case, the uniform LXX reading for this passage is τὰς αἰνέσεις σου, "your praises," as Sunnia and Fretela
report (Rahlfs 204). When Jerome says that the "Seventy" translated τὰς
ἐπαγγελίας σου, "your proclamations" (or "promises"), he clearly has the
hexaplaric LXX in mind. We may conclude that the hexaplaric LXX gave
τὰς ἐπαγγελίας σου at Ps 72:28.

Related to the common biblical Hebrew word מלאך, "messenger,"
classical Hebrew has a word מלאכות, "message" (e.g., Hag 1:13; Gen. Rab.
50.2). Aquila provided a rendering based on this root: ἀγγελίας σου, "your
messages" (*nuntios tuos*). In *Ep.* 106, Jerome cites Aquila simply to show
that the Hebrew word is, strictly speaking, closer to "proclamation" than to
"praise," and he defends his Gallican Psalter rendering against this nitpicky

---

120. A single medieval Hebrew manuscript registered by Kennicott (2:369) reads
תהילתך at Ps 73:28. The Syriac Peshitta has *tdmrtk*, "your marvels," perhaps reflecting
נפלאותיך (cf. BHS 1155; Pesh 84).

question by saying that *praedicatio*, "proclamation," and *laus*, "praise," ultimately indicate (*significet*) the same thing, presumably because praise must be proclaimed, and the sensible thing to proclaim about God is praise. In the IH Psalter, Jerome decides to follow Aquila's interpretation: *adnuntiationes tuas*.

46.1.4–5. *ut quid, deus, reppulisti in finem,* "Why, O God, did you reject unto the end?" Ps 73:1 (Heb 74:1), GPsal. Jerome's Gallican Psalter translation, which puts the vocative *deus*, "O God," before the verb (*reppulisti*) matches the Hebrew text, which has אלהים before the verb (זנחת). In agreement with the MT and Gallican Psalter are the Lucianic manuscripts, Theodoret's *Commentary**, the Syro-Hexapla, MS 1219 Washington, and Eusebius (Rahlfs 204; PG 23:852–53). Aquila and Symmachus are preserved for this passage, and they both give the word order as in the Hebrew (Field 2:216). It is likely that the hexaplaric LXX contained this reading, with θεός, "God" placed before the verb (cf. Caloz 225). On the whole, the best-attested word order for the LXX has the noun "God" after the verb: ἵνα τί ἀπώσω, ὁ θεός. This order, which Jerome regards as a mistake, is also the standard wording of the OL (Sabatier 148; Weber 172; Thibaut 100).

46.2.7. *in sancto,* "in the sanctuary." Ps 73:3 (Heb 74:3), GPsal. The Hebrew has the singular בקדש, "in the sanctuary." Most LXX witnesses, including Codex Vaticanus, Codex Sinaiticus, MS 1219 Washington, the Greek text of the Verona Psalter, the Bohairic and Sahidic Coptic versions, and the OL reflect the plural τοῖς ἁγίοις, "saints" (Rahlfs 204; Sabatier 148–49; Thibaut 100).[121] The singular (ἐν τῷ ἁγίῳ) appears in the Lucianic manuscripts and Theodoret's *Commentary** (Rahlfs 204) and also in the hexaplaric LXX Psalter, Symmachus, and Theodotion (Field 2:216). Theodoret comments: οὔτε Ἑβραῖος οὔτε οἱ λοιποὶ ἑρμηνευταὶ οὔτε μὲν οἱ Ἑβδομήκοντα ἐν τῷ Ἑξαπλῷ πληθυντικῶς ἐν τοῖς ἁγίοις τεθείκασιν, ἀλλ' ἑνικῶς ἐν τῷ ἁγίῳ σου, "Neither the Hebrew, nor the other translators, nor the Seventy in the Hexapla put the plural, 'among the saints,' but the singular, 'in your holy (place)'" (PG 80:1456).

Jerome translated with the singular *in sancto*, "in the holy (place)," following the hexaplaric LXX Psalter in harmony with the Hebrew. Apparently, the copy of Jerome's translation consulted by Sunnia and Fretela contained an error at this point, where some scribe had changed Jerome's

---

121. For most OL witnesses, the reading is *in sanctis tuis*, but a key manuscript of the Mozarabic Psalter has *in sanctuariis tuis*, "in your sanctuaries," and in Codex Casinensis 557 the plural is *super sanctos*, "over the saints" (Weber 173; Amelli 51).

singular (*in sancto*) into the plural of the standard Greek text (τοῖς ἁγίοις) and OL (*in sanctis*).

In previous cases where Sunnia and Fretela quoted Jerome's text back to him in erroneous form, Jerome first cites the corrupted text and then he corrects their text in his comments (see introduction, §3.2). In this instance, he cites the biblical text initially in the original form in which he wrote it and then merely refers to their corrupted reading in the course of correcting it. In the IH Psalter Jerome translates בקדש as *in sanctuario*, so as to identify more clearly the *sancto* as a building ("sanctuary") rather than a "holy" people.

46.2.7–9. *in codice vestro emendando ... in nostro codice*, "in emending your codex ... in our codex." *Ep.* 106 contains a number of discussions of books and manuscripts; see introduction, §8.3.

46.3.10. *incendamus omnes dies festos dei a terra*, "Let us burn all the festival days of God from the land." Ps 73:8 (Heb 74:8). In order to understand Jerome's discussion of this passage, it is useful to begin with the OL tradition. The Old Latin rendering of this passage as witnessed by Codex Sangermanensis, the Roman Psalter, the Sinai Psalter, Augustine's *Enarrations*, and Cassiodorus's *Explanation* was *comprimamus*: "let us suppress" the Lord's festival days (Sabatier 149; Thibaut 100; CC 39:1011; CC 98:677). The Greek underlying this rendering is καταπαύσωμεν, "let us make to cease." In the Gallican Psalter Jerome kept the basic meaning of the OL as he knew it, but he updated the language to better fit the Greek: *quiescere faciamus*, "let us cause to cease." The problem he faces is that this rendering follows neither the Hebrew nor the hexaplaric LXX. Apparently, Sunnia and Fretela quoted back to him a text (*incendamus*, "let us burn") that essentially matches the hexaplaric LXX (see below) and differs from the Gallican Psalter. Jerome must explain the various textual sources in detail to prove that he is competent and that his initial translation was not simply made out of ignorance.

46.3.13–14. *e latere adnotationem nostram ... in corpore*, "our marginal notation ... in the body (of the text)." On this marginal notation, see introduction, §8.3. As indicated here, Jerome produced an annotated edition of at least some parts of the Gallican Psalter in which he noted certain textual phenomena in the margin. Alternative translations in these marginal notes were not meant to replace the text but were intended to provide deeper understanding of the text's history and meaning. Although in the Gallican Psalter Jerome translated *quiescere faciamus*, "let us cause to cease," in keeping with the familiar Greek reading καταπαύσωμεν, in his marginal note he explained that the true Greek reading is κατακαύσωμεν, "let us burn" (*incendamus*). This is the reading of the hexaplaric LXX, as Jerome explains below. This hexaplaric-Hebraic interpretation occurs in a different form in Codex Casinensis 557: *comburemus*, "we will burn up" (Amelli 51).

46.4.17. *sanctus presbyter Firmus, qui huius operis exactor fuit*, "the holy presbyter Firmus, who had requested that work." On Firmus, see **2.2.1.** According to Jerome, Firmus was the one who requested this annotated copy of the Psalms; in fact, he describes him as *huius operis exactor*, "demander/exactor of this work." Jerome often presented his work as the fulfillment of an urgent, imperious request from a friend or friends.

46.4.19. *sarphu chol moedahu hel baares.* The previous Hebrew line reads: אמרו בלבם נינם יחד, "They said in their heart, 'let us oppress them altogether.'" This is followed by the line Jerome transliterates: שרפו כל מועדי אל בארץ, "They burned all the solemn festivals of God in the land." Based on the first-person plural in the first line (נינם), it has been proposed that the second line should read ונשרף, "and let us burn." This is the reading or interpretation presupposed by the LXX (cf. BHS 1156). Jerome does not explain the issue of the first-person vis-à-vis the third-person. He is able to quote the transliteration, but he does not exhibit any grammatical knowledge. He merely cites all the Greek versions in favor of the meaning "burn," with Aquila, Symmachus, and Quinta giving the third-person, and *Sexta* and Theodotion giving the first-person (see Field 2:217).

46.4.24. *Septuaginta iuxta exemplorum veritatem*, "the Seventy ... according to its true copies." When Jerome says that the Seventy translated καταχαύσωμεν "according to the truth of the copies" (*iuxta exemplorum veritatem*), he means that this is the reading of the hexaplaric LXX. The Benedictine edition of *Ep.* 106 emends this to *iuxta Hexaplorum veritatem*, "according to the truth of the Hexapla" (Gasquet 26). This is certainly the correct sense.

46.5.2. *Hebraica veritas*, "the Hebrew truth." On the *Hebraica veritas*, see **1.1.9.**

46.5.1–4. *sic psallendum, ut nos interpretati sumus.... quod Septuaginta transtulerunt ... in ecclesiis decantandem est*, "the psalm should be sung as we translated it.... What the Seventy translated should be sung in the churches." Jerome could mean one of two things: either (1) the text should be sung (*psallendum*) "as we translated" (*ut nos interpretati sumus*), that is, *quiescere faciamus* (= the Gallican Psalter, what Jerome regards as the popular LXX); or (2) the text should be sung (*decantandem*) as "the Seventy translated" (*Septuaginta transtulerunt*), that is, *incendamus/comburamus* (= a Latin equivalent of the hexaplaric LXX). Typically, we would expect Jerome in *Ep.* 106 to mean the hexaplaric LXX when he refers to *quod Septuaginta transtulerunt*. If this were his meaning, then by the phrase *propter vetustatem*, "in view of its antiquity," he would be indicating that κατακαύσωμεν/*incendamus* should be sung because it is the original LXX. Nevertheless, we should not lose sight of his overall purpose in this treatise: to defend the Gallican Psalter. Jerome is probably suggesting that we should sing what he translated in the Gallican Psalter: *quiescere faciamus*, which he understands to represent the popular LXX reading (καταπαύσωμεν; cf. the mainstream OL) that has been hallowed by long (even if erroneous) usage in the churches. This is what he means by *propter vetustatem*. To be sure, this argument does not sit well with his admonitions to prefer true readings above all (**41.6**), but elsewhere Jerome shows deference to customary usage (see introduction, §7.2), and in this case appealing to popular tradition was the only strategy available to justify the Gallican Psalter.

As for the Hebrew truth, when he comes to the IH edition, Jerome will follow the Hebrew שרפו more closely: *incenderunt*, "they burned." I think it likely that awkward explanations such as this motivated Jerome to improve his Hebrew and produce a fresh translation of the Psalter that was actually based on the Hebrew.

46.6.7–8. *contribulasti ... tu confregisti*, "you crushed ... you—you broke." Ps 73:13–14 (Heb 74:13–14), GPsal. The LXX has σύ, "you" in front of both verbs: σὺ συνέτριψας ... σὺ συνέθλασας. In the Gallican Psalter, Jerome uses the pronoun (*tu*) with the second verb only, which I indicated in my translation with the repeated "you." Jerome's omission of the first "you" matches the Hebrew text and Aquila (Field 2:217). In Latin, Codex Sangermanensis, Codex Casinensis 557, Augustine's *Enarrations*, and Cassiodorus's *Explanation* likewise omit the first "you" in agreement with the Hebrew (Sabatier 150; Amelli 51; CC 39:1014; CC 98:679). In this instance, Jerome does not report what Sunnia and Fretela claimed about the Greek; instead, he simply gives his own rendering and points out what is correct about it vis-à-vis the questions they apparently asked.

46.6.10–11. *plurali numero ... non singulari*, "not in the singular, but in the plural." See **8.2.1**.

46.6.11–12. *Aquila verbum Hebraicum 'amaim' τῶν ὑδάτων, id est 'aquarum' interpretatus est*, "Aquila translated the Hebrew word *amaim* as τῶν ὑδάτων, that is, 'waters.'" Greek witnesses to the LXX uniformly give "water" in the singular for this passage (τοῦ ὕδατος). The Hebrew word מים,

waters/water (here הַמַּיִם, "the waters" with the definite article) appears to have a plural, or (strictly speaking) dual form.

46.7.13. *voces inimicorum tuorum*, "the voices of your enemies." Ps 73:23 (Heb 74:23), GPsal. First of all, Jerome gives the plural *voces*, "voices" against the singular in the Hebrew (קוֹל), the LXX (φωνῆς), and much of the OL tradition (*vocem*). The Roman Psalter contains the plural (Weber 177), which likely reflects the text-form with which Jerome was familiar in his youth and that he followed in the Gallican Psalter. When he comes to the IH Psalter, he will correct this to the singular and also give the genitive case as Latin idiom expects for this verb (*ne obliviscaris vocis*).

The issue at hand is Jerome's rendering *inimicorum*, "enemies." The majority of LXX witnesses give τῶν ἱκετῶν, "those who entreat." This is the text proposed by Sunnia and Fretela. A minority of Lucianic manuscripts and some copies of Theodoret's *Commentary** contain the reading τῶν οἰκετῶν, "servants" (Rahlfs 207). Jerome offers a transliteration of the Hebrew: *sorarach*—in other words, צֹרְרֶיךָ, from צרר II, "attacker, enemy."[122] According to Jerome, the Sixth Edition and the Seventy (i.e., the hexaplaric LXX) support his interpretation, *inimicorum* (i.e., τῶν ἐχθρῶν). Symmachus is said to have translated *bellantium contra te*, "those fighting against you," perhaps reflecting τῶν πολεμούντων or τῶν πολεμίων (cf. Field 2:219).

Jerome renders Aquila into Latin as *hostium*, "foes," a Latin word that like *inimicus* often translates ἐχθρός but that probably stands for something else here, since he is distinguishing *Sexta* and the Seventy (*inimicus*) from Aquila (*hostis*). Perhaps he is reporting for Aquila ἀντικείμενος, or else πολέμιος.[123] According to the Syro-Hexapla, Aquila reads *'sryn*, "those who bind" (i.e., τῶν ἐνδεσμούντων; see Field 2:219), as from צרר I.[124] Because Jerome's Aquila (*hostium*, "foes") and the Syro-Hexapla's Aquila (*'sryn*, "those who bind") presuppose two different interpretations of the root צרר, they cannot go back to the same Greek word. Perhaps this is a case where there was a first rendering ("edition") and second rendering ("edition") of Aquila.[125] Each rendering would have offered an etymological equivalent, but for different understandings of the Hebrew root.

---

122. *HALOT*, s.v. "צרר II."

123. On ἀντικείμενος, cf. Jerome's IH edition and the LXX on 2 Sam 8:10. On πολέμιος, cf. Field 2:216; in this case, Symmachus could be the participle πολεμούντων.

124. Cf. Aquila at Exod 23:22; Pss 6:8; 7:7; 8:3; Hos 4:19.

125. For Jeremiah, Ezekiel, and Daniel, Jerome reports readings for a "second edi-

46.8.17–18. *est sensus pendens ex superioribus*, "The sense depends on
what precedes." Jerome explains how the meaning "your enemies" for *sorarach* in v. 23 fits coherently into the general flow of thought. On Jerome's
appeal to the surrounding context in explaining the basic sense of the text,
see introduction, §9.1.

There is some ambiguity as to the textual form of v. 22 regarding *quae*
(or *qui*): Both for *Ep.* 106 and the Gallican Psalter, there is manuscript
support both for (1) *inproperiorum tuorum eorum quae ab insipiente sunt*
= the text of *Ep.* 106 according to Hilberg (270) and the Vulgate according
to the Sixto-Clementine edition (Van Ess 78); and also for (2) *inproperiorum tuorum eorum qui ab insipiente sunt* = the text of *Ep.* 106 according to Gasquet (26) and the Gallican Psalter according to Weber-Gryson
(WG 862). The use of *eorum* after *tuorum* is an imitation of the Greek
repetition of the article (σου τῶν) that is awkward in Latin and no doubt
contributed to the confusion. Based on Jerome's paraphrase in *Ep.* 106 (*id
est, voces quae te blasphemant*, "that is, the voices that revile you"), I am
inclined to think that *quae* was the intended form in *Ep.* 106 and also in
the Gallican Psalter, with *qui* having arisen because someone construed
eorum as the people who are reproaching—in other words, masculine
instead of neuter.

47.1.25–26. *narrabimus mirabilia tua*, "We will recount your wonders." Ps 74:2 (Heb 75:2), GPsal. The reading presumably suggested by
Sunnia and Fretela is the standard LXX reading: διηγήσομαι πάντα τὰ
θαυμάσιά σου, "I will recount all your wonders." The two points in question are the LXX's addition of πάντα, "all" and the singular versus plural
verb. As for "all," the Hebrew textual tradition mostly lacks it, although
there is a single medieval Hebrew manuscript that agrees with the LXX
by reading כל נפלאתיך, "all your wonders" (Kennicott 2:371; cf. Pss 9:2;
26:7). The word "all" is absent from P.Bod. 24, Codex Sinaiticus, the Syro-
Hexapla, two codices mentioned by Field (2:219), and an early copy of the
Sahidic Coptic Psalter (Rahlfs 207; KT 148). As for the verb, evidence for
the LXX uniformly points to the first-person singular form (διηγήσομαι, "I
will recount") as Sunnia and Fretela proposed. Jerome brushes this aside

---

tion" of Aquila, which were probably nothing more than variant readings written in the
margins of Jerome's copies of these books. Jerome does not mention a second edition
of Aquila in relation to the Psalms, but there are enough double attestations for Aquila
in the Psalms that one might suppose that such marginal readings existed; see Field,
Origenis Hexaplorum, 1:xxv, xxxvi–xxxvii; and Marcos, *Septuagint in Context*, 119–20.

as an error "among the Greeks." The fact that Jerome does not mention a Greek source with the correct reading perhaps suggests that the hexaplaric LXX had the singular. If so, Jerome in the Gallican Psalter presumably followed one of the hexaplaric versions that gave the verb in the first-person plural in continuation of the previous three verbs.

As for the verb in Hebrew, the preserved Hebrew text reads סֵפְּרוּ, which could be an imperative but is vocalized as a perfect in the MT: סִפְּרוּ, "They recounted." One might suspect that the final *vav* (ו) of this verb is a reduplication of the following *nun* (נ), and that סִפַּר along with the preceding קָרוֹב (or קָרוֹא) were meant as infinitive absolutes. In any case, the early Hebrew text presented some difficulty for the Greek versions, requiring them to unpack the sense as best they could. By the time Jerome makes his IH translation, he is clearly looking at a text whose consonants and vocalic interpretation are like those of the MT, for there he translates with the third-person plural: *narrabunt mirabilia tua*, "they will recount your wonders." A different rendering with the third-person plural is given in Codex Casinensis 557: *proferantur mirabilia tua*, "let your wonders be announced" (Amelli 52).

48.1.1–2. *omnes viri divitiarum manibus suis*, "All the men of wealth with their hands." Ps 75:6 (Heb 76:6), GPsal. According to the Hebrew, "And all the men of strength did not find their hands" (ולא מצאו כל אנשי חיל ידיהם). This might mean that they "found no strength." But a closely related and more common expression in Hebrew is that a person would find something בידו, "in his hand," or the like (e.g., Exod 21:16; 22:3; 1 Sam 9:8; 12:5).[126] Most LXX witnesses translated οὐχ εὗρον οὐδὲν πάντες οἱ ἄνδρες τοῦ πλούτου ταῖς χερσὶν αὐτῶν, "And all the men of wealth found nothing with their hands." As for the idea "in their hands," this would normally be expressed by ἐν ταῖς χερσὶν αὐτῶν. In fact, the preposition ἐν was added in the Greek text of the Verona Psalter, and it is reflected in the Syro-Hexapla, Bohairic and Sahidic Coptic versions, and the OL tradition (*in manibus suis*) as seen in Codex Sangermanensis, the Verona Psalter, the Sinai Psalter, and the Roman Psalter (Rahlfs 209; Sabatier 152; Weber 179; Thibaut 102). This was the reading adopted by the Sixto-Clementine Vulgate (Van Ess 78). Evidently, the expression *in manibus suis*, "in their hands" felt more idiomatic in Latin. Nevertheless, Jerome persisted with

---

126. The collocation ביד can also be instrumental, "by means of/with"; e.g., Exod 3:19; 1 Sam 18:25; 2 Chr 24:11; Ps 77:21.

the hexaplaric Greek text, which in this case represents the majority LXX reading: ταῖς χερσὶν αὐτῶν/*manibus suis*, "with their hands."[127]

Symmachus gave a translation that more closely approximates the Hebrew, with τὰς χεῖρας αὐτῶν, "their hands," being the direct object of the verb (Field 2:221). This is what Jerome will do in the IH edition: *et non invenerunt omnes viri exercitus manus suas*, "And all the men of the army did not find their hands."

48.2.3–4. *terribili et ei, qui aufert spiritus principum*, "to the terrifying one, and to him who removes the spirits of rulers." Ps 75:12–13 (Heb 76:12–13), GPsal. The reading of the LXX is as follows: τῷ φοβερῷ καὶ ἀφαιρουμένῳ πνεύματα ἀρχόντων, "to the terrifying one, and to the one who removes the spirits of rulers." The issue raised by Sunnia and Fretela is that the dative article (τῷ) appears before the first word (φοβερῷ) but not the second (ἀφαιρουμένῳ), so, they ask, why does Jerome have *ei*, "to him," before the second element?

The Gallican Psalter took its start from translation options already found in the OL tradition. Codex Sangermanensis has: *terribili et ei auferenti spiritum principum*, "To the terrifying one, and to him, the one removing the spirit of rulers" (Sabatier 153). The Roman Psalter gives a similar rendering: *terribili et ei qui aufert spiritum principum*, "To the terrifying one, and to him who removes the spirit of rulers" (Weber 180). Jerome made "spirits" (*spiritus*) plural in order to match the LXX's plural (πνεύματα), and he translated the Greek participle ἀφαιρουμένῳ not with a Latin participle as in Codex Sangermanensis (*ei auferenti*) but with a relative clause as in the Roman Psalter (*ei qui aufert*). Jerome must have thought the dative singular pronoun *ei*, "to him," was awkwardly redundant alongside the dative singular participle *auferenti*, so he chose the relative clause (*qui aufert*). This is acceptable as far as the sense goes, but it constitutes a departure from the LXX, which has a participle (ἀφαιρουμένῳ).

48.2.5–6. *Latinus sermo non resonat*, "It does not sound correct in the Latin language." Jerome's explanation for why he included *ei* in his translation is that Latin idiom requires it (see introduction, §7.2). As Jerome correctly points out, if the Greek participle ἀφαιρουμένῳ is translated with a relative clause in Latin (*qui aufert*), it must be preceded by a dative singular pronoun. If Sunnia and Fretela were allowed a follow-up question, they

---

127. In the Gallican Psalter, Jerome's *divitiarum*, "of wealth," imitates the LXX's τοῦ πλούτου. In the IH edition, Jerome uses *exercitus*, "of the army," reflecting another construal of the underlying Hebrew חיל.

might have asked: Why not just use a dative singular participle (*auferenti*) in Latin (= Codex Sangermanensis) and simply eliminate the unnecessary pronoun (*ei*)? This would be an obvious solution, but Jerome does not bring it up because his task in *Ep.* 106 is to defend the Gallican Psalter. Yet this is precisely what he will do when he translates the IH Psalter (*terribili auferenti spiritum ducum*).[128]

49.1.9–10. *et scopebam spiritum meum*, "And I searched my spirit." Ps 76:7 (Heb 77:7), GPsal. Jerome quotes the entire verse according to the Gallican Psalter and then immediately gives a translation based on the Hebrew (matching the IH edition) to which he does not subsequently refer. Following this, he offers information on the Greek versions, primarily the verb in the LXX underlying *scopebam*, namely, ἔσκαλλον. Unlike his normal practice in *Ep.* 106, Jerome does not begin by stating what Sunnia and Fretela proposed, and he does not follow up with a statement that their understanding of the Greek is wrong. I suspect that his Gothic interlocutors challenged his translation *scopebam*, "to search," by appealing to a different meaning of the word σκάλλω, for example, "to stir up" or "to hoe."[129] Jerome must have thought they had a legitimate point, because instead of presuming to correct their mistake, he sets forth his various sources in order to show that his decision to translate ἔσκαλλον as *scopebam* was not made in ignorance but is fully defensible from an informed vantage point.

The preserved Hebrew text reads: אזכרה נגינתי בלילה עם לבבי אשיחה ויחפש רוחי, "Let me remember my song in the night, with my heart let me meditate, and so my spirit searched." This is close to Jerome's Hebrew rendering, except that Jerome (along with some LXX witnesses, Symmachus, Theodotion, and the Syriac Peshitta) has the first-person singular *scopebam*, "I searched," in place of the preserved Hebrew third-person: ויחפש רוחי, "and so my spirit searched" (BHS 1158; Pesh 88). There is considerable confusion in the Greek manuscripts. Two difficulties in the Hebrew may have generated this confusion: (1) the switch from first-person to third-person is abrupt; and (2) רוח, "spirit," is being construed as gram-

---

128. Jerome matches Symmachus (τῷ νομοδότῃ ἀφαιροῦντι, "To the lawgiver [cf. מוֹרֶה], to the one who removes"; Field 2:222) in lacking a conjunction (καί or *et*). Its omission might simply signal a perceived sentence break. One suspects that the LXX had a Hebrew text that read ובצר instead of יבצר in v. 13 (cf. one manuscript in Kennicott 2:372), thus generating the participle.

129. LSJ, s.v. "σκάλλω."

matically masculine, which, although not impossible, is unusual.[130] This could cause a copyist to construe רוחי as the verb's object.

The LXX rendered אזכרה, "let me remember," as ἐμνήσθην, "I remembered," and נגינתי, "my song," as ἐμελέτησα, "I meditated," (perhaps reading והגיתי) and joined at least the first (if not both) of these words to the previous verse. To explain his translation *exercitabar*, "I was vexed," Jerome refers to the LXX's ἠδολέσχουν, which he takes to mean "I meditated" or "I repeated" (cf. LSJ: "meditate, prate").[131] As for Jerome's handling of the third verb, *scopebam*, "I searched," the LXX reading Jerome knows is the first-person singular ἔσκαλλον. This reading is supported by P.Bod. 24, Codex Sinaiticus, the Greek text of the Verona Psalter, the majority OL tradition, and the Bohairic and Sahidic Coptic versions (Rahlfs 210; KT 152).[132] Other forms for this verb are preserved in Greek witnesses: for example, the third-person singular ἔσκαλλεν (most Lucianic manuscripts, Theodoret's *Commentary**, MS 1219 Washington), ἔσκαλεν (Codex Vaticanus, a few Lucianic manuscripts, and MS 55 Rome), ἐσκάλευον, ἤσχαλε, and others (see Rahlfs 210). The reading ἔσκαλον (with one λ) is written by a corrector in Codex Vaticanus. Jerome was clearly aware of this reading; perhaps this is the spelling cited by Sunnia and Fretela. Jerome makes the interesting remark that the form with double λ is frequentative.

Jerome's main objectives are to show that he understands that σκαλισμός in its proper sense refers to hoeing and to make clear how this meaning fits with his translation of ἔσκαλλον as *scopebam*, "I searched." When someone "stirs up" or "weeds" (*sariendo*) with a hoe, he or she digs into the ground, searching for weeds to remove. According to Jerome, this metaphor explains why the Greek word that means "to hoe" (σκάλλω) also means "to search."[133] In this way, Jerome's Gallican Psalter translation *scopebam* is justified.

---

130. E.g., Num 11:31; Isa 57:16; Jer 4:12; Pss 51:12; 78:39.

131. LSJ, s.v. "ἀδολεσχέω."

132. As for the OL tradition, Codex Sangermanensis, the Verona Psalter, the Roman Psalter, and the Sinai Psalter have *ventilabam*, "I fanned," and Augustine's *Enarrations* gives *scrutabar*, "I scrutinized" (Sabatier 154; Weber 181; Thibaut 103; CC 39:1059). The third-person *dubitavit spiritum meum*, "he pondered my spirit," appears in Codex Casinensis 557, although *et scopebam spiritum meum* (= GPsal at v. 7) appears in v. 4 (Amelli 53).

133. Cf. LSJ, s.v. "σκάλλω"; LD, s.v. "sariendo."

49.2.20. μεταφορικῶς, "metaphorically." Jerome references several figures of speech in *Ep.* 106; see introduction, §9.1.

49.3.2. *a generatione in generationem*, "from generation to generation." Ps 76:9 (Heb 77:9), GPsal. In keeping with Jerome's explanation, the phrase *consummavit verbum*, "He has completed the word" is absent from the Gallican Psalter. Most LXX witnesses agree with Jerome's minus. This Greek phrase (συνετέλεσεν ῥῆμα) is present in the Lucianic manuscripts, Theodoret's *Commentary**, the Syro-Hexapla, and MS 1219 Washington, but according to these texts it is found before "from generation to generation" (Rahlfs 210). This corresponds to the Hebrew: גמר אמר לדר ודר, "He has completed the word from generation to generation." Moreover, Symmachus provides a rendering for the phrase in question, likewise before the "generation" reference: συνετέλεσε ῥῆσιν περὶ γενεᾶς ἑκάστης, "He completed his speaking concerning each generation" (Field 2:223; see Theodoret's *Commentary*).

When Jerome says *in nullo habetur interpretum*, "It is not present in any of the translators," Jerome is correct that no translator has *consummavit verbum* after "from generation to generation," but he is wrong to say that Symmachus lacks the phrase entirely; and since the preserved Hebrew contains this phrase, we might guess that it was found in at least one of the other hexaplaric versions. Did Sunnia and Fretela mistakenly ask about the presence of *consummavit verbum* after *a generatione in generationem*, and Jerome answer without checking the text carefully enough to notice that it occurs just before? Did Jerome simply misunderstand what Sunnia and Fretela were asking? This discussion does not give the impression that Jerome is consistently checking the Hebrew. Moreover, his reporting of the hexaplaric evidence here must be either careless or highly selective (see introduction, §8.2).

Jerome's goal in *Ep.* 106 is to defend the Gallican Psalter, which was based on the hexaplaric LXX as understood to be the genuine LXX. From this perspective, the edition of the Septuagint based on the Hexapla, supported by its surrounding versions, is the practical standard of truth. As Jerome sums up, the phrase in question "is not correctly present in the Latin, because it is not present in any of the translators."

In the IH edition, Jerome provides a translation that follows the Hebrew: *consummabit verbum de generatione et generatione*, "He will complete the word from generation to generation."

50.1.4. *et narrabunt filiis suis*, "and they will recount to their sons." Ps 77:6 (Heb 78:6), GPsal. Jerome reports that the Greek reads ἀναγγελοῦσιν, "they will announce," which is the LXX text according to Codex Sinaiticus, the Greek text of the Verona Psalter, Hesychius of Jerusalem, a few Lucianic manuscripts, and MS 55 Rome (Rahlfs 212). The closely related word ἀπαγγελοῦσιν is found in most witnesses, including P.Bod. 24 (KT 154), Codex Vaticanus, most Lucianic manuscripts, and Theodoret's *Commentary**. It seems that ἀναγγελοῦσιν was the Greek word quoted by Sunnia and Fretela, and Jerome appears to accept it as the correct form of the Greek.

Most OL witnesses have the translation *narrabunt*, "they will recount" (Sabatier 156; Weber 185), and Jerome in the Gallican Psalter followed suit. Apparently, Sunnia and Fretela not only quoted the Greek ἀναγγελοῦσιν but also suggested that the correct meaning of this word is *adnuntiabunt*, "they will announce." This rendering is found in the Sinai Psalter (Thibaut 104). Jerome responds to their suggestion by appealing to the Hebrew word ויספרו, which he transliterates (without the *vav* conjunction): *iasaphpheru* (the doubling of the *ph* should be noted; MT וִיסַפְּרוּ). He interprets the meaning of the Hebrew through Aquila and Symmachus, whose translation he reports as *narrabunt* (probably διηγήσονται; Field 2:225), which supports his Gallican Psalter rendering.

Jerome's comments could be interpreted as saying that, although the LXX says ἀναγγελοῦσιν (i.e., *adnuntiabunt*), the true meaning based on the Hebrew is *narrabunt*. However, I think it is more likely that when Jerome says ἀναγγελοῦσιν, *quod est 'adnuntiabunt,'* he means that the Greek has ἀναγγελοῦσιν, which Sunnia and Fretela wrongly construe as *adnuntiabunt*, whereas the Hebrew word (as interpreted through Aquila and Symmachus) gives us the correct interpretation of ἀναγγελοῦσιν, namely, *narrabunt*.

50.2.7–8. *et occidit pingues eorum*, "And he killed their fat ones." Ps 77:31 (Heb 78:31), GPsal. Most preserved witnesses to the LXX read πλείοσιν, "more" (dative, plural, comparative of πολύς), yielding the sense: "And he killed among more of them." Most OL witnesses offer a text roughly equivalent to: *et occidit plurimos eorum/illorum*, "And he killed most of them" (Sabatier 158; Weber 188; Thibaut 106). Sunnia and Fretela must have suggested the meaning "more/most" based on the Greek πλείοσιν.

Jerome takes this to be a scribal miscopying of the original reading πίοσιν, "fat ones" (Rahlfs 214). Jerome supports his explanation by citing the hexaplaric LXX, Theodotion, and Quinta (ἐν τοῖς πίοσιν αὐτῶν, "among their fat ones"), Aquila (ἐν λιπαροῖς αὐτῶν, "among their oily/rich ones"), and Symmachus, who removes the preposition for clarity's sake (τοὺς λιπαρωτέρους αὐτῶν, "their most oily/richest ones"). According to Jerome, the hexaplaric versions give the correct interpretation of the Hebrew, *bamasmnehem*, that is, במשמניהם, from משמן, "fat, corpulence."[134] In the Latin tradition, Codex Casinensis 557 offers this meaning, giving the preposition *in* as one finds in Theodotion, Quinta, and Aquila: *et interfecit in pinguis* (Read: *pinguibus*) *eorum*, "And he slayed among their fat ones" (Amelli 54). Undoubtedly Codex Casinensis 557 here reflects influence from a Hebraized Greek source.

A passage in Origen's *Homilies on the Psalms*, preserved in Codex Monacensis Graecus 314 and only recently published, shows how Origen treated this passage in light of the hexaplaric versions:

> So, this wrath having come against them, "He killed among their fat ones." He did not say that He killed the people or that He killed more of the people, as some think who have not understood the text as πίοσιν but have made it: "He killed among more (πλείοσιν) of them." But it is: "He killed among their fat ones." First, we need to convince the hearer that the copy reading "He killed among more of them" has been corrupted. For in the first place the remaining editions do not have the equivalent of "more," but "their most oily/rich ones" (τοῖς λιπαρωτέροις αὐτῶν), and this is what the Hebrew has.[135] If it had been written "among more," you would not be able to make sense of the statement that six hundred thousand, three thousand, and five hundred came out of the land of Egypt (cf. Num 1:46), since if "He killed among more of them," it is clear that fewer of them would have been left remaining.[136] Therefore, it is not "He killed among more of them," but "among their fat ones," and indeed he added "among their fat ones" with good reason: Undoubtedly the people sinned that sin: "they desired a desire in the wilderness" (cf. Num 11:4), but only certain people sinned, either more or less, and probably some people did not sin. So, however many sinned, they became fat in the flesh, they took part in the sin. Therefore, it is written "He killed"—not "among their lean ones" nor "among their thin ones," but "among their fat ones," that is, those having traces left in their flesh of what was desired.[137]

---

134. *HALOT*, s.v. "משמן."

135. Origen gives the comparative form as Symmachus does, but he uses the dative in keeping with Aquila.

136. In other words, if the majority of Israelites were killed in the wilderness, it is unlikely that the number of Israelites who survived according to this census would be so high.

137. Lorenzo Perrone, ed., *Die neuen Psalmenhomilien. Eine kritische Edition des Codex Monacensis Graecus 314*, GCS 19 (Berlin: de Gruyter, 2015), 411–12. The Greek text is: Αὕτη τοίνυν ἀναβᾶσα ἐπ' αὐτοὺς ἡ ὀργὴ ἀπέκτεινεν ἐν τοῖς πίοσιν αὐτῶν. Οὐκ εἴρηκεν ὅτι ἀπέκτεινε τὸν λαὸν ἢ ἀπέκτεινε πολλοὺς ἀπὸ τοῦ λαοῦ, ὡς οἴονται τινες

In his *Enarrations*, Augustine gives the reading: *et occidit in plurimis eorum, hoc est, plurimos eorum*, "And he killed among most of them, that is, (he killed) most of them," but then he adds: *vel sicut nonnulli codices habent, pingues eorum. Quod quidem in graecis quos habuimus, non invenimus. Sed si hoc est verius, quid aliud intelligendi sunt pingues eorum, nisi superbia praevalentes, de quibus dicitur: prodiet quasi ex adipe iniquitas eorum*, "Or, as several codices have, 'their fat ones,' although we have not found this in the Greek codices we have. But if this is more correct, how else are 'their fat ones' to be understood except as those who prevail in pride, about whom it says: 'he will go forth as if out of the fat of their iniquity' (see Ps 72:6–7)" (CC 39:1081). It is very likely that Augustine knows the variant *pingues eorum* because he has read Jerome's *Ep.* 106. It should also be noted that Augustine explains *pingues eorum* with reference to the phrase *prodiet quasi ex adipe*, which Jerome discusses at **45.1**.

50.3.12. *dilexerunt eum*, "they loved him." Ps 77:36 (Heb 78:36), GPsal. There is an issue in the Gallican Psalter for Ps 77:36 that Jerome does not address but is worthy of mention. The Hebrew for this verb is from פתה, "deceive." The LXX translated this ἠπάτησαν, "they deceived." In a few Greek manuscripts, however, this was miscopied as ἠγάπησαν, "they loved" (Rahlfs 215). This became a widespread reading in the OL tradition (*dilexerunt*).[138] Codex Sangermanensis reflects a further corruption to *dixerunt*, "they said" (see Sabatier 158; Weber 189; Thibaut 106). In the Gallican Psalter, Jerome gives the OL rendering *dilexerunt*, even though the proper Hebrew meaning was probably available among the hexaplaric versions, for example,

---

τῶν μὴ νοησάντων τὸ πίοσιν καὶ πεποιήκασιν: ἀπέκτεινεν ἐν τοῖς πλείοσιν αὐτῶν, ἀλλά: ἀπέκτεινεν ἐν τοῖς πίοσιν αὐτῶν. Πρῶτον δὲ θέλομεν πεῖσαι τὸν ἀκροατήν, ὅτι ἡμάρτηται τὸ λέγον ἀντίγραφον: ἀπέκτεινεν ἐν τοῖς πλείοσιν αὐτῶν. Πρῶτον μὲν γὰρ οὐκ ἔχουσιν αἱ λοιπαὶ ἐκδόσεις τὸ ἀνάλογον τοῖς πλείοσιν ἀλλ' ἐν τοῖς λιπαρωτέροις αὐτῶν, καὶ αὐτο δὲ τὸ Ἑβραϊκὸν οὕτως ἔχει. Ἐὰν δὲ ᾖ γεγραμμένον ἐν τοῖς πλείσιν, οὐδὲν δύνασαι νοηθῆσαι τῷ ῥητῷ ἐξακόσιαι χιλιάδες ἐξῆλθον ἐκ γῆς Αἰγύπτου καὶ τρισχίλιοι πεντακόσιοι. Εἰ οὖν ἀπέκτεινεν ἐν τοῖς πλείοσιν αὐτῶν, δῆλον ὅτι ἐλάττονες κατελείφθησαν. Οὐκ ἄρα ἐστὶν ἐν τοῖς πλείοσιν αὐτῶν, ἀλλ' ἐν τοῖς πίοσιν αὐτῶν καὶ ἀναγκαίως προσέθηκε τὸ ἐν τοῖς πίοσιν αὐτῶν. Τάχα δὲ οὐχ ὁ λαὸς ἥμαρτε τὴν ἁμαρτίαν ἐκείνην: ἐπεθύμησαν ἐπιθυμίαν ἐν τῇ ἐρήμῳ, ἀλλά τινες ἢ πλεῖον ἢ ἔλαττον ἥμαρτον, τάχα δὲ καὶ τινες οὐχ ἥμαρτον. Ὅσοι οὖν ἥμαρτον, ἐγένοντο πίονες ἀπὸ τῶν σαρκῶν, ἀπέλαβον τὴν ἁμαρτίαν. Διὸ γέγραπται: ἀπέκτεινεν οὐκ ἐν τοῖς ἰσχνοῖς αὐτῶν οὐδὲ ἐν τοῖς λεπτοῖς αὐτῶν, ἀλλ' ἐν τοῖς πίοσιν αὐτῶν, τοῖς τὰ ἴχνη ἔχουσιν ἐν ταῖς σαρξὶ τοῦ ἐπιθυμουμένου.

138. The imperfect rather than then perfect appears in Codex Casinensis 557: *diligebant* (Amelli 55).

Symmachus according to the Syro-Hexapla reads *mṭʿyn*, "lead astray" (Field 2:226). Sunnia and Fretela seem not to have asked about it, so Jerome does not take up the question. But in the IH Psalter, Jerome gives a rendering closer to the Hebrew: *lactaverunt*, "they duped/deceived."

50.3.13. *mentiti sunt ei*, "they lied to him." Ps 77:36 (Heb 78:36), GPsal. The Hebrew for this phrase is: יכזבו לו, "they lied to him" (with the ל for "to"). Jerome transliterates this as one word, *icazbulo*—that is, *icazbu lo*—and defends his use of the dative in Latin (*ei*) by stating that all the hexaplaric versions used the dative in Greek (αὐτῷ). This shows his ability to work with hexaplaric materials as a tool, but it does not indicate much by way of specific knowledge of Hebrew.

Jerome gives the translation options in Latin, preferring the dative *ei*, "to him," to the accusative *eum*, "him." The verb *mentior* regularly takes the dative of the person lied to (OLD 1100). The dative appears in OL witnesses such as Codex Sangermanensis, Codex Casinensis 557 (*illi*), the Roman Psalter, and the Sinai Psalter (*ei*), whereas the Verona Psalter lacks this element altogether (Sabatier 158; Weber 189; Amelli 55; Thibaut 106; Rahlfs 215).

The real question, however, concerned the Greek text: αὐτῷ, "to him," versus αὐτόν, "him." The Greek word ψεύδομαι regularly takes the accusative, but most preserved LXX witnesses give the dative (αὐτῷ) in imitation of the Hebrew (לו).[139] Sunnia and Fretela must have proposed the accusative (αὐτόν), which is also attested by numerous Lucianic manuscripts, the Zürich Greek Psalter, and Hesychius of Jerusalem (Rahlfs 215). In this instance, Jerome's preservation of the dative maintains an expression that is less natural in Greek but is the majority reading of Greek witnesses and is closer to the surface structure of the Hebrew. It also translates directly into proper Latin (*mentior* plus the dative).

50.4.17–18. *et propitius fiet peccatis eorum et non disperdet eos*, "And he will make atonement for their sins and will not destroy them." Ps 77:38 (Heb 78:38), GPsal.[140] As Sunnia and Fretela apparently pointed out and as

---

139. LSJ, s.v. "ψεύδομαι."

140. Most Gallican Psalter witnesses read *disperdet*, but a few important manuscripts (e.g., the Cathach Psalter) have *perdet*. WG reads *perdet*, whereas the Sixto-Clementine Vulgate has *disperdet*. As for *Ep.* 106, the Benedictine edition reads *perdet*, in keeping with the original reading of one of the earliest witnesses (Gasquet 28). Hilberg favors *disperdet*, as found in several later manuscripts and a correction to Vatican, Reg. lat. 11 (Hilberg 272). In terms of possible influence from the Old Latin, the common

Jerome affirms, the LXX lacks an object for the second verb, stating merely οὐ διαφθερεῖ, "will not destroy/corrupt."[141]

50.4.20. *Latinum sermonem sua proprietate conplevimus*, "We filled out the Latin expression according to Latin's own particular idiom." On Jerome's concern for the particular idiom of each language in translation, see introduction, §7.2.

50.4.23. *et non, ut plerique* κακοζήλως *interpretantur*, "and not as most translate using an affected manner (κακοζήλως)." On Jerome's objection to translating in an affected manner, see introduction, §7.2. The rendering to which Jerome objects, *ne corrumpas*, "Do not corrupt" is attested at Ps 56:1 in Latin witnesses such as the Mozarabic Psalter, Hilary's *Tractatus*, and Augustine's *Enarrations* (Weber 125; CC 61:160; CSEL 94.1:222). Hilary reports both translation options: *nunc 'ne corrumpas' vel 'disperdas' praescribitur, quod uno verbo* τῷ μὴ διαφθείρῃς *utrumque graecus sermo complexus est*, "Now, 'Do not corrupt' or 'destroy' is written, both of which the Greek language encompasses with one word, διαφθείρῃς (CC 61:160). Augustine also uses *ne corrumpas*, "Do not corrupt" at Pss 57:1 and 58:1 (CSEL 94.1:259, 316). At Ps 74:1, *ne corrumpas* is even more widely attested, for example, in Codex Sangermanensis, the Roman Psalter, the Corbie Psalter, the Sinai Psalter, Augustine, and Cassiodorus (Sabatier 151; Thibaut 101; CC 39:1024; CC 98:685; also the Sixto-Clementine Vulgate). When Jerome says that "most" (*plerique*) translate *ne corrumpas*, he probably has in mind Ps 74:1 and perhaps Ps 56:1.

50.5.2–3. *montem quem adquisivit dextera eius*, "the mountain that his right hand acquired." Ps 77:54 (Heb 78:54), GPsal. To understand Jerome's point and resolve the confusion in the text of *Ep.* 106, it is helpful to begin with the Hebrew. The first line of the Hebrew text reads: ויביאם אל גבול קדשו, "And he led them to the border of his holiness." For גבול, "border," the LXX translated ὅριον, "border," although a few manuscripts listed by Rahlfs and P.Bod. 24 read ὅρος, "mountain," based on the second line (Rahlfs 216; KT 160). This latter reading (with "mountain" in both lines) was adopted

---

OL had *disperdet* (Sabatier 158; Weber 189). One might argue that *perdet* was the original reading for the Gallican Psalter, which was corrected in manuscripts towards the OL. If *Ep.* 106 originally had *perdet*, this might have been copied later as *disperdet* through harmonization to corrected Vulgate texts. However, the fact that Jerome here quotes Ps 74:1 with the form *disperdas* gives slight preference to Hilberg's text for the lemma of *Ep.* 106, *disperdet*.

141. LSJ, s.v. "διαφθείρω."

by the OL tradition (Sabatier 160; Weber 192; Thibaut 107; Amelli 55), and Jerome used it in the Gallican Psalter. Given that ὄρος, "mountain," belongs in the text only once based on the Hebrew and many LXX witnesses, we may imagine that Sunnia and Fretela had a Greek manuscript in which someone had mistakenly deleted the second reference to "mountain," ὄρος τοῦτο. This is the text with which they challenged the Gallican Psalter.

Here, then, is Jerome's response: (1) The correct text of the LXX for the second line is ὄρος τοῦτο ὃ ἐκτήσατο ἡ δεξιὰ αὐτοῦ, "the mountain that his right hand acquired." It is not, as Sunnia and Fretela suggest, ὃ ἐκτήσατο ἡ δεξιὰ αὐτοῦ, "which his right hand acquired" (i.e., with ὄρος τοῦτο omitted). (2) If one wonders why Jerome translated ὄρος τοῦτο simply as *montem* rather than *montem istum*, "this mountain" (or the like), it is because he was translating according to the Hebrew idiom (*secundum Hebraicam proprietatem*), for which Symmachus serves as witness.[142] In the IH edition, Jerome gives *montem* only once in agreement with the Hebrew (but against the Gallican Psalter), and he uses *montem istum* as opposed to what here he calls "Hebrew idiom."

The issue at hand is the presence or absence of ὄρος τοῦτο in the second line. Because Jerome, when reporting the text proposed by Sunnia and Fretela, signaled the omission simply by skipping the omitted text and going straight to the next words, "and not as you put: ὃ ἐκτήσατο," some confusion arose in the interpretation of *Ep.* 106 as to how the text proposed by Sunnia and Fretela differs from the Gallican Psalter. In a few manuscripts of *Ep.* 106, ὃ is omitted from Jerome's citation of the Greek (ὄρος τοῦτο ἐκτήσατο ἡ δεξιὰ αὐτοῦ), which becomes the key difference (ὃ instead of τοῦτο). The Benedictine edition follows this reading (Gasquet 28); yet, Hilberg retains ὃ (Hilberg 273), correctly in my view. For his part, Hilberg changes ἐκτήσατο to ἐκτίσατο, so that the change in verb becomes the point at issue. But if matters stand as I described above, this change is not needed.

50.6.8–9. *non servaverunt pactum*, "they did not maintain the covenant." Ps 77:57 (Heb 78:57), GPsal. The Hebrew underlying the verb in question is ויבגדו, from בגד ("act treacherously"). According to Jerome, "all"

---

142. On the translation of זה as τοῦτο ὃ (i.e., as both a demonstrative and relative), see Adrian Schenker, *Hexaplarische Psalmenbruchstücke: Die hexaplarischen Psalmenfragmente der Handschriften Vaticanus graecus 752 und Canonicianus graecus 62*, OBO 8 (Göttingen: Vandenhoeck & Ruprecht, 1975), 166–67. On the text of Symmachus, see Schenker, *Hexaplarische Psalmenbruchstücke*, 73.

the Greek versions rendered this word as ἠσυνθέτησαν, from ἀσυνθετέω ("break covenant, be faithless").[143] This appears to be a case where Jerome has collapsed the hexaplaric versions together because he takes them all to support his general point, even though they do not read precisely the same. Manuscript evidence suggests that Aquila had ἠσυνθέτησαν, but Symmachus translated ἠσυνθήκουν (from ἀσυνθηκέω).[144] In any case, Jerome's point is that the Greek verb is etymologically related to the noun συνθήκη (i.e., *pactum*/covenant; see **2.3**). He does not dispute the charge that the word *pactum* in his Gallican Psalter has no direct analogue in the Hebrew. His argument, however, is that the Greek verb ἀσυνθετέω entails the idea of "covenant." If the hexaplaric Greek translators chose to render the sense of the Hebrew using ἠσυνθέτησαν, he is justified in giving the translation *servaverunt pactum*, which uses two Latin words for one Greek word, but correctly preserves the "covenant" idea. For Jerome, a correct translation does not need to maintain the same number of constituent elements, one-for-one.

Witnesses to the Old Latin tradition such as Codex Sangermanensis (*repulerunt*), the Roman Psalter, the Corbie Psalter, and the Sinai Psalter (*observaverunt*) offer renderings of this word that do not introduce the noun *pactum* (Sabatier 160; Weber 193; Thibaut 107). Moreover, the Greek text of the Verona Psalter, the Lucianic manuscripts, Theodoret's *Commentary**, the Syro-Hexapla, and MS 1219 Washington read ἠθέτησαν, "they rejected," which lacks the clear connection to συνθήκη, "covenant." A great many LXX witnesses, however, read ἠσυνθέτησαν, which is the rendering Jerome says "all" (*omnes*) gave; these include Codex Vaticanus, Codex Sinaiticus, and P.Bod. 24 (Rahlfs 217; KT 160).

In a surprising statement at the conclusion of his discussion, Jerome says: *licet Septuaginta* ἠθέτησαν *posuerint*, "Yet the Seventy put ἠθέτησαν." Does Jerome mean by this that the authentic (i.e., hexaplaric) LXX gave ἠθέτησαν? Did Jerome translate *servaverunt pactum*, "maintain the covenant," in the Gallican Psalter and then defend his translation by claiming that "all" translated ἠσυνθέτησαν, when in fact the hexaplaric LXX read ἠθέτησαν against the grain of the hexaplaric versions? Masséo Caloz argues that this is so, citing as support the fact that Eusebius also reads ἠθέτησαν (PG 23:932; Caloz 373). The only alternative interpretation

---

143. LSJ, s.v. "ἀσυνθετέω."
144. See Schenker, *Hexaplarische Psalmenbruchstücke*, 75, 178.

would be to suggest that by *Septuaginta* Jerome means the "popular" LXX, whereas the "true" (= hexaplaric) LXX was included in the "all" who gave ἠσυνθέτησαν.

Although we might expect Jerome to include the hexaplaric LXX in the company of "all" the translators, I do not think this is what happened here. In all likelihood, the hexaplaric LXX had ἠθέτησαν. There is no reason for Jerome to tack on a reference to what the "popular" LXX contains, and he does not label this *Septuaginta* as κοινά or *vulgata*. Moreover, the very manner in which he slips in this terse comment suggests that it is an uncomfortable admission. The most likely scenario is that for this passage in the Gallican Psalter Jerome followed the hexaplaric versions rather than the hexaplaric LXX. At this stage of his career, he was incapable of interpreting the Hebrew בגד apart from the hexaplaric versions; in translating the Gallican Psalter Jerome appealed to their understanding of the Hebrew to give him the true meaning of the word (i.e., ἠσυνθέτησαν), which differed from the hexaplaric LXX (i.e., ἠθέτησαν). On this issue, in the course of defending the Gallican Psalter, Jerome is forced to acknowledge that the hexaplaric LXX is not as close as possible to the Hebrew text as he presently understands it.

Later, Augustine in his *Enarrations* gives a Latin text that follows the Gallican Psalter: *non servaverunt pactum* (CC 39:1092). In the IH Psalter, Jerome will render ויבגדו as *praevaricati sunt*, "acted corruptly," dispensing with the Greek versions entirely.

50.6b.14–15. *in terra quam fundavit in saecula*, "in the land that he founded unto the ages." Ps 77:69b (Heb 78:69b), GPsal. As is often the case, unpacking the Hebrew will help explain the confusion among the versions. The first half of this verse includes the idea that God built his sanctuary: ויבן ... מקדשו, καὶ ᾠκοδόμησεν ... τὸ ἁγίασμα αὐτοῦ, *et aedificavit ... sanctificium suum*, "and he built his sanctuary." For the second half, the Hebrew text according to the Leningrad Codex has כְּאֶרֶץ יְסָדָהּ לְעוֹלָם, "Like the land; he founded it to the age" (the feminine singular "it" agrees the with the feminine singular "land"). The phrase כְּאֶרֶץ, "like the land" is far less common than בְּאֶרֶץ, "in the land," so not surprisingly the LXX read the more common ב, "in," instead of כ, "like," = ἐν τῇ γῇ, "in the land."[145] Thus the LXX has ἐν τῇ γῇ ἐθεμελίωσεν αὐτὴν εἰς τὸν αἰῶνα, "In the land, he

---

145. In presuming ב, the LXX is supported by the Syriac Peshitta and numerous medieval Hebrew manuscripts (Pesh 93; De-Rossi 4:54).

founded it unto the age." But this leaves a significant point of unclarity: If "it" (feminine singular) agrees grammatically with "land" (feminine singular), what does it mean to say that God founded "it" (i.e., "the land") in the land? Because "sanctuary" is the wrong grammatical gender (masculine in Hebrew, neuter in Greek and Latin), the feminine pronoun "it" in the second half of the verse cannot go back to "sanctuary" in the first half.[146] This is the difficulty confronting the Greek versions and Jerome.

Symmachus resolves the difficulty by taking יְסָדָהּ as a relative clause, thus producing: τὴν γῆν, ἣν ἐθεμελίωσεν, "the land that he founded."[147] In the Gallican Psalter, Jerome followed Symmachus (*terra quam fundavit*), taking this to be the correct sense of the Hebrew. ("In Hebrew it is written thus, as Symmachus rendered.") Sunnia and Fretela must have objected to the relative pronoun (ἣν/*quam*). Jerome explains that, given the feminine pronoun αὐτήν, the text does not make sense without the relative pronoun. If "sanctuary" were the intended referent, the pronoun should be neuter (αὐτό/*illud*).

Of course, Symmachus's interpretation is possible, but it is not the only way to construe the Hebrew. In his IH edition, Jerome returns to the Hebrew by giving "like" (*quasi*) instead of "in" (*in*), making *saeculum* singular to match עוֹלָם, and he uses the neuter pronoun (*illud*) to refer back to "sanctuary" instead of construing יְסָדָהּ as a relative clause: *et aedificavit ... sanctuarium suum; quasi terram fundavit illud in saeculum*, "And he built ... his sanctuary; like the land, he founded it (i.e., the sanctuary) unto the age."

50.7.23–24. *et in intellectibus manuum suarum deduxit eos*, "And by the comprehensions of his hands he guided them." Ps 77:72 (Heb 78:72), GPsal. The issue at hand is whether the noun for "comprehension" (*intellectibus*) is plural or singular.

The Leningrad Codex gives a plural form for the Hebrew: וּבִתְבוּנוֹת, "and by the understandings." Jerome transliterates the Hebrew without the *vav* conjunction as *bathabunoth*. At some point in his career Jerome understood Hebrew well enough to know that the *-oth* ending signifies the plural (see **8.2.1**), but it is unclear whether he grasps that specific detail here.

---

146. Codex Sinaiticus gives a neuter singular pronoun (αὐτό) instead of αὐτήν, allowing the pronoun to refer back to "sanctuary" and thereby resolving the issue (Rahlfs 218).

147. Jerome erroneously (it seems) reports Symmachus as εἰς τὴν γῆν, "into the land." Other sources (including Theodoret's *Commentary*) attest Symmachus as ὡς τὴν γῆν (Field 2:230).

Evidence for the plural form in Greek includes P.Bod. 24, the Lucianic manuscripts, Theodoret's *Commentary**, the Syro-Hexapla, and the Berlin manuscript of the Sahidic Coptic version (Rahlfs 218; KT 162). There is also testimony from Eusebius that ascribes the plural to Aquila: φρονήσεσι (Field 2:230).

On the other hand, nearly thirty-five medieval Hebrew manuscripts read the singular (וּבִתְבֻנַת, De-Rossi 4:55), as does Symmachus, Theodotion, and some reports for Aquila (Field 2:230), along with important LXX witnesses such as Codex Vaticanus, Codex Sinaiticus, the Greek text of the Verona Psalter, MS 1219 Washington, and the Bohairic Coptic version (Rahlfs 218). The singular is also the reading of the OL according to Codex Sangermanensis, Codex Casinensis 557, the Verona Psalter, the Roman Psalter, Augustine's *Enarrations*, the Sinai Psalter, and other witnesses (Sabatier 161–62; Weber 195; Amelli 56; Thibaut 108).

In the Gallican Psalter, Jerome gave the plural. Sunnia and Fretela challenged this by suggesting that the Greek has the singular. Jerome replies with (1) a transliteration of the Hebrew word and (2) a quotation of the Greek that gives the plural. The Greek quotation might signify that the hexaplaric LXX had the plural: ἐν ταῖς συνέσεσιν.

In the IH Psalter, Jerome reverses his decision, giving the singular: *et in prudentia manuum suarum dux eorum fuit*, "and by the discretion of his hands he was their leader." Perhaps this change reflects his later encounter with a Hebrew text that had the singular (תְבֻנַת). It is also possible that he followed Symmachus or Theodotion.

51.1.27–1. *posuerunt Hierusalem in pomorum custodiam*, "They made Jerusalem into a keep of fruits." Ps 78:1 (Heb 79:1), GPsal. Obviously, Sunnia and Fretela questioned Jerome's rendering of ὀπωροφυλάκιον as *pomorum custodiam*, but we do not know specifically what they suggested instead. The compound word ὀπωροφυλάκιον (from ὀπώρα, "summer," "fruit," and φυλακεῖον, "watchtower") occurs several times in the LXX, referring to an "orchard guard's shed" (see Mic 1:6; 3:12; Isa 1:8) or a "tottering, unstable structure" as in Isa 24:20.[148] In the Latin tradition, Codex Sangermanensis translated this as *casam pomarii*, "fruit-garden hut"; the Roman Psalter and Hilary have *pomorum custodiarium*, a "keeping place of fruits"; the Sinai Psalter has *pomeri custodia*, "a keep of fruit"; and Codex Casinensis 557 matches the Gallican Psalter: *pomorum custodiam*, "a keep

---

148. *GELS*, s.v. "ὀπωροφυλάκιον."

of fruits" (Sabatier 162; Weber 195; CC 61B:172; Amelli 56; Thibaut 108). When Jerome says it is not possible to translate this word differently, he probably means that you cannot accurately translate this single Greek word with a single Latin word but in some way or another need two Latin words to capture the sense. In all likelihood, Sunnia and Fretela pointed out that ὀπωροφυλάκιον is just one word, and they asked why Jerome used two words. Underlying Jerome's response is a general point of translation philosophy: sometimes two or more words in the receptor language are needed to capture the meaning of a single word in the source language (see introduction, §7.2).

The discussion above relates to Jerome's rendering of ὀπωροφυλάκιον, which is without dispute the correct Greek reading. In Hebrew, however, the word is *lichin* (לעיים), made up of the preposition ל ("They made Jerusalem *into*") and the noun עי, "heap of ruins."[149] It is not clear how much of the Hebrew grammar Jerome understands. The word itself is uncommon and surely outside Jerome's vocabulary at this point. For the meaning of the Hebrew, Jerome appeals to Aquila, whom he cites as giving λιθαόριον, "boundary stone," although Eusebius says that Aquila translated λιθολογίαν, "unworked stone" (see Field 2:230). For this passage, Jerome seems comfortable acknowledging that even the correct Greek reading does not give precisely the same meaning as the Hebrew but offers merely an acceptable Greek rendition of the general sense. In the IH Psalter, he gives a translation close to his explanation of Aquila here: *in acervis lapidum*, "into a heap of stones."

52.1.8–9. *et plantasti radices eius hinc*, "And you planted its roots here." Ps 79:10 (Heb 80:10). As Jerome explains, the Gallican Psalter has: *et plantasti radices eius*, "And you planted its roots." This follows the preserved LXX: καὶ κατεφύτευσας τὰς ῥίζας αὐτῆς. The addition of *hinc*, "here," reflects a peculiar error in the source consulted by Sunnia and Fretela.

53.1.12–13. *hereditate possideamus sanctuarium dei*, "Let us possess by inheritance the sanctuary of God." Ps 82:13 (Heb 83:13), GPsal. The LXX does in fact read κληρονομήσωμεν ἑαυτοῖς, "let us inherit for ourselves," as Sunnia and Fretela assert. The word "for ourselves" in the LXX (ἑαυτοῖς) was represented consistently (*nobis*) in the Old Latin tradition (Sabatier 168; Weber 206; Amelli 59; Thibaut 112; CC 98:765), but it is absent from the Gallican Psalter and also from Augustine's text in the *Enarrations* (CC

---

149. *HALOT*, s.v. "עי."

39:1144). Jerome dropped *nobis* from the Gallican Psalter for purely sty-listic reasons, not because it was lacking in the hexaplaric LXX text or was under obelus (cf. Caloz 281–82). On this "point of question" (*quaestio*) being "superfluous" (*superflua*), see introduction, §8.5.

Noteworthy is Jerome's rendering of the single Greek word κληρονομήσωμεν, "let us inherit" with two Latin words: *hereditate possidea-mus*, "let us possess by inheritance." Some OL witnesses such as Codex Sangermanensis and the Roman Psalter give the noun in the accusative *hereditatem possideamus*, "let us possess the inheritance," whereas others such as the Verona Psalter, the Mozarabic Psalter, and the Sinai Psalter tes-tify to the ablative (*hereditate*) as in the Gallican Psalter. Jerome may have simply inherited the ablative from the Old Latin tradition as he knew it, or he may have chosen the ablative because it is slightly less cumbersome than the accusative. Perhaps this roundabout manner of handling the verb led Jerome to drop *nobis*.

The word ἑαυτοῖς, "for ourselves," in the LXX is based on the Hebrew, נירשה לנו, "let us possess/inherit for ourselves." In the IH Psalter, Jerome will simplify his translation of κληρονομήσωμεν and reintroduce *nobis*: *pos-sideamus nobis*, "let us possess for ourselves."

Jerome treats Ps 82:13 twice in his *Homilies on the Psalms*. In one instance, his citation matches the Gallican Psalter exactly (CC 78:94), and in the other instance, he quotes the text primarily according to the Gal-lican Psalter, but he adds *nobis* from the IH version (CC 78:388). In *Ruf.* 2.6, Jerome criticizes the translation of κληρονομήσουσιν using two words (*hereditate potientur*, "they possess by inheritance") as a flawed attempt to be ornate, preferring instead to use one word, *hereditabunt* (CC 79:38).

54.1.17–18. *cor meum et caro mea exultavit in deum vivum*, "My heart and my flesh has rejoiced in the living God." Ps 83:3 (Heb 84:3), GPsal. Evidence for the Greek and Latin versions mostly points to the plural form of the verb (ἠγαλλιάσαντο, *exultaverunt*), as Sunnia and Fretela propose, although P.Bod. 24 gives the singular ἠγαλλιάσατο.[150] The Hebrew verb is plural, so we do not expect to find the singular in the hexaplaric ver-sions. Jerome's choice of the singular (*exultavit*) in the Gallican Psalter may depend on a Greek tradition along the lines of P.Bod. 24, or else the singu-lar may have come from his sense of Latin style and idiom. Jerome's only

---

150. For P.Bod. 24, see KT 170. On the plural form, see Rahlfs 226; Sabatier 169; Weber 208; Thibaut 113; Amelli 59 (*exulta[ve]re*). Jerome used the plural *exultaverunt* in the *Commentaries on the Psalms* (CC 72:220).

defense for the Gallican Psalter is to request that Sunnia and Fretela stop asking pointless questions that do not touch on the meaning. In the IH Psalter, Jerome will use the plural: *cor meum et caro mea laudabunt*.

54.2.24. *beatus vir cuius est auxilium abs te*, "Blessed is the man whose help is from you." Ps 83:6 (Heb 84:6), GPsal.[151] In Hebrew, this sentence reads: אשרי אדם עוז לו בך, literally: "Blessed is the man, strength to him (is) in you." The majority of LXX witnesses have μακάριος ἀνήρ, οὗ ἐστιν ἡ ἀντίλημψις αὐτοῦ παρὰ σοῦ, literally, "Blessed is the man of whom his help is from you," with both the genitive relative pronoun οὗ ("of whom," "whose") before the noun ἀντίλημψις, "help," and also a possessive pronoun (αὐτοῦ) after it. In P.Bod. 24, most Lucianic manuscripts, and Theodoret's *Commentary**, one finds the dative pronoun αὐτῷ, "to him" (cf. Heb: לו) in place of the genitive pronoun αὐτοῦ, resulting in: μακάριος ἀνήρ, οὗ ἐστιν ἡ ἀντίλημψις αὐτῷ παρὰ σοῦ, "Blessed is the man, of whom there is help to him from you" (Rahlfs 226).[152] The Latin translation proposed by Sunnia and Fretela has the dative case for the relative pronoun and the genitive for the possessive pronoun: *cui est auxilium eius abs te*, "to whom his help is from you." The key issue from a Latin stylistic perspective is the combination of the relative pronoun (*cui*, "to whom") with the following possessive pronoun (*eius*, "his") referring to the same individual.

In the OL tradition one finds various renderings. For example, some texts (e.g., Codex Sangermanensis; Sabatier 169) have *beatus vir cui est auxilium a te*, "Blessed is the man to whom help is from you" (with the dative *cui*), while others (e.g., the Roman Psalter; Weber 208) have *beatus vir cuius est auxilium abs te*, "Blessed is the man whose help is from you" (with the genitive *cuius*). In neither of these Old Latin readings is the relative pronoun followed by a possessive pronoun. Yet such translations

---

151. For this text in *Ep.* 106, Hilberg follows three manuscripts (one eighth century) in reading *cuius*, "whose" (Hilberg 274). Other manuscripts (including two ninth-century witnesses) have *cui*, "to whom," which is adopted by the Benedictine edition (Gasquet 30). Most Gallican Psalter manuscripts have *cuius*, but a few witnesses, including the Cathach Psalter and Corbie Psalter read *cui*, as adopted by WG 876. The textual situation is complex, but it seems clear that Jerome intended the same form in *Ep.* 106 as he thought he wrote in the Gallican Psalter. It would not be surprising if Jerome followed the Greek and Latin tradition of using a genitive relative pronoun (see below) on account of its idiomatic quality. On the other hand, if the hexaplaric LXX (not preserved) gave the dative case (ᾧ) in imitation of the Hebrew (לו), then it is possible that Jerome wrote *cui*.

152. P.Bod. 24 has ἀντίλημψις instead of ἡ ἀντίλημψις (KT 171).

are found in the Sinai Psalter: *beatus vir cuius est susceptio eius abs te*, "Blessed is the man of whom his undertaking is from you" (Thibaut 113); in Ambrose, *Fug.* 1.2: *beatus vir cuius est auxilium eius abs te*, "Blessed is the man of whom his help is from you" (CSEL 32:164); and in Codex Casinensis 557: *beatus populus cuius virtus illi in te*, "Blessed is the people of whom strength (is) to him in you" (Amelli 59).[153] These last three examples are awkwardly redundant in Latin. Jerome avoided this redundancy in the Gallican Psalter: *beatus vir cuius est auxilium abs te*, "Blessed is the man whose help is from you."

54.2.3. *apertissimum vitium*, "a clear fault," in this case a "stylistic fault." See also **30.1**; introduction, §7.2.

54.3.5. *in valle lacrimarum*, "In the valley of tears." Ps 83:7 (Heb 84:7), GPsal. Sunnia and Fretela must have cited the Greek word κλαυθμῶνος, from κλαυθμών, "weeping" or "place for weeping," and suggested that this should be translated *plorationis*, "of weeping."[154] This is the Latin word used in many OL texts, for example, Codex Sangermanensis, the Corbie Psalter, the Sinai Psalter, and Augustine's *Enarrations* (Sabatier 170; Thibaut 113; CC 39:1155). On the other hand, the Roman Psalter, the Mozarabic Psalter, Codex Casinensis 557, and Cassiodorus's *Explanation* have *lacrimarum*, "of tears" (Sabatier 170; Weber 208; Amelli 59; CC 98:770), matching the Gallican Psalter and Jerome's *Commentaries on the Psalms* (CC 72:220). The phrase *in valle lacrimarum*, "in the valley of tears," clearly sounded better to Jerome than *in valle plorationis*, "in the valley of weeping."

54.3.8–9. *nos hoc sequimur, ut, ubi nulla de sensu est inmutatio, Latini sermonis elegantiam conservemus*, "We follow this principle, that where there is no change with regard to the sense, we should maintain the elegance of the Latin expression." Preserving the sense of the text was a primary goal for Jerome as a translator; see introduction, §7.2.

55.1.10–11. *benedixisti, domine, terram tuam*, "You blessed, O Lord, your land." Ps 84:2 (Heb 85:2), GPsal. In this case, the form of the Greek is not in dispute. The question pertains strictly to the translation into Latin. The LXX has εὐδόκησας, κύριε, τὴν γῆν σου, "You were well pleased, O Lord, with your land," where the verb εὐδόκησας, "you were well pleased with" takes the accusative object γῆν, "land."[155] In terms of lexical mean-

---

153. Several features of this translation, especially *virtus*, "strength" (cf. עז), and *in te*, "in you" (cf. בך), reflect the Hebraizing character of this manuscript.

154. See *GELS*, s.v. "κλαυθμών."

155. For εὐδοκέω with the accusative, see Gen 33:10; Lev 26:34, 41; Pss 50:21;

ing, a straightforward Latin equivalent for εὐδοκέω is *placet*, "it is pleasing." But whereas εὐδοκέω in biblical Greek can take an accusative object (even if other constructions, e.g., εὐδοκέω + ἐν, are more common), the intransitive *placet* in classical Latin takes the pleasing item as the subject and requires the dative for the one to whom it is pleasing (GL §346 R.2). In the OL tradition, the precise meaning of the verb was set aside, but the syntax of the Greek (second-person verb + accusative) was preserved by translating εὐδόκησας as *benedixisti*, "you blessed" (Sabatier 170; Weber 209).[156] Jerome followed this rendering in the Gallican Psalter. Sunnia and Fretela challenged Jerome on why he used *benedixisti*, since *benedico*, "bless," is not the nearest semantic equivalent of εὐδοκέω, "be well pleased with."

Jerome's defense is that Latin idiom forbids him from translating εὐδοκέω with the best Latin match, *bene placet*, "it is well pleasing." If Jerome were to be scrupulous about rendering the precise meaning—which Jerome describes as *si contentiose verba scrutamur et syllabas*, "If we contentiously scrutinize words and syllables"—he would need to use the intransitive *placuit* and make "your land" into the subject (*terra tua*), in which case the sentence now reads awkwardly, "It was well pleasing, O Lord, your land." Jerome describes this awkwardness as the loss of *ordo sensus*, "the order of the sense" or "proper sequence of thought," by which he means that the intended sense, namely, that the Lord himself was very pleased with his land, is obscured by the roundabout and elliptical mode of expression. If Jerome were to clarify the sense in keeping with *ordo eloquii*, "the right order of expression" or "proper style," he would need to add the dative *tibi* ("It was pleasing *to you*"), which would leave him open to the charge of inserting a pronoun without any basis in the Greek or Hebrew. In sum, Jerome asserts that the precise meaning of εὐδοκέω in this context cannot be conveyed clearly in natural Latin, but he has preserved the essential sense in accordance with the requirements of Latin idiom.

In the IH Psalter Jerome will use *placo*, "reconcile, placate," in the second-person with the dative: *placatus es, domine, terrae tuae*, "You have been reconciled, O Lord, to your land" (Hebrew: רצית יהוה ארצך). This appears to be Jerome's attempt to get closer to the sense and surface structure of the

---

101:15; 118:108; Eccl 9:7.

156. In Codex Casinensis 557, natural Latin idiom was set aside but the specific sense of the verb and the syntax of the Greek were followed by translating *beneplacuisti domine terram tuam*, "You were well pleased, O Lord, (with) your land" (Amelli 60).

Hebrew and Greek, while at the same time respecting the requirements of Latin usage.

55.1.13. *syllabas*, "syllables." See **29.2.5; 8.2.1.**

55.1.20–21. *ubi non fit damnum in sensu, linguae, in quam transferimus*, εὐφωνία *et proprietas conservetur*, "wherever there is no damage to the sense, the euphony (εὐφωνία) and particular idiom of the language into which we are translating should be maintained." This is one of Jerome's clearest articulations of this "rule of translating" (*interpretandi regula*); see introduction, §7.2.

55.2.21–22. *misericordia et veritas obviaverunt sibi*, "Mercy and truth met themselves." Ps 84:11a (Heb 85:11a), GPsal. The Hebrew for this passage is: חסד ואמת נפגשו, "mercy and truth met," that is, they "met one another" as expressed by the verb פגש in the *niphal* stem.[157] In the LXX as preserved, this was translated ἔλεος καὶ ἀλήθεια συνήντησαν, "Mercy and truth met." In the OL tradition, some witnesses (e.g., Codex Sangermanensis, Codex Casinensis 557) render this simply as *misericordia et veritas obviaverunt*, "Mercy and truth met," but many sources (e.g., Cassiodorus's *Explanation*, the Roman Psalter, and the Corbie Psalter) add the word *sibi*, "themselves" (Sabatier 171; Weber 210; Amelli 60; CC 98:778).[158] In the Gallican Psalter, Jerome preserved the OL rendering as he must have encountered it, including *sibi*. Sunnia and Fretela questioned Jerome's use of *sibi*, which does not correspond to anything in the Greek and (as Jerome concedes) represents no specific word in the Hebrew.[159]

According to Jerome, *sibi* represents a word in the hexaplaric LXX text that was marked with an obelus: *apud Septuaginta obelo praenotatum est* (see introduction, §8.2). If Jerome is correct that the hexaplaric LXX contained this word, a plausible reconstruction is: ἔλεος καὶ ἀλήθεια συνήντησαν ἀλλήλοις, "mercy and truth met one another" (cf. Prov 22:2), with ἀλλήλοις under obelus. Perhaps the Greek text employed by Origen for his fifth column contained the word ἀλλήλοις, an otherwise unattested

---

157. *HALOT*, "פגש."

158. In place of *obviaverunt sibi*, Augustine in his *Enarrations* gives the text as *occurrerunt sibi* (CC 39:1172), probably influenced by Jerome's IH Psalter: *misericordia et veritas occurrerunt*.

159. Of course, the *niphal* stem conveys a reciprocal sense, but this is not in Jerome's mind here. The reciprocal relation would be better expressed in Latin by *inter se* rather than by *sibi* (GL §221); on the use of the reflexive for the reciprocal in later Latin, see Blaise, *A Handbook of Christian Latin*, §183.

LXX reading added by a previous scribe to clarify the sense, and Origen placed it under obelus because it does not match the Hebrew. This could be what Jerome is reporting.

If one did not wish to posit the reading ἀλλήλοις (under obelus) for Origen's edition, another explanation is possible. Perhaps when Jerome produced the Gallican Psalter, he marked *sibi* with an obelus in his Latin text simply because it was an inherited OL element with no basis in the Greek. In other words, Jerome may have done more than simply copy the hexaplaric LXX with its critical signs; he may have employed these same signs to mark problem passages in the OL vis-à-vis the Greek. According to this scenario, when he wrote *Ep.* 106, Jerome saw *sibi* marked with an obelus in his copy of the Gallican Psalter and assumed this notation went back to the hexaplaric LXX, having forgotten that he supplied this obelus himself. Because corroborating evidence is lacking, it is impossible to know whether or not ἀλλήλοις (or the like) was present under obelus in the hexaplaric LXX Psalter.

As is often the case, Jerome wants to make clear that he is not unaware of the textual evidence behind the challenge to his translation. In this case, Jerome states clearly that he knows that the original LXX (= the hexaplaric LXX) lacks an equivalent for *sibi*, and he adds the additional fact that the Hebrew lacks such an equivalent, too. If the Gallican Psalter had been properly copied with the critical signs, it would have been obvious to the reader that *sibi* was marked as an addition to the text. This provides Jerome opportunity to lament the failure of scribes to faithfully record the hexaplaric signs (see also **22.1**). At the same time, Jerome offers a justification for the addition: the presence of *sibi* in the text makes clear that mercy and truth encounter "themselves"—that is, "one another"—rather than that mercy and truth encounter some other thing. Despite its lack of textual support, Jerome nevertheless justifies his Gallican Psalter rendering by noting that *sibi* makes the sense of the passage clearer.

56.1.1–2. *et non proposuerunt te in conspectu suo,* "and they did not set you in their sight." Ps 85:14 (Heb 86:14), GPsal. The majority of LXX witnesses contain "you" as Jerome states: καὶ οὐ προέθεντό σε ἐνώπιον αὐτῶν, "and they did not set you before them" (Rahlfs 230 cites no variants). But P.Bod. 24 offers a text that lacks σε: καὶ οὐ προσέθεντο ἐναντίον αὐτῶν, "and they did not set opposite them" (KT 174–75). Sunnia and Fretela based their question on a Greek text that lacked σε. Jerome considers their reading nothing more than a simple miscopying, so he tells them that they should correct their faulty text.

56.2.1–2. *et tu, domine deus*, "and you, O Lord God." Ps 85:15 (Heb 86:15), GPsal. The text proposed by Sunnia and Fretela, which includes "my" (i.e., καὶ σύ, κύριε ὁ θεός μου), is supported by the Lucianic manuscripts, Theodoret's *Commentary**, the Syro-Hexapla, MS 1219 Washington, and the Roman Psalter (Rahlfs 230; Weber 213). Jerome regards the addition of "my" as "superfluous" and notes its absence from the Hebrew and (true) Greek texts; see introduction, §8.5.

57.1.8. *magnus et horrendus*, "great and horrible." Ps 88:8 (Heb 89:8), GPsal. Jerome's aim in this comment is to defend his striking translation of φοβερός, "fearful, frightful," as *horrendus*, "horrible, dreadful." Most OL witnesses have *terribilis*, "terrible, frightful," although the Roman Psalter uses *metuendus*, "to be feared" (Sabatier 176–77; Weber 218).[160] Aquila and Symmachus are reported as ἐπίφοβος, "very frightful" (Field 2:242), so it does not appear that Jerome was basing his translation on either of them. A remarkable congruence with the Gallican Psalter is found in Codex Casinensis 557, which has *magnus et (h)orrendus* (Amelli 62). Either Jerome inherited his translation of φοβερός as *horrendus* from an Old Latin tradition as represented in Codex Casinensis 557, or else this manuscript has been influenced by the Gallican Psalter at this point. In his comments, Jerome gives the impression that he chose *horrendus* specifically because of what it conveys in the *Aeneid*, for which Jerome gives three examples (*Aen.* 3.29–30, 658; 2.755) and insists that many more could be found (e.g., *Aen.* 6.10; 7.172; 11.507). Jerome's discussion of this rendering illustrates what others have observed, namely, that Jerome's translation choices were sometimes influenced by his knowledge of classical authors.[161]

In the IH Psalter, Jerome will revert to the Old Latin rendering, *terribilis*. Moreover, it is *terribilis*, not *horrendus*, that made its way into the Sixto-Clementine Vulgate (Van Ess 87).

57.2.20. *sanctis tuis*, "to your saints." Ps 88:20 (Heb 89:20), GPsal. The Hebrew for this word as found in the Leningrad Codex and many masoretic manuscripts is לחסידיך, "to your pious ones," although the singular לחסידך, "to your pious one," appears in some masoretic witnesses (De-Rossi 4:59).

---

160. Jerome will later quote this text as *magnus et metuendus* in his *Homilies on the Psalms* (CC 78:411).

161. E.g., see Kraus, *Jewish, Christian, and Classical Exegetical Traditions in Jerome's Translation of the Book of Exodus*, 180–212; and Neil Adkin, "*Biblia Pagana*: Classical Echoes in the Vulgate," *Aug* 40 (2000): 77–88.

A different lexeme altogether, לבחריך, probably לִבְחִרֶיךָ, "to your chosen ones" (cf. Pss 89:4; 105:6, 43; 106:5, 23), is given in 4QPsˣ (Ulrich 652–53). Jerome's transliteration of the Hebrew, *laasidach*, shows that he is working with the word חסיד, "pious one, saint," but because of the loose connection between Jerome's transcriptions and the later masoretic vocalization, it is impossible to ascertain clearly whether this transliteration represents the singular or plural form.

The vast majority of LXX witnesses read τοῖς υἱοῖς σου, "to your sons," as Sunnia and Fretela proposed. Furthermore, the OL tradition consistently supports "to your sons" (*filiis tuis*; Sabatier 177; Weber 220). The reading τοῖς ὁσίοις σου, "to your saints," is limited to a small number of Lucianic manuscripts, and in Latin *sanctis tuis* is found in Codex Casinensis 557 (Rahlfs 234; Ameli 62). In translating *sanctis tuis*, "to your saints," in the Gallican Psalter, Jerome was following all the hexaplaric versions, as he reports, which gave τοῖς ὁσίοις σου in order to match the Hebrew לחסידיך. Jerome also reports that the Sixth edition (*sexta*) translated τοῖς προφήταις σου, "to your prophets" (Field 2:243), which Jerome explains as a free rendering of the sense.

This last detail about the Sixth edition in particular links Jerome's discussion here to his treatment of this passage in the *Commentaries on the Psalms*, where he first quotes the passage with *filiis*, "sons," and then comments: *Omnes reliqui interpretati sunt 'sanctis tuis.' Denique sexta editio 'prophetas' pro filiis posuit: ostendit autem illam prophetiam, quae ad eum facta est per Nathan prophetam*, "All the remaining (versions) translated 'to your saints.' But the Sixth edition put 'prophets' in place of 'sons.' This represents the prophecy that was given to him through the prophet Nathan" (*Comm. Ps.* 88:20a). Here in *Ep.* 106.57, when Jerome says: *sensum magis quam verbum exprimens*, "expressing the sense rather than the word," the "sense" to which he is referring is this interpretation whereby God spoke to David (v. 21) through the prophet Nathan (see 2 Sam 12:1–15).

In this instance, Jerome's information about the hexaplaric versions and the reading of the Sixth edition in particular go back to Origen through the *Commentaries on the Psalms*. In a brief fragment of Origen's exegesis preserved in the catenae, Origen explains τοῖς υἱοῖς σου, "to your sons," as διὰ τῶν ἁγίων προφητῶν, "through the holy prophets" (PG 12:1549). Another probable source for Jerome is Apollinaris of Laodicea, who refers this passage to the prophecy of Nathan, quotes the text as "sons of God," and adds "or, as others translate, 'saints' " (ἢ ὡς οἱ λοιποὶ ἑρμηνεύουσιν ὁσίους).[162] In his later *Homilies on the Psalms*, Jerome cites the text as *tunc locutus es in aspectu filiis tuis*, "Then you spoke in an appearance to your sons," but he paraphrases it as *in visione sanctis tuis, prophetis tuis atque electis*, "in a vision to your saints, to your prophets, and to the elect" (CC 78:411–12).

Two questions arise from the information Jerome reports: (1) Did the hexaplaric LXX Psalter (or Jerome's copy of it) contain the correction from υἱοῖς, "sons" to ὁσίοις, "saints"? When Jerome says that only the κοινή edition has "sons," he certainly gives the impression that the hexaplaric LXX contained ὁσίοις. Caloz tentatively favors the hypothesis that the text of the hexaplaric LXX at Ps 88:20 read ὁσίοις, as Jerome suggests (Caloz 373–75). I think this is a likely conclusion. (2) Is Jerome correct that the Hebrew text underlying the Sixth edition had חסיד, "saint," and the translator chose to render it loosely as προφήτης, "prophet"? Given the completely different lexeme found in 4QPs^x, we may be justified in thinking that the Hebrew text for this passage was somewhat in flux and that the Hebrew underlying *Sexta* could have been לנביאיך, "to your prophets."

57.3.26. *respexisti*, "looked back." Ps 88:39 (Heb 89:39). The question posed by Sunnia and Fretela is based on an error in their copy of Jerome's translation. Whereas their manuscript of the Gallican Psalter had *respexisti*, the actual translation given by Jerome is *despexisti*.[163] Their opinion that Jerome had mistranslated the Greek is due to the fact that their manuscript had "r" instead of "d." As Jerome points out, his choice of *despicio*, "look down on, despise" correctly matches the LXX's ἐξουδενέω, "despise, regard as nothing." In addition to his own rendering, *despexisti*, Jerome also gives the meaning as "reckoned as nothing" (*pro nihilo duxisti*), which is the translation found in Codex Sangermanensis, and which also appears in a slightly different form (e.g., *ad nihilum deduxisti*) in sources such as the Verona Psalter and Augustine's *Enarrations* (Sabatier 179; Weber 222; CC 39:1237).[164]

---

162. Mühlenberg, *Psalmenkommentare aus der Katenenüberlieferung*, 1:60.

163. Jerome's correct Gallican Psalter translation, *Tu vero reppulisti et despexisti*, "But you rejected and looked down on," was also the rendering given in the *Commentaries on the Psalms* (CC 72:223), where Jerome (perhaps following Origen) says that God the Father rejected and looked down on the Son at Christ's passion when he said: "My God, My God, Why have you forsaken me?" (Matt 27:46; Mark 15:34). Cf. the similar exegesis given by Didymus of Alexandria (Mühlenberg, *Psalmenkommentare aus der Katenenüberlieferung*, 2:176–78).

164. See also Augustine, *Civ.* 17.10: *ad nihilum deduxisti* (CC 48:574); Ambrose, *De fide* 3.11.76: *ad nihilum redegisti* (CSEL 78:136); and *De fide* 3.14.121: *pro nihilo*

57.3.3–4. *secundum disertissimum istius temporis interpretem*, "in accordance with the most fluent translator of this time." The identity of this individual is not entirely certain. The most likely candidate is Rufinus of Aquileia, although some recent scholars have favored Augustine. See Intro. **6.2**.

57.3.4–5. *adnihilasti vel adnullasti vel nullificasti*, " 'nothingafy,' or 'nothingize,' or 'nullificate.' " The verb *adnihilo* is extremely rare in late antiquity. It appears in Jerome and was employed by Cassiodorus in his *Explanation of the Psalms* (CC 97:566; CC 98:728, 1010).[165]

There is one appearance of *adnullo* in the Latin Bible, and this occurs at Sirach (Ecclesiasticus) 21:5. It does not appear in classical authors. In late antiquity, *adnullo* is found in at least three authors of the fourth century. The North African bishop Optatus of Milevis (fourth century) used *adnullo* in his *Against the Donatists* (SC 412:260). Chromatius of Aquileia (d. 408) employed *adnullo* in his *Tractatus on Matthew* 14.5 (CC 9A:255). The word *adnullo* also appears in the Latin translation that Calcidius (fourth century) made of Plato's *Timaeus*.[166]

As for *nullifico*, although it is not a common word, it occurs in a number of different sources. The word *nullifico* was employed by Tertullian in *On Fasting* 15.3 (CC 2:1273), and it also appears in the Latin translation of Irenaeus's *Haer.* 4.20.12 and 4.29.1 (SC 100:674, 766). Other Latin authors who used this word are the poet Commodian, *Instr.* 2.35 (CC 128:70), Pseudo-Ambrose, *Laps. virg.* 46 (PL 16:381), and Faustus and Marcellinus, *Confession of the True Faith* (CC 69:368). In terms of the Latin Bible, the word *nullifico* appears at Ps 118:118 in Codex Casinensis 557 (Amelli 87).

Jerome regards these word formations as lexical monstrosities (*portenta verborum*, "portents of words"), so I have not given them proper English translations (e.g., "annihilate," "annul," "despise") but instead have rendered them using unconventional English so as to match the register of the Latin in keeping with Jerome's assessment.[167] One may ascribe Jerome's

---

dispulisti (CSEL 78:150). Cf. Ambrose, *Enarratio* 43:23: *Tu vero repulisti pro nihilo, Domine, distulisti Christum tuum* (PL 14:1130).

165. LD, s.v. "adnihilo."

166. Jan H. Waszink, ed., *Timaeus, A Calcidio Translatus Commentarioque Instructus*, Corpus Platonicum Medii Aevi (Leiden: Brill, 1962), 12.

167. Cf. Jerome's observation in his *Commentary on Galatians* 1:11–12 that Cicero, in coining new words, had to create *verborum portenta*, "portents of words," that were unknown to the Latin ear; see G. Q. A. Meershoek, *Le latin biblique d'après*

disapproval of these words to his general respect for natural Latin idiom and his esteem for classical authors and usage. At the same time, there are other Latin words that Jerome accepts that are likewise unclassical in their background. Meershoek is probably correct that Jerome's negative reaction to these words arises from the fact that they are not only unclassical but also did not appear in the Latin Bible of Jerome's youth (except perhaps *adnullo* in Sir 21:5).[168] Therefore, they not only lacked pedigree in respected authors but also lacked the consecration and familiarity that comes from biblical usage.

58.1.7–8. *a saeculo et usque in saeculum tu es, deus,* "From age unto age you are, O God." Ps 89:2 (Heb 90:2), GPsal.[169] The Hebrew for this passage reads ומעולם עד עולם אתה אל, "And from age unto age, you are God," transcribed by Jerome as *meolam ad olam ath hel.* It is not fully clear whether Jerome intends *deus* as vocative ("O God") or as a predicate ("You are God"). The LXX interpreted אל not as אֵל, "God," but as אַל, "not," and joined it to the following verse to produce μὴ ἀποστρέψῃς ἄνθρωπον εἰς ταπείνωσιν, "Do not turn back humanity to humiliation." Naturally, the Hebrew for this next verse lacks the negation (תשב אנוש עד דכא, "You return man to dust"). Jerome says that he is following the Hebrew, the Seventy (i.e., the hexaplaric LXX), and all the translators (in other words, Aquila, Symmchaus, Theodotion, and others) in translating the word "God," giving the Greek as ἀπὸ τοῦ αἰῶνος καὶ ἕως τοῦ αἰῶνος σὺ εἶ, ὁ θεός. Field punctuates this text with θεός as vocative (Field 2:245), which is entirely possible but not required by the syntax of Biblical Greek (e.g., 2 Sam 7:28).

The text proposed by Sunnia and Fretela, that is, without *deus,* "God" is the standard LXX reading, whereas Jerome's translation follows the hexaplaric versions and the Hebraized Greek text of the hexaplaric LXX (cf.

---

saint Jérôme: Aspects linguistiques de la rencontre entre la Bible et le monde classique (Nijmegen-Utrecht: Dekker & Van de Vegt, 1966), 33.

168. Meershoek, *Le latin biblique d'après saint Jérôme,* 49.

169. Manuscripts differ both for *Ep.* 106 and the Gallican Psalter with regard to the presence or absence of *et.* Hilberg 277 in agreement with Vatican, Reg. lat. 11 includes *et* for *Ep.* 106, and the Sixto-Clementine edition includes *et* for Ps 89:2, following the Cathach Psalter, the ninth-century *Psalterium Augiense triplex,* the Dagulf Psalter, and other manuscripts. The Benedictine edition of *Ep.* 106 and Weber-Gryson's text of Ps 89:2 omit *et* (Gasquet 32; WG 884). OL witnesses are also divided on whether or not to include *et* (Sabatier 181). Jerome does not indicate any question of difference between their copy of the Gallican Psalter and his original translation on this point.

Eusebius; PG 23:1124). Interestingly, in keeping with the majority OL tradition (Sabatier 181; Weber 224),[170] Jerome preserves the LXX's negation of the following verse (*ne avertas hominem*), thereby unwittingly representing the Hebrew אל twice.

In the IH Psalter, the negation in v. 3 is dropped (*convertes hominem*), but surprisingly, in some witnesses to the IH Psalter, *deus* also disappears from v. 2.[171] The absence of *deus* from the IH Psalter appears to find support in Jerome's citation of this verse in *Ep.* 140.6 (CSEL 56.1:274–75). The omission of *deus* from the IH Psalter may be an oversight on Jerome's part or a copying error on the part of an early transmitter of this work.

58.1.8–9. *quod apud eos deesse manifestum est*, "But it is clear that this was left out in their copies." When Jerome uses *desum* for the absence of *deus*, he means not just that the word is "lacking" from their copies but that it was "neglected"—that is, "left out."[172] What does he have in mind by saying that *deus* was left out *apud eos*? He has just spoken to Sunnia and Fretela in the second-person (*dicitis*, line 8). Perhaps Jerome is saying that this word was left out "in them," i.e., "in your copies," although for this we would expect *in codicibus vestris* (cf. **2.2.23**; **7.2.10**; **28.1.9–10**) or *in codice vestro* (**46.2.7–8**), or else *in libris vestris* (cf. **7.2.12**; **41.6.14**). Otherwise, he refers to *exemplaria*, "copies" (**2.3.5**; **20.1.23**; **46.4.24**; **50.3.16**; **78.1.6**), which is neuter and cannot be in view here. It is more likely that he is saying that *deus* was left out "among/with them," that is, in the sources that Sunnia and Fretela were using, imagining these sources in personal terms (cf. **22.1.7**), as in *apud Septuaginta*, "among the Seventy" (e.g., **44.2.5**; **55.2.23–24**), or *apud Hebraeos*, "among the Hebrews" (e.g., **59.1.18**). In other words, Jerome gives the impression that Sunnia and Fretela are relying on copies of the Greek Psalter (or texts containing selections from the Greek Psalter) borrowed from or otherwise associated with some others (*apud eos*, "among *them*," i.e., "*their* copies"), perhaps people with whom Sunnia and Fretela consulted on the Greek text. On Jerome's perspectives on books and copies, see introduction, §8.3.

---

170. Codex Casinensis 557, however, represents אל as *[al]tissimus* and does not begin v. 3 with a negative particle (Amelli 63).

171. E.g., Vatican, Reg. lat. 11; Codex Toletanus; and the Theodulfian manuscripts. Neither Henri de Sainte-Marie, *Sancti-Hieronymi Psalterium iuxta Hebraeos*, Collectanea Biblica Latina 11 (Vatican: Abbaye Saint-Jérôme, 1954), 130, nor Weber-Gryson (WG 885) include *deus* in their text of IH Ps 89:2.

172. LD, s.v. "desum II."

58.2.12–13. *quoniam supervenit mansuetudo et corripiemur*, "Because gentleness came upon, and we shall be corrected." Ps 89:10 (Heb 90:10), GPsal. The Hebrew for this passage is not fully clear, but a plausible interpretation is as follows: כי גז חיש ונעפה, "Because it (i.e., רהבם, their pride/span) passes quickly, and we fly away." In the LXX, in place of the first three words in this passage we find ὅτι ἐπῆλθεν πραΰτης, "Because gentleness came upon." This generated the addition of ἐφ᾽ ἡμᾶς, "upon us," to complete the sense. In place of the final word (ונעפה), the Greek has καὶ παιδευθησόμεθα, "and we shall be corrected." The additional phrase, ἐφ᾽ ἡμᾶς, "upon us," is found in virtually all LXX and OL (*super nos*) witnesses, either before or after πραΰτης (Rahlfs 238; Sabatier 182; Weber 225). Thus, with some minor variation in placement, the preserved LXX reads essentially as Sunnia and Fretela suggest: "Because gentleness came upon us, and we shall be corrected."

None of the hexaplaric versions represent ἐφ᾽ ἡμᾶς. Aquila and Symmachus provided fresh renderings closer to the preserved Hebrew (cf. Jerome, *Ep.* 140.14), and Theodotion gave the Greek according to the LXX, minus ἐφ᾽ ἡμᾶς (see Field 2:246–47). In all likelihood, the hexaplaric LXX omitted "upon us," and Jerome followed suit in the Gallican Psalter. In *Ep.* 106, he explains that ἐφ᾽ ἡμᾶς, "upon us," is "superfluous" (see introduction, §8.5) since it is lacking in the authoritative sources and is obvious from the context.

In the IH Psalter, Jerome will give a completely different translation: *quoniam transivimus cito et avolavimus*, "Because we passed by quickly, and we flew away." As Jerome reports in *Ep.* 140.14, this rendering includes elements both from Symmachus and from the Fifth edition (*quinta*), although there is some uncertainty as to the reading of Quinta (see Field 2:247). Jerome's IH translation may be compared to the rendering given in Codex Casinensis 557, *quia transitus repentinus et evolatio*, "because a sudden passing by and a flying away" (Amelli 64), which is more a Hebraic crib than a translation.

59.1.16–17. *susceptor meus es tu*, "You are my protector." Ps 90:2 (Heb 91:2), GPsal. The issue in this instance has to do with translation theory and involves basic Hebrew knowledge. The LXX for this sentence is ἀντιλήμπτωρ μου εἶ, "(you) are my protector." The pronoun "you" is understood from the verb (εἶ) but not explicitly stated. Some OL witnesses (e.g., Codex Sangermanensis) use both the pronoun and the verb in Latin as Jerome does (*susceptor meus es tu*), but others (e.g., the Roman Psalter) use only the verb (*susceptor meus es*) in strict conformity to the Greek (Sabatier

183; Weber 226). Sunnia and Fretela challenged Jerome as to why he followed the former approach (*es tu*) in the Gallican Psalter, when fidelity to the Greek demands the latter approach (*es*).

This is a quibbling question, to be sure, and Jerome's reply is slightly condescending (*ego vobis amplius dicam*, "Let me explain to you more fully"), but the discussion is not without interest. In Hebrew, the text has nothing except מחסי, "my refuge/protector." The sentence starts as follows: אמר ליהוה מחסי, "I/He will say to the LORD: 'my protector.'"[173] The Hebrew explicitly states neither the pronoun nor the verb. Therefore, in translating ἀντιλήμπτωρ μου εἶ, "(you) are my protector," the Seventy themselves added the verb (εἶ, "are") without strict lexical basis in the Hebrew. They were justified in doing so, however, because this addition was necessary for Greek idiom (*verborum consequentia*, "natural sequence of words," "verbal flow") and it makes the text sound better (εὐφωνία, "euphony"). If the Seventy can add εἶ based on the principles of *verborum consequentia* and εὐφωνία, Jerome is justified in adding not only the verb (*es*) but also the pronoun (*tu*) for the sake of Latin idiom and euphony. As Jerome explains, elements were added both *apud Septuaginta* and *apud Latinos*. Even if the Latins added more, the reason was the same. Even as he departs from the literal form of the Seventy, Jerome is following their translation theory.

In the IH edition, Jerome will rewrite the Latin so as to eliminate both the second-person verb (*es*) and the pronoun (*tu*) in closer conformity to the Hebrew: *dicens Domino spes mea et fortitudo mea*, "saying to the Lord: my hope and my strength." When Jerome quotes Ps 90:2 in his *Homilies on the Psalms*, he gives the Gallican Psalter version rather than the IH version, but he omits the pronoun *tu* in keeping with the latter (CC 78:127).

60.1.21–22. *beatus homo, quem tu erudieris, domine*, "Blessed is the man whom you instruct, O Lord." Ps 93:12 (Heb 94:12), GPsal. Sunnia and Fretela asserted that the Greek does not explicitly express the second-person singular pronoun σύ/*tu* as Jerome does in the Gallican Psalter. Jerome acknowledges that this is true, but he defends his inclusion of *tu* by appealing to the εὐφωνία of the text in Latin (see introduction, §7.2).

---

173. The Hebrew אמר could be read as third-person masculine singular perfect, but it is vocalized in MT as first-person singular imperfect (אֹמַר), "I will say," supported by 18 medieval Hebrew manuscripts (אומר; Kennicott 2:388). The LXX (ἐρεῖ), on the other hand, seems to presuppose the third-person masculine singular imperfect, יאמר, "he will say," but cf. 11QapocrPs, האומר, which appears to be the *qal* active participle, "who says" (Ulrich 654).

This suggests that the Greek hexaplaric Psalter lacked σύ (cf. Caloz 285) in conformity with the Hebrew (אשרי הגבר אשר תיסרנו יה). The absence of σύ is attested by Codex Alexandrinus, MS 1219 Washington, the Lucianic manuscripts, Theodoret's *Commentary**, and the Syro-Hexapla, and in Latin most significantly by Codex Sangermanensis (Rahlfs 244; Sabatier 187–88; Weber 233).

60.1.24–25. *conpositionis elegantiam*, literally "elegance of composition," that is, "literary elegance." For Jerome, the requirements of Latin idiom and basic stylistic concerns should be taken into consideration when there is no harm to the sense. On Jerome's concern for *elegantia*, see introduction, §7.2.

60.1.25. *apostrofa.* The rhetorical figure ἀποστροφή involves "turning away from someone to address someone else specifically."[174] In a judicial setting, the speaker would turn away from the judge and suddenly address a second audience, such as an adversary in court or an absent person, or personified objects, such as hills or groves (*Inst.* 9.2.38–39; 9.3.24–26; 4.1.63–69).[175] On Jerome's use of rhetorical figures in *Ep.* 106, see introduction, §9.1.

60.2.1–2. *et in malitia eorum disperdet eos*, "And in their wickedness he will destroy them." Ps 93:23 (Heb 94:23), GPsal. In order to understand what is happening in this discussion, it is necessary to set forth two lines of the Hebrew:

(23) (b) וברעתם יצמיתם
(23) (c) יצמיתם יהוה אלהינו

In other words:

(23) (b) And in their wickedness he will destroy them
(23) (c) He will destroy them, the LORD our God

Kennicott (2:390) lists ten medieval Hebrew manuscripts in which one of the two occurrences of יצמיתם is omitted. The LXX similarly represented יצמיתם only once, creating at least two major textual forms in the Greek:

---

174. R. Dean Anderson Jr., *Glossary of Greek Rhetorical Terms* (Leuven: Peeters, 2000), 25.

175. For further examples, see Lausberg, *Handbook of Literary Rhetoric*, §762.

1. καὶ <u>κατὰ</u> τὴν πονηρίαν αὐτῶν ἀφανιεῖ αὐτους κύριος ὁ θεὸς ἡμῶν, "And <u>according</u> to their wickedness he will destroy them, the Lord our God." See Codex Alexandrinus, Eusebius, MS 55 Rome, the Greek text of the Verona Psalter, the Lucianic manuscripts, Theodoret's *Commentary**, and the Syro-Hexapla. In Latin, the Verona Psalter and Augustine's *Enarrations* support this reading with κατά: *et secundum malitiam eorum* (Rahlfs 245; PG 23:1208; Sabatier 188–89; CC 39:1328).

2. καὶ τὴν πονηρίαν αὐτῶν ἀφανιεῖ αὐτους κύριος ὁ θεὸς ἡμῶν, "And their wickedness he will destroy them, the Lord our God." See Codex Vaticanus, Codex Sinaiticus, and the Bohairic Coptic. As for Latin witnesses, Codex Sangermanensis follows this reading, adding another *et* before *disperdet* (ἀφανιεῖ) so that the phrase *et malitiam eorum* goes with what precedes and *et disperdet* begins a new clause: (*et reddet illis iniquitatem ipsorum) et malitiam eorum; et disperdet eos dominus deus noster*, "(And he will render to them their iniquity) and their wickedness; and he will destroy them, the Lord our God." Codex Casinensis 557 also gives the noun in the accusative (*malitiam*) without a preposition, but it avoids redundancy by representing both occurrences of יצמיתם, albeit without the object pronoun on the first verb, in what amounts to a partly Hebraized translation: *et malitiam eorum damnabit damnabis eos domine deus noster*, "And their wickedness he will condemn, you will condemn them, O Lord our God" (Amelli 66).

In the Gallican Psalter, apparently following the hexaplaric LXX, Jerome gave a translation that closely approximates the Hebrew: *et in malitia eorum disperdet eos, disperdet illos dominus deus noster*, "And in their wickedness he will destroy them, he will destroy them, the Lord our God."[176] Jerome translated both occurrences of יצמיתם, and he rendered ב in וברעתם as *in*, "in," as opposed to κατά, "according to." There are a few OL witnesses that likewise have *in*, for example, the Roman Psalter, *et in malitia eorum*, and the Corbie Psalter, *et in malitiam eorum* (Sabatier 188; Weber 234). The Gallican Psalter also resembles the Greek text of P.Bod. 24, which uses the dative without preposition, τῇ πονηρίᾳ, "in their wickedness" (KT 188).[177] The Greek text of Sunnia and Fretela, however, apparently had τὴν πονηρίαν in the accusative with no preposition (= the Greek text in the

---

176. The link between the Gallican Psalter and the hexaplaric LXX is apparent in, e.g., the second צמיתם/ἀφανιεῖ αὐτούς, which was supplied under asterisk in the Hexapla (Field 2:252).

177. Since P.Bod. 24 lacks a preposition such as ἐν, it is unclear whether it should be seen as reflecting correction towards the Hebrew.

previous paragraph), so they questioned Jerome as to why he added the preposition *in*.

Jerome defends his translation with two arguments. First, the preposition *in* is found in the Hebrew and "all the translators" (i.e., the hexaplaric LXX and all the hexaplaric versions). Second, the Greek text consulted by Sunnia and Fretela is redundant, in that it provides two different objects for the verb ἀφανιεῖ, "he will destroy": καὶ τὴν πονηρίαν αὐτῶν ἀφανιεῖ αὐτούς, "And their wickedness he will destroy them." Unless one takes "and their wickedness" with the previous clause (cf. Codex Sangermanensis above), both τὴν πονηρίαν αὐτῶν, "their wickedness," and αὐτούς, "them," function as objects of the verb "he will destroy." As Jerome points out, this would make αὐτούς, "them," superfluous (see introduction, §8.5).

61.1.9–10. *recordatus est misericordiae suae*, "He has remembered his mercy." Ps 97:3 (Heb 98:3), GPsal. Most witnesses to the LXX include the name "Jacob" in the first half line of this verse: ἐμνήσθη τοῦ ελέους αὐτοῦ τῷ Ιακωβ, "He has remembered his mercy toward Jacob." Codex Alexandrinus and a few Lucianic manuscripts have the genitive: τοῦ Ιακωβ (Rahlfs 250). The preserved Hebrew text lacks "Jacob," as does Codex Sinaiticus. We may assume that at least one of the hexaplaric versions and perhaps the hexaplaric LXX omitted "Jacob." Consequently, Jerome did not translate it in the Gallican Psalter.

From a stylistic standpoint, one might suggest that the addition of "Jacob" in this first half line provides balance vis-à-vis its parallel in the second half line: "He has remembered his mercy toward Jacob; and his truth to the house of Israel" (LXX). But for Jerome, because the recipient of God's mercy and truth is obvious from the reference to "the house of Israel" in the second half line, the name "Jacob" in the first half line is superfluous (see introduction, §8.5).

62.1.12–13. *ut sederent mecum*, "that they may dwell with me." Ps 100:6 (Heb 101:6), GPsal. Jerome supplies the Greek of the LXX: τοῦ συγκαθῆσθαι αὐτοὺς μετ᾽ ἐμοῦ, for which his Gallican Psalter translation is a sound Latin rendering. Proper Latin does not express final clauses through an infinitive with subject accusative, so he employs *ut* + subjunctive. Sunnia and Fretela obviously criticized Jerome's rendering for not staying close enough to the Greek. Jerome imagines a translation that would satisfy their demand for a "word for word" rendering (*verbum ad verbum*) by offering an absurd caricature: *ut consederent ipsi mecum*, "that they themselves may co-dwell with me." Based on this, we can discern two specific criticisms that were levelled against Jerome:

(1) Why did Jerome not translate αὐτούς? For example, the OL as represented in Codex Sangermanensis rendered this final clause as *ut sedeant hi simul mecum* (Sabatier 196), representing both the verb, συγκαθῆσθαι (*sedeant*) and the subject pronoun, αὐτούς (*hi*). Jerome only represented the verb (*sederent*). Presumably, his response is that the Latin construction of finite verb with *ut* makes it unnecessary to express the subject with a separate word. To do so (as with *ipsi*, "that they *themselves* may co-dwell") would be stylistically cumbersome.

(2) Since the Greek uses a compound verb συγκάθημαι, "dwell with," why does Jerome only use the simple verb *sedeo*, "dwell." Perhaps Sunnia and Fretela had in mind the use of *sedeant ... simul* in the OL to represent both the base verb (κάθημαι) and the preposition (συν-).[178] Jerome's reply appears to be as follows: if one reproduced the compound Greek verb literally, the result would be the artificial, non-Latin compound *consedeo*, "co-dwell."[179] Such a translation that ignores Latin usage and euphony is unthinkable.

63.1.18. *in tecto*, "on the roof." Ps 101:8 (Heb 102:8), GPsal. The LXX does indeed have ἐπὶ δώματι as Sunnia and Fretela stated, and *in aedificio*, "on a building," is well attested as a rendering of this phrase in the OL tradition in, for instance, Codex Sangermanensis, Cassiodorus's *Explanation*, Ambrose's *Exp. Luc.* 12:6–7, the Roman Psalter, and the Corbie Psalter. Other OL renderings attested are *domo*, "house," in Ambrose's *Fug.* 5.30 (CSEL 32:188); *super tectum*, "above the roof," in Codex Casinensis 557; and (matching Jerome) *tecto*, "roof," in the Verona Psalter and Augustine's *Enarrations* (see Sabatier 197; Weber 245; CC 98:903; CC 14:250; Amelli 70; CSEL 95.1:34).

In classical authors, δῶμα typically means "house," "household," or "chief room, hall."[180] In the LXX, on the other hand, δῶμα consistently stands for the Hebrew גג, "flat roof," and in biblical Greek δῶμα normally refers to "the level surface of a flat roof, roof, housetop."[181] The meaning "top of the house" is attested in the papyri and related sources (e.g., P.Oxy.

---

178. Not all OL witnesses do this, e.g., the Roman Psalter: *ut sedeant hii mecum* (Weber 243).

179. Some copyists of *Ep.* 106 changed this word into a form of *consido*, "be seated, settle," which is an actual Latin word (see the apparatus in Hilberg 278; and Gasquet 33).

180. LSJ, s.v. "δῶμα."

181. BDAG, s.v. "δῶμα"; *GELS*, s.v. "δῶμα"; HRCS 358.

3.475²²), although δῶμα continues to be used simply for "house" in some of these texts (e.g., Rylands Papyrus 2.233³).[182] It seems that "building, chief room" is the normal sense of δῶμα down to the Hellenistic (or Roman) era, at which time the meaning "flat roof" came into usage.[183] The meanings "house/palace/temple" and "central hall," however, persisted in the later period (e.g., *Vit.* 7.7; *Pyrrh* 9; *Frat. amor.* 11; *Comm not.* 14; *Diatr.* 1.24; *2 Regn.* 38; *Comp.* 5; *Pun.* 19.127). Jerome justifies his translation of δῶμα as *tectum,* "roof," by quoting biblical examples and also by explaining how houses were constructed in the eastern lands of the Bible. Jerome was fond of utilizing whatever information he had at hand about the world of the East to unravel biblical obscurities for his western readers (e.g., *Qu. hebr. Gen.* 10:2–29; 21:30–31; *Comm. Zech.* 12:3; *Comm. Nahum,* Pref.; *Comm. Jonah,* Pref.; *Comm. Ezech.* 9:4–6a; *Comm. Jer.* 2:22; 3:2a; 4:15; 6:1, 20; 9:25–26).[184]

63.1.20. *in orientalibus provinciis,* "In the Eastern provinces." By "Eastern provinces" Jerome means Palestine and Egypt. By the fourth century, the Near Eastern provinces of the Roman Empire were categorized by divisions such as *Syria* (*Syria Prima* and *Syria Secunda*), *Euphratensis, Phoenicia* (*Phoenicia Prima* and *Phoenicia Secunda*), *Arabia, Mesopotamia,* and *Palestina* (*Palestina Prima, Palestina Secunda, Palestina Tertia*).[185] Naturally, Jerome refers to Palestine most frequently, but among the Eastern

---

182. In addition to BDAG, see also James H. Moulton and George Milligan, *Vocabulary of the Greek Testament* (London: Hodder and Stoughton, 1930), 174.

183. See Franco Montanari, *The Brill Dictionary of Ancient Greek,* ed. Madeleine Goh and Chad Schroeder (Leiden: Brill, 2015), 574: "house, abode … room, central hall … temple … residence … *later* terrace, flat roof" (citing Deut 22:8; Matt 24:17). Evangelinus A. Sophocles, *Greek Lexicon of the Roman and Byzantine Periods* (New York: Scribner, 1900), 408, gives "flat roof, housetop" as the meaning for δῶμα, citing the LXX; the NT; Babrius, *Fab.* 5.5 (Perry); Clement of Alexandria; Epiphanius; and Jerome. According to H. A. A. Kennedy, *Sources of New Testament Greek* (Edinburgh: T&T Clark, 1895), 152–53, δῶμα is one of several ancient Greek words that took on a fresh sense in the period of the LXX and preserved that sense in modern Greek.

184. Cf. Fergus Millar, "Jerome and Palestine," in *Empire, Church and Society in the Late Roman Near East,* Late Antique History and Religion 10 (Leuven: Peeters, 2015), 423–48.

185. See Fergus Millar, "Bishops and their Sees at the Sixth Session of the Council of Chalcedon: The Near Eastern Provinces," in *Empire, Church and Society in the Late Roman Near East,* 33–45. Jerome shows that he is aware of the subdivision of Palestine into provinces in *Qu. hebr. Gen.* 21:30–31; see Millar, "Jerome and Palestine," 436. Cf. Jerome's reference to the "provinces of Palestine" (*Pref. IH Chron.*).

provinces he also mentions Egypt and Syria regularly. For examples, see *Comm. Jer.* 2:22 (on the province of Palestine); *Tract. Marc.* 11:15–17 ("from the whole province of Palestine, Cyprus, and the other provinces"); *Vit. Hil.* 22 (on Palestine, Egypt, Syria, "and the more distant provinces"); *Jov.* 2.7 and *Comm. Matt.* 23:8–10 (on Egypt and Palestine); *Comm. Ezech.* 16:56–58 and *Qu. hebr. Gen.* 10:23 (on Syria/Coele-Syria and Palestine); and *Ep.* 33.5 (on Palestine, Arabia, Phoenicia, and Achaia).

63.1.5–6. *et in euangelio: quae, inquit, auditis in aure, dicite super* δώματα, "And in the gospel it says: 'What you hear in the ear, speak on the δώματα'" (Matt 10:27). The Vulgate rendering, *quod in aure auditis praedicate super tecta*, is closer to the Greek. The Vulgate has *quod* (not *quae*) for ὅ, translates "in the ear" before "you hear" (not vice versa), and gives *praedicate* (not *dicite*) for κηρύξατε. Jerome is probably quoting from memory. He does remember correctly that the plural of the word δῶμα (ἐπὶ τῶν δωμάτων) is used in this verse.

63.1.6. *et in Esaia*, "and in Isaiah." Evidence for the OL tradition is varied at Isa 22:1.[186] The wording of Jerome's quotation agrees with other OL witnesses in certain details, but it does not match any other witness precisely. The idiosyncratic form of this quotation is likely due to the fact that he is quoting from memory.

63.2.8–9. *factus sum sicut* νυκτικόραξ *in domicilio*, "I became like a νυκτικόραξ in a house." Ps 101:7 (Heb 102:7), GPsal. In his original Gallican Psalter translation, Jerome transliterated the Greek word νυκτικόραξ into Latin as *nycticorax*, but here he gives the actual Greek in the lemma in order to emphasize that this is a Greek word that he imported into Latin. The Hebrew word found in most manuscripts is כוס, "small owl."[187] Jerome gives this word as *bos* (i.e., בוס), as it appears in at least five medieval Hebrew manuscripts (De-Rossi 4:66). As he notes, the LXX translated νυκτικόραξ, "owl" (literally, "night raven"), as did Aquila, Theodotion, and Quinta. Jerome reports Symmachus as *upupa*, "hoopoe" (an ἔποψ, a kind of bird; see Field 2:257). Although in the Gallican Psalter Jerome followed the LXX by using *nycticorax*, in *Ep.* 106 he says that he favors the meaning as given by *Sexta*: *noctua*, "night owl" (probably γλαύξ; Field 2:257). See also Jerome's brief comment at **86.2.**

---

186. Gryson, *Esaias 1–39*, 477–78.
187. *HALOT*, s.v. "כוס."

Jerome adds two further comments on the translation of this passage. First he contrasts his own rendering, which matches the (true) Greek version, with what is found *apud Hebraeos*, "among the Hebrews." This Hebrew version not only has *noctua*, "night owl" instead of the LXX's *nycticorax* (νυκτικόραξ) but also has *ruinosis*, "ruins," instead of the LXX's *domicilio* (οἰκόπεδον), "house." This latter translation ("ruins") comes from Symmachus, as Theodoret's *Commentary* shows (see also Field 2:257).

Second, Jerome observes that most who interpret *contentiose*, "stringently," understand this bird to be a "horned owl" (*bubo*). In *Ep*. 106, the impression one receives is that such precision is useful to read about in a commentary but excessive for the purpose of translation. After all, Jerome earlier complained about those who "contentiously scrutinize words and syllables" (*si contentiose verba scrutamur et syllabas*; **55.1**). It is worth noting that in the IH Psalter he decides to translate this word *bubo*.

Jerome recognizes elsewhere in this work that even the true LXX does not need to be strictly literal with reference to the Hebrew (e.g., **33.1**; **50.6**; **51.1**). So, it is not totally unexpected for him to place his preferred translation of the Greek alongside a different, strict rendering of the Hebrew. The LXX can be correct, even when it is not scrupulously literal. Moreover, his Gallican Psalter was meant to render the LXX into sensible Latin, not literalistic Latin. Still, discussions such as this one, where Jerome says the bird is a "night owl" according to the LXX but that according to the Hebrew it should really be a "horned owl," probably encouraged him to turn his attention more toward the Hebrew text.

63.3.18. *a facie irae et indignationis tuae*, "from the face of your anger and wrath." Ps 101:11 (Heb 102:11), GPsal. Both the Hebrew (מפני זעמך וקצפך) and the LXX (as reported by Jerome) contain both words, "anger" and "wrath." The Greek text consulted by Sunnia and Fretela must have been faulty on this passage, lacking the words καὶ τοῦ θυμοῦ σου, which presumably dropped out by homoioteleuton.

In *Ep*. 106, Jerome gives the Greek with σου, "your," appearing twice, but in the Gallican Psalter *tuae*, "your," appears only after the second word, just as in P.Bod. 24 and a few Lucianic manuscripts (Rahlfs 254; KT 199). Were it not for Greek witnesses such as these, the obvious explanation for the Gallican Psalter would be that Jerome used *tuae* only once because it sounded better in Latin. Given the existence of Greek manuscripts that lack the first "you," however, it remains worth considering whether the Greek version Jerome followed when he translated the Gallican Psalter read as follows: ἀπὸ προσώπου τῆς ὀργῆς καὶ τοῦ θυμοῦ σου.

63.4.23. *terrae*, "land." Ps 101:15 (Heb 102:15), GPsal. Some OL witnesses read *terrae*, "land," such as the Roman Psalter, the Corbie Psalter, the Mozarabic Psalter, and Cassiodorus's *Explanation* (Sabatier 198; Weber 246; CC 98:907). Jerome was no doubt aware of this rendering when he made the Gallican Psalter, and this is what he chose to adopt. Other witnesses to the OL have some form of the word *pulvis*, "powder" or "dust," for instance, Codex Sangermanensis, Codex Casinensis 557, the Verona Psalter, the Sinai Psalter, and Augustine's *Enarrations* (Sabatier 198; Amelli 70; Thibaut 114; CSEL 95.1:43). Clearly, Sunnia and Fretela asked Jerome why he used *terra*, "land," when the Greek word used by the LXX, χοῦς, means "dust" (e.g., Gen 2:7).

Jerome does not dispute the suggestion that χοῦς is not the normal word for "land." As is often the case, he is eager to show that he is familiar with the textual and linguistic data and that his translation choice was well informed. By supplying the Hebrew word (*afar*, עפר) and reporting the consensus of all the hexaplaric versions, he no doubt provides even more information than what Sunnia and Fretela asked about in their query. As he explains, χοῦς can certainly mean "dust" (*pulvis*), but it can also be used for "ground, earth" (*humus*), which is an acceptable synonym for "land" (*terra*).

This discussion illustrates the fact that Jerome's primary goal in *Ep.* 106 is to defend the Gallican Psalter. It seems unlikely that he selected *terrae* based on his careful consideration of the relevant linguistic and stylistic factors; rather, he simply adopted *terrae* from the OL as known to him because it was familiar and sufficient. Now that *terrae* is being challenged, however, he marshals his textual and linguistic knowledge in order to justify it. His aim here is to prove that the Gallican Psalter is valid. Later, when he produces the IH Psalter, he will use *pulverem*.

64.1.1. *non in perpetuo irascetur*, "Not forever will he be angry." Ps 102:9 (Heb 103:9). The Gallican Psalter reads *in perpetuum*, and the manuscript evidence for *Ep.* 106 strongly supports *in perpetuo*. Either Jerome or (more likely) an early copyist of *Ep.* 106 mistakenly wrote *perpetuo* instead of *perpetuum*.

The Hebrew text has לנצח, made up of נצח, "splendor, duration, successful" plus the preposition ל, the combination לנצח often meaning "endless, forever."[188] The LXX translated this as εἰς τέλος, literally "to the end"

---

188. *HALOT*, s.v. "נצח."

(Latin: *in finem* = the standard OL at Ps 102:9). Sunnia and Fretela must have asked why Jerome did not translate εἰς τέλος literally as *in finem*.

Jerome reports the Hebrew word (נצח) as *nese*, and he defends his Gallican Psalter translation by stating that this Hebrew word has three possible senses: *finis*, "end"; *perpetuum*, "forever"; and *victoria*, "victory." His point is that *in perpetuum* is just as valid a translation as *in finem*.

In the LXX Psalter, the standard rendering of לנצח is εἰς τέλος, which usually comes into Latin as *in finem* (Pss 9:7, 19, 32; 43:24; 48:10; 51:7; 73:1, 10, 19; 76:9; 78:5; 88:47; 102:9).[189] The meaning *victoria* derives from passages where the Hebrew root נצח was translated into Greek as νῖκος/ νίκη, "victory" in the LXX: for example, 2 Sam 2:26; Amos 1:11; 8:7; Jer 3:5; Lam 3:18; 5:20; 1 Chr 29:11; and frequently in the hexaplaric versions (HRCS 945).[190]

As for *perpetuum* and Jerome's sense of how the Hebrew and Latin correspond, Jerome will use the phrase *in perpetuum* six times in the IH Psalter for לנצח (Pss 9:31; 73:19; Job 14:20; 36:7; Isa 28:28; Lam 5:20), three times for לעד/עד (Pss 9:18; 47:5; Prov 12:19), twice for לצמיתת (Lev 25:23, 30), and twenty times for some collocation using עולם.[191] As for the various ways that Jerome renders לנצח into Latin in the IH Psalter, these include not only *in perpetuum* but also *usque ad* (2 Sam 2:26), *in aeternum* (Ps 9:18), *semper* (Ps 67:17), *in sempiternum* (e.g., Isa 25:8), *in saeculum* (Isa 34:10), *usque ad finem* (Isaiah 57:16), and *in finem* (Jer 3:5). At Ps 102:9 in the IH Psalter, Jerome will translate לנצח as *in sempiternum*.

64.1.3–4. *pro locorum ... qualitate*, "depending on the nature of the passage." As a translator, Jerome did not strive for lexical concordance between his source text and the translation he was producing; on the contrary, he regularly rendered different occurrences of the same Greek or Hebrew word with diverse Latin equivalencies, both to capture the proper nuance of meaning for a given context and to enhance stylistic variety (see introduction, §9.1). Moreover, he was at liberty to use a single Latin term

---

189. At Ps 67:17, εἰς τέλος is rendered *in aeternum* according to Codex Sangermanensis, but it appears as *in finem* in the Coislin Psalter, the Roman Psalter, the Mozarabic Psalter, Augustine's *Enarrations*, Cassiodorus's *Explanation*, and other witnesses (Sabatier 132; Weber 248; CC 39:887; CC 97:593).

190. In particular, Aquila regularly translates מְנַצֵּחַ in the Psalter as νικοποιός; see Reider, *Index to Aquila*, 163.

191. Exod 19:9; 1 Chr 17:14, 23, 27; 2 Chr 23:13; Pss 5:11; 40:13; Eccl 2:16; 3:14; Isa 26:4; 60:21; Jer 3:5, 12; 31:40; Ezek 27:36; 28:19; 37:25, 26, 28; Mic 2:9.

to translate multiple Greek or Hebrew words.[192] According to Jerome's approach, the linguistic context in which a word occurs is an important factor in deciding how to interpret its meaning and translate it. Later, in his *Commentary on Jeremiah* (ca. 414–419 CE), Jerome explains that the Hebrew word רוח can mean *ventum*, "wind," or *spiritus*, "spirit," depending on the nature of the passages (*pro locorum qualitate*) in which the word is used (*Comm. Jer.* 4:11–12a). He also notes that the Hebrew consonants אבנים may be interpreted as "stone" (i.e., אֲבָנִים) or a "potter's wheel" (i.e., אָבְנַיִם), depending on the nature of the passage and the diversity of pronunciation (*pro qualitate loci et diversitate pronuntiationis*) for the Hebrew consonants involved (*Comm. Jer.* 18:1–10). By the time he wrote his commentary on the book of Jeremiah, his Hebrew skills were strong enough to apply this principle of linguistic context to the interpretation of individual Hebrew words at an advanced level. It does not seem that his Hebrew skills were quite so advanced when he composed *Ep.* 106. Still, Jerome is already aware that the unique linguistic context or specific quality of each passage must be considered when determining how best to translate a given word.

65.1.5–6. *qui facis angelos tuos spiritus*, "you who make your angels spirits." Ps 103:4 (Heb 104:4), GPsal. The Hebrew text of this psalm includes a few changes in grammatical person interspersed with a series of participles, all of which created ambiguity for ancient readers as to who was being addressed or who was being spoken about.

After the first line directs a command to the psalmist's "soul" (v. 1a), the next two lines contain verbs in the second-person addressed to God (vv. 1b–c: "you are great ... you put on"). This is followed by two lines that begin with indefinite participles (vv. 2a–b: "covering ... stretching"), which could be construed as addressing God in keeping with the previous lines. Suddenly, a switch in perspective takes place in vv. 3–4, where God is spoken about in the third-person, as is clear from the pronouns used: עליותיו, "his upper rooms"; רכובו, "his chariot"; מלאכיו, "his messengers"; and משרתיו, "his servants." The verbs in these clauses remain participles, however, so that their subject (second- or third-person) must be discerned from the context. In the MT, the psalm proceeds as follows: in v. 5, the main verb is third-person singular (יָסַד)—although 4QPs[d] (יוסד) and some witnesses to the Greek suggest a participle (יֹסֵד), which leaves the subject

192. See Michael Graves, "1.3.5 Vulgate," in Lange and Tov, *Overview Articles*, 278–89, esp. 283–84.

ambiguous.[193] Verse 6 has a second-person verb (בְּסִיתוֹ, "You covered it")—
although the LXX (τὸ περιβόλαιον αὐτοῦ) presupposes a third-person reference (בְּסוּתוֹ, "his clothing"); and v. 7 returns clearly to the second-person
("your rebuke … your thunder"), along with vv. 8–9 ("you founded … you
set"). Most of this ambiguity was preserved in the LXX, which employed
ambiguous participles where the Hebrew did. This ambiguity was then
passed on to the Latin tradition.

In many OL witnesses (e.g., Codex Sangermanensis, the Sinai Psalter,
Cassiodorus's *Explanation*), all the verbs in vv. 3–5 are construed as third-
person (e.g., *qui tegit … qui ponit … qui facit*). In other witnesses to the
OL, the verbs in v. 3 (*qui protegis … ponis*) are second-person (e.g., the
Verona Psalter, Prosper of Aquitaine's *Exposition of the Psalms*).[194] As for
v. 4, which is the passage under direct discussion, Latin witnesses consistently render the verb and pronouns in the third-person (see also Tertullian, *Marc.* 2.8; 3.9; 4.26) in accordance with the Hebrew and Greek, as
Sunnia and Fretela suggest.

Jerome's translation of this entire passage as addressed to God in the
second-person is supported by neither the Hebrew nor the Greek. Consequently, in defense of his own rendering he makes no reference to the
Hebrew, the LXX, or the hexaplaric versions. We may assume that he found
no support for the Gallican Psalter in any of these sources. His consistent
use of the second-person throughout was based on the initial appearance
of the second-person in v. 1b–c, on the second-person in vv. 7–9, and on
his expectation that the psalm should present a logical, consistent discourse. Based on these factors, he translated all of the verbs and pronouns
as second-person, even where the verbs in the Greek text are participles
or infinitives (e.g., vv. 3–5, 10, 14). When Jerome produced the Gallican

---

193. On 4QPs[d], see Ulrich 667. For the participle in Greek (θεμελιῶν), the wit-
nesses are P.Bod. 24, Codex Alexandrinus, MS 1219 Washington, MS 55 Rome, the
Bohairic Coptic, the Lucianic manuscripts, Theodoret's *Commentary**, and the Syro-
Hexapla (Rahlfs 258; KT 204).

194. See Sabatier 202; Weber 252; Thibaut 116; CC 68A:17–18; CC 98:925–27. In
the Roman Psalter (*tegis*) and Augustine's *Enarrations* (*protegis*), v. 3a has the second-
person, and then third-person thereafter (CSEL 95.1:140). In Codex Casinensis 557,
the first two verbs in v. 3 are kept as participles (*coperiens, ponens*), but the third verb
is third-person (*qui ambulat*); the only verb in v. 4 is a participle (*faciens*); and the only
verb rendered in v. 5 is second-person (*fundasti*), with בל תמוט becoming *sine errore*
(Amelli 72). This reflects a measure of correction toward the Hebrew or Greek along
with some translation or scribal confusion.

Psalter, he translated against the grain of the third-person grammatical forms so as to avoid the sudden (*subito*) introduction of the third-person in a manner that violated the *ordo* of the discourse (*extra ordinem*, "out of sequence").

Elsewhere, Jerome comments on the sudden introduction of new speakers in the Psalms and prophets, for example: *Prophetae et psalmi ideo obscuri sunt, quoniam subito, cum nescis, persona mutatur*, "The Prophets and the Psalms are obscure, because suddenly, when you do not expect it, there is a shift in person" (*Tract. Psal.* 80:8; CC 78:79); and *consuetudinis autem est prophetarum repente personas introducere sine ulla praefatione verborum—ut est illud in psalmo tricesimo primo*,"It is a custom of the prophets to introduce speakers suddenly without any introductory words, as in the Thirty-First Psalm" (*Expl. Dan.* 11:1; CC 75A:897; see also *mutatio personarum*, "the switching around of the speakers" in *Comm. Jer.* 8:14–15; 31:25–26). At some point Jerome came to understand that the switching around of speakers was a feature of Hebrew poetry as preserved in the Bible. This insight might have helped him sort out the switching around of participant references in this psalm. Still, however much he might grasp an element of biblical style for the sake of comprehension, Jerome was disinclined to produce a translation that did not make coherent sense (e.g., see his comments at **65.4**).

65.2.23. *a voce tonitrui tui formidabunt*, "at the sound of your thunder they will be afraid." Ps 103:7 (Heb 104:7), GPsal. It seems that Sunnia and Fretela had a copy of the Greek text that omitted *tui*, "your" from this verse. As Jerome notes, the pronoun "your" is present in the Hebrew (רעמך); it is likewise present in most Greek and Latin manuscripts (Rahlfs 258; Sabatier 202; Amelli 72; Thibaut 116).[195] The text consulted by Sunnia and Fretela was faulty at this point, and Jerome expresses astonishment (*miror*) at the error.

65.3.25–26. *hoc mare magnum et spatiosum manibus*, "this sea, great and spacious in hands." Ps 103:25 (Heb 104:25), GPsal. As Sunnia and Fretela pointed out and Jerome acknowledges, the word for "in hands" (χερσίν,

---

195. P.Bod. 24 has ἀπὸ ἐπιτ[ιμ]η$^\sigma$εως ου, with the letters ου marked as fragmentary or uncertain by the editors (KT 204). It is easy to see how the σ of σου, "your," could drop out after the final *sigma* of the previous word, and then a later copyist who did not know how to interpret ου in this context might eliminate it. In Latin, *tui* is lacking in the uncorrected text of Saint Zenon of Verona's Psalter and in a key manuscript of the Mozarabic Psalter (Weber 253).

manibus) is absent from preserved Greek manuscripts.[196] But as Jerome reports, χερσίν was added from Theodotion into the text of the hexaplaric LXX with an asterisk, so as to correspond to the Hebrew, which Jerome gives as *ze haiam gadol uarab idaim*, that is, זה הים גדול ורחב ידים.[197]

When Jerome states that "in Greek" it does not have this word, and then he concedes the point (*et ego novi*, "And I am aware of this"), it could be taken to imply that the original LXX lacked the word and needed to be corrected toward the Hebrew by the addition of χερσίν from Theodotion. In some cases, to be sure, Jerome recognizes that the hexaplaric LXX does not precisely match the Hebrew; these cases occur especially in the second half of *Ep.* 106 (see introduction, §6.2). If he were thinking along these lines, then *in Graeco* would refer to the "original" hexaplaric LXX, and the addition from Theodotion would be seen as bringing the LXX's proper but idiomatic translation into closer conformity with the Hebrew. Alternatively, early in *Ep.* 106 Jerome insists that the Hebrew and the true (i.e., hexaplaric) LXX are in accord with each other against the popular edition of the LXX. If he were thinking this way, then *in Graeco* would mean "in popular, uncorrected Greek copies," and the addition from Theodotion would be seen as restoring the original LXX. Jerome probably intends the latter option in this case, because he cites the hexaplaric versions in favor of an interpretation based on χερσίν, "in hands," and describes this as a metaphor expressed "according to the particular idiom of Hebrew." If this word enjoys such strong textual support and plays such a key role in the text's meaning, it seems likely that Jerome means to say that it belongs to the "original" (i.e., hexaplaric) LXX.

Jerome reports Aquila as αὐλὴ καὶ πλατεῖα χερσίν, "(open) courtyard and (broad) street in hands." Field doubts that Aquila would represent גדול as freely as αὐλή and suggests instead that αὐλή is a corruption for μεγάλη (Field 2:260). This is a reasonable proposal that fits Aquila's normal pattern for rendering the root גדל (Reider, *Index to Aquila*, 270). The second Greek option, αὕτη ἡ θάλασα ἡ μεγάλη καὶ εὐρύχωρος χερσίν, "this great sea and spacious in hands," is what Jerome followed in the Gallican Psalter. Jerome

---

196. The word *manibus*, "in hands," is likewise lacking in the text as quoted in the *Commentaries on the Psalms* (CC 72:229).

197. In BHS 1184, it is stated that זה is absent from a Qumran manuscript, but based on Ulrich 668, it appears that the evidence of the manuscript (4QPs^d) is not clear on this word.

introduces this rendering with the words *et omnes interpretes*, by which he means "and all the (other) translators"—that is, besides Aquila.

65.3.6. *secundum Hebraicam … proprietatem* μεταφορικῶς, "metaphorically according to the particular idiom of Hebrew." On Jerome's concern for the "particular idiom" of Hebrew, see introduction, §7.2. On his references to rhetorical figures such as metaphor, see introduction, §9.1.

65.4.8. *ut educas panem de terra*, "so that you might bring out bread from the earth." Ps 103:14 (Heb 104:14), GPsal. On Jerome's handling of this passage, see **65.1.5–6**. In Hebrew, the verb is an infinitive: לְהוֹצִיא לחם מן הארץ, "to bring out bread from the earth." The LXX preserved the infinitive: τοῦ ἐξαγαγεῖν, "to bring out." In the Gallican Psalter, Jerome translated using a second-person verb (*ut educas*, "that you might bring out") in keeping with his view that the entire passage is addressed to God. In the IH Psalter, he changes his mind and renders this verb in the third-person: *ut educat*, "that he might bring out."

65.5.13. *herodii domus dux est eorum*, "The house of the heron is their leader." Ps 103:17 (Heb 104:17), GPsal. The Gallican Psalter uses the spelling *erodii* in place *herodii*. This is merely an orthographic variation. In the IH edition, one finds *erodionem* at Lev 11:19 but *herodii* at Job 39:13.

Jerome begins his comments by giving the Hebrew for "heron," *asida* (חסידה), adding that Symmachus translated the word as ἰκτίν, "kite." The LXX has ἐρωδιός, "heron," so Jerome's *erodius*, "heron," appears to be a straightforward representation of the Greek. Perhaps Sunnia and Fretela had some question about the identification of this bird, so Jerome starts with this detail.

In the LXX, v. 17b reads as follows: τοῦ ἐρωδιοῦ ἡ οἰκία ἡγεῖται αὐτῶν, "The house of the heron leads them." The best attested Hebrew reading is חסידה ברושים ביתה, "the heron, the junipers are its house." The LXX's ἡγεῖται, "leads," reflects a different Hebrew text: rather than ברוש, "juniper," the LXX presupposes some form of ראש, "head, leader."[198] The Gallican Psalter essentially followed the LXX, so as to produce *erodii domus dux est eorum*, "The house of the heron is their leader." But where the LXX had a verb, ἡγεῖται, "leads," Jerome used a noun, *dux*, "leader." This might have been the main objection raised by Sunnia and Fretela. It is also possible that Sunnia and Fretela had a Greek text that contained a hexaplaric gloss

---

198. There are five medieval Hebrew manuscripts that read ברשים, and one that fills out the text as בראשים (Kennicott 2:397).

on ἡγεῖται (see below), which served as the basis for their query. In either case, Jerome was forced to deal with the Greek evidence for ברושים.

When Jerome says, *denique et nos ita vertimus in Latinum*, what does he mean? He is not wrapping up his whole argument but rather summing up the main piece of evidence for this section. Consequently, *denique* means "in fact," not "at last" or "finally."

Is *vertimus* present tense or perfect? And what is the translation that Jerome gives? In the Gallican Psalter Jerome followed the LXX, including *passeres*, "sparrows," for the LXX's στρουθία, "sparrows" (for צפרים). Now, so as to address the meaning of ברושים, Jerome gives a new translation that follows Aquila closely in the first half (ἐκεῖ ὄρνεα νοσσεύσουσιν, *ibi aves nidificabunt*, "There the birds will build their nests"), and then in the second half combines Symmachus's ἰκτῖνι, "kite," with a loose rendition of Aquila (ἐρωδιῷ ἐλάται οἶκος αὐτῷ, "to the heron, silver firs (are) house to it"), so as to produce: *milvi abies domus est*, "of the kite, the silver fir is house."[199] In the IH Psalter, Jerome will again reproduce Aquila in the first half, but in the second half he will adjust "kite" (from Symmachus) to the dative case, drop the verb *est*, and add a pronoun (*eius*) to come closer to Aquila (αὐτῷ), thereby giving: *milvo abies domus eius*, "to the kite, the silver fir (is) its house." In other words, this translation is not the same as what Jerome will give in his IH Psalter, although it is moving in that direction. In *Ep.* 106, Jerome is giving a fresh translation based on Aquila and Symmachus so as to make clear what is present in the Hebrew. Therefore, *vertimus* is present tense—that is, he is now giving a translation in addition to the Gallican Psalter, so as to explain his point.

The citation of the Sixth edition (*sexta editio*) gives the meaning in clearer syntax, but unfortunately it identifies the trees as κυπαρίσσους (*cupressos*, "cypress trees"), which Jerome has to clarify with reference to the Hebrew *barusim* (ברושים), which he takes to mean "silver fir" rather than "cypress tree."

Although Jerome does not report what Sunnia and Fretela asked, it seems their questions had to do with (1) identifying the bird in v. 17b and (2) understanding Jerome's decision to use *dux*, "leader," for what the LXX put as ἡγεῖται, "leads." Jerome mentions two Hebrew words, *asida* and *barusim*, but he does not make direct connections between the Hebrew

---

199. Symmachus has ὅπου στρουθία ἐννοσσεύσει, τῷ ἰκτῖνι βόρατον οἴκησις, "where sparrows built their nest, to the kite the juniper is dwelling" (see Field 2:260; Theodoret's *Commentary*; and Jerome's *Comm. Jer.* 8:7).

words, their spellings and pronunciations, and the various Greek versions—as he will do regularly in his prophetic commentaries. At this stage, he moves straight from citing the Hebrew words to discussing the hexaplaric versions. He does not yet unpack details about individual Hebrew words to illuminate the various Greek options. Nevertheless, we see in this discussion that, in order to answer the challenges Sunnia and Fretela put to him, Jerome needed to set aside the Gallican Psalter and deploy whatever resources he could to undertake fresh analysis of the Hebrew. Ultimately, his experience offering explanations of this sort helped show him the necessity of making a new translation based directly on the Hebrew.

65.6.21. *petra refugium erinaciis,* "The rock is a refuge for hedgehogs." Ps 103:18 (Heb 104:18), GPsal. The Hebrew word in question is שפנים (Jerome's *sphannim*), from שׁפן, understood today as "rock badger, hyrax, dassie."[200] According to Jerome, the LXX translated this word as λαγῶος, "hare," whereas all the other hexaplaric translations rendered it as χοιρογρύλλιος, "*Hyrax syriacus,* rock coney."[201]

In terms of preserved witnesses, the evidence for the LXX is mixed. The word λαγῶος, "hare" finds support in P.Bod. 24, Codex Alexandrinus, MS 55 Rome, the Lucianic manuscripts, Theodoret's *Commentary**, and as an addition to the text (i.e., "for hedgehogs and hares") in the Verona Psalter, the Sinai Psalter, Augustine's *Enarrations,* and the Syro-Hexapla (Rahlfs 259; KT 206; Weber 254; Thibaut 117; CSEL 95.1:177). Most other witnesses to the LXX contain χοιρογρύλλιος, "*Hyrax syriacus,* rock coney." As for the hexaplaric versions, there is some evidence that Theodotion had λαγῶος in agreement with the LXX (Field 2:260). This contradicts Jerome's statement that *omnes* τοῖς χοιρογρυλλίοις *voce simili transtulerunt,* "all translated with a similar voice τοῖς χοιρογρυλλίοις." But as I suggested before in *Ep.* 106 (see introduction, §8.2), it is not impossible that Jerome has reported the majority of the hexaplaric versions as "all" of them, perhaps reckoning Theodotion as so closely aligned to the LXX that it could be counted together with it.

In his *Comm. Matt.* 7:25, Jerome quotes this verse and identifies the animal as a *lepor,* "hare," or *herinaceus,* "hedgehog" (CC 77:47). Jerome describes it as a timid creature that hides itself in rocky crevices. He also notes that it is covered all around with a rough hide that can protect it even

---

200. *HALOT,* s.v. "שׁפן."
201. LSJ, s.v. "χοιρογρύλλιος."

from javelins. According to Ilya Dines, this animal "hides itself among the rocks in the Middle East" and is noteworthy from a zoological point of view for being the smallest elephant in the world.[202]

66.1.6. *dedit terra eorum ranas*, "Their land gave frogs." Ps 104:30 (Heb 105:30), GPsal. Most LXX manuscripts have ἐξῆρψεν, "brought forth."[203] This was the reading known to Sunnia and Fretela, and Jerome does not contest it. The Hebrew has שׁרץ, "swarmed." No evidence for the hexaplaric versions is preserved.

Among the various OL renderings that survive, widespread evidence is preserved both for *dedit*, "gave," as attested by Codex Sangermanensis, Saint Zenon of Verona's Psalter, and Augustine's *Enarrations*; and also for *misit*, "sent," as in the Roman Psalter, Corbie Psalter, Mozarabic Psalter, and Cassiodorus's *Explanation* (Sabatier 208; Weber 260; CSEL 95.1:226; CC 98:951). Jerome inherited *dedit* in his Latin Psalter and employed it in the Gallican Psalter on the principle of preserving a well-established reading (*antiquam interpretationem sequentes*) when there is no change in the meaning (*in hoc nulla est in sensu mutatio*) or harm to the sense (*quod non nocebat*). See introduction, §7.2.

Jerome acknowledges that the Greek has ἐξῆρψεν, which can be rendered *ebullivit*, "brought forth." In fact, Codex Casinensis 557 contains *ebullivit*, "brought forth" (Amelli 74; cf. Exod 8:3). Nevertheless, Jerome defends the Gallican Psalter's *dedit* on grounds of tradition and not harming the basic sense. In the IH Psalter, however, he decides to use *ebullivit*, as Sunnia and Fretela proposed.

66.2.10–11. *et contrivit lignum finium eorum*, "And he broke the tree of their borders." Ps 104:33 (Heb 105:33), GPsal. The word "every" is absent from the Hebrew, but this word (πᾶν) is present in the vast majority of LXX witnesses, although it is lacking in P.Bod. 24 and Codex Sinaiticus (Rahlfs 263; KT 211). In all likelihood, πᾶν was either absent altogether from the

---

202. Ilya Dines, "The Textual and Pictorial Metamorphoses of the Animal Called *Chyrogrillius*," in *Science Translated: Latin and Vernacular Translations of Scientific Treatises in Medieval Europe*, ed. Michèle Goyens, Pieter De Leemans, and An Smets (Leuven: Leuven University Press, 2008), 73–89. Dines includes a useful picture on p. 73 and three artistic depictions. See also Joshua T. Katz, "Aristotle's Badger," in *The Frontiers of Ancient Science: Essays in Honor of Heinrich von Staden*, ed. Brooke Holmes, Klaus-Dietrich Fischer, and Emilio Capettini (Berlin: de Gruyter, 2015), 267–88.

203. The Greek text of the Verona Psalter has ἐξηρεύξατο, "vomited forth," and both the Verona Psalter and the Sinai Psalter have the corresponding Latin word, *eructuabit* (for *eructuavit*; see Rahlfs 23, 263; Weber 260; Thibaut 119).

hexaplaric LXX or was marked with an obelus (*hoc additum est*, "this was added"), so Jerome omitted it from the Gallican Psalter and reckons it as *superfluum* (see introduction, §8.5).

66.3.13–14. *quod habuit*, "which he had," Ps 104:42 (Heb 105:42), GPsal. The present passage serves as an example where Jerome in the Gallican Psalter took a middle position between what he probably thought were extreme translation options. This left him ground to stand on when responding to Sunnia and Fretela, but without the privilege of claiming that his translation is precisely accurate.

According to the Hebrew, God remembered his holy word את אברהם עבדו, "with Abraham his servant." In the LXX, which Jerome quotes in full, this became: πρὸς Αβρααμ τὸν δοῦλον αὐτοῦ, "to/with Abraham his servant." Perhaps because of the tediousness of the phrasing, τοῦ λόγου τοῦ ἁγίου αὐτοῦ, τοῦ πρὸς Αβρααμ, literally, "the word, the holy one of him, the one toward Abraham," a significant stream in the OL tradition filled out the expression thus: *quod locutus est ad Abraham*, "which he spoke unto Abraham" (e.g., the Roman Psalter, Corbie Psalter, and Mozarabic Psalter). Another stream of the OL added the relative pronoun *quod*, but no verb: *quod ad Abraham*, "which (was) unto Abraham" (e.g., Codex Sangermanensis, the Verona Psalter). To Jerome, adding *quod locutus est*, "which he spoke," probably seemed too much, but leaving the clause with no verb, that is, *quod ad Abraham*, "which (was) unto Abraham," seemed too little.[204] In the Gallican Psalter, therefore, Jerome used the relative pronoun *quod* and added the bland verb *habuit*, "had," in order to satisfy Latin idiom's need for a verb while at the same time intruding as little as possible into the sense. This resulted in the Gallican Psalter: *quod habuit ad Abraham puerum suum*, "which he had unto Abraham his servant."[205]

Sunnia and Fretela had a Greek text that added the words ὃν διέθετο, probably reading: ὅτι ἐμνήσθη τοῦ λόγου τοῦ ἁγίου αὐτοῦ, ὃν διέθετο πρὸς Αβρααμ τὸν δοῦλον αὐτοῦ, "Because he remembered his holy word, *which*

---

204. In the Ambrosian Psalter, the verb *fuit* appears: *quod fuit ad Abraham*, "which was unto Abraham." This represents an even more minimalistic translation. On the Latin options for this passage, see Sabatier 209; Weber 262. The Sinai Psalter offers: *quod iuravit ad Abraam*, "which he swore unto Abraham" (Thibaut 120). In Codex Casinensis 557, one finds: *Quoniam fuit memor sermonis sancti sui cum Abraham servo suo*, "Since he recollected his holy speech with Abraham his servant" (Amelli 74). This is closer to the Hebrew; it is similar to but not identical with Jerome's IH translation.

205. Augustine, *Enarrat. Ps.* 104.40 matches the Gallican Psalter (CSEL 95.1:234).

he set forth unto Abraham his servant" (cf. the Bohairic and Sahidic Coptic versions; Rahlfs 264). As Jerome explains, ὅν διέθετο does not directly represent anything in the Hebrew and is not part of the original LXX. Although these words are found in v. 9, in this passage (*in hoc loco*) they are superfluous (see introduction, §8.5) and "should be scratched out."

66.3.19. *radendum*, "should be scratched out." In Tacitus's *Ann.* 3.17, someone's name is to be scratched out (*radendum*) from official records. Ovid's *Pon.* 2.4 refers to a book that has been scratched out (*rasus*) by a file (*lima*), resulting in erasure (*litura*). This gives some sense of what Jerome has in mind. Elsewhere, Jerome ironically advises others to "scratch out" the material under asterisk in his hexaplaric translation if they do not approve of his scholarly work (*Pref. IH Job*; *Ep.* 112.19). In his *Comm. Matt.* 5:22, he concludes that the words *sine causa*, "without cause," which appear "in certain codices" (*in quibusdam codicibus*), are inauthentic and should be "scratched out" (CC 77:27–28). See also Jerome's *Comm. Gal,* 2:11–13 (CC 77A:56).

In the IH Psalter, Jerome stays closer to the Hebrew: *quia recordatus est verbi sancti sui cum Abraham servo suo*, "Because he remembered his holy word with Abraham his servant." He avoids the awkward *quod* relative clause by translating the Hebrew את, "with," as *cum* plus the ablative.

67.1.20–21. *confitemini domino, quoniam bonus*, "Give thanks to the Lord, because he is good." Ps 105:1 (Heb 106:1), GPsal. The LXX has ὅτι χρηστός, which appears in many OL witnesses (e.g., Codex Sangermanensis; Codex Casinensis 557; the Roman Psalter) as *quoniam bonus*, "because he is good."[206] Jerome kept this translation when he made the Gallican Psalter. The question posed by Sunnia and Fretela stems from the fact that ἀγαθός, not χρηστός, is the standard equivalent for *bonus*. How can Jerome justify using *bonus*, if the Greek is χρηστός rather than ἀγαθός? A standard Latin equivalent for χρηστός might be *suavis*, "sweet, pleasant, delightful."

Jerome cites the Hebrew *chi tob*, that is, כי טוב, in his defense. In order to verify the meaning of the Hebrew, he appeals to the agreement of all the hexaplaric versions (*quod omnes voce simili transtulerunt*) in rendering this word as *bonus* (i.e., ἀγαθός; cf. Field 2:262). The hexaplaric versions make clear (*ex quo perspicuum est*) that the Greek word used by the LXX, χρηστός, can have the meaning *bonus*, "good." Jerome is not saying that the

---

206. Sabatier 209; Weber 262; Amelli 74. The Verona Psalter and the Sinai Psalter have *quoniam bonus est* (Thibaut 120). For Augustine, see below.

LXX gave the wrong translation. Rather, he explains that the LXX used χρηστός in the sense of *bonus*, which we know because the hexaplaric versions tell us the meaning of χρηστός in this context. Although the Hebrew word *tob* (טוב) plays little role in this discussion, the basic assumption is that when we are searching for the proper sense of χρηστός in the LXX, we are looking for what it means as a translation of the underlying Hebrew. For this, the hexaplaric versions serve as the interpretive key.

In his *Enarrat. Ps.* 105.2, Augustine makes the following comment on *quoniam bonus* at v. 1: *Quod autem habent aliqui codices 'quoniam bonus,' alii habent, 'quoniam suavis,' Ita unum verbum Graecum, quod dicitur* χρηστός, *diversa interpretatio secuta est*, "Where some codices have 'Because he is good (*bonus*),' others have 'Because he is pleasant (*suavis*).' These differing translations derive from one Greek word, which is said χρηστός." (CSEL 95.1:238). It is not impossible that Augustine was aware of copies of the Latin Psalter that contained *suavis*, in keeping with what Sunnia and Fretela suggested. But given the close echo Augustine makes of Jerome's discussion, I think it is more likely that Augustine took this information directly from Jerome's *Ep.* 106. Augustine's claim that some codices have *suavis* may be nothing more than an inference based on Jerome's comments.

67.2.3–4. *non fuerunt memores multitudinis misericordiae tuae*, "They were not mindful of the multitude of your mercy." Ps 105:7a (Heb 106:7a), GPsal. Sunnia and Fretela challenged the Gallican Psalter on the basis of a Greek text that put the conjunction καί, "and," before this clause: καὶ οὐκ ἐμνήσθησαν, "*And* they did not remember." This text is supported by Codex Vaticanus, the Greek text of the Verona Psalter, Theodoret's *Commentary**, MS 55 Rome, the Syro-Hexapla, and many OL witnesses such as Codex Sangermanensis, the Roman Psalter, the Sinai Psalter, and Codex Casinensis 557 (*neque* for *et non*) (Rahlfs 265; Sabatier 210; Weber 263; Thibaut 121; Amelli 74). In addition, at least nine medieval Hebrew manuscripts (ולא) and the Syriac Peshitta (*wl'*) use the conjunction (Kennicott 2:401; Pesh 126).

The Gallican Psalter, which lacks the conjunction, reflects the best Hebrew manuscripts and many Greek texts. No doubt hexaplaric materials helped Jerome recognize the absence of καί; but specific evidence is lacking. Jerome dismisses the conjunction as *superflua* (see introduction, §8.5).

67.2.5. *'et' coniunctio*, "the conjunction 'and.'" See **25.1.5**.

67.3.5–7. *et inritaverunt ascendentes in mare, Mare Rubrum*, "And they provoked, going up into the sea, the Red Sea." Ps 105:7b (Heb 106:7b),

GPsal. Two difficulties confronted the LXX in translating the Hebrew for this passage, which is normally construed as וימרו על־ים בים־סוף, "and they rebelled (מרה) by (על) the sea, at the Sea of Reed." First, what is the lexical root for the word וימרו? Second, what is the meaning of על־ים? Is it "upon the sea"? Can it mean "by the sea"? Does על ים convey the same basic idea as בים־סוף, "at the Sea of Reed"?

The LXX interpreted וימרו as if it were a *hiphil* verb from the root מרר, "to make bitter."[207] Therefore the LXX translated this word as παρεπίκραναν, "they embittered" (cf. πικρία, "bitterness"), as Sunnia and Fretela correctly pointed out. Furthermore, instead of the preposition על, "over, upon, by," plus the word ים, "sea," the LXX interpreted these letters as a single word, עלים, the *qal* active participle of עלה, "to go up" (עלים), and thus translated ἀναβαίνοντες (עלים) ἐν τῇ ἐρυθρᾷ θαλάσσῃ (בים סוף), "going up in the Red Sea." In full, the LXX had καὶ παρεπίκραναν ἀναβαίνοντες ἐν τῇ ἐρυθρᾷ θαλάσσῃ, "And they embittered, going up in the Red Sea" (Rahlfs 265).

In the Gallican Psalter, Jerome translated *et inritaverunt ascendentes in mare, Mare Rubrum*, "And they provoked, going up into the sea, the Red Sea." It should be observed that Jerome followed the LXX in using the verb "going up" (*ascendentes*, ἀναβαίνοντες), which presumes reading עלים as a participle, but he also rendered both occurrences of "sea" (*mare, Mare*), which presumes reading על־ים. Jerome supplied the additional *mare*, "sea," based on hexaplaric evidence, in conformity with the Hebrew, which uses ים, "sea," twice.[208] Augustine remarks that an asterisk (*stella*, "star") was placed before the second occurrence of *mare* in the codex he consulted.[209] This suggests that the Gallican Psalter had an asterisk on this word, which presumably reflects an asterisk in the hexaplaric LXX. Apparently, Jerome did not realize that *ascendentes*, "going up" (עלים) and *in mare*, "into the sea" (על־ים) represent the same Hebrew consonants. Perhaps he thought

---

207. By analogy, see the *hiphil* וַיָּפֵרוּ from פרר (Ezek 44:7) and וַיָּסֵבּוּ from סבב (Judg 8:23; 1 Sam 5:8). For מרר, one might expect the *piel* וימררו, e.g., Exod 1:14; but see also המר (*hiphil*) in Ruth 1:20.

208. E.g., Quinta is reported as ἐπὶ θαλάσσης, θαλάσσῃ ἐρυθρᾷ, "over the sea, in the Red Sea" (Field 2:262).

209. *Codex quem intuebar, sic habebat, et his quidem duobus verbis ultimis, quod dictum est Mare Rubrum, stella fuerat praenotata, qua significantur quae in Hebraeo sunt, et in interpretatione septuaginta non sunt*, "The codex that I looked at had it thus; and before these two last words that are said, 'Red Sea,' a star was placed, by which things are indicated that are in the Hebrew and are not in the Seventy Translators" (*Enarrat. Ps.* 105.7; CSEL 95.1:246).

the second *mare* brought the text into stricter conformity with the Hebrew, and he assumed that *ascendentes* had been added by the LXX idiomatically so as to complete the sense; in other words: The Israelites provoked God, ("going up") into the sea, the Red Sea.

67.3.8. *verbum e verbo*, "word for word." Apparently, Sunnia and Fretela asked why Jerome did not use the verb *amaricaverunt*, based on *amaritudo*, "bitterness," in order to translate παρεπίκραναν, "they embittered." Jerome's reply harkens back to previous comments he has made about not pursuing excessive linguistic precision at the expense of natural idiom (see introduction, §7.2).

Jerome does not consider the verb *amarico* to be proper Latin. As a verb, *amarico* seems to be biblical in origin (see Rev 10:9–10; 2 Esd 8:34) and otherwise appears in writers of the fourth century and later who reflect biblical usage; for example, Lucifer of Cagliari, *Non parc.* 9 (CC 8:211–12); Ambrosiaster, *Quaes.* 76 (CSEL 50:129); Augustine, *Enarrat. Ps.* 54.13–15; 65:3, 7; 67:7; and elsewhere; and Augustine, *Locut. Hept.* 5.69 (CC 39:668, 844, 849, 872; CC 33:452).[210] On several occasions, Jerome explains that the Greek verb πικραίνω (or παραπικραίνω) indicates that someone is being made to experience "bitterness" (*amaritudo*).[211] That this Greek verb is associated with "bitterness" is clear to Jerome, but he prefers to communicate this in Latin through phrases that use the noun *amaritudo*. In his *Book of Hebrew Names*, however, when giving literalistic Latin equivalents for Hebrew proper names, Jerome is willing to use the verb *amarico* (CC 72:74, 85).

In Jerome's view, to say *amaricaverunt* in Latin would be like saying "embitterized" in English. Although the expression may capture the correct etymological connection, it is entirely unacceptable in terms of style. Jerome likens this to the absurd Latin word formations he discussed earlier at **57.3**: *adnihilasti*, "nothingafy" and *adnullasti*, "nothingize." In *Ep.* 106, the idea of word-for-word translation does not meet with approval (see **17.1**; **29.2**; **57.3**; **62.1**; **67.3**; **3.3.4–3.3.9**).

In his *Enarrations on the Psalms*, Augustine makes the following comment: *Plures autem codices, quos inspicere potui, et Graeci et Latini sic habent: et irritaverunt, vel, quod expressius de Graeco est, et amaricaverunt,*

---

210. On the verb *amarico* in Christian writers of late antiquity and afterward, see Meershoek, *Le latin biblique d'après saint Jérôme*, 49–53.

211. *Comm. Mich.* 7:5–7 (CC 76:511); *Comm. Ezech.* 2:3c (CC 75:27); 2:8b (CC 75:29); 12:1–2 (CC 75:126).

"Many codices that I have been able to inspect, both Greek and Latin, have 'and they provoked,' or, that which better expresses the Greek, '*et ama-ricaverunt*'" (*Enarrat. Ps.* 105.7; CSEL 95.1:246). I am not sure whether Augustine actually saw any codices that contained *et amaricaverunt*, but his statement that *amaricaverunt* better expresses the Greek along with his observation in the previous line about the asterisk and the Hebrew (see n. 209) suggests that Augustine was making use of Jerome's *Ep.* 106. Augustine, however, took a more positive view than Jerome on *amaricaverunt* as an accurate translation of the Greek.

67.3.11–12. οἶκος παραπικραίνων. As shown by the citations of Lucifer of Cagliari (see **67.3.8**), there was an OL tradition of translating οἶκος παραπικραίνων in Ezekiel (Ezek 2:5–8; 3:9, 26–27; 12:2–3, 9, 25, 27; 17:12; 24:3; 44:6) as *domus amaricans*, "an embittering house." In contrast to this, Jerome claims that the phrase οἶκος παραπικραίνων illustrates the fact that other words, such as *inritatio*, "provocation," and *exacerbatio*, "exasperation," serve as regular Latin equivalents for παραπικρασμός.[212] Oddly enough, when Jerome translates the phrase οἶκος παραπικραίνων, he uses another word altogether, *exasperans*, "vexing." The best sense I can make of Jerome's argument is that the Old Latin text of Ezekiel as he knew it did not use the word *amaricans* to translate παραπικραίνων in the expression οἶκος παραπικραίνων.

67.4.12–14. *et vidit cum tribularentur et audivit orationem eorum*, "And he saw when they were afflicted, and he heard their prayer." Ps 105:44 (Heb 106:44), GPsal. The manuscript evidence for *Ep.* 106 consistently reads *audivit* (perfect) for this verse. As for the Gallican Psalter, three significant manuscripts likewise read *audivit*: the eighth-century Dagulf Psalter (Vienna, Lat. 1861), the ninth-century *Psalterium Augiense triplex,* and the ninth-century Psalter of St. Gallen (WG 906). This was the reading adopted by the Sixto-Clementine Vulgate (Van Ess 99). Otherwise, most manuscripts of the Gallican Psalter have *audiret* (imperfect), which is the text of the Gallican Psalter given in the Weber-Gryson edition and is also the reading of the IH Psalter. It is tempting to argue that the original Gallican Psalter contained *audivit* as preserved in *Ep.* 106 and the three Psalters mentioned above, and that the Gallican Psalter witnesses that have *audiret* represent harmonization to the IH edition. On closer inspection, however,

---

212. See *inritavo* for παραπικραίνω in the OL of Pss 5:11; 105:7 (Sabatier 15, 210), and *exacerbo* for παραπικραίνω in the OL of Pss 65:7; 67:7; 77:8, 17, 40, 56; 104:28; 105:33, 43; 106:11 (Sabatier 128, 131, 156, 157, 159, 160, 207, 212, 213, 214).

the best interpretation of these Latin readings in relationship to the underlying Greek and Jerome's typical translation practice favors *audiret* as the
original Gallican Psalter.

The Greek text of Ps 105:44 has καὶ εἶδεν ἐν τῷ θλίβεσθαι αὐτοὺς ἐν τῷ
αὐτὸν εἰσακοῦσαι τῆς δεήσεως αὐτῶν, "And he saw, when they were afflicted,
when he heard their prayer." The first verb is finite (εἶδεν, "he saw"), and the
next two verbs are infinitives within circumstantial clauses (ἐν plus infinitive). This roughly corresponds to the Hebrew: (1) וירא, "And he saw," (2)
בצר להם, "in distress to them," (3) בשמעו את רנתם, "in his hearing their
cry." There would be no reason for the hexaplaric LXX to change the verb
"hear" (εἰσακοῦσαι) into a finite verb. We may therefore assume that the
hexaplaric LXX read very much like the preserved LXX, with the second
two verbs as part of subordinate clauses. In such a case, Jerome is more
likely to have used *audiret* (imperfect subjunctive), so that the verb "heard"
is construed with *cum* as part of the subordinate clause: *et vidit, cum tribularentur et audiret orationem eorum*, "And he saw, when they were afflicted
and (when) he heard their prayer."

This conclusion finds modest support from two further arguments: (1)
First, in the Gallican Psalter Jerome typically uses *audio* for ἀκούω (Pss
29:11; 58:8; 77:21, 59; 80:6, 12; 96:8), whereas *exaudio* is the regular and
frequent rendering for forms of εἰσακούω (Pss 4:2; 6:9, 10; 9:38; 17:7, 42;
21:25; 27:6; 33:7, 18; 39:3; 65:19; 68:34; 119:1) and also ἐπακούω (Pss 3:5;
33:5; 117:5).[213] When Jerome saw a form of εἰσακούω and wrote the Latin
third-person perfect indicative, he wrote *exaudivit*, not *audivit*. By contrast, the subjunctive *audiret* is much less common, occurring elsewhere
in the Gallican Psalter only at Ps 101:21 (for the infinitive ἀκοῦσαι); moreover, *exaudiret* appears nowhere in the Gallican Psalter. Therefore, I tentatively suggest that the association εἰσακούω = *exaudio* was firmly fixed in
Jerome's mind when he wrote the perfect indicative, but not necessarily for
the imperfect subjunctive. Therefore, if some form of *audio* (rather than
exaudio) were to be used for εἰσακοῦσαι, it is more likely to be the imperfect
subjunctive.

(2) Second, Jerome shows his understanding of this verse later in the
IH Psalter when he adds *cum* right before the verb *audiret*, thus clarifying what he means: *et vidit tribulationem eorum cum audiret eos rogantes*,

---

213. Many LXX manuscripts of Ps 17:7 have ἤκουσεν, but Jerome's Greek text
probably had εἰσήκουσεν as does the Greek text of the Verona Psalter (Rahlfs 101).

"And he saw their affliction, when he heard them petitioning." This does not appear to be a new interpretation based on some perspective freshly gleaned from the Hebrew or from Aquila or Symmachus, such as was not already available in the Septuagint. On the function of this clause, I suspect this was Jerome's reading of the text all along. In this instance, I propose, the IH edition confirms what Jerome meant in the Gallican Psalter.

In sum, I think it probable that Jerome wrote *audiret* at Ps 105:44 in the Gallican Psalter.

What, then, is the origin of *audivit* in *Ep.* 106 manuscripts and the three Psalters noted above? Here is a suggestion: If one were not looking at the Greek or Hebrew, the lines work better as poetic parallelism with *audivit*: (1) *et vidit cum tribularentur*, "And he saw when they were afflicted," (2) *et audivit orationem eorum*, "and he heard their prayer." For anyone accustomed to the structure of Hebrew poetry (even in translation), it would be natural to expect the perfect *audivit*, in order to balance out the lines (*vidit ... audivit*). Furthermore, as noted above, the perfect *audivit/exaudivit* occurs much more frequently than the imperfect subjunctive *audiret* in the Gallican Psalter. Therefore, it would be easy for someone to write *audivit* instead of *audiret* by mistake. Perhaps this was Jerome in *Ep.* 106, or else an early copyist of *Ep.* 106. From here, the erroneous *audivit* could have made its way into the previously mentioned Vulgate Psalters at Ps 105:44.

As for Jerome's comment, clearly Sunnia and Fretela proposed additional words based on their Greek text, which Jerome regarded as too cumbersome to discuss in detail. I am not aware of evidence in Greek for the additional material that Sunnia and Fretela may have suggested. Jerome's curt response is simply that whatever beyond this (*quidquid extra hoc*) they claim to have found in Greek is superfluous (see introduction, §8.5).

68.1.16–17. *et statuit procellam eius in auram et siluerunt fluctus eius*, "And he settled its tempest into a breeze; and its waves were silent." Ps 106:29 (Heb 107:29), GPsal. In Hebrew according to the MT, this verse reads: יקם סערה לדממה ויחשו גליהם, "He appointed (literally "raised up") the storm for calm, and their waves were silent." As for the second half of the verse, the antecedent for the third-person masculine plural suffix on גל, "waves," is not clear ("their" waves?). In Qumran fragment 4QPs^f, the text appears as גלי ים, "the waves of the sea" (Ulrich 673).[214] For this second half, the LXX has καὶ ἐσίγησαν τὰ κύματα αὐτῆς, "and its waves

---

214. Cf. v. 25 in the Peshitta: *gllwhy dym'*, "the waves of the sea" (Pesh 130).

were silent." Whatever the LXX's Hebrew text may have read, the Gallican Psalter reflects the third-person singular suffix of the Greek ("its waves," i.e., the waves of the tempest).

The specific issue raised by Sunnia and Fretela, however, pertains to the first half of the verse. In place of the shorter Hebrew text, "And he settled its tempest into a breeze," Sunnia and Fretela quoted to Jerome a longer reading from the LXX: καὶ ἐπετίμησεν τῇ καταιγίδι αὐτῆς καὶ ἔστη εἰς αὔραν, "And he rebuked its tempest, and it settled (literally: "stood") into a breeze." In reality, most LXX manuscripts have ἐπέταξεν, "he commanded," instead of ἐπετίμησεν, "he rebuked," the latter being the language of the gospels: "he rebuked the sea" (see Matt 8:26; Mk 4:39; Lk 8:24). As for ἐπετίμησεν, "he rebuked," it is found in several Greek sources at Ps 106:29, including the Greek text of the Verona Psalter, a few Lucianic manuscripts, and a correction to Codex Sinaiticus (Rahlfs 271). In either case, the LXX gives an expanded reading: rather than one verb ("he settled"), the Greek has two ("he rebuked/commanded, and it settled"). In the Gallican Psalter Jerome provided a shorter reading closer to the Hebrew with only one verb. The additional words in the LXX (καὶ ἐπετίμησεν or καὶ ἐπέταξεν) Jerome regards as "superfluous" (see introduction, §8.5).[215]

In agreement with the LXX (τῇ καταιγίδι αὐτῆς), the Gallican Psalter offers a third-person pronoun after the word "tempest": *procellam eius*, "its tempest." But in agreement with the MT, the Gallican Psalter places an obelus on *eius*, "its," in order to indicate its absence from the Hebrew (Gasquet 237). Whereas the MT vocalizes this word as the feminine noun סְעָרָה, "tempest," the LXX presupposes the masculine noun סַעַר, "tempest," plus a third-person feminine singular suffix ("its").[216]

The hexaplaric versions give us some insight into what the hexaplaric LXX might have contained. Aquila, Symmachus, and Theodotion each give the shorter text with only one verb, as in the Hebrew and Gallican Psalter. Both Aquila and Symmachus signal the absence of the pronoun "its" by omitting it, although each one handles the verb קָם, "settled/raised up," differently than the Gallican Psalter does.[217] Theodotion looks like a plausible model for the Gallican Psalter, except that Theodotion gives a plural

---

215. Codex Sinaiticus gives a very short text: καὶ ἔστησεν καταιγίδα αὐτῆς, "And he settled its tempest" (without εἰς αὔραν), which probably arose through a combination of correction toward the Hebrew and scribal error (Rahlfs 271).

216. *HALOT*, s.v. "סַעַר."

217. Aquila: ἀναστήσει λαίλαπα εἰς αὔραν, "He will settle/raise up the storm into a

pronoun after "tempest" (cf. "their waves" in the following clause).[218] So, what did Jerome find in the hexaplaric LXX? Perhaps Origen's text of the LXX contained: καὶ ἔστησεν καταιγίδα αὐτῆς εἰς αὔραν, "And he settled its tempest into a breeze," and he marked αὐτῆς with an obelus because of its absence in Aquila and Symmachus.[219] This would account for the Gallican Psalter.

68.2.20. *voluntatis eorum*, "their wish." Ps 106:30 (Heb 107:30), GPsal. The Greek text suggested by Sunnia and Fretela is θελήματος αὐτοῦ, "his wish." This reading is found in many witnesses, including the fourth-century MS 2029 Sinai, Codex Sinaiticus, Codex Alexandrinus, MS 1219 Washington, MS 55 Rome, the Lucianic manuscripts, Theodoret's *Commentary**, and the Syro-Hexapla (Rahlfs 271). According to Jerome, he followed "all the translators" who put θελήματος αὐτῶν, "their wish." This reading is also attested by P.Bod. 24, the Sahidic Coptic version, the Greek text of the Verona Psalter, and in Latin by witnesses such as the Verona Psalter, Codex Sangermanensis, the Roman Psalter, and Augustine's *Enarrations* (Rahlfs 271; KT 216; Weber 272).

As Jerome explains, his translation agrees with the Hebrew, *ephsam*, (חפצם). He is able to show his basic knowledge of Hebrew by supplying what the Hebrew would be if the third-person pronoun were correct: *ephsau*, (חפצו; see **6.1.9–10**).

69.1.1. *exurge, gloria mea*, "Arise, my glory." Ps 107:3 (Heb 108:3). Jerome does not begin this discussion with his customary phrase "You say that you found/read," followed by the text proposed by Sunnia and Fretela. That is because Jerome's original Gallican Psalter did not contain these additional words, *exurge, gloria mea*. This addition was present in the flawed copy of the Gallican Psalter consulted by Sunnia and Fretela. Jerome agrees with them that *exurge, gloria mea* is not the correct Latin reading (*in Latino non esse*, "is not in the Latin"), and he assures them that it finds no support in the Hebrew or Greek translations. Both the Hebrew (עורה הנבל וכנור) and the LXX (ἐξεγέρθητι, ψαλτήριον καὶ κιθάρα) begin with the words: "Arise, O harp and lyre." This is also how the genuine Gallican Psal-

---

breeze." Symmachus: στήσαντος αὐτοῦ τὴν καταιγίδα εἰς γαλήνην, "when he settled the tempest into calm" (Field 2:263).

218. Theodotion: καὶ ἔστησε τὴν καταιγίδα αὐτῶν εἰς αὔραν, "And he settled their tempest into a breeze" (Field 2:263).

219. Origen's text may have resembled Codex Sinaiticus (n. 215). Also, the Syro-Hexapla has: *'b 'qym l'l' dylh*, "The Hebrew: he settled its tempest" (Field 2:263).

ter for this passage begins: *exsurge, psalterium et cithara*. For other passages where Sunnia and Fretela quote back to Jerome a mistaken version of the Gallican Psalter, see introduction, §3.2.

As Jerome explains, this additional phrase (i.e., *exurge, gloria mea*) that Sunnia and Fretela wrongly thought was present in the Gallican Psalter at Ps 107:3 likely crept into this passage because a scribe mistakenly remembered the similar wording of Ps 56:9, ἐξεγέρθητι, ἡ δόξα μου, ἐξεγέρθητι, ψαλτήριον καὶ κιθάρα, "Arise, my glory; arise, O harp and lyre." As it turns out, this error did not simply arise in the Latin tradition but can be traced back to a miscopying in the Greek text; the words ἐξεγέρθητι, ἡ δόξα μου (*exurge, gloria mea*) are found at the beginning of Ps 107:3 in the Lucianic manuscripts, Theodoret's *Commentary**, the Syro-Hexapla, MS 1219 Washington, the Bohairic Coptic, and the Roman Psalter (Rahlfs 273; Weber 274).

69.2.5–6. *mihi alienigenae amici facti sunt*, "Foreign tribes became friends to me." Ps 107:10 (Heb 108:10), GPsal. According to the preserved Hebrew text, this verse reads as follows: "(1) Moab is my washbasin, (2) over Edom I cast my sandal, (3) over Philistia I shout in jubilation" (עלי פלשת אתרועע). The verb אתרועע is *hithpolal* imperfect from רוע.[220] This same poetic line appears at Ps 60:10 (Heb), except that at (3) the verb is התרעעי, which is *hithpolal* imperative from רוע, thus producing: "shout in jubilation over Philistia!"[221] Looking at the Hebrew is helpful for understanding the origins of the Greek versions, but Jerome does not discuss the Hebrew in any detail, except for giving a transliteration of the Hebrew word.

At both passages, Ps 59:10 (Heb 60:10) and Ps 107:10 (Heb 108:10), the LXX translated: ἐμοὶ ἀλλόφυλοι ὑπετάγησαν, "Foreign tribes were subjected to me."[222] Perhaps the LXX encountered or interpreted the verb as התרדד, from רדד, "to subjugate" (see Ps 143:2 [Heb 144:2]). As for the Gallican Psalter, at Ps 59:10 Jerome matches the preserved LXX reading: *mihi alienigenae subditi sunt*, "Foreign tribes were subjected to me." Sunnia and

---

220. *HALOT*, s.v. "רוע."

221. At least one medieval Hebrew manuscript attempted to correct this toward Ps 108:10 (Heb) by putting אתרועעי (Kennicott 2:356).

222. The Hebrew פלשת/פלשתי, "Philistia/Philistine" was typically rendered into Greek as Φυλιστιιμ in the Pentateuch and Joshua, and as ἀλλόφυλος in the later books of the LXX (HRCS 57–59, 155 in app. 1); see Emanuel Tov, "The Septuagint," in *Mikra*, ed. Martin J. Mulder and Harry Sysling (Assen: Van Gorcum, 1988), 161–88, esp. 169.

Fretela apparently questioned Jerome as to why he did not translate this way at Ps 107:10.

Jerome agrees with Sunnia and Fretela that *subditi sunt*, "were subjected" is the correct translation at Ps 59:10, but he cites the Hebrew word (*ethrohe*) and the unified testimony of the hexaplaric Greek versions in favor of the reading ἐφιλίασαν, "became friends," or, as it is in the Gallican Psalter, *amici facti sunt*. The Hebrew transliteration is primarily ornamental; Jerome's understanding of what the word means comes entirely from the Greek translations. In reality, the sense "became friends" derives from construing the Hebrew word as a *hithpael* verb from רעה II, "befriend."[223] For a more advanced discussion of this Hebrew word from later in Jerome's career, see his *Comm. Jer.* 15:12.

What is one to make of Jerome's claim that he found "in all the translators" the verb ἐφιλίασαν, "became friends"? This was the reading of Theodotion at Ps 59:10 (Field 2:189), so it may well have been Theodotion's reading here, too. Another hexaplaric witness, a marginal note in the Syro-Hexapla at Ps 107:10, reports the reading of ὁ Ἑβρ as *hww rḥm'*, "became friends" (Field 2:265). But for Aquila, evidence for Ps 59:10 (ἡταιρήσατο, "kept company with") and for Ps 107:10 (συνεταιρισθήσομαι, "I will keep company together with") suggests a different word. Still, each of these renderings has a lexical meaning similar to ἐφιλίασαν, which presupposes the same basic interpretation of the Hebrew root (Field 2:189, 264). Perhaps when Jerome says that all the Greek translators have "ἐφιλίασαν, that is, 'became friends,'" what he means is that Theodotion and the hexaplaric LXX read this way (cf. Caloz 193–94) and that Aquila and Symmachus give roughly equivalent translations that support the same general sense (see introduction, §8.2). It should be noted that a reading preserved for Quinta, ἐντιμωθήσομαι, "I will be honored," does not necessarily provide support for Jerome's *amici facti sunt*, "became friends" (Field 2:264). If this reading for Quinta is correct, then we must assume that by "all the translators," Jerome is referring strictly to Aquila, Symmachus, and Theodotion.

70.1.11–12. *virtutis tuae*, "of your strength." Ps 109:2a (Heb 110:2a), GPsal. Sunnia and Fretela had a Greek copy of the text that lacked the words δυνάμεως σου, "of your strength." But these are found consistently in preserved witnesses to the LXX and also in the Hebrew text: עֻזְּךָ.

---

223. *HALOT*, s.v. "רעה II."

70.2.14–15. *dominare in medio inimicorum tuorum*, "Rule in the midst of your enemies!" Ps 109:2b (Heb 110:2b), GPsal. In this case, the Greek text consulted by Sunnia and Fretela, which contained the conjunction καί, "and," accords with the consistent witness of LXX manuscripts (Rahlfs 277). But there is no conjunction in the Hebrew: רדה בקרב איביך, "Rule in the midst of your enemies!" It is no surprise, then, that the conjunction is absent from the preserved reading for Theodotion (Field 2:266), and it was likely absent from the hexaplaric LXX (*nec apud Septuaginta*, "nor among the Seventy"). As an element not needed for the sense and lacking in the genuine LXX and Hebrew, it is reckoned by Jerome as "superfluous" (see introduction, §8.5).

71.1.18–19. *confitebor tibi, domine, in toto corde*, "I will confess to you, Lord, with all heart." Ps 110:1 (Heb 111:1). This lemma presents a puzzling problem, in that manuscript evidence for the Gallican Psalter uniformly suggests that Jerome included *meo*, "my," in his translation (*in toto corde meo*, "with all my heart"), but in *Ep.* 106 Jerome clearly judges *meo* to be a superfluous addition (see introduction, §8.5). Jerome says that "here" (*hic*) this word is superfluous because he recognizes that the phrase *in toto corde meo* does occur elsewhere (e.g., Pss 9:2; 85:12; 118:10; 137:1; Jer 32:41).

Although LXX witnesses consistently attest to the presence of *meo* (μου), this pronoun is lacking in the Hebrew. A first question to ask is this: Why did Jerome include *meo* in the Gallican Psalter? One possibility is that Jerome kept *meo* because the hexaplaric LXX contained μου and did not mark it with an obelus. Another possibility is that the hexaplaric LXX marked μου with an obelus to indicate its absence from the Hebrew, but Jerome kept *meo* in the Gallican Psalter due to a slip of the eye or else for the sake of euphony. Otherwise, perhaps he followed another hexaplaric version that kept μου. By the time *Ep.* 106 was composed, whether by checking the Hebrew for the presence of *yod* attached to לבב (e.g., לבבי, Heb Ps 86:12), by checking another hexaplaric version, or perhaps by checking the hexaplaric LXX for an obelus, Jerome realized that, if he were adhering strictly to the Hebrew, he would need to remove *meo*.

So, what series of events stands behind what we see in *Ep.* 106? If Jerome already wrote *in toto corde meo* in the Gallican Psalter, why did Sunnia and Fretela propose that *meo* should be added? Two possible scenarios come to mind: (1) Sunnia and Fretela wrote Jerome to tell him to remove *meo* based on a corrected Greek text in their possession, and in reporting their statement Jerome reversed the communication—making their proposed text his version and the erroneous Gallican Psalter their text—in order to avoid having to acknowledge his mistake. (2) The copy of Jerome's version consulted by Sunnia and Fretela had been corrected at this point toward the Hebrew, probably *via* the Hexapla. The two Goths challenged Jerome to add *meo*, not realizing that his original translation contained *meo*. When Jerome checked his sources, he saw that the text they wrongly ascribed to him, *in toto corde*, "with all heart," is actually closer to the Hebrew, so he responded as briefly as possible that *meo* is superfluous. Anyone who saw this letter and had access to hexaplaric evidence would assume that Jerome was correct all along.

If the preserved readings for the Gallican Psalter and *Ep.* 106 are correct, this lemma presented a dilemma for Jerome because it shows a flaw in the Gallican Psalter that is not easily explained away. Issues such as this contributed to his decision to retranslate the Psalter directly out of the Hebrew. In the IH Psalter, Jerome does, in fact, remove *meo*.

72.1.21–22. *deus autem noster in caelo*, "But our God is in the heaven." Ps 113:11 (Heb 115:3), GPsal. The Hebrew has: כל (2) ואלהינו בשמים (1) אשר חפץ עשה, which means (1) "But our God is in the heavens; (2) everything that he wishes, he does." This reading represents the MT, and it finds support in 4QPs^b (Ulrich 677). The Gallican Psalter essentially reproduces this text: (1) *deus autem noster in caelo*, (2), *omnia quaecumque voluit fecit.* (1) "But our God is in the heaven, (2) all things whatsoever he wished, he did." We may assume that Jerome followed hexaplaric evidence in this rendering.

In the mainstream LXX tradition, material is added between the two half lines of this verse. The textual evidence for the Greek is complex. The longest text preserved in important witnesses has ἄνω, "above," added to the end of the first half line ("But our God is in the heaven above"), and then inserts the following before the second half line: ἐν τοῖς οὐρανοῖς καὶ ἐν τῇ γῇ, "in the heavens and on the earth." This longest text is found in Codex Sinaiticus (ἐπι τῆς γῆς), the Bohairic Coptic version, Codex Sangermanensis, and Augustine's *Enarrations* (Rahlfs 281; CSEL 95.2:37). For a slightly shorter reading, Codex Alexandrinus does not have ἄνω or ἐν τοῖς οὐρανοῖς, but it does add καὶ ἐν τῇ γῇ, "and on the earth," at the end of the first half line (see also RH 127).[224] This Alexandrinus reading is essen-

---

224. P.Bod. 24 gives a short Greek text that is close to the Hebrew. For the first half line, this manuscript reads (1) ὁ δὲ θς ἡμῶν ἐν τοῖς οὐρανοῖς ἄνω, "But our God (is) in the heavens (pl.) above (ἄνω)," and then for the second half line it reads (2) πάντα ὅσα ἐβούλετο ἐποίησεν, "all things whatsoever he wished, he did"—with the verb ἐβούλετο,

tially the Greek text upon which Sunnia and Fretela based their suggestion. Jerome rejects the added phrase καὶ ἐν τῇ γῇ as superfluous (see introduction, §8.5).

73.1.1–2. *et in diebus meis invocabo te*, "And in my days I will call on you." Ps 114:2 (Heb 116:2), GPsal. Neither the Hebrew (אקרא) nor the LXX (ἐπικαλέσομαι) have a word that corresponds to "you." A few potential witnesses to the Old Greek supply the pronoun "him," for example, the Syro-Hexapla, the Verona Psalter, the Roman Psalter, and Cassiodorus's *Explanation* (Rahlfs 283; Sabatier 227; Weber 287; CC 98:1038). At least this fits the context, which speaks of God in the third-person. But Jerome's *te*, "you," is not suitable for this passage. Presumably Jerome added *te*, "you," in order to improve readability and fill out the sense; only, he inserted the wrong pronoun. This left him with a word in his translation that has no basis in the Hebrew or Greek and cannot be justified on grounds of Latinity or preserving the sense. His response is to acknowledge succinctly that their observation is correct (*et bene*, "and you are correct") and then agree that the offending word should be scratched out (*eradendum est*) from their codices. When he says *quoque*, "too" (*e vestris quoque codicibus*, "out from your codices, too"), this is perhaps his way of admitting that *te* must be scratched out from his own copy, first. Based on the manuscript evidence for the Gallican Psalter, it seems that this is an error that goes back to Jerome himself. But his vague reply leaves open the possibility that this is a scribal mistake that crept into these copies (i.e., theirs and Jerome's) during the text's transmission.

In the IH Psalter, Jerome omits *te*. This pronoun is likewise absent from Jerome's citation of Ps 114:2 in his later *Homilies on the Psalms* (CC 78:235). The editors of the Sixto-Clementine Vulgate did not include *te* in their edition (Van Ess 104).

73.2.3–4. *placebo domino in regione vivorum*, "I will be pleasing to the Lord in the land of the living." Ps 114:9 (Heb 116:9), GPsal. The phrase in question is *placebo domino*, "I will be pleasing to the Lord." This Latin rendering appears in Old Latin sources such as Hilary's *Tractatus* and the Roman Psalter (Sabatier 227; Weber 287; CC 61:105; CC 61A:27). Jerome clearly brought it over into the Gallican Psalter from his own OL text. In his *Comm. Ps.* 114:9, he translates: *placebo domino in regione viventium*, "I will

---

"he wished," like Sinaiticus (ἠβούλετο), rather than ἠθέλησεν, "he wished," like Alexandrinus (KT 225).

be pleasing to the Lord in the land of those who live." In the LXX, however, the passage reads εὐαρεστήσω ἐναντίον κυρίου, "I will be pleasing before the Lord." Sunnia and Fretela asked why Jerome had not represented ἐναντίον, "before," in his translation. Either they or he provided the Latin phrase *in conspectu*, "in the sight," as an equivalent for ἐναντίον. In other words, if the Greek says ἐναντίον κυρίου, "before the Lord," why does Jerome just say *domino*, "to the Lord"? What about ἐναντίον?

Matters only become more complicated if one looks at the Hebrew, according to which this passage reads אתהלך לפני יהוה, "I will walk before the Lord." Literal Greek renderings were available to Jerome in the hexaplaric versions (Field 2:269). Apparently, Jerome did not correct this passage according to the hexaplaric materials as scrupulously as he had done with other passages. Perhaps, as happened with his revision of the gospels, he revised the traditional text less and less often as he progressed through the book.[225]

All Jerome can say is: *sed hoc superfluum est*, "But this is superfluous." In most places in *Ep.* 106, when Jerome says something is "superfluous," he means that it is unsupported by the genuine texts and unnecessary for the meaning (see introduction, §8.5). In this instance, his position is that *in conspectu* is not needed to convey the sense, even though it better matches the Greek (ἐναντίον) and especially the Hebrew (לפני). In the IH Psalter, Jerome will represent ἐναντίον as *coram*: *deambulabo coram domino*, "I will walk before the Lord."

Interestingly, Codex Casinensis 557 shows adaptation toward the Hebrew and nearly matches Jerome's IH edition. For the Hebrew אתהלך לפני יהוה בארצות החיים, "I will walk before the Lord in the *lands* of the living," the IH Psalter has: *deambulabo coram domino in terris viventium*, "I will walk before the Lord in the *lands* of the living," and Codex Casinensis 557 gives: *deambulabo coram domino in generationibus vi[v]orum*, "I will walk before the Lord in the *generations* of those alive" (Amelli 82).

74.1.6–7. *et in nomine domini, quia ultus sum in eos*, "and in the name of the Lord, because I have taken vengeance on them." Ps 117:10 (Heb 118:10), GPsal. In Hebrew this passage reads: "All the nations surround me;

---

225. See H. F. D. Sparks, "Jerome as Biblical Scholar," in *From the Beginnings to Jerome*, vol. 1 of *The Cambridge History of the Bible*, ed. Peter R. Ackroyd and Christopher F. Evans (Cambridge: Cambridge University Press, 1970), 510–41, esp. 524. In his revision of the Gospel of Matthew, Jerome regularly converted finite verbs into participles at first, but as the work progressed, he did so less and less consistently.

in the name of the LORD, indeed (כִּי), I oppose them." The particle כִּי is used in a corroborative sense: "yea," "verily," "indeed" (see GKC 148d; 159ee).[226] This function of כִּי is far less common than its uses to express "because" or "that." In the mainstream LXX tradition, the particle כִּי is left untranslated. In the hexaplaric LXX, ὅτι, "because, that," was supplied under asterisk (Field 2:270). Since ὅτι does not normally convey a corroborative meaning, this translation would not have been very clear in Greek; the presence of ὅτι introduced by an asterisk in the hexaplaric LXX Psalter served as a note to the reader that, for whatever reason, the word "because" or "that" appears in the Hebrew.

When Jerome translated the Gallican Psalter, he supplied *quia*, "because," with an asterisk in order to represent ὅτι in the hexaplaric LXX. Jerome probably included the asterisk precisely because *quia* does not make obvious sense in the context; he wanted to present this word as a note to the reader, not as an integral part of the translation. Apparently, the copy of the Gallican Psalter owned by Sunnia and Fretela did not have the asterisk (see introduction, §8.2). They challenged Jerome as to why he included this element, which neither makes sense in Latin nor appears in the Greek source they consulted. Jerome might have justified *quia* by pointing to the Hebrew and the hexaplaric LXX, but in this instance, since the word is semantically and stylistically out of place in Latin, he merely explains that it should have an asterisk in the Latin copies (*in Latinis sub asterisco legendum est*). In other words, *quia* is just a footnote. In the IH Psalter, Jerome decides to leave כִּי untranslated, despite its presence in the Hebrew. As for the presence of this Hebraic element in the Latin tradition, Codex Casinensis 557 represents כִּי/ὅτι in the text as *quoniam* (Amelli 83).

75.1.9–10. *et meditabar in mandatis tuis, quae dilexi*, "And I meditated on your commandments, which I loved." Ps 118:47 (Heb 119:47), GPsal. In preserved copies of the LXX, the word σφόδρα, "intensely," is present. This came into the OL tradition in a variety of ways, for example, as *valde*, "exceedingly" (e.g., Codex Sangermanensis; the Verona Psalter), as *nimis*, "excessively" (e.g., the Roman Psalter), and as it is reported by Sunnia and Fretela, *vehementer*, "intensely," which is found in the Corbie Psalter, the Lyon Psalter, and Hilary's *Tractatus* (Sabatier 236; Weber 296; CC 61A:65). There is nothing to correspond to σφόδρα in the Hebrew text. In all likelihood, the word σφόδρα was omitted or marked with an obelus in the

---

226. *HALOT*, s.v. "כִּי."

hexaplaric LXX. Because its absence causes no harm to the sense, Jerome simply left it out of the Gallican Psalter. On *hoc superfluum est*, see introduction, §8.5.

In his *Enarrationes in Psalmos*, Augustine makes the following comment after citing this verse: *sive, quod nonnulli codices habent in utroque uersu, dilexi ualde, aut nimis, aut uehementer, sicut interpretari placuit quod Graece dicitur* σφόδρα, "Or, what some codices have in both verses: 'I loved exceedingly,' or else 'excessively,' or else 'intensely,' just as it seemed best to translate what is said in Greek: σφόδρα" (CSEL 95.2:126). This shows Augustine's awareness of various Latin renderings and illustrates his practice of checking the Greek. Augustine's comment may have been intended to counter Jerome's discussion in *Ep.* 106. When Jerome says that *vehementer* is superfluous, he does so on the basis of hexaplaric evidence and in conformity with the Hebrew. Most LXX manuscripts, however, contain the word σφόδρα, although based on Jerome's *Ep.* 106 one would not know how well attested a reading it is. He simply says: *sed hoc superfluum est*. Augustine's response was to give the Greek word and report the various ways it had been translated into Latin. This justifies Augustine's inclusion of the word in his commentary.

75.2.11–12. *levavi manus meas ad mandata tua, quae dilexi*, "I lifted up my hands unto your commandments, which I loved." Ps 118:48 (Heb 119:48). The text of *Ep.* 106 as given by the majority of witnesses does not make sense. According to the preserved text, Jerome gives the lemma with *tua*, "your," included (i.e., *mandata tua*, "your commandments"), and then he says: *in Graeco legisse vos dicitis: ad mandata tua, sed hoc superfluum est*, "You say that you read in Greek: 'unto your commandments.' But this is superfluous." Obviously, if Jerome includes *tua* in his own quotation of the passage, he will not also dismiss it as superfluous. The text of *Ep.* 106 has been corrupted at this point. What did Jerome actually say?

The first piece of information relevant to this question is the reading of the Gallican Psalter. Just as most witnesses to *Ep.* 106 have *tua* (it is omitted in only one manuscript), the majority of witnesses to the Gallican Psalter include *tua*, although *tua* is absent from two important manuscripts (the Lyon Psalter and Vatican, Reg. lat. 11; WG 922).

The first possible solution to our textual difficulty is to suppose that the Gallican Psalter lacked *tua* and that the original text of the lemma in *Ep.* 106 also lacked *tua*, with the resulting sense: "'I lifted up my hands unto the commandments, which I loved.' You say that you read in Greek: 'unto your commandments.' But this is superfluous." In other words, the Gallican Psalter lacked *tua*; Sunnia and Fretela wrote to Jerome that it should be added, but he rejects their proposal, dismissing "your" as superfluous. From a textual standpoint, this is the simplest solution, and it is the one adopted by the Benedictine edition of *Ep.* 106 (Gasquet 39).

Although this is a plausible reconstruction, I do not favor it. One obstacle is that the Hebrew (מצותיך) has "your," and consequently the main body of hexaplaric evidence likely had "your," which leads us to expect that the Gallican Psalter probably had "your" as well. Given this line of thinking and the fact that most manuscripts of both *Ep.* 106 and the Gallican Psalter read *tua*, I find it hard to reject. Therefore, I suggest that the original Gallican Psalter contained *ad mandata tua*, "unto your commandments," and that *ad mandata tua* is also the correct reading of the lemma in *Ep.* 106. This is the text of the biblical lemma adopted by Hilberg 285. If so, there must be an error in the transmission of Jerome's commentary in *Ep.* 106. As noted above, Jerome's argument cannot be that *tua* is superfluous.

Further illumination can be derived from looking at the evidence for the Greek text. Several witnesses to the Greek, including Papyrus 2014, Codex Sinaiticus, Codex Alexandrinus, the Bohairic Coptic version, Codex Sangermanensis (*nimis*), and Hilary's *Tractatus* (*valde*) attest to the presence of σφόδρα, "intensely" in v. 48 right after ἃς ἠγάπησα, "which I loved" (Rahlfs 292; RH 133; Sabatier 236; CC 61A:66). The addition of σφόδρα in v. 48 harmonizes this passage to its parallel in v. 47. If we assume that Sunnia and Fretela based their challenge on a Greek text that contained τὰς ἐντολάς σου, ἃς ἠγάπησα σφόδρα, "unto your commandments, which I loved intensely," then Jerome's brief response, *sed hoc superfluum est*, makes sense. Just as σφόδρα was superfluous in the previous text (v. 47), so also it is superfluous here in v. 48 (see introduction, §8.5). In line with this solution, Hilberg added *quae dilexi vehementer* in his edition as the final words of the text proposed by Sunnia and Fretela. I take this to be the most likely reading.

75.3.14–15. *cogitavi vias meas*, "I have contemplated my ways." Ps 118:59a (Heb 119:59a), GPsal. Most copies of the LXX have σου, "your" (Rahlfs 293).[227] This is the reading suggested by Sunnia and Fretela. The

---

227. Hilberg 285 inserts the word *iuxta*, thus producing *iuxta vias tuas*, "according to your ways," which brings the text proposed by Sunnia and Fretela in line with the reading of Codex Alexandrinus and Codex Sinaiticus: κατὰ τὰς ὁδούς σου. But I do not think this is necessary. Evidence is preserved for the Greek text without κατά.

Hebrew (דרכי), the hexaplaric versions, and the hexaplaric LXX have "my" (see Field 2:273), which is how Jerome translated in the Gallican Psalter. It is notable that the difference between *tuas* and *meas* is qualitative, not quantitative. When Jerome says that *tuas* is "superfluous" (see introduction, §8.5), he means that the reading *tuas*, "your" (σου) arose as a miscopying of the correct reading *meas*, "my" (μου), so that to suggest a change is unnecessary.

75.4.16–17. *et averti pedes meos in testimonia tua*, "And I turned my feet unto your testimonies." Ps 118:59b (Heb 119:59b). The Latin text is uncertain for this passage. I will briefly explain the text as I understand it.

For the *Ep.* 106 readings, Hilberg 285 prints *verti*, "I turned," for the lemma and *averti*, "I turned/averted," for what Sunnia and Fretela proposed. In favor of this text, Codex Casinensis 247 (eleventh–twelfth century) reads *verti* for the lemma, and most manuscripts read *averti* for the proposed reading. What makes me regard this text as unlikely is that Augustine is aware of two readings: *averti*, "I turned," and *avertisti*, "you turned" (CSEL 95.2:134–35), both of which appear in the manuscript evidence for *Ep.* 106 and the Gallican Psalter. This meaningful variation between "I turned" and "you turned" is more likely the basis of Sunnia and Fretela's question, rather than the mere lexical difference between *verti* and *averti*.

The Benedictine edition of *Ep.* 106 prints *avertisti*, "you turned," as the Gallican Psalter lemma and *averti*, "I turned," as the reading Sunnia and Fretela suggested (Gasquet 39). As stated above, *averti* as the proposed reading has good manuscript support. As for *avertisti* as the lemma, it is attested by several manuscripts of *Ep.* 106, and it is also the reading of the Gallican Psalter according to three important manuscripts (WG 922). This is a plausible text, and it would read: "'And you turned my feet unto your testimonies.' You say that in Greek you read: 'I turned.' But this is also superfluous." My concern about this text arises from the fact that the Hebrew (ואשיבה), the hexaplaric versions (Field 2:273), and the uniform Greek evidence for the LXX (Rahlfs 293) all give the first-person for this verb. It is difficult to imagine why Jerome in the Gallican Psalter would have translated the second-person.

As for the Gallican Psalter and the lemma in *Ep.* 106, there is solid evidence for the first-person: for the Gallican Psalter, three major witnesses have *averti* and two have *converti* (WG 922); for *Ep.* 106, not only does Codex Casinensis 247 have *verti* as already noted, but three other manuscripts of *Ep.* 106 have *averti* for Jerome's lemma (Hilberg 285). Given the

Hebrew and hexaplaric evidence for the first-person, I think it is likely that the Gallican Psalter had a first-person verb (e.g., *averti*, "I turned"), and that this is the text quoted back to Jerome by Sunnia and Fretela that serves as the lemma in *Ep.* 106.

As for the reading proposed by Sunnia and Fretela, two manuscripts listed by Hilberg, Berolinensis lat. 17 (ninth century) and Oxoniensis Balliolensis 229 (twelfth century) read *avertisti*, "you turned" (Hilberg 285). This reading was known to Augustine (see above) and appears in the Corbie Psalter and Lyon Psalter (Weber 298). I suggest that this is the reading suggested by Sunnia and Fretela.

Therefore, the text I propose is as follows: *et averti pedes meos in testimonia tua. In graeco legisse vos dicitis: et avertisti. Sed et hoc superfluum est,* "'And I turned my feet unto your testimonies.' You say that in Greek you read: 'you turned.' But this is also superfluous." The text and translation I provide follows this reconstruction.

On Jerome's comment *hoc superfluum est*, see introduction, §8.5. Again (see also **75.3**), Jerome says their suggestion is "superfluous" as a way to brush aside the variant as not worth discussing. The issue here is not one of additional, unnecessary material; rather, the question concerns a different word.

75.5.18–19. *ego autem in toto corde scrutabor mandata tua*, "But I will search out your commands with all heart." Ps 118:69 (Heb 119:69), GPsal. Most witnesses to the LXX have the word "my": ἐν ὅλῃ καρδίᾳ μου, "with all my heart" (Rahlfs 294). The Hebrew, however, does not have this word: בכל לב, "with all heart." We may assume that Jerome in the Gallican Psalter followed some evidence from the Hexapla. On *sed hic 'meo' superfluum est*, "but this 'my' is superfluous," see introduction, §8.5. On the presence or absence of *meo* in the expression *in toto corde*, see **71.1**.

75.6.1–2. *anima mea in manibus meis semper et legem tuam non sum oblitus*, "My life is in my hands always, and I have not forgotten your law." Ps 118:109 (Heb 119:109), GPsal. As Jerome observes, the Hebrew (בכפי) has the first-person pronoun ("my"). In the MT, the word is vocalized as singular: בְכַפִּי, "in my hand," whereas according to masoretic conventions the Gallican Psalter presupposes the vocalization בְכַפַּי, "in my hands." Jerome's transliteration into Latin, *bachaffi*, resembles masoretic pronunciation in the spirant כ (i.e., without the *dagesh lene*) and the doubled פ (i.e., with the *dagesh forte*), but the final vowel (*i*) corresponds to the pronunciation of the word as singular rather than plural. Given the challenge of knowing how various sounds were represented in different languages and heard by different ears, it is impossible to determine whether a variation like this represents a mistake on the part of Jerome or his source, a change in pronunciation from late antiquity to the Middle Ages, or some other phenomenon.

Evidence for the Greek reading presupposed by Sunnia and Fretela, ἐν ταῖς χερσίν σου, "in your hands," is found in the Greek text of the Verona Psalter, the Lucianic manuscripts, Theodoret's *Commentary**, the Syro-Hexapla, MS 1219 Washington, the Bohairic Coptic version, the Syriac Peshitta, and many OL witnesses such as Codex Sangermanensis, the Verona Psalter, the Roman Psalter, Augustine's *Enarrations*, and Hilary's *Tractatus* (Rahlfs 297; Pesh 147; Sabatier 242; CC 61A:137). Jerome's rendering of the pronoun in the first-person was guided by the hexaplaric LXX (*apud Septuaginta*, "among the Seventy"). It seems that Aquila, Symmachus, and Quinta all gave some form of the singular, "my hand," but Theodotion kept the plural, ἐν ταῖς χερσί μου, "in my hands" (Field 2:276). Theodotion was likely the basis for the hexaplaric LXX text, which served as the basis for the Gallican Psalter.

75.6.6–7. *omnes apud Graecos ecclesiastici interpretes istum locum sic edisserunt,* "This is how all the ecclesiastical interpreters among the Greeks explain this passage." Jerome claims that all interpreters in the Greek church explained this passage as he does, with the first-person pronoun ("in my hands"). As noted above (**75.6.1–2**), this is not true for Theodoret. Athanasius likewise offered an interpretation based on the second-person pronoun, "in your hands."[228] Based on the brief explanation of the sense that he gives (*et est breviter hic sensus*), Jerome probably has in mind the exegesis offered by Origen:

Ἡ ψυχή τινος ἐν χερσὶν αὐτοῦ ἐστιν εἴ ποτε ἐν κινδύνοις γεγένηται. καὶ τοῦτο ἡ συνήθεια λέγει, ὅτι τὴν ψυχήν μου εἶχον εἰς τὰς χεῖράς μου. Ἐγὼ οὖν, φησὶν ὁ δίκαιος, καθ᾽ ἡμέραν ἀποθνῄσκω, ἀεὶ κινδυνεύω διὰ τὸν λόγον σου, διὰ τὴν ἀλήθειαν, διὰ τὸν ἔλεγχον, διὰ τὴν βασιλείαν ἣν βασιλεύω, καὶ διὰ ταῦτα ἡ ψυχή μου ἐν ταῖς χερσί μου διὰ παντός, ἀλλ᾽ οὐκ ἐπελαθόμην τοῦ νόμου σου.

---

228. Athanasius: Εἰ δ᾽ ἐν ταῖς χερσί σου εἴη, νοήσομεν χεῖρας εἶναι τοῦ θεοῦ τὴν δημιουργίαν αὐτοῦ, ἧ προσιτέον διὰ παντός, "And if it be 'in your hands,' let us think of the hands of God as his supervision, to which one must cling continually"; see Marguerite Harl and Gilles Dorival, eds., *La chaîne palestinienne sur le Psaume 118*, 2 vols., SC 189–190 (Paris: Cerf, 1972), 1:368.

The life of a person is 'in his hands' if ever he comes into dangers. This is what this expression is saying, that "I held my life in my hands." Therefore, the just one says: "I die daily. I am in danger always for the sake of your word, for the sake of the truth, for the sake of reproof, for the sake of the kingdom that I rule; and for the sake of these things, my life is in my hands always, but I did not forget your law."[229]

Origen goes on to give an understanding of this passage that is more sublime (ὑψηλότερον), according to which "My life was in my hands always" means that "good deeds" were in his hands, on the grounds that "hands" are often used in Scripture for "deeds."

75.7.10–11. *exitus aquarum deduxerunt oculi mei quia non custodierunt legem tuam,* "My eyes let down issues of water, because they did not keep your law." Ps 118:136 (Heb 119:136), GPsal. The Hebrew text gives the verb in the third-person plural, שמרו, "they kept," as is also found in many witnesses to the LXX: ἐφύλαξαν, "they kept." The reading proposed by Sunnia and Fretela is ἐφύλαξα, "I kept," which is supported by Codex Alexandrinus, MS 1219 Washington, MS 55 Rome, most Lucianic manuscripts, and the Syro-Hexapla (Rahlfs 300).

In his *Enarrations*, Augustine observes that it is the psalmist's own eyes that let down tears (*ipsi oculi mei,* "my very own eyes"), which he seeks to illuminate by citing the variant reading proposed by Sunnia and Fretela: *Nam in quibusdam codicibus et hoc legitur: quia non custodivi legem tuam,* "For in certain codices also this is read: 'Because I did not keep your law'" (CSEL 95.2:189). This may reflect Augustine's dependence on Jerome's *Ep.* 106.

Jerome rejects the proposed reading as "superfluous" (see introduction, §8.5), by which he simply means that it is incorrect. Perhaps what Jerome has in mind is that it is superfluous or unnecessary to make a change, since the Hebrew agrees with the Gallican Psalter in giving "they did not keep" rather than "I did not keep." In his translation according to the Hebrew, Jerome uses *fluebant,* "flowed," for the Hebrew ירדו, "came down." This matches what is preserved for Theodotion, Quinta, and Sexta (ἔρρευσαν).[230] This rendering of the Hebrew agrees with what he will use in his IH Psalter (see introduction, §§5.3; 6.2).

---

229. Harl, *La chaîne palestinienne sur le Psaume 118,* 1:366–68. Cf. 1 Cor 15:30–31; 2 Cor 4:8–12; Rom 8:35–39.

230. See Giovanni Mercati, *Alla ricerca dei nomi degli "Altri" traduttori nelle Omelie*

75.8.15–16. *pronuntiabit lingua mea eloquium tuum*, "My tongue will announce your declaration." Ps 118:172 (Heb 119:172), GPsal. Some Greek witnesses reflect the aorist optative, φθέγξαιτο, "may it utter" (e.g., Codex Sinaiticus, some Lucianic manuscripts, Theodoret's *Commentary**), whereas other witnesses give the future indicative, φθέγξεται, "it will utter" (e.g., Codex Alexandrinus, MS 1219 Washington, MS 55 Rome, and the Greek text of the Verona Psalter) as Sunnia and Fretela propose (Rahlfs 303). We may assume that Sunnia and Fretela pointed to the Greek word φθέγγομαι, "utter," and asked why Jerome did not translate it using *effor*, "utter."

Jerome's response is twofold: First, the basic meaning of the passage is the same whichever near synonym one chooses, whether "announce" (as Jerome put in the Gallican Psalter), "utter" (as Sunnia and Fretela suggest), or "speak" (as the Hebrew says, according to Jerome). Second, to be precise, the Hebrew does not say *effabitur*, "will utter," but *loquetur*, "will speak." Jerome's point is not that the LXX is wrong, but that even the Seventy Translators gave the general sense of the Hebrew according to the needs of Greek idiom, so Jerome should not be blamed if he has done the same thing in moving from Greek into Latin.

The Hebrew word in question is תַעַן, from עָנָה, which today is often interpreted to mean "sing" but looks like the common verb עָנָה, "answer, reply."[231] It is hard to see how Jerome could say that the Hebrew, in precise terms, means *loquor*, "speak." In all probability, he is following one of the hexaplaric versions in this rendering, although evidence is lacking. Jerome recognizes that going back to the Hebrew is necessary for getting the best possible grasp of the sense, but he does not seem to know how to handle the meaning of עָנָה in this context on his own. As with the previous lemma (see **75.7**), he keeps this translation when he produces the IH Psalter.

76.1.21–22. *domine, libera animam meam a labiis iniquis, a lingua dolosa*, "O Lord, free my soul from unjust lips, from a deceitful tongue." Ps 119:2 (Heb 120:2), GPsal. The word "and" is lacking in the Leningrad Codex and most masoretic manuscripts, but it consistently appears in LXX and OL witnesses, and it is also found in nine medieval Hebrew manuscripts (Rahlfs 304; Sabatier 249; Weber 313; Amelli 89; Kennicott 2:421).

---

sui Salmi di s. Giovanni Crisostomo e variazioni su alcune catene del Salterio, StT 158 (Vatican City: Biblioteca Apostolica Vaticana, 1952), 128–29. Field (2:277) suggests ἔρρευσαν for Quinta, based on the Syro-Hexapla: *h. 'rdyym*, "let flow," *aphel* from *rd'*.

231. *HALOT*, s.v. "עָנָה."

Jerome will later quote Ps 119:2 with the *et* ("and") in his *Homilies on the Psalms* (CC 78:251). In the Gallican Psalter, he omitted *et* despite its presence in the LXX and OL, no doubt following hexaplaric evidence. On his simple explanation: *et superfluum est*, "The 'and' is superfluous," see introduction, §8.5.

77.1.25. *beatus vir*, "Blessed is the man." Ps 126:5 (Heb 127:5), GPsal. Both the Hebrew (הגבר) and many witnesses to the LXX (ἄνθρωπος) contain "man." The word ἄνθρωπος, however, is absent from Codex Sinaiticus, MS 1219 Washington, the Lucianic manuscripts, Theodoret's *Commentary**, and the Syro-Hexapla (Rahlfs 310). In Latin, the word *vir*, "man" is lacking in the Ambrosian Psalter and Prosper of Aquitaine's *Exposition of the Psalms* (Weber 319; CC 68A:138). Sunnia and Fretela apparently consulted a Greek text that did not contain ἄνθρωπος.

The Hebrew for this verse has אשרי הגבר אשר מלא את אשפתו מהם, "Blessed is the man who fills his quiver with them." In place of the word "quiver" (אשפה), the LXX contains ἐπιθυμία, "desire."[232] Jerome followed this in the Gallican Psalter, but in the IH edition he uses *pharetra*, "quiver." This reflects knowledge that he gained when he produced the *Commentaries on the Psalms*, where he says: *Pro desiderio, in hebraeo 'pharetram' habet*, "In place of 'desire,' in Hebrew it has 'quiver'" (CC 72:238). Cf. **11.2.18–19**.

78.1.4–5. *propter legem tuam sustinui te, domine*, "For the sake of your law, I wait on you, O Lord." Ps 129:4 (Heb 130:4–5), GPsal. According to the Leningrad Codex, the Hebrew for this passage reads לְמַעַן תִּוָּרֵא קִוִּיתִי יְהוָה, which, if construed as a single unit (against the MT), can be taken to mean "so that you may be feared, I wait, O LORD." With this vocalization, תורא is a *niphal* imperfect verb from the root ירא, "fear," in the *niphal* meaning "be feared." This vocalization is clarified in 13 medieval Hebrew manuscripts that read תיורא (Kennicott 2:424). There is a single Hebrew manuscript listed in Kennicott that reads תירא, that is, תִּירָא, the *qal* imperfect form, which produces "so that you will fear."

Some witnesses to the LXX read ἕνεκεν τοῦ νόμου σου, "for the sake of your law," for example, the Greek text of the Verona Psalter and most OL witnesses, including Hilary's *Tractatus* (Sabatier 257; Weber 321; CC 61B:106). This presupposes the Hebrew תּוֹרָתֶךָ, or perhaps simply תורה, "law," with the pronoun σου, "your," having been supplied by the Greek

---

232. On this word, Codex Casinensis 557 gives a familiar OL rendering that follows the LXX: *desideria*, "desires" (Amelli 92), although most OL witnesses give the singular: *desiderium* (Sabatier 255; Weber 319).

translator for the sake of clarity. It should be noted that Codex Casinensis 557 reads simply *propter legem*, "for the sake of law," without the pronoun "your" (Amelli 93). In any case, ἕνεκεν τοῦ νόμου σου, "for the sake of your law," was very likely the reading of the hexaplaric LXX (see below), which Jerome followed in the Gallican Psalter.

Many other witnesses to the LXX read ἕνεκεν τοῦ ὀνόματος σου, "for the sake of your name," for example Codex Sinaiticus, Codex Alexandrinus, the Lucianic manuscripts, Theodoret's *Commentary**, the Syro-Hexapla (Rahlfs 311), and in Latin the Ambrosian Psalter (Weber 321).[233] This presupposes the Hebrew שמך למען as in Pss 25:11; 31:4; 79:9; 109:21; 143:11; Jer 14:7, 21; 1 Kgs 8:41; and 2 Chr 6:32. This was the reading of the Greek text used by Sunnia and Fretela. Why, they ask, did Jerome put *legem*, "law" when the Greek has ὀνόματος, "name"?

Jerome's discussion of this textual difficulty shows his growing conviction that the Hebrew can and should function as an independent court of appeal in relation to the Greek versions and cannot simply be equated with the hexaplaric LXX. He admits that *plura exemplaria*, "many copies," exist in Greek that contain ὀνόματος, "name." Of course, many times in *Ep.* 106 Jerome has favored the hexaplaric LXX against the "popular text" on the grounds that the hexaplaric LXX correctly renders the underlying Hebrew. But here it appears that he has checked the Hebrew and the hexaplaric versions and has reached the conclusion that the Hebrew does not support either option. He therefore endeavors to correct the mistake, perhaps in the same spirit of scholarly integrity he later expresses in his *Comm. Isa.* 19:16–17: *Melius reor etiam proprium errorem reprehendere quam, dum erubesco imperitiam confiteri, in errore persistere*, "I think it is better to censure an error, even my own, rather than to persist in error because I am ashamed to admit my mistake" (CC 73:197).

In addressing this problem in Ps 129:4, Jerome reports the Hebrew as *thira*, which in all likelihood represents תירא, "you will fear." He distinguishes this from *thora*, (תורא), which he understands to be capable of bearing the meaning "law," as if it were תורה. It is noteworthy that Jerome's Hebrew text seems to match the single Hebrew manuscript reported by Kennicott that has תירא, as opposed to what today is the majority masoretic reading, תורא. As for Jerome's Hebrew competence at this stage, he knows enough to connect *thora* to "law" and *thira* to "fear," but he makes

---

233. See also Curti, *La Catena Palestinese sui Salmi Graduali*, 145, 152, 154, 158.

no reference to the issue of תורא versus תורה, and he shows no awareness of the syntax of the clause or even the status of the word as a verb or noun. He does, however, comment on the similarity between *yod* (י) and *vav* (ו), which are distinguished primarily by the larger size of the *vav*. Sorting out the Greek versions by appealing to the Hebrew and commenting on the confusion of similar letters become common features of Jerome's prophetic commentaries.[234]

The evidence for the hexaplaric versions is not entirely consistent. According to Jerome, Aquila translated this word as φόβος, "fear" (*timor*), Symmachus and Theodotion gave νόμος, "law" (*lex*), Quinta agreed closely with Aquila by translating "terror" (*terror*), and Sexta gave "word" (*verbum*). As reported by Theodoret, however, Aquila and Theodotion put φόβος, "fear," and Symmachus alone gave νόμος, "law."[235] In John Chrysostom's *Exposition of the Psalms*, after citing the text as ἕνεκεν τοῦ ὀνόματος σου, "for the sake of your name," Chrysostom reports (1) "another" (ἄλλος) who translated ἕνεκεν τοῦ νόμου σου, "for the sake of your law," and then (2) "another" (ἕτερος) who translated ἕνεκεν τοῦ γνωσθῆναι τὸν λόγον σου, "for the sake of your word being made known." Later, he cites (3) "another" (ἄλλος) as ἕνεκεν φόβου ὑπέμεινα κύριον, "for the sake of fear, I waited on the Lord," and finally (4) "another" (ἄλλος) as ἕνεκεν νόμου ὑπέμεινα κύριον, "for the sake of law, I waited on the Lord" (PG 55:375–76). Field suggests that the two instances of νόμος, "law" reported by Chrysostom in (1) and (4) are Theodotion and Symmachus, which supports Jerome.[236] Chrysostom's version (3), which gave φόβος, "fear," would be Aquila, and version (2), which used λόγος, "word," would be Sexta (Field 2:286–87). If these identifications are correct, Chrysostom supports Jerome's testimony for the hexaplaric versions.

As for the Quinta reading that Jerome reports, John Chrysostom offers further useful evidence. According to Chrysostom, there is another source (ἄλλος φησίν) that says ὅπως ἐπίφοβος ἔσῃ, προσεδόκησα τὸν κύριον, "As you are frightful, I waited for the Lord" (PG 55:375). This is Quinta (ἐπίφοβος), which Jerome translated as *terror*.

---

234. See Graves, *Jerome's Hebrew Philology*, 26–61; and Martin Meiser, "Hieronymus als Textkritiker," 266–68. Cf. introduction, §§6.2; 8.1.

235. See Theodoret, *Commentary*; and Curti, *La Catena Palestinese sui Salmi Graduali*, 153.

236. The Syro-Hexapla also reports Symmachus as *nmws'*, νόμος (Field 2:287).

Although Jerome acknowledges that the reading suggested by Sunnia and Fretela is found in many copies, he does not accept their correction to his translation. But in a remarkable change of tack for *Ep.* 106, Jerome admits that his rendering in the Gallican Psalter, *legem*, "law" was based on a misunderstanding of the Hebrew. Symmachus and Theodotion mistranslated *thira*, "fear," as if it were *thora*, (i.e., νόμος, "law"). This same mistranslation underlies the hexaplaric LXX and Jerome's Gallican Psalter. Even if his treatment of the Hebrew is rudimentary, Jerome shows greater willingness here than earlier in this work to appeal to the Hebrew against all Greek witnesses. In the IH Psalter, he provides a rendering that adheres closely to Quinta: *cum terribilis sis, sustinui dominum*, "Since you are frightful, I waited for the Lord."

79.1.14–15. *sicut iuravit domino, votum vovit deo Iacob*, "Just as he swore to the Lord; he vowed a vow to the God of Jacob." Ps 131:2 (Heb 132:2), GPsal. Behind Jerome's *votum vovit*, "he vowed a vow," the Hebrew has a single word: נדר, "perform a vow" or "make a solemn promise."[237] As Sunnia and Fretela correctly point out, LXX translated this as ηὔξατο, "he prayed," or else "he vowed."[238] The more common meaning for this word is "pray," which is what Sunnia and Fretela presumably had in mind when they inquired as to why Jerome had not rendered it as *oravit*, "he prayed."

Jerome answers them by noting that εὔχομαι can also mean "vow." He illustrates this with the phrase: *redde deo vota tua*, "render to God your vows." There are several close approximations of this phrase in the Psalter that use the word εὐχή. Examples include ἀπόδος τῷ ὑψίστῳ τὰς εὐχάς σου, "render to the Most High your vows," in Ps 49:14 (Heb 50:14) and τὰς εὐχάς μου τῷ κυρίῳ ἀποδώσω, "my vows I will render to the Lord," in Ps 115:9 (Heb 116:18). See also Pss 21:26 (Heb 22:26); 55:13 (Heb 56:13); 60:9 (Heb 61:9); 64:2 (Heb 65:2); 65:13 (Heb 66:13).

79.1.17–18. *pro locorum qualitate*, "depending on the nature of the passage." See **64.1**; and introduction, §9.1.

80.1.20–21. *qui fecit luminaria magna*, "who made the great lights." Ps 135:7 (Heb 136:7), GPsal. The Hebrew at v. 7 reads לעשה אורים גדלים, "to the one who made the great lights." At v. 4 the Hebrew has לעשה נפלאות גדלות לבדו, "to the one who does great wonders alone."[239] In most LXX wit-

---

237. *HALOT*, s.v. "נדר."

238. See LSJ, s.v. "εὔχομαι."

239. The word לבדו, "alone," is absent from one preserved medieval Hebrew manuscript (Kennicott 2:427).

nesses, however, the word μόνῳ, "alone," occurs at the end of both verses. Sunnia and Fretela asked why at v. 7 Jerome wrote: *qui fecit luminaria magna*, "who made the great lights," when the Greek says τῷ ποιήσαντι φῶτα μεγάλα μόνῳ, that is, *qui fecit luminaria magna solus*, "who alone made the great lights." When Jerome quotes their proposed translation, he gives only the final two words, *magna solus*, highlighting the addition of *solus*, "alone."

Jerome omitted *solus*, "alone," in v. 7 in agreement with the Hebrew, presumably guided by hexaplaric evidence. The word "alone" (μόνῳ) is also absent from MS 1219 Washington, the Sahidic Coptic version, and the Syro-Hexapla (Rahlfs 318). Jerome dismisses *solus* in v. 7 as *superfluum*; see introduction, §8.5.

81.1.25–1. *quoniam magnificasti super omne nomen sanctum tuum*, "Because you magnified your Holy (one) above every name." Ps 137:2 (Heb 138:2), GPsal. The evidence for the LXX is complex for this passage. Jerome claims that the LXX reads ὅτι ἐμεγάλυνας ἐπὶ πᾶν τὸ ὄνομα τὸ ἅγιόν σου, which, as he makes clear through his explanation, he takes to mean: "Because you magnified your Holy one (τὸ ἅγιόν σου) above every name (ἐπὶ πᾶν τὸ ὄνομα)." This Greek might also be construed as: "Because you magnified your holy name above everything." The reading πᾶν, "every," is attested by Codex Sinaiticus, the Lucianic manuscripts, Theodoret's *Commentary**, the Syro-Hexapla, MS 55 Rome, and in Latin by Augustine's *Enarrations* (Rahlfs 321; CSEL 95.4:109). Presumably the text Jerome reports is what he found in the hexaplaric LXX (*in Septuaginta*, "in the Seventy").

In place of πᾶν, "every," some witnesses to the Greek read πάντας, "all" (masculine accusative plural), which presumably means: "Because you magnified your holy name above all (people)." This reading is attested by Codex Alexandrinus, the Greek text of the Verona Psalter, the Zürich Greek Psalter, Hesychius of Jerusalem, the Bohairic and Sahidic Coptic versions, and one manuscript representing the Mozarabic Psalter (Rahlfs 321; Weber 333). This was the reading contained in the text consulted by Sunnia and Fretela.

Instead of πᾶν or πάντας, some witnesses offer the neuter accusative plural πάντα/*omnia* (thus "above all things"), for example, MS 1219 Washington; Codex Sangermanensis; and Hilary's *Tractatus* (CC 61B:186). Furthermore, some key Latin witnesses have *nos*, "us" (thus "above us"), for example, the Verona Psalter and the Roman Psalter. These variants, however, do not play into Jerome's discussion. What is of prime importance is that most LXX witnesses have λόγιον, "word," instead of ἅγιον, "holy" (cf. the first line of the verse), the latter extant in just a few Greek manuscripts. The reading λόγιον, "word," is a closer match to the Hebrew, as explained below.

81.1.4–6. *ceterum apud Hebraeos ita esse cognoscite: quia magnificasti super omne nomen tuum verbum tuum,* "Besides, you should know that among the Hebrews it is thus: 'Because you magnified your word above all your name.'" In most Hebrew manuscripts, this passage reads: כי הגדלת על כל שמך אמרתך, "Because you magnified your word above all your name," just as Jerome reports.[240] It appears that Jerome could have learned this Hebrew rendering, which has *verbum*, "word" (אמרה), instead of *sanctum*, "holy," from Aquila or Quinta, each of whom translated τὸ λόγιόν σου, "your word" (Field 2:291). Jerome's rendering according to the Hebrew here is close to what he will give in the IH Psalter, except that in the IH Psalter he uses *eloquium* instead of *verbum* for אמרה, "speech" or "word."

Jerome concedes in this case that the Hebrew reads differently from the LXX, whether the "popular" edition or the hexaplaric edition. Whereas the Hebrew has *verbum*, "word," the hexaplaric LXX has *sanctum*, "holy." The Gallican Psalter is a rendering of the hexaplaric LXX, and as such it is accurate to its purpose. But does the difference between the Greek and the Hebrew mean that the LXX, and by implication Jerome's Gallican Psalter, is wrong? Not necessarily, suggests Jerome, who explains the sense of his Latin edition with an expanded paraphrase: *quoniam magnificasti super omne nomen, hoc est, quod in caelo et in terra dici potest, sanctum filium tuum,* "Because you magnified your holy Son above every name, that is, (above every name) that can be spoken in heaven and on earth."

In paraphrasing the text in this way, Jerome identifies the "word" or "holy (one)" as Jesus the Son, whom God the Father has magnified. This means that, whether one says *verbum*, "Word" (e.g., John 1:1), or *sanctum*, "Holy One" (e.g., John 6:69), the reference to Jesus is communicated correctly. In Jerome's mind, this shows that the LXX and Gallican Psalter have given a correct, if somewhat free, translation. What is more, by adding *quod in caelo et in terra dici potest*, "that can be spoken in heaven and on earth," Jerome alludes to Eph 1:20–21 and Phil 2:9–10, which allows him to use his Gallican Psalter rendering *nomen*, "name," for the

---

240. There is a single medieval Hebrew manuscript that omits אמרתך, "your word," thus producing a Hebrew text that reads כי הגדלת על כל שמך, "Because you magnified your name above all" (Kennicott 2:428).

sake of christological interpretation. In referring this passage to Jesus and connecting it to Phil 2:5–11, Jerome matches Didymus of Alexandria, although Didymus's text reads: ὅτι ἐμεγάλυνας ἐπὶ πάντας τὸ ὄνομα τὸ ἅγιόν σου, "Because you magnified your holy name above all (people)."[241] Moreover, through this paraphrase, Jerome makes clear his understanding of the syntax of the verse.

82.1.9–10. *quia non est sermo in lingua mea*, "Because there is no discourse on my tongue." Ps 138:4 (Heb 139:4), GPsal. The Hebrew text has בי אין מלה בלשוני, "Because there is no speech (מלה) on my tongue." The sense of the whole line in Hebrew may be taken as: "Because there is no speech on my tongue but that you, O Lord, know all of it." In other words, there is no speech on the psalmist's tongue that the Lord does not know. It might have seemed strange, however, to declare "there is no speech on my tongue" when "speech" itself is not negative. Consequently, in many Greek witnesses this text appears as ὅτι οὐκ ἔστιν λόγος ἄδικος ἐν γλώσσῃ μου, "because there is no unjust word on my tongue"; for instance, this reading appears in Codex Alexandrinus, Codex Vaticanus, Codex Sinaiticus, the Bohairic Coptic version, and Hesychius of Jerusalem (Rahlfs 322). Alternatively, in some Greek texts the word δόλος, "deceit" appears instead of λόγος, "word," for example, in the Lucianic manuscripts, Theodoret's *Commentary**, the Syro-Hexapla, MS 1219 Washington, the Sahidic Coptic version, and many OL witnesses such as Codex Sangermanensis, the Roman Psalter, Hilary's *Tractatus*, and Augustine's *Enarrations*.[242] This is the text consulted by Sunnia and Fretela that served as the basis for their challenge to the Gallican Psalter.

Jerome acknowledges that, among the hexaplaric versions, the Sixth edition (*sexta editio*) gave δόλος, "deceit," as Sunnia and Fretela suggest. But he insists that all of the other translators use either λαλιά, "speech," or λόγος, "word." Both of these correspond to the Hebrew *mala* (MT: מִלָּה). Field, citing Nobilius and Codex Vat. 754 (tenth century), proposes Aquila as λαλιά, Symmachus as ἑτερολογία, and Theodotion as δόλος (Field 2:292).[243] The Symmachus reading ἑτερολογία is not surprising, despite Jerome's claim that all (other) translators (*omnes interpretes*) have either

241. See Mühlenberg, *Psalmenkommentare aus der Katenenüberlieferung*, 2:321–22.

242. The Greek text of the Verona Psalter combines the two solutions: δόλος ἄδικος, "unjust deceit" (see Rahlfs 322; Sabatier 268; Weber 334; CC 61B:199; CSEL 95.4:133).

243. Chrysostom's text was δόλος, "deceit," but he reports ἑτερολογία, "other speech," i.e., "false speech," as another reading without identifying the source (PG

λαλιά or λόγος, because ἑτερολογία is related to λόγος and agrees generally with his translation against δόλος, and we have seen Jerome simplify
the evidence in this manner previously (see introduction, §8.2). Is it true
that Theodotion had δόλος, "deceit"? On the basis of Jerome, Montfaucon
proposed λόγος, not δόλος, for Theodotion (Field 2:292), and I am inclined
to agree with this reconstruction. If Aquila translated λαλιά and Theodotion translated λόγος, based on Jerome's *sermo* (rather than *verbum*) in the
Gallican Psalter, it is likely that he followed Aquila's rendering, and perhaps
also the hexaplaric LXX.

83.1.15–16. *funes extenderunt in laqueum*, "They stretched out cords
as a snare." Ps 139:6 (Heb 140:6), GPsal. The present text in Greek begins
with the words καὶ σχοινία διέτειναν, "And they stretched out cords," which
corresponds to the Hebrew: וחבלים פרשו. After this, virtually all Greek
witnesses have παγίδας τοῖς ποσίν μου, "snares for my feet." The Hebrew,
however, has only רשת, "net" or "snare." In the Gallican Psalter, Jerome
followed the hexaplaric LXX or one of the hexaplaric versions, so he translated the Hebrew וחבלים פרשו רשת, "And they stretched out cords (as) a
snare," straightforwardly as *funes extenderunt in laqueum*. Sunnia and Fretela consulted a standard LXX text that included the additional words τοῖς
ποσίν μου, "for my feet." Therefore, they challenged Jerome as to why he did
not represent these words in his translation.

Two interesting elements in the LXX may be observed. First, in place
of the Hebrew singular רשת, "net, snare," most LXX witnesses give the
plural παγίδας, "snares," whereas Jerome and the text consulted by Sunnia
and Fretela have the singular *laqueum*, "snare," which agrees with the Lucianic manuscripts, Theodoret's *Commentary**, the Syro-Hexapla, MS 1219
Washington, and the Greek text of the Verona Psalter (Rahlfs 324). Second,
the additional words in the LXX, τοῖς ποσίν μου, "for my feet," probably
arose as an attempt to make sense of the following words in Hebrew, ליד
מעגל, "by the path," as if they were לרגלי, "for my feet." Eventually, a better
representation in Greek was given for ליד מעגל, "by the path," in the form
of ἐχόμενα τρίβου, "near to the path." But instead of replacing the earlier
mistranslation, some scribe placed this corrected version next to it, thereby
producing a double rendering.

55:412). The Syro-Hexapla identifies Symmachus as *'ḥrnywt mmll'*, "other speech"
(Field 2:292).

Jerome comments that "in this passage" (*in hoc loco*) the additional phrase is "superfluous" (see introduction, §8.5). He says "in this passage" because elsewhere (Ps 56:7) the phrase does occur and is rendered in the Gallican Psalter: *laqueum paraverunt pedibus meis*, "They prepared a snare for my feet."

83.2.18–19. *habitabunt recti cum vultu tuo*, "The upright will dwell with your countenance." Ps 139:14 (Heb 140:14), GPsal. Most LXX witnesses include καί, "and," as Sunnia and Fretela propose. Jerome in the Gallican Psalter omits "and" in agreement with the Hebrew, in harmony also with Codex Alexandrinus in Greek and Augustine's *Enarrations* in Latin (BHS 1219; Rahlfs 325; CSEL 95.4:189). We may assume that the omission of the conjunction was indicated in the hexaplaric Septuagint.

Jerome dismisses the *coniunctio*, "conjunction," as "superfluous" (see introduction, §8.5). The conjunction (*et*) appears in most OL witnesses (Weber 340) and was included in the Sixto-Clementine Vulgate (Van Ess 118).

83.2.20. *'et' coniunctio*, "the conjunction 'and.'" See **25.1.5**.

84.1.21–22. *dissipata sunt ossa nostra secus infernum*, "Our bones were scattered by the side of the inferno." Ps 140:7 (Heb 141:7), GPsal. Several notable Greek witnesses contain the reading τὰ ὀστᾶ αὐτῶν, "their bones," namely, a correction in Codex Alexandrinus, MS 1219 Washington, MS 55 Rome, the Bohairic Coptic version, MS 2011 Cambridge, the Lucianic manuscripts, Theodoret's *Commentary**, and the Syro-Hexapla (Rahlfs 326). This was the text consulted by Sunnia and Fretela.

The Hebrew, however, reads עצמינו, "our bones." In agreement with the Hebrew are many LXX witnesses, the OL tradition (Sabatier 274; Weber 341; Amelli 98), and most if not all hexaplaric translations. That the hexaplaric versions had τὰ ὀστᾶ ἡμῶν, "our bones," is suggested by alternative renderings given without names in John Chrysostom (PG 55:440–41), the Syro-Hexapla, Eusebius of Caesarea, and other sources.[244] Moreover, Jerome says in his *Commentaries on the Psalms* that Symmachus translated *ossa nostra*, "our bones" (CC 72:244), and Didymus of Alexandria (in the tradition of Origen) cites Ps 140:7 with τὰ ὀστᾶ ἡμῶν, "our bones."[245] This Hebraic-hexaplaric and OL text is what Jerome followed in the Gallican

---

244. See Field 2:297; Mercati, *Alla ricerca dei nomi degli "Altri" traduttori*, 113–15.

245. Mühlenberg, *Psalmenkommentare aus der Katenenüberlieferung*, 2:337. Epiphanius (who preserves Methodius against Origen) likewise quotes the text with τὰ ὀστᾶ ἡμῶν, "our bones," in *Panarion* 64.15.6; see Karl Holl and Jürgen Dummer, eds.,

Psalter. Because the reading proposed by Sunnia and Fretela offers no improvement on the sense and has no basis in the best witnesses, Jerome dismisses it as "superfluous" (see introduction, §8.5).

85.1.1–2. *nec in tibiis viri bene placitum erit ei,* "Nor will he take pleasure in the legs of a man." Ps 146:10 (Heb 147:10), GPsal. The alternative text cited by Sunnia and Fretela arose from a peculiarity of Latin idiom and a textual confusion.

In Hebrew, this passage reads לא בשוקי האיש ירצה, "Not in the legs ("fibula," "shank") of man will he delight." This was translated straightforwardly into Greek as οὐδὲ ἐν ταῖς κνήμαις τοῦ ἀνδρὸς εὐδοκεῖ, "Nor in the legs ("shins") of man will he delight." In Latin, instead of the single verb ירצה, or εὐδοκεῖ, "he will delight," the future for this concept is expressed through the complex expression: *bene placitum erit,* "it will be well pleasing," which requires a dative to indicate the one to whom it will be pleasing, in this case *ei,* "to him." Thus, *bene placitum erit ei,* "it will be well pleasing to Him" or "He will take pleasure." This translation is found in many OL witnesses (Sabatier 283; Weber 353), and Jerome kept it in the Gallican Psalter to suit the requirements of Latin idiom.

However, Sunnia and Fretela did not object to the addition of *ei,* "to him." Rather, they claimed that the Greek has "Lord" instead of "him." The explanation for this can be found in the following verse (v. 11), which begins: εὐδοκεῖ κύριος, "The Lord will delight (in those who fear him)." Sunnia and Fretela, or their source, must have seen Jerome's *ei,* "to him," at the end of v. 10 (*bene placitum erit ei*), noticed the word *domino,* "to the Lord," at the start of v. 11 and mistakenly transferred *domino* in v. 11 back to the similar expression just before it in v. 10.

What was Jerome to say? Jerome might have explained that *domino* does not belong to v. 10 but to the following verse and that strictly speaking v. 10 in Greek does not have anything that corresponds to *ei,* even though this word is required by Latin idiom. But instead of this long and complicated explanation, Jerome merely states *quod non habetur,* "but it does not have this."

86.1.4. *in fine scedulae,* "at the end of your note." See *iuxta digestionem schedulae vestrae,* "following the arrangement set out in your note" at **2.1.17.** It is not clear whether Sunnia and Fretela asked about these spe-

---

Epiphanius, Zweiter Band. Panarion haer. 34–64, GCS 31 (Berlin: Akademie-Verlag, 1980), 425; see also Perrone, *Die neuen Psalmenhomilien,* 454 n. g.

cific words. It is unlikely that Avitus "frequently" demanded to know the meanings of the exact same Greek words that puzzled Sunnia and Fretela. Perhaps the two Goths concluded their note with a request for clarification on various Greek terms, and Jerome chose to discuss a few on which he thought he had something useful to say. If Avitus frequently asked Jerome about Greek words, he could say that he chose to address only those words that Avitus also mentioned. Jerome appeals to Avitus to justify writing projects at *Ep.* 79.1 and 124.1.

86.1.5. *sanctus filius meus Avitus,* "my holy brother Avitus." See **2.2.25.**

86.1.6. νεομηνία. In Hebrew, the adjective חדש (חָדָשׁ) means "new," and the noun חדש (חֹדֶשׁ) means "new moon," or simply "moon" in place of the earlier ירח, "moon."[246] In the LXX, חֹדֶשׁ is regularly translated μήν, "month" (HRCS 922), although it can also be rendered as νουμηνία, or else using the uncontracted form νεομηνία.[247] The uncontracted form (νεομηνία) does not appear in inscriptions or papyri before the second half of the second century, but it occurs in Col 2:16 and is well known in Christian literature (see also Philo, *Somn.* 2.257; otherwise, Philo uses the contracted form νουμηνία).[248] Jerome interprets the word according to its constituent elements, νεο-, "new," and μήνη (a poetic form of μήν), "moon," to make up νεομηνία, "new moon: the first of the month."[249]

The Greek loanword *neomenia* appears in Tertullian (e.g., *Idol.* 14; *Marc.* 1.20) and was used occasionally by Jerome (e.g., Ps 80:4, Gallican and IH). More often, however, Jerome employed the Latin word *kalendae*, "Kalends," that is, the first day of the month.[250] According to Varro, the Kalends (*kalendae*) received their name because on the first day of the month the *Nones* (i.e., the ninth day before the Ides) were "announced" (*calantur; Ling.* 6.27).

The question was put to Jerome: What is the meaning of νεομηνία? What probably stands behind this question is the fact that Jerome typi-

---

246. *HALOT*, s.v. "ירח."

247. For νουμηνία, see e.g., Exod 40:2, 17; Num 10:10; 29:6; 1 Sam 20:18; 2 Chr. 2:3; 29:17; 31:3; Ezra 3:5; Neh 10:34; Hos 2:13; Isa 1:13–14; Ezek 45:17; 46:1, 3, 6. For νεομηνία, see Num 28:11; 1 Sam 20:5; 2 Kgs 4:23; 1 Chr 23:31; Ps 80:4; Ezek 23:34.

248. BDAG, s.v. "νεομηνία"; "νουμηνία."

249. LSJ, s.v. "μήνη"; "νεομηνία."

250. E.g., Num 10:10; 28:11; 29:6; 1 Sam 20:5, 18, 24, 27, 34; 2 Kgs 4:23; 1 Chr 23:31; 2 Chr 8:13; 31:3; Ezra 3:5; Neh 10:33; Isa 1:14; Ezek 45:17; 46:1, 3, 6; see LD, s.v. "kalendae."

cally employs a cultural translation into Latin by using *kalendae* rather than using the form closer to the Greek: *neomenia*. In his explanation, Jerome shows that he understands the linguistic and conceptual basis for the underlying Hebrew and Greek words.

86.1.7. *secundum Latinae linguae proprietatem,* "according to the particular idiom of the Latin language." In addition to showing his knowledge of how the Hebrews calculate months and what the Greek word νεομηνία means, Jerome also offers a defense for his regular use of the Latin *kalendae* for this word. To be sure, *kalendae* is not a literal rendering of the underlying Hebrew custom or Greek word, but it represents a translation of the correct meaning into the "particular idiom" (*proprietas*) of the Latin language. In Jerome's eyes, this is a commendable method of translation (see introduction, §7.2).

86.2.10. ἔρημος. This Greek word means "desolate, lonely, solitary" and is used in the LXX with the sense "uninhabited desolate land, wilderness."[251] Jerome identifies it as meaning either *desertum*, "desert," or *solitudo*, "solitude." These are the two words employed in the OL according to Codex Sangermanensis to translate ἔρημος: *desertus* (Pss 28:8; 62:1, 2; 64:13; 67:8; 74:7; 77:15, 19, 40, 52; 94:8; 105:9, 14, 26; 106:33, 35; 135:16) and *solitudo* (Pss 28:8; 54:8; 106:40). In the Gallican Psalter, Jerome employs these two words: primarily *desertus* but twice *solitudo* (Pss 54:8; 106:4) and also once *heremo* (Ps 77:15). In the IH Psalter, he relies primarily on *desertus*, also using *solitudo* (Pss 74:7; 77:19; 106:4) and *invius* (Ps 62:2).

86.2.11. The two Latin equivalents Jerome suggests for θρόνος are *sedes*, "seat," and *solium*, "throne." In the OL according to Codex Sangermanensis, the standard rendering is *sedes* (Pss 9:8; 10:4; 44:7; 46:9; 88:5, 15, 30, 37, 45; 92:2; 93:20; 96:2; 102:19; 121:5; 121:5; 131:11, 12). In one passage, Ps 9:5, the Latin word *thronus* is found. Both words are also found in the Gallican Psalter: *sedes* in Pss 10:4; 44:7; 46:9; 88:5, 15, 45; 92:2; 93:20; 96:2; 102:19; 121:5; 131:11, 12 and *thronus* in Pss 9:5, 8; 88:30, 37. The noun *solium*, "throne," is not used for θρόνος in the Gallican Psalter.

Jerome's mention of *solium* as a translation for θρόνος in *Ep.* 106 is therefore something of a surprise. Perhaps as Jerome reflected on this question and came up with a response, it occurred to him that *solium* is another way to express the meaning of θρόνος in Latin, a way that had not been used in the OL tradition. In the IH Psalter, Jerome does make use of *solium* (Pss

---

251. LSJ, s.v. "ἔρημος"; GELS, s.v. "ἔρημος."

9:5, 8; 92:2; 96:2) alongside *sedes* (Pss 121:5; 131:11) and *thronus* (Pss 10:4; 44:7; 46:9; 88:5, 15, 30, 37, 45; 93:20; 102:19; 131:12).

86.2.11. νυκτικόραξ. Jerome discussed this word in detail earlier (*ut diximus*, "as we said"). See **63.2**.

86.2.12. κυνόμυια. This is the Greek word used in the LXX to describe what God sends against the Egyptians as the fourth plague in the book of Exodus; see Exod 8:17, 18, 20, 25, 27; Pss 77:45 (Heb 78:45); 104:31 (Heb 105:31). The spelling κυνόμυια is a later form of κυνάμυια, "dog-fly."[252] The underlying Hebrew is ערב (MT: עָרֹב), the original meaning of which is uncertain.[253] Like the LXX, Philo employs the word κυνόμυια, "dog-fly," for this plague (*Mos.* 1.130–131, 133, 145).

Many ancient sources, however, interpret the Hebrew as if it were related to ערב II, "be mixed with" (cf. Aramaic עָרֵב).[254] In Midrash Tanhuma, it is suggested that God sent חיות מערבבות, "beasts mixed together," such as lions and bears (Tan., Va'era, 14).[255] According to Exod. Rab. 11.2, the fourth plague consisted of חיות ועפות מערבבין, "beasts and birds mixed together."[256] Midrash on Psalms 78.11 reports various views whereby God sent a mixture of beasts including lions, bears, wolves, and leopards, and possibly birds of prey as well (cf. also Tg. Ps.-J. on Exod. 8:17). Interpretations such as these served as the basis for Josephus's statement that God plagued the Egyptians with beasts of all sorts and many kinds (θηρίων … παντοίων καὶ πολυτρόπων; A.J. 14.303). The same tradition probably underlies the description of God's punishment against Egypt in Wis 11:15–19.

The interpretation of ערב as "be mixed with" can be seen in Aquila's translation reported by Jerome: πάμμικτον, "all mixed" (Field 2:227, 261).[257] Jerome interprets this through the lens of the LXX, κυνόμυια, "dog-fly," so he translates Aquila as *omnimodam muscam*, "fly of every kind."

86.2.14. *per* δίφθογγον … οι. "with the diphthong οι." The term δίφθογγος, an utterance "composed of two sounds" (δίς, φθόγγος), was employed by

---

252. LSJ, s.v. "κυνάμυια."

253. *HALOT*, s.v. "ערב."

254. *HALOT*, s.v. "ערב II"; Jastrow, s.v. "ערב."

255. Avrohom Davis, trans. and annotated, *The Metsudah Midrash Tanchuma: Shemos I*, ed. Yaakov Y. H. Pupko (Monsey, NY: Eastern Book, 2004), 158–59.

256. Mosheh A. Mirkin, *Midrash Rabbah*, 11 vols. (Tel-Aviv: Yavneh, 1992), 5:138.

257. At Exod 8:17, the Syro-Hexapla reports Aquila as ḥlwṭ', "mixed" and Theodotion as ḥlṭ', "mixture" (Field 1:94). The same equivalents are given at Ps 77:45, although here Ceriani suggests that for Aquila there is visible an earlier reading: kl ḥlwṭ', "all mixed," i.e., πάμμικτον; see Ceriani, *Codex Syro-Hexaplaris Ambrosianus*, 30.

Greek grammarians in antiquity.[258] Six letter combinations were recognized as diphthongs in the Τέχνη γραμματική traditionally ascribed to Dionysius Thrax: αι, αυ, ει, ευ, οι, ου.[259] In Donatus's *Ars grammatica*, it is said that a *diphthongus* in Latin is made when two vowels are joined (*duae vocales iunguntur*), such as *ae, oe, au, eu, ei*.[260] In *Ep.* 106 Jerome makes reference to the Greek diphthong οι. On Jerome's training in technical grammar and use of grammatical terminology, see **8.2.1**.

86.3.16. λαξευτήριον. This word refers to a stonecutter's tool.[261] It is derived from the verb λαξεύω, "to hew in stone." The OL translated it as *ascia*, "axe, hatchet" (Sabatier 149; Weber 173). Jerome likewise used *ascia* in the Gallican Psalter. When Jerome says *Latinus 'asciam' vertit*, "the Latin rendered 'hatchet,'" he is referring both to the OL and to his own Latin version. In fact, the Gallican Psalter is nearly identical with the OL as witnessed by Codex Sangermanensis, the only exceptions being Jerome's *securi*, "axe," for OL's *bipenni*, "(double-edged) axe" (for the Greek πελέκει), and at the end of the verse Jerome's *eam*, "it," in place of OL's *ea*, "them." In all probability, the hexaplaric LXX was close to the popular LXX text for this verse, so in the Gallican Psalter Jerome stayed close to the OL tradition. The reason why Jerome says "the Latin (tradition) rendered" rather than "I rendered" is that he is about to give an alternative translation to represent the Hebrew that differs considerably from this, and he wishes to downplay the gap between the Gallican Psalter (and the hexaplaric LXX), on the one hand, and the Hebrew, on the other.

86.3.18. *denique ex Hebraeo vertentes ita diximus*, "So, translating from the Hebrew we said thus." Ps 73:6 (Heb 74:6). The translation *ex Hebraeo* in *Ep.* 106 matches what Jerome gives in his IH Psalter. It is instructive to compare this rendering with the only preserved hexaplaric version, Symmachus: νῦν δὲ καὶ τὰς πύλας αὐτῆς ὁμοῦ ἐν μοχλοῖς καὶ δικράνοις κατέρριψαν, "And now they threw down its gates with bars and pitchforks" (Field 2:217). Jerome's rendering *ex Hebraeo* is similar to Symmachus in overall structure: *et nunc sculpturas eius pariter bipinne et dolatoriis deraserunt*, "And now they have together cut down its carved works

---

258. Montanari, *The Brill Dictionary of Ancient Greek*, 540.

259. Δίφθογγοι δὲ εἰσιν ἕξ: αι αυ ει ευ οι ου. See Jean Lallot, *La grammaire de Denys le Thrace*, 2nd ed., Collection sciences du langage (Paris: CNRS, 1998), 44, 100–101.

260. Keil, *Grammatici Latini*, 4:368.

261. LSJ, s.v. "λαξευτήριον."

with axe and hewers."[262] But Jerome gives *deraserunt*, "cut down," instead of Symmachus's κατέρριψαν, "threw down" (for הלם, "strike, beat"); translates *sculpturas*, "carved works," instead of Symmachus's πύλας, "gates" (for פתוח, from "opening" or "engrave"); and handles the tools differently, giving *bipinne*, "axe," and *dolatoriis*, "hewers" (like the LXX), instead of Symmachus's μοχλοῖς, "bars," and δικράνοις, "pitchforks" (for כשיל and בילפת, neither clear in meaning). We might suppose that the other hexaplaric versions (e.g., Aquila or Quinta) also influenced Jerome's *ex Hebraeo* rendering (e.g., for *deraserunt*, "cut down," and *sculpturas*, "carved works"). Perhaps Jerome is following another hexaplaric version verbatim. But he may also be picking and choosing among them for each word, consulting the Hebrew text as his guide.

In this final discussion, Jerome seems to be operating with a *hebraica veritas* mindset that has moved beyond the notion expressed earlier in *Ep.* 106 that faithfulness to the hexaplaric LXX constitutes conformity to the Hebrew (**2.2–4**). There have been instances in *Ep.* 106 where Jerome's Hebrew-based rendering matches his IH Psalter (**31.2**; **49.1**; **75.7**; **75.8**). Here Jerome says *ex Hebraeo vertentes ita diximus*, "translating from the Hebrew, we *said* thus" (*diximus*, past tense). Does this mean that Jerome had already translated the IH Psalter prior to his composing *Ep.* 106? I do not think this is likely (see introduction, §6.2). Several Hebrew-based translations in *Ep.* 106 disagree with the IH Psalter, and many discussions in this treatise run counter to what Jerome does in the IH Psalter.[263] Furthermore, Jerome's confident and unqualified assertion at **2.2–4** about the agreement between the hexaplaric LXX and the Hebrew is incongruent with what Jerome would have known if the IH Psalter were already finished. I think it is likely, therefore, that in the course of composing *Ep.* 106, Jerome began making translations of individual passages in the Psalter that were truly grounded in the Hebrew in response to his growing awareness that the hexaplaric LXX Psalter was not sufficient for a proper return to the Hebrew.

---

262. This may be contrasted with the Gallican Psalter: *exciderunt ianuas eius in id ipsum in securi et ascia deiecerunt eam*, "They chopped down its gates, together, with hatchet and cleaver they felled it."

263. For disagreements between *Ep.* 106 and the IH Psalter, see **9.6.24**; **26.2.18–19**; **33.2.19–20**; **35.2.15**; **38.1.56**; **41.6.7–8**; **63.2.8–9**; **65.5.13**; **81.1.4–6**. For discussions in *Ep.* 106 running counter to Jerome's IH Psalter, see, e.g., **23.2.15**; **29.2.3**; **33.1.13–14**; **37.1.21**; **45.1.11**; **47.1.25–26**; **48.2.3–4**; **49.3.2**; **50.5.2–3**; **50.6b.14–15**; **50.7.23–24**; **53.1.12–13**; **54.1.17–18**; **66.1.6**; **73.2.3–4**.

Why does Jerome say *ita diximus*, "we said thus," in relation to his translation *ex hebraeo*? I think it is probable that, by the end of composing this letter, he had designs to translate the entire Psalter based on the Hebrew and had already made a formal start. But this does not mean that he had finished the IH Psalter, let alone the whole IH edition. As an analogy, consider how Jerome talks about his hexaplaric revision at **2.2** as if it were complete ("which I faithfully translated into the Latin language"), when at the time he wrote *Ep.* 106 he certainly had not translated the entire hexaplaric LXX (see introduction, §2.2 n. 15). Jerome also spoke as if he had finished translating the entire New Testament (e.g., "I translated the New Testament faithfully from the Greek," *Vir. ill.* 135, 393 CE), when he had not.[264] Once he set his mind to a task with intent to finish, the task seems to have reached completion in his mind before it did in reality. I do not, therefore, think we can take Jerome's wording in *Ep.* 106.86.3, "translating from the Hebrew, we said thus," as evidence that he had finished the IH edition.

---

264. See also *Ep.* 71.5; 112.20. It is unclear whether Jerome ever finished translating the New Testament. He wrote no prefaces for New Testament books besides the gospels, he does not cite the New Testament according to the preserved Vulgate text, and the Latin New Testament outside the gospels does not necessarily fit his style. On the origins of the Vulgate New Testament, see Bogaert, "The Latin Bible," 517–18; Bruce M. Metzger, *The Early Version of the New Testament* (Oxford: Clarendon, 1977), 356–62; and Kurt Aland, *Die alten Übersetzungen des Neuen Testaments, Die Kirchenväterzitate und Lektionare* (Berlin: de Gruyter, 1972), 116–19.

BIBLIOGRAPHY

Editions and Translations of *Epistle* 106

Cola, Silvano. *San Girolamo. Le Lettere.* Vol. 3. Rome: Città Nuova, 1997.
Gasquet, Francis Aidan. *Liber Psalmorum ex recensione sancti Hieronymi cum praefationibus et Epistula ad Sunniam et Fretelam.* Vol. 10 of *Biblia Sacra iuxta latinam vulgatam versionem ad codicum fidem.* Rome: Libreria Editrice Vaticana, 1953.
Hilberg, Isidorus. *Epistulae LXXI–CXX.* Vol. 2 of *Sancti Eusebii Hieronymi Epistulae.* CSEL 55. Vienna: Verlag der Österreichischen Akademie der Wissenschaften, 1996.
Labourt, Jérôme. *Saint Jérôme Lettres.* Vol. 5. Collection des Universités de France. Paris: Les Belles Lettres, 1955.

Biblical Texts

Amelli, Ambrogio M., ed. *Liber Psalmorum iuxta antiquissimam latinam versionem nunc primum ex Casinensi cod. 557.* Collectanea Biblica Latina 1. Rome: Pustet, 1912.
Brooke, Alan E., Norman McLean, and Henry St. J. Thackeray, eds. *The Old Testament in Greek according to the Text of Codex Vaticanus.* 9 vols. Cambridge: Cambridge University Press, 1906–1940.
Ceriani, Antonio M. *Codex Syro-Hexaplaris Ambrosianus: Photolithographice editus.* 1874. Repr., Piscataway, NJ: Gorgias, 2013.
Field, Frederick. *Origenis Hexaplorum Quae Supersunt: Sive Veterum Interpretum Graecorum in Totum Vetus Testamentum Fragmenta.* 2 vols. Oxford: Clarendon, 1875.
Fischer, Bonifatius, ed. Genesis. VL 2. Freiburg: Herder, 1951.
Gryson, Roger, ed. *Altlateinische Handschriften/Manuscrits vieux latins, Première partie: Mss 1–275.* VL 1/2A. Freiburg: Herder, 1999.

————, ed. *Altlateinische Handschriften/Manuscrits vieux latins, Deuxième partie: Mss 300–485.* VL 1/2B. Freiburg: Herder, 2004.

————, ed. *Esaias 1–39.* VL 12.1. Freiburg: Herder, 1987–1993.

Holmes, Robert, and James Parsons, eds. *Vetus Testamentum Graecum cum Variis Lectionibus.* Vol. 3. Oxford: Clarendon, 1823.

Mercati, Giovanni. *Psalterii Hexapli Reliquiae, Pars Prima: Codex Rescriptus Bybliothecae Ambrosianae O 39 SVP.* Rome: Vatican Library, 1958.

————. *Psalterii Hexapli Reliquiae, Pars Prima: 'Osservazioni,' Commento Critico al Testo dei Frammenti Esaplari.* Rome: Vatican Library, 1965.

Ofer, Yosef, and Mordechai Glatzer, eds. *Jerusalem Crown: The Bible of the Hebrew University of Jerusalem.* 2nd ed. Jerusalem: N. Ben-Zvi, 2004.

Peshiṭta Institute. *The Book of Psalms.* Part 2, fasc. 3 of *The Old Testament in Syriac according to the Peshiṭta Version.* Leiden: Brill, 1980.

Rahlfs, Alfred. *Psalmi cum Odis.* 3rd ed. SVTG 10. Göttingen: Vandenhoeck & Ruprecht, 1979.

Sabatier, Pierre. *Bibliorum Sacrorum Latinae Versiones Antiquae, seu Vetus Italica.* Vol. 2. Paris: Apud Franciscum Didot, 1751.

Sainte-Marie, Henri de. *Sancti-Hieronymi Psalterium iuxta Hebraeos.* Collectanea Biblica Latina 11. Rome: Abbaye Saint-Jérôme, 1954.

Schenker, Adrian. *Hexaplarische Psalmenbruchstücke: Die hexaplarischen Psalmenfragmente der Handschriften Vaticanus graecus 752 und Canonicianus graecus 62.* OBO 8. Göttingen: Vandenhoeck & Ruprecht, 1975.

————. *Psalmen in den Hexapla: Erste kritische und vollständige Ausgabe der hexaplarischen Fragmente auf dem Rande der Handschrift Ottobonianus Graecus 398 zu den Ps 24–32.* StT 295. Vatican City: Biblioteca Apostolica Vaticana, 1982.

Weber, Robert. *Le Psautier Romain et les autres anciens psautiers latins.* Collectanea Biblica Latina 10. Rome: Abbaye Saint-Jérôme, 1953.

Weber, Robert, and Roger Gryson, eds. *Biblia Sacra iuxta vulgatam versionem.* 5th ed. Stuttgart: Deutsche Bibelgesellschaft, 2007.

White, Emanuel. "A Critical Edition of the Targum of Psalms: A Computer Generated Text of Books I and II." PhD diss., McGill University, 1988.

Patristic Works

Ambrose

Adriaen, Marcus, ed. *Sancti Ambrosii Mediolanensis Opera, Pars IV. Expositio Evangelii Secundum Lucam. Fragmenta in Esaiam.* CC 14. Turnhout: Brepols, 1957.
Faller, Otto, ed. *Sancti Ambrosii Opera, Pars Octava. De Fide [Ad Gratianum Augustum].* CSEL 78. Vienna: Hölder-Pichler-Tempsky, 1962.
Sancti Ambrosii Mediolanensis Episcopi Opera Omnia: Enarrationes in XII Psalmos Davidicos. PG 14:921–1180.
Schenkl, Karl, ed. *Sancti Ambrosii Opera, Pars Altera.* CSEL 32. Vienna: Tempsky, 1897.

Pseudo-Ambrose

Sancti Ambrosii Mediolanensis Episcopi Opera Omnia: De Lapsu Virginis Consecratae Liber Unus. PG 16:367–84.

Ambrosiaster

Souter, Alexander, ed. *Pseudo-Augustini: Quaestiones Veteris et Novi Testamenti CXXVII.* CSEL 50. Vienna: Tempsky, 1908.

Augustine

Dekkers, Eligius, and Jean Fraipont, eds. *Sancti Aurelii Augustini Opera, Pars 10, 1. Enarrationes in Psalmos I–L.* CC 38. Turnhout: Brepols, 1956.
———, eds. *Sancti Aurelii Augustini Opera, Pars 10, 2. Enarrationes in Psalmos LI–C.* CC 39. Turnhout: Brepols, 1956.
Dombart, Bernhard, and Alphonse Kalb, eds. *Aurelii Augustini Opera, Pars 14, 2: De Civitate Dei Libri XI–XXII.* CC 48. Turnhout: Brepols, 1955.
Fraipont, Jean, ed. *Sancti Aurelii Augustini. Locutiones in Heptateuchum Libri VII.* CC 33. Turnhout: Brepols, 1958 .
Gori, Franco, ed. *Augustinus. Enarrationes in Psalmos 101–150, Pars 2: Enarrationes in Psalmos 110–118.* CSEL 95.2. Berlin: de Gruyter, 2015.

Gori, Franco, and Claudio Pierantoni, eds. *Sancti Augustini Opera. Enarrationes in Psalmos 101–150, Pars 1: Enarrationes in Psalmos 101–109.* CSEL 95.1. Vienna: Österreichischen Akademie der Wissenschaften, 2011.

Gori, Franco, and Francisca Recanatini, eds. *Sancti Augustini Opera. Enarrationes in Psalmos 101–150, Pars 4: Enarrationes in Psalmos 134–140.* CSEL 95.4. Vienna: Österreichischen Akademie der Wissenschaften, 2002.

Müller, Hildegund, ed. *Sancti Augustini Opera. Enarrationes in Psalmos 51–100, Pars 1: Enarrationes in Psalmos.* CSEL 94.1. Vienna: Österreichischen Akademie der Wissenschaften, 2004.

Cassiodorus

Adriaen, Marcus, ed. *Magni Aurelii Cassiodori Senatoris Opera, Pars 2, 1. Expositio Psalmorum I–XX.* CC 97. Turhout: Brepols, 1958.

———, ed. *Magni Aurelii Cassiodori Senatoris Opera, Pars 2, 2. Expositio Psalmorum LXXI–CL.* CC 98. Turhout: Brepols, 1958.

Catenae

Curti, Carmelo. *La Catena Palestinese sui Salmi Graduali.* Catania: Centro Di Studi Sull'Antico Cristianesimo, 2003.

Harl, Marguerite, and Gilles Dorival. *La chaîne palestinienne sur le Psaume 118.* 2 vols. SC 189–190. Paris: Cerf, 1972.

Mühlenberg, Ekkehard. *Psalmenkommentare aus der Katenenüberlieferung.* 2 vols. PTS 15–16. Berlin: de Gruyter, 1975–1977.

Chromatius of Aquileia

Étaix, Raymond, and Joseph Lemarié, eds. *Chromatii Aquileiensis Opera.* CC 9A. Turnhout: Brepols, 1974.

Commodian

Martin, Joseph, ed. *Commodianus. Claudius Marius Victorius. Commodiani Instructionum.* CC 128. Turnhout: Brepols, 1960.

Cyprian

Weber, Robert, ed. *Sancti Cypriani Episcopi Opera: Ad Quirinum*. CC 3. Turnhout: Brepols, 1972.

Didymus of Alexandria

Blumell, Lincoln H., Thomas W. Mackay, and Gregg W Schwendner, eds. *Didymus the Blind's Commentary on Psalms 26:10–29:2 and 36:1–3*. P.BYU 1. Turnhout: Brepols, 2019.

Epiphanius

Holl, Karl, and Jürgen Dummer, eds. *Epiphanius, Zweiter Band. Panarion haer. 34–64*. GCS 31. Berlin: Akademie-Verlag, 1980.

Eusebius of Caesarea

Curti, Carmelo. *Eusebiana I: Commentarii in Psalmos*. 2nd ed. Catania: Centro Di Studi Sull'Antico Cristianesmo, 1989.
Eusebii Pamphili Opera Omnia Quae Exstant: Commentaria in Psalmos. PG 23:66–1396; 24:9–76.

Faustus and Marcellinus

Günther, Otto, ed. *Gregorius. Iliberritanus. Faustinus Luciferianus: Marcellinus et Faustinus Presbyteri, De Confessione Verae Fidei*. CC 69. Turnhout: Brepols, 1967.

Hilary of Poitiers

Doignon, Jean, ed. *Sancti Hilarii Pictaviensis Episcopi Opera, Pars 1, 1. Tractatus Super Psalmos, Instructio Psalmorum in Psalmos I–XCI*. CC 61. Turnhout: Brepols, 1997.
———, ed. *Sancti Hilarii Pictaviensis Episcopi Opera, Pars 1, 2. Tractatus Super Psalmos, In Psalmum CXVIII*. CC 61A. Turnhout: Brepols, 2002.
———, ed. *Sancti Hilarii Pictaviensis Episcopi Opera, Pars 1, 3. Tractatus Super Psalmos, In Psalmos CXIX–CL*. CC 61B. Turnhout: Brepols, 2009.

Irenaeus

Rousseau, Adelin, ed. *Irénée de Lyon: Contre les Hérésies, Vol. 2.* SC 100. Paris: Cerf, 2008.

Jerome

Adriaen, Marcus, ed. *S. Hieronymi Presbyteri Opera, Pars I: Opera Exegetica VI. Commentarii in Prophetas Minores.* CC 76. Turnhout: Brepols, 1969.

———, ed. *Commentariorum in Esaiam libri I–XI.* CC 73. Turnhout: Brepols, 1963.

Canellis, Aline, ed. *Jérôme: Préfaces aux livres de la Bible.* SC 592. Paris: Cerf, 2017.

Glorie, Franciscus., ed. *S. Hieronymi Presbyteri Opera, Pars I: Opera Exegetica IV. Commentariorum in Hiezechielem Libri XIV.* CC 75. Turnhout: Brepols, 1964.

Gryson, Roger, ed. *Commentaire de Jérôme sur le Prophète Isaïe, Livres I–IV.* Freiburg: Herder, 1993.

Hilberg, Isidorus, ed. *Epistulae I–LXX.* Vol. 1 of *Sancti Eusebii Hieronymi Epistulae.* CSEL 54. Vienna: Österreichischen Akademie der Wissenschaften, 1996.

———, ed. *Epistulae LXXI–CXX.* Vol. 2 of *Sancti Eusebii Hieronymi Epistulae:* CSEL 55. Vienna: Österreichischen Akademie der Wissenschaften, 1996.

———, ed. *Epistulae CXXI–CLIV.* Vol. 3 of *Sancti Eusebii Hieronymi Epistulae.* CSEL 56.1. Vienna: Österreichischen Akademie der Wissenschaften, 1996.

Hurst, David, and Marcus Adriaen, eds. *S. Hieronymi Presbyteri Opera, Pars I: Opera Exegetica VII. Commentariorum in Matheum Libri IV.* CC 77. Turnhout: Brepols, 1969.

Lagarde, Paul de, ed. *S. Hieronymi Presbyteri Opera, Pars I: Opera Exegetica I. Liber Interpretationis Hebraicorum Nominum.* CC 72. Turnhout: Brepols, 1959.

Lardet, Pierre, ed. *S. Hieronymi Presbyteri Opera, Pars III: Opera Polemica I. Contra Rufinum.* CC 79. Turnhout: Brepols, 1982.

Morin, Germain, ed. *S. Hieronymi Presbyteri Opera, Pars 2. Opera Homiletica.* CC 78. Turnhout: Brepols, 1958.

Raspanti, Giacomo, ed. *S. Hieronymi Presbyteri Opera, Pars 1. Opera Exegetica 6. Commentarii in Epistulam Pauli Apostoli ad Galatas.* CC 77A. Turnhout: Brepols, 2006.

Risse, Siegfried, trans. and intro. *Hieronymus. Commentarioli in Psalmos: Anmerkungen zum Psalter.* Fontes Christiani 79. Turnhout: Brepols, 2005.

John Chrysostom

Sancti Patris Nostri Joannis Chrysostomi Opera Omnia Quae Exstant: Expositio in Psalmos. PG 55:35–528.

Lucifer of Cagliari

Diercks, G. F., ed. *De non parcendo in deum delinquentibus.* CC 8. Turnhout: Brepols, 1978.

Optatus of Milevis

Labrousse, Mireille, ed. *Optat de Milève. Traité contre les Donatistes, Vol. 1.* SC 412. Paris: Cerf, 1995.

Origen

Cadiou, René. *Commentaires inédits des Psaumes: Études sur les textes d'Origène contenus dans le manuscript* Vindobonensis 8. Collection d'études anciennes. Paris: Les Belles Lettres, 1936.

Origenis Opera Omnia: Selecta in Psalmos. PG 12:1053–1686.

Origenis Opera Omnia: Excerpta in Psalmos. PG 17:105–50.

Perrone, Lorenzo, ed. *Origenes Werke, Dreizehnter Band. Die neuen Psalmenhomilien. Eine kritische Edition des Codex Monacensis Graecus 314.* GCS 19. Berlin: de Gruyter, 2015.

Prosper of Aquitaine

Callens, P. ed. *Prosperi Aquitani Opera, Pars 2. Expositio Psalmorum. Liber Sententiarum.* CC 68A. Turnhout: Brepols, 1972.

Tertullian

Braun, René, ed. *Tertullien: Contre Marcion, Vol. 3.* SC 399. Paris: Cerf, 1994.

———, ed. *Tertullien: Contre Marcion, Vol. 4.* SC 456. Paris: Cerf, 2001.

Reifferscheid, August, and Georg Wissowa, eds. *Quinti Septimi Florentis Tertuliani Opera, Pars II: Opera Montanistica. De Ieiunio Adversus Psychicos.* CC 2. Turnhout: Brepols, 1954.

Theodore of Mopsuestia

Hill, Robert C., trans. *Theodore of Mopsuestia: Commentary on Psalms 1–81.* WGRW 5. Atlanta: Society of Biblical Literature, 2006.

Theodoret of Cyrus

Theodoreti Cyrensis Episcopi Opera Omnia: Interpretatio in Psalmos. PG 80:857–1997.

Other Resources and Studies

Abel, F.-M. "Parallélisme exégétique entre S. Jérôme et S. Cyrille d'Alexandrie." *Vivre et Penser* 1 (1941): 94–119, 212–30.

Adkin, Neil. "*Biblia Pagana:* Classical Echoes in the Vulgate." *Aug* 40 (2000): 77–88.

Aitkin, James K. "Psalms." Pages 320–34 in *The T&T Clark Companion to the Septuagint.* Edited by James K. Aitkin. London: Bloomsbury T&T Clark, 2015.

Aland, Kurt. *Die alten Übersetzungen des Neuen Testaments, Die Kirchenväterzitate und Lektionare.* Berlin: de Gruyter, 1972.

Allgeier, Arthur. "Der Brief an Sunnia und Fretela und seine Bedeutung für die Textherstellung der Vulgata." *Bib* 11 (1930): 86–107.

Altaner, Berthold. "Wann Schrieb Hieronymus Seine Ep. 106 Ad Sunniam et Fretelam De Psalterio?" *VC* 4 (1950): 246–48.

Alter, Robert. *The Art of Biblical Poetry.* New York: Basic Books, 1985.

Anderson, R. Dean, Jr.. *Glossary of Greek Rhetorical Terms.* Leuven: Peeters, 2000.

Arns, Paulo E. *La technique du livre d'après saint Jérôme.* Paris: Boccard, 1953.

Bady, Guillaume. "La 'vérité hébraïque' ou la 'vérité des Hexaples' chez Jérôme d'après un passage de la *Lettre 106*." Pages 91–99 in *L'exégèse de saint Jérôme*. Edited by Élie Ayroulet and Aline Canellis. Saint-Étienne: Publications de l'Université de Saint-Étienne, 2018.

Bailey, D. R. Shackleton, ed. and trans. *Cicero: Letters to Atticus, Volume 2*. LCL 8. Cambridge: Harvard University Press, 1999.

Barsby, John, ed. and trans. *Terence: Phormio. The Mother-in-Law. The Brothers*. LCL 23; Cambridge: Harvard University Press, 2001.

Bartelink, G. J. M. *Hieronymus: Liber de optimo genere interpretandi (Epistula 57). Ein Kommentar*. Leiden: Brill, 1980.

Barthélemy, Jean-Dominique. "Quinta ou Version selon les Hébreux?" *TZ* 16 (1960): 342–53.

Blaise, Albert. *A Handbook of Christian Latin: Style, Morphology, and Syntax*. Translated by Grant C. Roti. Washington, DC: Georgetown University Press, 1994.

Bogaert, Pierre-Maurice. "Les bibles d'Augustin." *RTL* 37 (2006): 513–31.

———. "The Latin Bible." Pages 505–26 in *The New Cambridge History of the Bible, Volume 1: From the Beginnings to 600*. Edited by James C. Paget and Joachim Schaper. Cambridge: CUP, 2013.

———. "Le psautier latin des origines au XIIe siècle. Essai d'histoire." Pages 51–81 in *Der Septuaginta-Psalter und seine Tochterübersetzungen*. Edited by Anneli Aejmelaeus and Udo Quast. Göttingen: Vandenhoeck & Ruprecht, 2000.

Bons, Eberhard, and Ralph Brucker. "Psalmoi/The Book of Psalms." Pages 297–316 in *Introduction to the Septuagint*. Edited by Siegfried Kreuzer. Translated by David A. Brenner and Peter Altmann. Waco, TX: Baylor University Press, 2019.

Boyd-Taylor, Cameron, Peter C. Austin, and Andrey Feuerverger. "The Assessment of Manuscript Affiliation within a Probabilistic Framework: A Study of Alfred Rahlfs's Core Manuscript Groupings for the Greek Psalter." Pages 98–124 in *The Old Greek Psalter: Studies in Honor of Albert Pietersma*. Edited by Robert J. V. Hiebert, Claude E. Cox, and Peter J. Gentry. Sheffield: Sheffield Academic, 2001.

Bredow, Iris von. "Getae." Pages 842–43 in *Brill's New Pauly: Encyclopaedia of the Ancient World*. Edited by Hubert Cancik and Helmuth Schneider. Leiden: Brill, 2004.

Burton-Christie, Douglas. *The Word in the Desert: Scripture and the Quest for Holiness in Early Christian Monasticism*. New York: Oxford University Press, 1993.

Cain, Andrew. "Apology and Polemic in Jerome's Prefaces to his Biblical Scholarship." Pages 107–28 in *Hieronymus als Exeget und Theologe: Interdisziplinäre Zugänge zum Koheletkommentar des Hieronymus.* Edited by Elisabeth Birnbaum and Ludger Schwienhorst-Schönberger. Leuven: Peeters, 2014.

———. *The Letters of Jerome: Asceticism, Biblical Exegesis, and the Construction of Christian Authority in Late Antiquity.* OECS. Oxford: Oxford University Press, 2009.

Caloz, Masséo. *Étude sur la LXX origénienne du Psautier.* OBO 19. Fribourg: Éditions universitaires; Göttingen: Vandenhoeck & Ruprecht, 1978.

Cañas Reíllo, José M. "Psalms 10.4.1 Vetus Latina." Pages 115–19 in *Writings.* Vol. 1C of *Textual History of the Bible: The Hebrew Bible.* Edited by Armin Lange. Leiden: Brill, 2017.

Cavallera, Ferdinand. *Saint Jérôme: Sa vie et son œuvre.* 2 vols. Paris: Champion, 1922.

Ceulemans, Reinhart. "Theodoret and the Antiochene Text of the Psalms." Pages 149–64 in *XV Congress of the International Organization for Septuagint and Cognate Studies. Munich 2013.* Edited by Wolfgang Kraus, Michaël N. van der Meer, and Martin Meiser. SCS 64. Atlanta: SBL Press, 2016.

Clarke, Emma C., John M. Dillon, and Jackson P. Hershbell, eds. *Iamblichus: De mysteriis.* WGRW 4. Atlanta: Society of Biblical Literature, 2003.

Courcelle, Pierre P. *Late Latin Writers and their Greek Sources.* Translated by Harry E. Wedeck. Cambridge: Harvard University Press, 1969.

Curti, Carmelo, and Maria A. Barbàra. "Greek Exegetical Catenae." Page 605–54 in *Patrology: The Eastern Fathers from the Council of Chalcedon (451) to John of Damascus (†750).* Edited by Angelo Di Berardino. Translated by Adrian Walford. Cambridge: James Clarke, 2006.

Davis, Avrohom, trans. and annotated. *The Metsudah Midrash Tanchuma: Shemos I.* Edited by Yaakov Y. H. Pupko. Monsey, NY: Eastern Book, 2004.

De Bruyne, Donatien. "La lettre de Jérôme à Sunnia et Fretela sur le Psautier." *ZNW* 28 (1929): 1–13.

———. "Notes sur le psautier de saint Augustin." *RBén* 45 (1933): 20–28.

———. "La Reconstitution de psautier hexaplaire latin." *RBén* 41 (1929): 297–324.

————. *Saint Augustin: Reviseur de la Bible*. Rome: Tipografia Poliglotta Vaticana, 1931.

Deléani, Simone. "Un emprunt d'Augustin à l'Écriture: 'Redite, praevaricatores, ad cor' (Isaïe 46, 8b)." *REAug* 38 (1992): 29–49.

Denecker, Tim. *Ideas on Language in Early Christianity: From Tertullian to Isidore of Seville*. Leiden: Brill, 2017.

Devreesse, Robert. "Chaines exégétiques grecques." Extrait du *Supplément du Dictionnaire de la Bible*. Paris: Librairie Letouzey et Ané, 1928.

Dines, Ilya. "The Textual and Pictorial Metamorphoses of the Animal Called *Chyrogrillius*." Pages 73–89 in *Science Translated: Latin and Vernacular Translations of Scientific Treatises in Medieval Europe*. Edited by Michèle Goyens, Pieter De Leemans, and An Smets. Leuven: Leuven University Press, 2008.

Estin, Colette. *Les Psautiers de Jérôme à la lumière des traductions juives antérieures*. Collectanea Biblica Latina 15. Rome: San Girolamo, 1984.

————. "Les traductions du Psautier." Pages 67–88 in *Le monde latin antique et la Bible*. Edited by Jacques Fontaine and Charles Pietri. Paris: Beauchesne, 1985.

Fairclough, H. Rushton, ed. and trans. *Horace: Satires, Epistles, and Ars Poetica*. LCL 194. Cambridge: Harvard University Press, 1929.

Fiedrowicz, Michael. "General Introduction." Pages 13–66 in *Saint Augustine: Exposition of the Psalms 1–32*. Translated by Maria Boulding. Edited by John E. Rotelle. The Works of Saint Augustine, Part III., Vol 15. Hyde Park, NY: New City, 2000.

Fisher, Elizabeth. "Greek Translations of Latin Literature in the Fourth Century A.D." Pages 173–215 in *Later Greek Literature*. Edited by John J. Winkler and Gordon Williams. YCS 27. Cambridge: Cambridge University Press, 1982.

Fürst, Alfons. *Hieronymus: Askese und Wissenschaft in der Spätantike*. Freiberg: Herder, 2003.

Gamble, Harry Y. *The New Testament Canon: Its Making and Meaning*. Minneapolis: Fortress, 1985.

Gentry, Peter J. "1.3.1.2 Pre-Hexaplaric Translations, Hexapla, Post-Hexaplaric Translations." Pages 211–35 in *Overview Articles*. Vol. 1A of *Textual History of the Bible: The Hebrew Bible*. Edited by Armin Lange and Emanuel Tov. Leiden: Brill, 2016.

————. "Did Origen Use the Aristarchian Signs in the Hexapla?" Pages 133–47 in *XV Congress of the International Organization for Septuagint and Cognate Studies. Munich 2013*. Edited by Wolfgang Kraus, Michaël N. van der Meer, and Martin Meiser. SCS 64. Atlanta: SBL Press, 2016.

———. "The Greek Psalter and the καίγε Tradition: Methodological Questions." Pages 74–97 in *The Old Greek Psalter: Studies in Honor of Albert Pietersma*. Edited by Robert J. V. Hiebert, Claude E. Cox, and Peter J. Gentry. Sheffield: Sheffield Academic, 2001.

Glare, P. G. W. *Oxford Latin Dictionary*. Oxford: Clarendon, 1997.

Goshen-Gottstein, Moshe H. "Hebrew Biblical Manuscripts: Their History and Their Place in the HUBP Edition." *Bib* 48 (1967): 243–90.

Graves, Michael, ed. "1.3.5 Vulgate." Pages 278–89 in *Overview Articles*. Vol. 1A of *Textual History of the Bible: The Hebrew Bible*. Edited by Armin Lange and Emanuel Tov. Leiden: Brill, 2016.

———. "21.8 Latin Church Fathers." Pages 759–63 in *Writings*. Vol. 1C of *Textual History of the Bible: The Hebrew Bible*. Edited by Armin Lange. Leiden: Brill, 2017.

———. *Biblical Interpretation in the Early Church*. Ad Fontes: Early Christian Sources. Minneapolis: Fortress, 2017.

———. "Glimpses into the History of the Hebrew Bible Through the Vulgate Tradition, With Special Reference to Vulgate MS θ^G." Pages 217–54 in *The Text of the Hebrew Bible and Its Editions*. Edited by Andrés P. Otero and Pablo T. Morales. Leiden: Brill, 2017.

———, trans. and intro. *Jerome: Commentary on Jeremiah*. Ancient Christian Texts. Downers Grove: IVP Academic, 2011.

———. *Jerome's Hebrew Philology: A Study Based on His Commentary on Jeremiah*. VCSup 90. Leiden: Brill, 2007.

———. "Jerome's Principles of Biblical Translation in the Context of Classical and Sacred Ideals." in *Shifting Paradigms in the Study of Jerome*. Edited by Andrew Cain, Jessica van 't Westeinde, and Matthew Kraus. Leuven: Peeters, forthcoming.

Gribomont, Jean. "Les plus anciennes traductions latines." Pages 43–65 in *Le monde latin antique et la Bible*. Edited by Jacques Fontaine and Charles Pietri. Paris: Beauchesne, 1985.

Grützmacher, Georg. *Hieronymus: Eine Biographische Studie zur Alten Kirchengeschichte*. 3 vols. Berlin: Trowitzsch & Sohn, 1901–1908.

Hagendahl, Harald. *Latin Fathers and the Classics: A Study on the Apologists, Jerome and Other Christian Writers*. Göteborg: Almquist & Wiksell, 1958.

Hakham, ʿÅmôs. *Sefer Tehillim*. 2 vols. Daʿat Miqra. Jerusalem: Mossad Harav Kook, 1979.

Harnack, Adolf. *The Origin of the New Testament.* Translated by John R. Wilkinson. London: Williams & Norgate, 1925.

Heine, Ronald E. *Origen: Scholarship in the Service of the Church.* Oxford: Oxford University Press, 2010.

Hiebert, Robert J. V. "The 'Syrohexaplric' Psalter: Its Text and Textual History." Pages 123–46 in *Der Septuaginta-Psalter und seine Tochterübersetzungen.* Edited by Anneli Aejmelaeus and Udo Quast. Göttingen: Vandenhoeck & Ruprecht, 2000.

Hong, Jonathan. *Der ursprüngliche Septuaginta-Psalter und seine Rezensionen: Eine Untersuchung anhand der Septuaginta-Psalmen 2; 8; 33; 49 und 103.* BWANT 224. Stuttgart: Kohlhammer, 2019.

Houghton, H. A. G. *The Latin New Testament: A Guide to its Early History, Texts, and Manuscripts.* Oxford: Oxford University Press, 2016.

Hritzu, John N. *The Style of the Letters of St. Jerome.* Washington, DC: Catholic University of America Press, 1939.

Hulley, Karl K. "Light Cast by St. Jerome on Certain Palaeographical Points." *HSCP* 54 (1943): 83–92.

Jackson, John, trans. *Tacitus: The Annals Books I–III.* LCL 249. Cambridge: Harvard University Press, 1931.

Jay, Pierre. "La datation des premières traductions de l'Ancien Testament sur l'hébreu par saint Jérôme." *REAug* 28 (1982): 208–12.

———. *L'exégèse de saint Jérôme d'après son "Commentaire sur Isaïe."* Paris: Études Augustiniennes, 1985.

———. "Jérôme à Bethléem: les Tractatus in psalmos." Pages 367–80 in *Jérôme entre l'Occident et l'Orient.* Edited by Yves-Marie Duval. Paris: Études Augustiniennes, 1988.

Jeanjean, Benoît. "Le *Dialogus Attici et Critobuli* de Jérôme et la Prédication Pélagienne en Palestine entre 411 et 415." Pages 59–71 in *Jerome of Stridon: His Life, Writings, and Legacy.* Edited by Andrew Cain and Josef Lössl. Farnham: Ashgate, 2009.

Jellicoe, Sidney. *The Septuagint and Modern Study.* Oxford: Oxford University Press, 1968.

Kaimio, Jorma. *The Romans and the Greek Language.* Commentationes Humanorum Litterarum 64. Helsinki: Societas Scientiarum Fennica, 1979.

Kamesar, Adam. *Jerome, Greek Scholarship, and the Hebrew Bible.* OCM. Oxford: Clarendon, 1993.

Katz, Joshua T. "Aristotle's Badger." Pages 267–88 in *The Frontiers of Ancient Science: Essays in Honor of Heinrich von Staden.* Edited by

Brooke Holmes, Klaus-Dietrich Fischer, and Emilio Capettini. Berlin: de Gruyter, 2015.

Keil, Heinrich, ed. *Grammatici Latini*. 7 vols. Leipzig: Teubner, 1864.

Kelly, J. N. D. *Jerome: His Life, Writings, and Controversies*. London: Duckworth, 1975.

Kennedy, H. A. A. *Sources of New Testament Greek*. Edinburgh: T&T Clark, 1895.

Kerrigan, Alexander. *St. Cyril of Alexandria: Interpreter of the Old Testament*. Rome: Pontifical Biblical Institute, 1952.

Kraus, Hans-Joachim. *Psalms 1–59: A Continental Commentary*. Minneapolis: Fortress, 1993.

Kraus, Matthew A. *Jewish, Christian, and Classical Exegetical Traditions in Jerome's Translation of the Book of Exodus*. VCSup 141. Leiden: Brill, 2017.

Kreuzer, Siegfried. "The Origins and Transmission of the Septuagint." Pages 3–56 in *Introduction to the Septuagint*. Edited by Siegfried Kreuzer. Translated by David A. Brenner and Peter Altmann. Waco, TX: Baylor University Press, 2019.

La Bonnardière, Anne-Marie. "Did Augustine Use Jerome's Vulgate?" Pages 42–51 in *Augustine and the Bible*. Edited by Paula Bright. Notre Dame, IN: University of Notre Dame Press, 1986.

Lallot, Jean. *La grammaire de Denys le Thrace*. 2nd ed. Collection sciences du langage. Paris: CNRS, 1998.

Lane, Edward W. *Arabic-English Lexicon*. 8 vols. Edinburgh: Williams & Norgate, 1863–1893.

Lange, Armin, and Brent A. Strawn. "Psalms 10.2 Ancient Hebrew Texts." Pages 24–81 in *Writings*. Vol. 1C of *Textual History of the Bible: The Hebrew Bible*. Edited by Armin Lange. Leiden: Brill, 2017.

Lausberg, Heinrich. *Handbook of Literary Rhetoric*. Edited by David E. Orton and R. Dean Anderson. Translated by Matthew T. Bliss, Annemick Jansen, and David E. Orton. Leiden: Brill, 1998.

Luhtala, Anneli. "On Definitions in Ancient Grammar." Pages 257–86 in *Grammatical Theory and Philosophy of Language in Antiquity*. Orbis Supplementa 19. Edited by Pierre Swiggers and Alfons Wouters. Leuven: Peeters, 2002.

Marcos, Natalio F. *The Septuagint in Context: Introduction to the Greek Versions of the Bible*. Translated by Wilfred G. E. Watson. Leiden: Brill, 2001.

Marotta, Giovanna. "Syllable and Prosody in Latin Grammarians." Pages

55–86 in *The Notion of Syllable Across History: Theories and Analysis.* Edited by Domenico Russo. Newcastle upon Tyne: Cambridge Scholars Publishing, 2015.

Marti, Heinrich. *Übersetzer der Augustin-Zeit.* Munich: Fink, 1974.

McElduff, Siobhán. *Roman Theories of Translation: Surpassing the Source.* Routledge Monographs in Classical Studies. New York: Routledge, 2013.

McGowan, Andrew B. *Ancient Christian Worship.* Grand Rapids: Baker Academic, 2014.

Meershoek, G. Q. A. *Le latin biblique d'après saint Jérôme: Aspects linguistiques de la rencontre entre la Bible et le monde classique.* Nijmegen-Utrecht: Dekker & Van de Vegt, 1966.

Meiser, Martin. "Hieronymus als Textkritiker." Pages 256–71 in *Die Septuaginta—Texte, Theologien, Einflüsse.* Edited by Wolfgang Kraus and Martin Karrer, with Martin Meiser. Tübingen: Mohr Siebeck, 2010.

Mercati, Giovanni. *Alla ricerca dei nomi degli "Altri" traduttori nelle Omelie sui Salmi di s. Giovanni Crisostomo e variazioni su alcune catene del Salterio.* StT 158. Vatican City: Biblioteca Apostolica Vaticana, 1952.

Metzger, Bruce M. *The Early Version of the New Testament.* Oxford: Clarendon, 1977.

———. "St. Jerome's Explicit References to Variant Readings in Manuscripts of the New Testament." Pages 199–210 in *New Testament Studies: Philological, Versional, and Patristic.* Leiden: Brill, 1980.

Millar, Fergus. "Bishops and their Sees at the Sixth Session of the Council of Chalcedon: The Near Eastern Provinces." Pages 33–45 in *Empire, Church and Society in the Late Roman Near East.* Late Antique History and Religion 10. Leuven: Peeters, 2015.

———. "Jerome and Palestine." Pages 423–48 in *Empire, Church and Society in the Late Roman Near East.* Late Antique History and Religion 10. Leuven: Peeters, 2015.

Minnich, Nelson H., ed. *Collected Works of Erasmus, Volume 84: Controversies.* Translated by Daniel Sheerin. Toronto: University of Toronto Press, 2005.

Mirkin, Mosheh A., ed. *Midrash Rabbah.* 11 vols. Tel-Aviv: Yavneh, 1992.

Montanari, Franco. *The Brill Dictionary of Ancient Greek.* Edited by Madeleine Goh and Chad Schroeder. Leiden: Brill, 2015.

Moulton, James H. and George Milligan. *Vocabulary of the Greek Testament.* Peabody, MA: Hendrickson, 1930.

Neuschäfer, Bernhard. *Origenes als Philologe.* 2 vols. Basel: Reinhardt, 1987.

Ohrloff, Otto. "Die alttestamentlichen Bruchstücke der gotischen Bibelübersetzung." *Zeitschrift für deutsche Philologie* 7 (1876): 251–95.

Olofsson, Staffan. *God Is My Rock: A Study of Translation Technique and Theological Exegesis in the Septuagint.* Stockholm: Almqvist & Wiksell, 1990.

Oulton, John E. L., trans. *Eusebius: Ecclesiastical History Books VI–X.* LCL 265. Cambridge: Harvard University Press, 1932.

Ozóg, Monika. "Saint Jerome and *Veritas Hebraica* on the Basis of the Correspondence with Saint Augustine." *Vox Patrum* 30 (2010): 511–19.

Peri, Vittorio. *Omelie origeniane sui Salmi: Contributo all'identificazione del testo latino.* StT 289. Vatican City: Biblioteca Apostolica Vaticana, 1980.

Perry, Ben E., trans. *Babrius and Phaedrus.* LCL 436. Cambridge: Harvard University Press, 1965.

Pfeiffer, Rudolf. *History of Classical Scholarship: From the Beginning to the End of the Hellenistic Age.* Oxford: Oxford University Press, 1968.

Pietersma, Albert. "The Edited Text of P. Bodmer XXIV." *BASP* 17 (1980): 67–79.

———. "The Present State of the Critical Text of the Greek Psalter." Pages 12–32 in *Der Septuaginta-Psalter und seine Tochterübersetzungen.* Edited by Anneli Aejmelaeus and Udo Quast. Göttingen: Vandenhoeck & Ruprecht, 2000.

Pitra, Jean B., ed. "Origenes in Psalmos." *Analecta sacra spicilegio Solesmensi parata.* Vol. 2. Paris: Tusculum, 1884.

Rackham, Harris, ed. and trans. *Cicero: De finibus bonorum et malorum.* LCL 40. Cambridge: Harvard University Press, 1931.

Rebenich, Stefan. *Jerome.* ECF. New York: Routledge, 2002.

Reider, Joseph. *An Index to Aquila.* Revised by Nigel Turner. Brill: Leiden, 1966.

Rice, Eugene F., Jr. *Saint Jerome in the Renaissance.* Baltimore: Johns Hopkins University Press, 1985.

Rogers, Justin. "Psalms: 10.3.7 Vulgate." Pages 104–10 in *Writings.* Vol. 1C of *Textual History of the Bible: The Hebrew Bible.* Edited by Armin Lange. Leiden: Brill, 2017.

Rondeau, Marie-Josèphe. *Les travaux des Pères grecs et latins sur le Psautier: Recherches et bilan.* Vol. 1 of *Les Commentaires patristiques de Psautier (IIIe – Ve siècles). Vol. 1 –.* OrChrAn 219. Rome: Pontificium Institutum Studiorum Orientalium, 1982.

Russell, D. A. *Criticism in Antiquity.* London: Bristol Classical, 1995.

Saxer, Victor. "La Bible chez les Péres latin du IIIᵉ siècle." Pages 339–64 in *Le monde latin antique et la Bible*. Edited by Jacques Fontaine and Charles Pietri. Paris: Beauchesne, 1985.

Schaper, Joachim. "The Origin and Purpose of the Fifth Column of the Hexapla." Pages 3–15 in *Origen's Hexapla and Fragments*. Edited by Alison Salvesen. Tübingen: Mohr Siebeck, 1998.

Schäublin, Christoph. *Untersuchungen zu Methode und Herkunft der antiochenischen Exegese*. Bonn: Hanstein, 1974.

Schenker, Adrian. "L'apport durable des Hexaples d'Origène. Bilan de la Lettre à Africanus, bilan aujourd'hui." Pages 385–94 in *Eukarpa: Études sur la Bible et ses exégètes en hommage à Gilles Dorival*. Edited by Mireille Loubet and Didier Pralon. Paris: Cerf, 2011.

Schironi, Francesca. "The Ambiguity of Signs: Critical ΣΗΜΕΙΑ from Zenodotus to Origen." Pages 87–112 in *Homer and the Bible in the Eyes of Ancient Interpreters*. Edited by Maren R. Niehoff. Leiden: Brill 2012.

———. *The Best of the Grammarians: Aristarchus of Samothrace on the Iliad*. Ann Arbor: University of Michigan Press, 2018.

Schulz-Flügel, Eva. "The Latin Old Testament Tradition." Pages 642–62 in *Antiquity*. Part 1 of *From the Beginnings to the Middle Ages (until 1300)*. Vol. 1 of *Hebrew Bible/Old Testament: The History of Its Interpretation*. Edited by Magne Sæbø. Göttingen: Vandenhoeck & Ruprecht, 1996.

Smith, Jannes. "Psalms: 10.3.1 Septuagint." Pages 82–88 in *Writings*. Vol. 1C of *Textual History of the Bible: The Hebrew Bible*. Edited by Armin Lange. Leiden: Brill, 2017.

———. "The Text-Critical Significance of Oxyrhynchus Papyrus 5101 (RA 2227) for the Old Greek Psalter." *JSCS* 45 (2012): 5–22.

Sophocles, Evangelinus A. *Greek Lexicon of The Roman and Byzantine Periods*. New York: Scribner's Sons, 1900.

Sparks, H. F. D. "Jerome as Biblical Scholar." Page 510–41 in *From the Beginnings to Jerome*. Vol. 1 of *The Cambridge History of the Bible*. Edited by Peter R. Ackroyd and Christopher F. Evans. Cambridge: Cambridge University Press, 1970.

———. "The Latin Bible." Pages 100–127 in *The Bible in Its Ancient and English Versions*. Edited by Henry W. Robinson. Oxford: Clarendon, 1940.

Strawn, Brent A. "10.1 Textual History of the Psalms." Pages 5–23 in *Writings*. Vol. 1C of *Textual History of the Bible: The Hebrew Bible*. Edited by Armin Lange. Leiden: Brill, 2017.

Sutcliffe, Edmund F. "The Name 'Vulgate.'" *Bib* 29 (1948): 345–52.

Taft, Robert F. *The Liturgy of the Hours in East and West.* Collegeville, MN: Liturgical Press, 1986.

Tawil, Hayim. b. Y. *An Akkadian Lexical Companion for Biblical Hebrew.* Jersey City, NJ: KTAV, 2009.

Taylor, Daniel J. "Latin Declensions and Conjugations: From Varro to Priscian." *Histoire Épistémologie Langage* 13 (1991): 85–109.

Thackeray, Henry St. J., trans. *Josephus: Jewish Antiquities Books I–IV.* LCL 242. Cambridge: Harvard University Press, 1930.

Tisserant, Eugene Cardinal. Forward to *A Monument to St. Jerome.* Edited by Francis X. Murphy. New York: Sheed & Ward, 1952.

Tov, Emanuel. "The Septuagint." Pages 161–88 in *Mikra.* Edited by Martin J. Mulder and Harry Sysling. Assen: Van Gorcum, 1988.

———. *Textual Criticism of the Hebrew Bible.* 3rd ed. Minneapolis: Fortress, 2011.

Ulrich, Eugene. "The Dead Sea Scrolls and Their Implications for an Edition of the Septuagint Psalter." Pages 323–36 in *Der Septuaginta-Psalter und seine Tochterübersetzungen.* Edited by Anneli Aejmelaeus and Udo Quast. Göttingen: Vandenhoeck & Ruprecht, 2000.

Vessey, Mark. "Jerome's Origen: The Making of a Christian Literary *Persona.*" StPatr 28 (1993): 135–45.

Waszink, Jan H., ed., *Timaeus, A Calcidio Translatus Commentarioque Instructus.* Corpus Platonicum Medii Aevi. Leiden: Brill, 1962.

Watson, Wilfred G. E. *Classical Hebrew Poetry.* JSOTSup 26. Sheffield: JSOT Press, 1986.

Weigert, Sebastian. *Hebraica Veritas: Übersetzungsprinzipien und Quellen der Deuteronomiumübersetzung des Hieronymus.* Stuttgart: Kohlhammer, 2016.

Wheeler, Arthur L., trans. *Ovid: Tristia. Ex Ponto.* Revised by G. P. Goold. LCL 151. Cambridge: Harvard University Press, 1996.

Williams, Megan H. *The Monk and the Book: Jerome and the Making of Christian Scholarship.* Chicago: University of Chicago Press, 2006.

Zeiller, Jacques. "La lettre de saint Jérôme aux Goths Sunnia et Fretela." *CRAI* 79 (1935): 238–50.

Zetzel, James E. G. *Critics, Compilers, and Commentators: An Introduction to Roman Philology, 200 BCE–800 CE.* New York: Oxford University Press, 2018.

Ancient Sources Index

Greco-Roman Literature

Modern Authors Index

SUBJECT INDEX

CPSIA information can be obtained
at www.ICGtesting.com
Printed in the USA
LVHW110843290422
717027LV00002B/63